ANGLO-AMERICAN
FOLKSONG SCHOLARSHIP
SINCE 1898

ANGLO-AMERICAN
FOLKSONG SCHOLARSHIP
SINCE 1898

BY D. K. WILGUS

RUTGERS UNIVERSITY PRESS

New Brunswick, New Jersey

Second Printing

Copyright © 1959 by Rutgers, The State University
SBN: 8135–0310–8
Library of Congress Catalogue Card Number: 59–7517
Manufactured in the United States of America
by H. Wolff, New York
Designed by Betty Crumley

Dedicated to the memory of

PHILLIPS BARRY

whose scholarship has been a constant inspiration.

ACKNOWLEDGMENTS

This book has grown out of a doctoral dissertation completed at The Ohio State University under the direction of Claude M. Simpson, Jr., whose continuing counsel and support have been invaluable. The decision to continue work on the history was effected by its being awarded the Chicago Folklore Prize in 1956 and by the encouragement of Wayland D. Hand. Further research and writing were made possible by a grant from the John Simon Guggenheim Memorial Foundation and a leave of absence granted by Western Kentucky State College, 1957–1958.

I am grateful to Miss Carolyn Jakeman and the staff of the Houghton Library at Harvard University, to Miss Winnie Allen and the staff of the Eugene C. Barker Texas History Center of the University of Texas Library, and to Duncan B. M. Emrich, formerly Chief of the Folklore Section, Library of Congress, for their aid and courtesy. Necessary information and material not otherwise available were provided by Edward Cray, Kenneth S. Goldstein, Hershel Gower, Hamish Henderson, Joseph Hickerson, Frank A. Hoffmann, Edward Kahn, Mrs. Rae Korson of the Archive of American Folk Song, Alan Lomax, and Holger O. Nygard.

Material to be considered for inclusion in the discography in Appendix Two was generously provided by Moses Asch of Folkways Recording and Service Corporation, Atlantic Records, Audio-Fidelity Records, Capitol Records, Counterpoint Records, E. O'Byrne Dewitt's Sons, Elektra Records, Bill Grauer Productions, Heirloom Records, Mercury Records, Radio Corporation of America, Stinson Records, Tradition Records, and George W. Williams and John A. Siegling of the Society for the Preservation of Spirituals.

Permission to use material from the indicated sources was granted by Miss Winnie Allen and Alan Lomax: The John A. Lomax Papers at the University of Texas; Robert Winslow Gordon: *Folk-Songs of America*; Wayland D. Hand: *Western Folklore*; Charlotte W. Hardy: *Minstrelsy of Maine* by Fannie Hardy Eckstorm and Mary Winslow Smyth; Harvard University Press: *Folk-Songs of the South* by John Harrington Cox; Houghton Mifflin Company: *English and Scottish Popular Ballads*, ed. Helen Child Sargent and George Lyman Kittredge, *The Popular Ballad* by Francis Barton Gummere; MacEdward Leach and the American

Folklore Society: *Journal of American Folklore, The British Traditional Ballad in North America* by Tristram P. Coffin, *Native American Balladry* by G. Malcolm Laws, Jr.; Methuen and Company: *English Folk-Song: Some Conclusions* by Cecil J. Sharp; Alton C. Morris: *Southern Folklore Quarterly*; Oxford University Press: *The Ballad of Tradition* by Gordon Hall Gerould; Archer Taylor: *"Edward" and "Sven i Rosengård"*; University of Chicago Press: *Modern Philology*; University of Pennsylvania Press: *American Folksongs of Protest* by John Greenway.

Numerous friends have contributed to whatever may be found valuable in this book, and I personally owe a great deal over a number of years to the advice and suggestions of Herbert Halpert and Francis Lee Utley. William Sloane and Miss Helen Stewart of Rutgers University Press and Mrs. Maria Leach have been extremely helpful in the final editing and the preparation of the manuscript for the press. My greatest debt, however, is to Ebby, Karen, and Cindy, without whose love and affection this work would never have been undertaken.

D. K. W.

Bowling Green, Kentucky
March, 1959

CONTENTS

INTRODUCTION

In 1953 Archer Taylor, in a succinct review of recent folksong study, noted the need of a history of ballad studies since 1898. Such a work, he wrote,

> will deal with the musical investigations begun by Cecil Sharp and continued by the English Folk-Song Society. It will review Hjalmar Thuren's investigations of Faeroic song and the implications of his findings and will survey once more the dispute over the communal origin of ballads. It will state the principles employed in the reconstruction of ballads and criticize them.[1]

Taylor had in mind a continuation of the histories of British and Scandinavian ballad scholarship by Sigurd Bernhardt Hustvedt, *Ballad Criticism in Scandinavia and Great Britain during the Eighteenth Century* (1916) and *Ballad Books and Ballad Men* (1930). It must be stated at the outset that this history does not meet the requirements.

Though beginning with 1898, the point at which Hustvedt rested his labors, this study is at the same time broader and narrower. These differences serve to point out the character of British-American ballad scholarship in the twentieth century; they point out limitations and emphases which this study tries to reflect. In two volumes Hustvedt found it possible to consider two centuries of Anglo-American-Scandinavian study, to include related studies of medieval poetry, and to indicate the literary influence of the ballad. But he focused largely on the popular ballad as defined by the collection of Francis James Child, *The English and Scottish Popular Ballads* (1882–1898). The present volume, covering roughly half of the twentieth century, does not consider such a wide geographical and literary area, nor yet concentrate on such a narrow aspect of folksong.

This is a history of British and American scholarship devoted to ballads and folksongs in English. No brief is held for the narrow approach which this decision reflects. The fact is that it does reflect the central tradition of twentieth-century ballad scholarship. Consideration is given the international scholarship of men like W. P. Ker and Archer Taylor. But Anglo-American study in general went its own limited way. Omitted is the study of Irish folksong,[2] which needs more thorough investigation, not only for itself, but because of important Anglo-Irish-American relationships. Also excluded is much of the slight but important attention that has been paid to the songs of other language groups in the United States.

This is not a history of men and personalities. A fascinating study could be written of the characteristics and relations of the giants of twentieth-century study and collection. There is something that marks a ballad man, though not always the same thing. George Lyman Kittredge and Phillips Barry, Cecil J. Sharp and Miss Lucy E. Broadwood, Henry Marvin Belden and Louise Pound (not to speak of the living) had vital relations with folksong and its study that transcend the printed page. But this study is concerned with the scholarship rather than the man, excepting where the character of the man has assumed in his work a prominence too great to be ignored.

This is not a history of literary and cultural trends. Interest in folksong has often been an index to cultural values, and the influence of folksong enthusiasm on popular culture in the United States is becoming fearful to behold. Generally excluded, however, are the promoters of "folk festivals," the proprietors of "folk workshops," the professional "folksingers," and the editors of "bankrupt treasuries." This history deals with folksong as a scholarly study, not as a force "to instruct the young, reform the old, correct the town, and castigate the age"—or even to line the pockets. But one cannot ignore motives and aims when they have influenced or determined the materials and tools of scholarship. Therefore, to that extent, account is taken of such influences as the cult of beauty in the English folksong renaissance and the cult of the common man in the United States.

The limitations of this history are perhaps balanced by the inclusion of the entire range of folksong scholarship. To be sure, this study emphasizes the ballad in the narrow sense, as has twentieth-century scholarship. But ballad scholarship no longer reigns alone; it has absorbed or has been absorbed by folksong study. Hustvedt, chronicling activities in the eighteenth and nineteenth centuries, could treat the ballad as literature. An historian of twentieth-century scholarship can no longer do so. He must consider the song and the singer, the performance and the function.

The material of this history is organized and apportioned to suggest in some measure the interests and accomplishments of twentieth-century folksong scholarship. Two chapters, approximately half the study, are devoted to the controversy over the communal nature of the ballad. Another chapter deals with the collection of folksong and its publication. The final chapter concerns methods, accomplishments, and promises of folksong studies. And the argument over the origin of Negro folksong in the United States is treated briefly in an appendix.

The chapters dealing with what may be termed the *Ballad War,* treat a problem of great historical importance—of international importance, it must be added. The concept that folksong is a spontaneous, autochthonous expression of the "collective soul" of the people needs thorough historical study. But the present concern is less with its origins than with its expression in and effect on British and American scholarship. Whatever the ultimate origin and Continental history of subservience to the *Gesammtgeist*, the focal point of the infection of Anglo-American studies is the work of Francis Barton Gummere. And it is symptomatic that not until 1934 did an English-language scholar thoroughly examine the works of Lachman, Ludwig Uhland, Steinthal, and the Grimms to determine what they really said and meant.[3] By that time the point was almost academic, for there was hardly a communalist to castigate. The dogma of communal composition lingered largely in the provinces of literary anthologies.

The first chapter treats the armchair scholars, those to whom the ballad problem was an exhumation and examination of literary remains. In Gummere's work are sought the approach and techniques by which he made, from his faith in the communal origin of poetry, a theory well nigh impregnable and one which captured the minds of a generation of scholars. The influence of the theory on its literary disciples is then appraised. Finally appears the opposition: the sneering rationalists of the literary school and the few scholars who attempted to weigh the evidence in the literary record.

Chapter 2 is devoted to the new generation, called *Emersonian* because it did not believe that the ballad was dead. The ballad sun shines today also, said these neo-Emersonians, and, however feeble the light, it will illuminate the problem. Communalist and individualist alike turned to the facts of contemporary folksinging during the period when the great collections were being built. Still the battle raged, until the communalists retreated and finally abandoned a theory that was never disproved—merely disavowed. The faith lost its defenders.

Chapter 3 follows the twentieth-century collectors, examines their collections, appraises the editorial methods. The tune collectors of the Folk-Song Society dominated the English quest and restricted it to a rather narrow path. They collected only the older tunes in oral circulation, printed selected tunes unembellished in the Society's journal, though they took less pains with the texts. They published collections of accompanied tunes and edited words in order to reform the public taste into an acceptance of what the leaders believed to be esthetically valuable in Anglo-Celtic tradition. North of the Border, the enthusiastic but incurious Scots collectors remained in the persons of Robert Ford and John Ord. In Aberdeenshire, Gavin Greig worked wisely and well and left a great legacy but until recently few legatees.

Across the Atlantic, a wider and richer area was combed by heterogeneous collectors united only by a faith in the value and use of folksong. Three traditions guided the collecting: the academic, which, following Child, sought accurate transcriptions of text first and music later for scholarly study; the local-enthusiastic, which searched out and displayed the quaint, the unusual, the exciting, the enjoyable in undisciplined and mercurial fashion; and the musical-esthetic, which sought the distinguishable art form of the folk tune for appreciation and performance. The collectors themselves were academics, whether somewhat detached leaders of regional activity or lone workers aided by chance location, early upbringing, or special interest. Or they were interested amateurs, in that they began and pursued their labors for a variety of reasons unrelated to the values of disinterested scholarship. A union of both types of collector, in the person of John A. Lomax, enriched the greatest collection of all, the Archive of American Folk Song (Library of Congress).

The published works of these collectors vary greatly in content, value, and method of presentation, not always in direct relation to the collectors, since the editor was not always the collector. The material itself was drawn from geographical and political units, or occupational and ethnic groups. The books can be divided on the basis of intention and method into a number of types. The academic collection presents texts (and sometimes tunes) in formal pattern imitative of Child's canon, with bibliographical and comparative notes. The running-comment collections surround the collectanea with essays, scholarly or colorful. An unordered, unannotated mass of texts characterizes the random-text collections. The singing books contain arranged folksongs for public or private performers. The collections of John A. and Alan Lomax are laws unto themselves, composite photographs of native American folksong selected for color and colored by the sentiments and prejudices of the compilers, mingling impeccably transcribed material with composite and butchered songs, informed and enlightening comment with "cute" and crude appeals to the emotions of the populace. But despite the great divergency among American published collections, there is a discernible pattern: the tendency to present accurately all the songs sung from memory by the American people in as many variants as possible. The collections tend to be inclusive and accurate as they tend to be American and academic.

Although collection and the controversy over origins occupy most of the history, as they occupied most of the time of folksong scholars, there is yet room to discuss the scholarship devoted to classification, analysis, and critical history of folksongs, and the place of folksong in folk culture. A consideration of these studies is undertaken in the final chapter. Much scholarship has been incidental to the display of texts and tunes. But the notes to collectanea often present extended and considered conclusions that reflect a great tradition of scholarship. And there have been independent studies as well, dealing with aspects of folksong and with individual folksongs. Most of the study has been American, though English scholarship, within the limitation of its interests, has been distinguished.

Analysis of ballad texts began with attempts to define and account for the Child ballads. The earlier definition applied formal tests for certain elements which, as a new and looser definition was accepted, came to be viewed as merely characteristics. These elements—themes, formulas, stanza, and meter—have been analyzed thoroughly if not definitively. The ballads outside the canon have received less attention. Some of the perceptive comments on the vulgar ballad have been almost lost in the revulsion at the modern connotation of the term and the snobbish attitude it seems to imply. But the perceptions have been revived to some extent in recent characterizations and analyses of the British broadside and of native American balladry.

Textual variation has occupied a considerable portion of ballad study. The study of variation was early used to support broad theories of ballad origin and development. Subsequently it was concerned with the minutiae of textual change, but is now considering more fully the relationship between alteration and the singer on the one hand and the whole ballad on the other.

While considerable effort has been expended in the attempt to determine the origin and authorship of individual ballads, particularly noncanon narratives, critical studies of ballads have been few. Even less frequently have scholars studied the international tradition of ballads current in more than one language. But a conclusion based on the number and extent of separate studies would be deceptive. The amount of scattered material awaiting synthesis is surprising, though one cannot fail to note the emphasis on the local and the national. In so far as this emphasis represents the mood that set in at the close of the Ballad War, the determination to study the narrow but verifiable contemporary tradition before advancing broad generalizations, it is salutary. And the current tendency is toward synthesis and extended study.

Types of folksong falling outside the widest definition of *ballad* have occupied less of the scholars' attention. Work songs and the American play-party have been somewhat attractive; and religious folksongs, both the English carol and the more American spiritual, have had serious consideration. The amorphous folk-lyric is only now becoming attractive as an object of investigation.

Serious attempts to index, classify, and assess folksong began at mid-century. They could not have begun while collection was at its height and before the material had been garnered. It is necessary to treat in detail the history and problems of classification, especially since recently published indices and syllabi tend to follow old patterns and multiply old errors. Despite the many voices raised against subservience to the Child canon, it still casts a long shadow.

In spite of some collection and comment, notoriously inaccurate, music did not assume a place in the study of folksong until the close of the nineteenth century. The founding of the Folk-Song Society in 1898 marks a beginning of serious study. The English emphasis on tune alone countered the American emphasis on text. Phillips Barry and a few others in the United States asserted the rights of ballad music, and the old attitude, at least in America, has been altered. But with the advance of study, the unified treatment of text and tune, valid as an ideal, now seems more remote, or at any rate postponed, in that tunes must be studied more fully before reliable methodology is achieved.

In the present state of folk-music study, appraisal of even its history is difficult. It is necessary either to oversimplify or to become involved in detail out of proportion to the place (but not the importance) of music in twentieth-century scholarship. Therefore the study traces briefly the growth of musical study from an almost esthetic hobby and outlines the two interrelated approaches to the study of folk tunes: the analytical and the genetic. The analytical, at first almost a mere display of "quaint" modes and figures, has developed into a scientific investigation of the complex patterns of a multifarious folk art. The genetic or historical study, while coeval with the analytical, progressed significantly only after analysis had determined the factors which indicate melodic relationships. The resulting study of tune families, or genetically related airs, has begun to add to the scanty knowledge of folk melodizing, but seems to make more distant the possibility of a simple melodic index for the general student.

The functional approach to folksong was the last to develop. Though the communalists commented extensively on the theoretical role of the ballad in primitive society, few students took note of the social and psychological function of folksong. There are scattered comments by collectors, but consideration of even the milieu of the folksong was more often an afterthought. Not until the 1930s were the questions significantly formulated. The functional approach is not yet keeping pace with the comparative and the esthetic, but there are greater emphasis and a little progress toward an understanding of folksong as an expression of the singer and of the community.

No Jim Crow technique is involved in the relegation to an appendix of the argument over the Afro-American origin of American Negro song. The complexity of the subject demands separate treatment. The section outlines the development of the argument, beginning in 1867 but flourishing after 1914, and attempts to dispel the sentimentality, prejudice, and confusion between origin and essence that have obscured the opportunities for an important study in acculturation.

This is a critical history of folksong study not only because any history must be critical, but because the writer is in no sense "above the battle." For the battle continues. The current folk-music revival is a product of many factors, but it is not causing a *renaissance* of scholarship. Folksong scholarship never died. Though it may be encouraged and used in popular trends and fads, it has a way of using and even absorbing popular enthusiasm without serious damage to its integrity.

In the twentieth century folksong study has developed from an antiquarian, esthetic, and literary pastime toward a disciplined study of a segment of traditional culture. Men of widely differing interests have deliberately and accidentally amassed materials beyond the ken of a Percy or a Scott—or even a Child. In the fire of acrimonious debate and on the anvil of reason are being forged the tools of a scholarship that is at once scientific and humane. And the scholarship is flourishing now more than ever. In 1937 Reed Smith suggested that to "the things that the Psalmist held to be past finding out—'the way of a man with a maid, the way of an eagle in the air, and the way of a serpent on the rocks' "—one might add "the way of a folksong in oral tradition." [4] To the glory of twentieth-century scholars, they have continued to track the untrackable with heat and light.

ANGLO-AMERICAN
FOLKSONG SCHOLARSHIP
SINCE 1898

THE BALLAD WAR I:
THE MORPHOLOGY OF
DRY BONES

For more than a century following the publication of Bishop Thomas Percy's *Reliques of Ancient English Poetry* in 1765, ballads had furnished a field for lively controversy on the Continent as well as in the British Isles. But in England the serious points of dispute were textual and, in a narrow sense, authorial. Joseph Ritson had challenged the authenticity of Percy's versions and even his sources and had attacked the assumption of minstrel authorship. The forgeries of such worthies as David Pinkerton and Lady Elizabeth Wardlaw had been exposed, and the texts of Sir Walter Scott and Peter Buchan had been questioned. Robert Chambers had stirred up a minor tempest with his claim that a large number of the Scots ballads came from the pen of Lady Wardlaw, and had been effectively answered.[1] It was generally felt that balladry was connected with the metrical romances. Robert Jamieson, insisting that ballads preceded all other types of compositions and were built up into romances, also held that ballads were in their turn broken-down romances, as did Scott and John Leyden. Even John Finley, who attributed the authorship of some ballads to "the people" and associated them with the popular poetry of uncivilized nations, expressed no conception of aggregate or group authorship, which was to furnish the grounds for what may be termed the *Ballad War*.

On the Continent, matters had taken a somewhat different turn. Pronouncements by Johann Gottfried von Herder and the brothers Grimm, rightly or wrongly interpreted, had led to a concept of folksong as a spontaneous, autochthonous expression of the "collective soul" of the people. The ensuing dispute over the alleged dichotomy between group or folk poetry and individual or art poetry spread throughout the Continent, but seems to have crossed neither the Channel nor the Atlantic Ocean until the last quarter of the nineteenth century, when the group concept was appropriated and, applied particularly to the traditional narratives, denominated ballads. Then arose the communal theory.

Because the theory of communal origins assumed so many shapes in the hands of its proponents, its essence can be stated only with difficulty. The orthodox communalist held that folk poetry is a genre which precedes and is antithetical to the poetry of art, that it springs spontaneously from a people, and that it is composed collectively by the people. It is simpler to understand what the communal theory was not. As George Lyman Kittredge wrote, the communal theory did not require us "to believe that 'Chevy Chase' or 'The Queen's Marie,' or 'Gil Breton,' was composed collaboratively by a tribe of neolithic, skin-clad enthusiasts dancing round a campfire to the notes of the tom-tom," or to "imagine some stanza in Mr. Child's thesaurus as created *sua sponte* by at least a score of tattooed improvisators chanting in unison." [2] That was, nevertheless, the conception of the theory held by some of its opponents, and perhaps by some of its supporters as well.

The distinguishing feature of the first phase of the British-American ballad controversy—despite its levies upon anthropology, ethnology, and folklore—was its concentration on literary and antiquarian problems. Scholars regarded the ballad as a surviving literary text, a fossil to be explained only in the light of historical evidence or by analogy with the verse of primitive peoples. One section of opinion held the ballad to be a relic of unrecorded culture poetry, historically interesting. On the other hand, the impact of German literary scholarship, the concept of biological evolution, and the influence of the Tylor school of anthropology upon Anglo-American scholarship had created a climate of ideas which nourished the theory of communal origin as a concept of literary evolution. But all parties to the dispute regarded the ballad as little more than a corpse to be wrangled over.

Credit seems to belong to Andrew Lang for the first enunciation in English of the doctrine that the ballad is the "immemorial inheritance at least of all European peoples" and that "its birth from the lips and hearts of the people may be contrasted with the origins of an artistic poetry." Writing for the *Encyclopaedia Britannica* of 1875, Lang introduced at least four of the principles which were to mark the work of later communalists: the use of the anthropological or comparative method; the formulation of the marks of popular poetry (repetition, assonance, etc.), the application of the test of impersonality to differentiate the poetry of the people from artistic poetry, and the connection of the ballad with improvisation at the dance. Despite the challenge of Lang's pronouncement, the war did not truly begin until the communal position was fortified by Francis Barton Gummere in 1894.

The ground, however, was already prepared. William Wells Newell, though never a communalist, gave assent, in his *Games and Songs of American Children* (1883), to at least two tenets of the literary evolutionist: that ballads are dance songs and that they survive from antiquity. The following year, in a review of Part I of Child's *The English and Scottish Popular Ballads*, Thomas Davidson [3] apparently called for just that type of theory which was to be formulated, an evolutionary theory which would trace the ballads "as distinguished from other species of popular literature" to "their sources in the natural faculties of the human mind." He made it clear that the theory would be one of evolution, which, "incapable of furnishing a rational explanation of anything . . . is teaching us that every reality . . . every institution, every idea, every word— had behind it an incalculable period of growth." Small wonder that proponents of the theory did not wait for the "definitive" edition of Child—a fact which, because of the nature of the theory and the character of its adherents, made no difference.

The Caution of
Francis James Child

Before plunging into the arena of the battle, it is well to consider briefly the limited pronouncements of Francis James Child. Later critics have almost uniformly regretted that the admitted paragon of ballad editors did not live to write the critical introduction to his collection; for his subsequent reputation, it may be as well that he wrote no more. His very silence tended to remove him from the conflict. His students—whom Louise Pound later termed "the Harvard School of communalists"—were, like other literary evolutionists, able to take shelter freely in his authoritative collection. Even the most violent opponents of the communalists revered Child's work and refused (or did not dare) to associate the "great scholar and a sane one" with the extravagances of "the school of Child."

What was Child's view of ballad origins? Though communalists believed that "he held in essentials the views Gummere developed at length," Walter Morris Hart, in his 1906 synthesis of Child's scattered remarks,[4] failed to prove the case. In addition to the "mere *obiter dicta*" of his ballad introductions, Child left only a résumé of "Ballad Poetry" in Johnson's *Universal Cyclopaedia* (1874), which Gummere reported Child wished "to be neither quoted nor regarded as final." Because the article is the one extended statement made by Child, and because Hart drew upon it for the comments most favorable to the communal position and found that "for at least forty years Professor Child retained without essential change his conception of the traditional ballad as a distinct literary type," it is necessary to consider the résumé.

Child explicitly denied three fundamental tenets of the communalists: that ballads were dance songs, that they were of group authorship, and that they originated among the peasantry or in a classless society. *Ballad* "means by derivation, a dance song, but . . . the application of the word in English is quite accidental"; ballads were made by "a man and not a people"; ballads are "popular, not in the sense of something arising from and suited to the lower orders of the people," for many of them "had their origin in that class whose acts and fortunes they depict—the upper class." But these statements are set in a context favorable to the views of the literary evolutionists, and consequently they have been accidentally or deliberately overlooked.

Child, for whom the ballad held a place "anterior to the appearance of the poetry of art," believed that this "truly national or popular poetry" developed in a stage of society in which "there is such a community of ideas and feelings that the whole people form one individual." His statement is undoubtedly metaphorical and cannot be understood by those who try to translate metaphor into scientific fact, or by those who refuse to understand metaphor at all. This community of thought and feeling (not the homogeneous society of his followers) explains why the composition of one man "will always be an expression of the mind and heart of a people as an individual and never the personality of individual men." Thus Child accounts for the objectivity of the popular ballads, for he grants nothing to transmission but change. In an oblique reference to the alleged uniformity of ballad style, Child writes that though ballad poetry is always "in its essence an expression of our common human nature [it] will in each case be differenced by circumstances and idiosyncrasy." Specific characteristics of ballad style may derive, then, not from universal poetic origins, but from the unique cultural situation. Child's comments on the age of ballads are reasonably clear. Although he considers as ballads the Germanic songs referred to by Tacitus, his avoidance of a formal definition places him outside the camp of those communalists who argued for the existence of ancient Germanic songs with the characteristics of extant ballads. Child's position is that popular narrative songs existed before the introduction of the rhymed stanza and "seem to have been in use from the earliest recorded time"; but he mentions no formal elements connecting the English and Scottish ballads with earlier popular narratives.

Child's conception of ballad authors is by no means precise. In a passage denying the necessity to go back to the "cradle of mankind" to explain resemblances among ballads of various nations, he refers to the transmission of at least ballad plots among professional entertainers of the Middle Ages. Yet he does not specifically connect these minstrels with ballad authorship. His recognition of individual authorship is, however, worth quoting:

> Though they do not "write themselves," as William Grimm has said, though a man and not a people has composed them, still the author counts for nothing, and it is not by mere accident, but with the best reason, that they have come down to us anonymous.

Although quoting correctly in *Old English Ballads,* Gummere later paraphrased this as "although men and not communities make the ballad," [5] a rendering that distorts Child's statement. Critics such as T. F. Henderson have made merry with the statement that the author counts for nothing, but more revealing is the fact that Gummere by inference did so, too, writing, in *Old English Ballads,* in reference to Ludwig Uhland's remarks on *Volkslied:*

> . . . what does Uhland really teach us? Certainly no distinctive notion about the making of a ballad. He rests too much in a phrase. He avoids the mystery in which the Grimms took refuge; but instead he flies to image and allegory. He concedes the individual act in authorship, and then denies its significance (p. lvi).

To this strategy Gummere applies Hosea Biglow's phrase, "frontin' south by north." Is there reason to wonder that Gummere did not wish Child's article quoted or regarded as final?

Child's statements are rather like those of John Geddie, who, in *The Balladists* (1896), could write of a "Ballad Age, when such poetry sprung up naturally and spontaneously" and of a "voice . . . not of an individual poet, but of an age and of a people" while still believing in "original ballad-writers." Geddie, however, was an early "Darwinian" critic in seeing the Scottish ballads as, "in their present form, the outcome of a long and strenuous process of selection. . . . As a rule, what was fittest . . . survived and was perpetuated in this evolution of the ballad" (pp. 11–13). Child had apparently no conception of transmission as evolution or progress.

If anywhere Child approaches the communal position, it is in his placing of national poetry "anterior to the appearance of the poetry of art, to which it formed a step." In classifying the "vulgar ballads of our day, the broadsides," as "a different genus . . . products of a low kind of *art*," he may have meant merely that the broadsides were conscious appeals to the lower classes as contrasted with the unconscious appeal made by the popular ballad in an era when knowledge, desires, and tastes were relatively uniform. But Child's remarks were certainly understood differently, and, using the opposed categories of art and nature, his pupil, Gummere, began a defense of popular poetry.

The Communal Theory of Gummere: A Faith and a Method

It is indeed surprising, in view of the dogmatic quality which the communal argument later assumed in the United States, that its greatest champion entered the lists with a defense of an older, minority position against the "band of sleek-headed men who work by day, sleep soundly o' nights, and are troubled by no dreams or mysteries" [6]—the contemporary scholars of language, comparative literature, ballads, and folksongs, who accepted imitation, diffusion, and individuality instead of spontaneity, instinct, and communality, who preferred nominalism to realism.

The folk is out of favor, and democracy itself put on the defensive. Ballads for a time held out bravely, but now even ballads, like folklore in general, have been annexed to the domain of art . . . one feels that one is losing old landmarks, and is swept by strange currents into a chartless and unsounded ocean.[7]

Gummere made no secret of his defense, in spirit at least, of Herder and Jacob Grimm. Although his complaints were directed chiefly against Continental writers—Wilhelm Scherer, Hermann Paul, Karl Müllenhoff, John Meier, Gabriel Tarde, and others—his ire was aroused by three representatives of the developing Anglo-American folktale scholarship whom he took to be infected with the modernism he wished to forestall.

The three offenders—F. J. Campbell, W. W. Newell, and Joseph Jacobs—were all "on the side of the artist." Gummere questioned the implication made by Campbell in *Popular Tales of the West Highlands* (1860) that the ballad was descended from epic or romance, and accused Newell of holding, at the International Folk-Lore Congress of 1891, that "folktales are a degenerate form amid a low civilization of something which was composed amid a higher civilization." Jacobs not only had suggested in his *English Fairy Tales* (1890) that the cante fable might be "the protoplasm out of which both ballad and folk-tale have been differentiated," but, in a paper read before the Folk-Lore Society in 1892, had affirmed his belief in the individual origin and the subsequent diffusion of folklore. He sought to break down the distinction between the folk of the past and the folk of the present, attacked the hard and fast line between folklore and literature, and refused to consider folklore the exclusive possession of the rustic and illiterate. "The Folk is simply a name for our ignorance." [8] Although Jacobs' remarks were directed at the anthropological school, they represented just that line of thought against which Gummere was to fight for the remainder of his life.

No adequate summary of Gummere's theory of communal origins has ever been made, possibly because no critic seems to have understood the peculiar union of faith and method by which Gummere convinced a generation of literary scholars that the ballad must be studied as a survival of primitive poetry. His supporters and detractors often understood him differently because of those very methods which make summary misleading. Gummere's theory can only be *followed*. One can perceive a number of devices—deceptive use of the term *common sense*, shifting definitions and limited statements, "the closed account and the open door," the "higher chronology," emphasis on slight evidence and the "adding of zeros," "unliterary" analysis—by which he sought to justify his faith; but only by tracing them through Gummere's work and observing how they operate is it possible to understand why they have been so convincing and why no summary can do justice to the theory.

Gummere waged his campaign from a fixed position, from which he never deviated. From his first clear statement in *Old English Ballads* (1894) to his final pronouncements in *Democracy and Poetry* (1911), his thesis remained unaltered and his arguments virtually the same. Pushing different phases of his argument, clarifying points, rephrasing pronouncements, responding to criticism, he kept his basic attack almost unchanged, even repeating the same examples time after time.

Apart from summary and popular articles, each of Gummere's publications touching the ballad emphasizes a major portion of his argument. In the introduction to *Old English Ballads*, he summarizes English and German ballad scholarship to 1893. *The Beginnings of Poetry* (1901) develops the process of poetic evolution in which he placed the ballad. In a series of articles, "Primitive Poetry and the Ballad," published in *Modern Philology* (1903–1904), Gummere replies directly to his critics and attempts to shift the burden of proof to the opposition. *The Popular Ballad* (1907) places the emphasis on the ballad of Child's collection as a literary genre and (apparently influenced by the work of George Morey Miller) its dramatic qualities. *Democracy and Poetry* (1911) focuses attention on the communal and individual elements in the poetry of art. Common to them all are basic aims, assumptions, and methods—

elements as pervasive as Gummere found the repetition in the ballad—which determine the character of the works.

The *Handbook of Poetics* (1885), though it disagrees at points with Gummere's later arguments, reveals the germ of the full-blown theory and will serve to point out certain assumptions which underlie all that followed. A study of the *Handbook* reminds one that Gummere's chief interest lay not in the ballad or folksong, but in historical poetics. The study of poetics was to him the contemplation of an evolutionary process which began in a ritual, choral dance with incoherent repetition: originally strophic with refrain, poetry early developed into continuous epic verse sung by minstrels. The process is roughly Spencerian in that it proceeds from the spontaneous to the designed, the objective to the subjective, the general to the particular, the simple to the complex. Furthermore, form, structure, and tone of poetry reveal this development, and elements such as impersonality are indications and tests of origin. These assumptions are clearly visible in the *Handbook,* amounting to a conviction that "poetry began in a human horde," but omitting "the assertion of simultaneous composition." The word *communal* nowhere appears, and there is only a hint that "something made by the whole people and not by individual poets" is more than a metaphor.

It is Gummere's refusal to rest in a metaphor that characterizes all his later writings. Jacob Grimm's oft-quoted statement, that "every epos must compose itself," presented a challenge. Gummere set out to explain "How got the apples in?" to clarify what he took as mystery. Recognizing in the ballad the communal *essence,* he interpreted it as part of an evolutionary process, a survival of communal *origin.* In effect, *Gummere's doctrine is an etiological myth which explains the essence of the popular ballad.*

Although it was the individualists who were accused of literal-mindedness and who charged Gummere with nebulous thinking, his writings on the ballad and poetic evolution are pervaded by literal acceptance of categories and terms, explicit application of a concept of evolution to acknowledged phenomena, and use of analogies as literal evidence. The categories of "art and nature," "individual and communal," "poetry of the schools and poetry of the people," "popular and artistic" are treated as fundamentally dualistic in the evolutionary process. His statement that "poetry, like music, is social" is meant literally, and this conviction is combined with the acceptance of rhythm as the essential fact of poetry. The theory that poetry originated in a communal dance seems inescapable. The poetry of the people is public poetry, made in public, by the public. The homogeneity affirmed for the folk among whom ballads arose or were preserved is extended to include all aspects of being and behavior. Gaston Paris' reference to medieval poetry "which everybody could have made" is applied exactly. Gummere insists on connecting "initial literary effort" with "the poetry that is written to be read." Elements and tone of ballads, increasing personality in "the poetry of art," and medieval concepts of literary property are for him *facts* in the evolution of folksong. The generally accepted conclusion that a ballad has no one text becomes the judgment that there is no *ur*-text or any organized beginning. The *a priori* nature of Gummere's dualism is often obscured by the adroitness and flexibility of the argument. A "brilliant scholarly ingenuity," it certainly was, a cunning strategy designed to confuse and disarm critics by a variety of techniques.

Deceptive Use of the Term Common Sense. After the tremendous range and fund of knowledge, the element which impresses the unprejudiced reader of Gummere is his apparent combination of common sense and scientific scholarship. Certainly, common sense was the last thing many of the individualist critics credited to Gummere; yet he uses it tellingly in combination with sharp distinctions, limitations, concessions, qualifications, often with the result of smuggling in the very sort of mystery or technique he disclaims. Denying any "belief in miraculous and folk-made verse," proclaiming a theory that "holds the middle way," he sets the problem in carefully restricted sociological terms, attaches it to studies in other areas, makes reasonable objections to assumptions and methods of other investigators—all this in such a way as to provide himself with a great deal of flexibility in dealing with evidence and to introduce techniques justified only by the rejection of other techniques.

In Chapter 1 ("Purpose and Method") of *The Beginnings of Poetry*, Gummere carefully limits his problem to "how aesthetic activity made itself seen and felt," rejecting any consideration of "the perplexing question why aesthetic activity first evolved." Thus, by avoiding uncertain psychological speculations, he reads out of court all serious consideration of individual activity and introduces without discussion the assumption that a consideration of the social aspects of poetry will justify conclusions about its beginnings. His language, drawn largely from nineteenth-century social science, makes an analogy never stated but assumed as fact. His statement that "facts of poetry ought to precede the theory" is immediately followed by the admonition that the "facts . . . should be brought into true relations with the development of social man." The importance of this admonition is not so much that it implies his levies upon social science and his acceptance of an evolutionary hypothesis which corresponds to the curve of Spencerian evolution (he admits this completely), but that it provides justification for great flexibility in handling "facts" to bring them into "true relations," while at the same time producing the impression of scientific objectivity.

So it is with his consideration of methods and materials to be employed. His considered rejection of the ontogenetic-phylogenetic hypothesis permits comments on the cautious uses of analogy which serve as a left-handed defense of his own usage. The way is left open for the use of social rather than psychological evidence from children. The cautions concerning the "abuse of ethnological facts" also express common-sense and scholarly objections to any simple use of analogy, any assumption that "the lower one goes in the scale of culture among living savage tribes, the nearer one has come to primitive culture." Without denying the seriousness of Gummere's objection, one notes immediately how it provides the opportunity to reject evidence on the ground that the tribe in question has "degenerated" or has become so "stunted" that the dance has progressed "from wild rhythmic leapings in festal throng to the rigid form it has found under the care of certain experts." Furthermore, the valid objection permits him to smuggle in a mystery by declaring, "It is a mistake of the first order to assume that a form of expression now unknown among men must have been unknown to those who made the first trials of expression in words and song." (This discussion also serves to introduce the policy of chronological flexibility discussed below as the "higher chronology.") When he advises caution in dealing with evidence, common sense supplies the reason for rejecting the extreme example of a rather graveyard-school translation of an Osage song; but the argument moves from objection to the language to objection to the sentiment, and finally serves to introduce the type of evidence which "can control the evidence of ethnology." This turns out to be not evidence at all, but "the sense of literary evolution."

Although one may grant at least the utility of *"theoretical or conjectural history"* in ordering facts, he may well question a method which suggests reducing the inquiry to a more limited field by seeking a narrower path than a "History of Human Thought," then proposes to trace "some particular characteristic of human nature . . . to a point where all records and traces of it cease." One may question such a method because it leads to conclusions based on traits which may be isolated from cultural or literary context. The conclusion specifically related to ballad criticism is that "the way to treat the ballad for historic, comparative, and genetic purposes is to follow these elements back to the point where they vanish in the mists of unrecorded time." The degree of preponderance of these elements in a given poem or genre is then justification for classifying it as either "communal" or "artistic."

The skillful placing of the ballad in this "curve of evolution" set a trap for many of Gummere's critics. Simply to deny or ignore the place of the ballad or its elements in poetic evolution was enough to bring down upon the critic's head the charge of ignorance, narrowness, and antipathy toward balladry in general. The critic who attempted to refute choral origins of poetry while denying that ballads had any connection with primitive poetry was made to appear like the defendant who pleaded self-defense while refusing to admit his presence at the scene of the crime. Even the spotting of Gummere's essential fallacy (concluding too hastily that "certain features of balladry" must be products of the "singing and dancing habits of savage tribes" instead of being, at best, no more than analogues) [9] cuts the Gordian knot without untying it.

Shifting Definitions and Limited Statements. To untie the knot of Gummere's criticism, it is necessary first to find the rope's end: the definition of *ballad.* And one never finds it unless he considers the mass of Gummere's work as an attempt at definition, the "definition by origins." For the term *ballad* means to Gummere not a poem or group of poems, not a genre or type in the usual sense, but a concept of the historical process of popular poetry reaching from the most primitive social organization to the eighteenth century. What seems to be Gummere's most succinct statement by way of definition occurs in his 1896 article in *Harvard Studies and Notes:* "Folk-poetry was a survival of prehistoric gregarious or communal verse of the horde; ballads are a crossed and disguised survival of folk poetry" (52*n*).

To take a narrower view, Gummere's work is an effort to explain the use of the definite article in *The English and Scottish Popular Ballads.* He seems to have foreseen Thelma James's conclusion that "a 'Child ballad' means little more than one collected and approved by Professor Child" [10] when in "Primitive Poetry and the Ballad" he almost pleads that the concept of the ballad as the detritus of "author-poetry" is "an attack upon balladry as a whole." Such a concept, he concludes, could only mean that "Mr. Child simply collected the things he liked out of a mass of things which seem to have been liked by the people." But Gummere's characterization of Child's admittedly heterogeneous collection as "itself a definition of balladry" is one of his characteristically limited statements, referring to only one aspect of the concept *ballad.*

The quantity of such limited statements scattered throughout Gummere's writings led to misunderstanding and confusion; yet their use is part of that method which makes the communal theory a faith still to be reckoned with. Despite his attempts to differentiate among the ballads of the collections, the "original poetic product," and the "ballad as ballad," despite his reiteration that the ballads of the collections are not communal in any literal sense, Gummere's practice is not always clear. The shifting senses in which the word *ballad* is used make many statements equivocal, even in context.

> For the earliest form of the ballad, now nowhere to be found, but easy to reconstruct by the help of an evident evolutionary curve, one must assume not the refrain as such, but rather choral form outright (p. 357).

In this statement from *The Beginnings of Poetry* it is hardly possible to determine whether Gummere has reference to the ballad as a poetic form, the ballad as it existed in the Middle Ages, or the original form of a ballad of the collections. In simple justice one might reject a consideration of the last alternative, that Gummere, in spite of his fervent denials, is asserting choral origins for an extant ballad. But in the same work he states, "Probably many of the English and Scottish ballads began as a kind of *vocero*." And in *Old English Ballads*, after writing that "*The Battle of Otterburn* . . . as the poem lies before us, at least," was not composed by a community, he postulates a number of laments and merry songs that would spring up among the men-at-arms and in the dances and choruses which would characterize the "homogeneous social condition still existing along the border, even in 1388. . . . Out of all this, by a survival, we will hope, of the fittest, some singer of note would in time chant a ballad into unity." This differs from his earlier statement concerning a ballad of the same class, that "only madness could regard such an altogether charming piece as mere gregarious making . . . jostled into unity by the chances of time" only in the introduction of an "artist" whose labors cannot affect the fundamentally communal nature of the production, at least as far as classification is concerned. Again, in *The Popular Ballad*, the ballad (an individual survival?) cannot be appreciated in excerpts, for "the whole ballad is the thing"; but the ballad (the species?) "is a conglomerate of choral, dramatic, lyric, and epic elements . . . forced into *more or less* poetic unity by the pressure of tradition in long stretches of time" (italics added). The basic technique is one of *concession and reaffirmation,* whereby a major point is conceded to the opposition in such a way that its essence can be reintroduced and the basic argument salvaged. The method is similar to the *argument by inference* which Gummere uses in approaching the definition of *ballad* by etymology.

Perhaps no one knew better than Gummere the difficulties of an etymological argument, but his handling of it evades the main issue. In the *Handbook of Poetics* he is content with the comment, "Both names, ballad and folk-song, are suggestive: *ballad* means a song to which one may dance; *folk-song* is something made by the whole people, not by individual poets" (p. 35). His almost parallel statement in *The Popular Ballad,* that "Popular is something which pertains to the people at large, and ballad is a song to which folk used to dance; yet nearly every variety of short poem in English has been called a ballad . . ." (p. 3) illustrates the almost querulous tone in which he discussed the problem. He was interested not so much in why a traditional narrative song *came to be* called a *ballad,* but why it *should be* called a *ballad.* He writes, in *The Beginnings of Poetry* (p. 175n), "The terminology of the whole subject [evolutionary poetics?] is notoriously bad, and 'ballad' is no exception to the rule." And in *Old English Ballads* (p. xviii), he writes, "Confusion is rife in the use of the term." Gummere's failure to dispel the confusion was not due to his lack of knowledge of the etymology. In *Old English Ballads* he presents the facts almost as thoroughly as does Louise Pound in *Poetic Origins and the Ballad* when she attacks the communal position for confusing the modern application of *ballad* with its derivation from *ballare.* Characteristically, Gummere makes no direct claim for associating the origin of the traditional narrative song with the derivation of its name. He presents the facts and adopts an air of injured innocence concerning the various uses of the term *ballad*. He nowhere gives assent to Child's statement that "the application of the term in English is quite accidental." Perhaps it was an act of God that eighteenth-century antiquaries applied the word *ballad* to traditional narratives. Gummere nowhere states that the name, like elements in the ballad, is a survival. Nor does he ask the embarrassing question of what the transmitters of the songs called them. He merely plants the etymology in the mind of the reader, asserting only that "in many tongues, dance and song are convertible terms," and that "our own words, like 'ballad' itself, 'carol,' and others, help the etymological argument" for the early connection of dance and song. But the insinuation, together with the flexible use of the term *ballad* itself, lends force to such uses as the following in *The Beginnings of Poetry*:

> The song that always went with a dance got its name thence, and was called a ballad; and in the ballad, whether strictly taken as a narrative song or as the purely lyrical outburst for which there is no better term than folksong, this consenting and cadenced series of words found its main refuge and record (p. 314).
>
> . . . the nearer one comes to the source of a ballad, that is, to the dancing throng, the more insistent and pervasive this refrain becomes (p. 320).
>
> For the ballad is a song made in the dance by the dance (p. 321).

On the other hand, Gummere is left free to call to task G. Gregory Smith for his use of the fifteenth-century term *ballate* in pleading for the ballad as a literary form. *Ballate*, says Gummere, in his article "Primitive Poetry and the Ballad," was a word then applied to almost anything from journalism to the Song of Solomon. This sort of flexibility applies to all aspects of Gummere's definition. In the *Handbook of Poetics*, he affirms that the characteristics of the ballad are the same as those of the "original epic," including "the trait of telling something known, or supposed, or feigned to have happened"; in *Old English Ballads*, he quotes with approval Ritson's distinction which confines *ballad* to "mere narrative compositions"; and in *The Popular Ballad* he can say, "The ballad of our quest is a narrative lyric handed down from generation to generation of a homogeneous and unlettered community." But later in the last-named work the flexibility of the approach is demonstrated by statements implying a basic contradiction. He can say of the ballad that "narrative is its vital fact," regardless of his earlier statement that, "despite its rank as necessary condition, narrative is not a fixed, fundamental, primary fact in the ballad scheme." The latter statement is qualified, of course, by his insistence that "ballads have not always been what they are." In this argument, the ballad is not static even in definition; as a genre it is dynamic, or it is the survival of a dynamic genre, depending on the needs of the moment.

Gummere's terms are "crossed and disguised." They mean what Gummere chooses them to mean—neither more nor less—to serve the needs of various arguments. A ballad is a number in the Child collection, a narrative poem, a dancing song, a genre of poetry, the primitive poetic "germ," a concept of evolutionary poetics. It is all of these, but none of them exclusively. This sort of strategy might be classed with another aspect of Gummere's method.

The Closed Account and the Open Door.   One of the peculiar "beauties" of Gummere's work is his ability to deal with only that evidence which suits his purpose, rejecting noncontributing or conflicting points. Ballad making is a closed account, in the opinion of Child and most of the scholars of his time. And Gummere writes in *The Popular Ballad* that the ballad must be viewed like "the medieval romance, the ancient epic, as an outcome of conditions which no longer exist." This conclusion, valid or not, has limitations. While eliminating the evidence of modern "ballads," it minimizes the use of any positive evidence outside the genre and requires the acceptance of all evidence provided by the species itself. Consequently, Gummere "opens the door" by postulating that, though ballad *making* is over, the surviving ballads comprise not the genre, but the survival of the genre, a survival from the "vanished world of poetry." A ballad is not pure popular poetry, but a blend, a compromise between tradition and art. Furthermore, *tradition* [11] can be apprehended in certain elements of the survivals, and the valid way to determine the nature of the genre is to trace those elements "back to the point where they vanish in the mists of unrecorded time."

The advantages of such a method are clear. In the surviving specimens Gummere can select those elements which are congenial to his theory and dispose of the others as incipient art. The particular configuration which makes a literary genre is not binding, for he can go far afield in tracing the elements. Time itself ceases to be a restriction, for he can search for elements in all sorts of survivals. And no example need be considered completely. Its essence may be distilled, or certain elements may be noted; but the relevance of all aspects of the material may be slighted. Thus contemporary children's games, songs of labor, and marching songs are grist for the mill in so far as they demonstrate survivals, improvisation, communal production. But conflicting evidence, such as lack of narrative and the presence of borrowed or degenerated material, may be conveniently dismissed. The carole and branle, forms of the round dance of medieval Europe, furnish valuable evidence for the origin of the ballad in the dance, but can later be conveniently rejected as nonnarrative and leading to the lyric instead of to the ballad. Then when Gummere's favorite example, the dance song of the Faeroe Islands, turns out to be intimately associated with a form of the carole, he reaffirms the branle's communal essence and connection with the ballad. Writing of the Scandinavian ballads in *The Beginnings of Poetry*, he seems willing to concede the borrowing of the material, the stanza form, "even now and then the peculiar rhythm of the lines," but salvages "the impulse that drives that throng to express its feelings by rhythm, movement, cry . . . the very dancing and singing," as sufficient indication of the communal nature of the ballad. This essence is enough. "Borrowing is, after all, incidental."

In Chapter 2 of *The Beginnings of Poetry*, where he champions rhythm as the distinguishing feature of poetry, Gummere not only sharply separates the origin of poetry and prose (granting priority to the former), but gives poetry to the throng and prose to the entertainer. The corollary to this becomes clear in *The Popular Ballad*: the *Märchen* or folk narrative, which "follows an entirely different line and springs from an entirely different impulse," is of no value in determining the origins of balladry. There is a valuable kernel in this conclusion: it emphasizes the necessity of making some distinction between the origin of the ballad type and the origin of the tale recounted in an individual ballad. But carried to an extreme, it leads to the failure to consider whatever evidence folktale scholarship might have to offer; it serves Gummere as an excuse to ignore or explain away the narrative element. When, in his chapter on "The Sources of the Ballads," he somewhat belatedly faces the problem, he never successfully explains how the narrative entered the ballad. Yet he is quite willing to accept anything toward his theory that a story element can offer, whether in terms of spontaneity, local legend, homogeneity, or custom and belief.

The Higher Chronology. Closely allied to what Gummere termed the "closed account" is his use of the concept of the "higher chronology," a reassessment of the age of ballad texts to conform to his "curve of evolution." As even the merest tyro in the study of folksong knows, the dates of collection of any individual song bear no necessary relation to the stage of development of the variants. And if one assumes, as did the Tylor school of anthropologists, a rather parallel development of cultures, chronology in the usual sense cannot be applied to existing so-called "savage" communities. In a somewhat similar fashion, but with somewhat less excuse, Gummere imposes a logical order on a mass of literary and ethnological data. A method which may appear merely debatable when applied to the Botocudo Indians of the Amazon region is almost shocking when turned on contemporary so-called "civilized" peoples. Calling the dances of the Faeroe Islanders *primitive* is disturbing; yet the method is even more alarming as applied to the corpus of English balladry. Ignoring almost completely or explaining away the problems of literary culture and literary record in the complex society of the Middle Ages, Gummere concludes that the various classes of extant ballads "fall into logical if not chronological order of development" from almost primitive choral to arrested epic, an order completely at variance with the historical record. Thus "Edward" lies close to the beginning of a process of which the *Gest of Robin Hood* is the end. Yet the conclusion is reached by an argument which, to support a sweeping generalization in *The Beginnings of Poetry*, can produce such a statement:

> Silent folk . . . tribes that neither sing nor dance, must not be brought into the account; if they do occur, and the negative fact is always hard to establish, they are clearly too abnormal to count (p. 90).

Limited Evidence and the Adding of Zeroes. The type of evidence is also important in a consideration of Gummere's method. Although a complete résumé of the evidence would require a book, one is surprised to discover how little objective evidence in the way of analogical texts can be found. Considering the vast ranges of time and space which Gummere covers—the whole of human society during the historic period—one might expect copious citation. But few of the adduced examples are accepted as communal in any strict sense. Instead they hint of something further or illustrate the stage of tradition or development in a period removed from communal conditions. Perhaps only the oft-repeated example of the Botocudos with their songs such as "Good Hunting" or "Brandy Is Good" completely qualifies. But of this and other "savage" examples, for which he seldom gives texts, one becomes distrustful, realizing that they are often drawn from "tribes about whom anthropologists know next to nothing," as Franz Boas [12] said of similar examples in A. S. MacKenzie's *The Evolution of Literature*. The number of Gummere's examples tends to obscure the absence of extended information in individual cases, and it comes as a surprise to discover that Gummere's prime example, that of the Faeroe fishermen who composed a satiric ballad while dancing around a hapless colleague, is based only on a description, with no text and little supporting information.

The same sort of evidence is drawn from medieval chronicles, although one senses a modification, a growing caution in Gummere's comments on the existence of ballads in the Anglo-Saxon and medieval periods. In *Old English Ballads* he can say, after his usual qualifications, that "we find ample evidence that poems in character and contents analogous to the later ballads were sung in Saxon England." By the time of the writing of *The Popular Ballad* he is prepared to admit more clearly the lack of any direct evidence and to be more cautious in assuming the existence of ballads behind the tales in the Anglo-Saxon and medieval chronicles. He can even say, "In the lack of actual material, any theory can be proved." But he takes nothing back. His admission that "only a reasonable probability springs from the facts at our command . . . and proof must be sought elsewhere" does not place the burden of proof on the anthropological analogies and the analysis of ballad elements. His full presentation of the negative evidence is so adroit as to give credence to the statement that the absence of any examples is a "defect of the record." This technique might be called the *adding of zeroes*. Zero plus zero equals zero; but when Gummere adds them, the answer is a positive number. It is this result, one suspects, which has been especially maddening to Gummere's critics. He has stolen all their thunder by readily admitting that "in a case where identity of subject matter is supposed to link an acknowledged ballad to a lost source of chronicle or poem . . . identity of subject matter cannot carry with it identity of structure or form." He does not crudely translate the *cantilenae* of William of Malmesbury as *ballads*; but he leaves the impression that they *should have been* ballads.

Unliterary Analysis. A detailed treatment of these assumptions and techniques may have served to establish the background in which can be set the core of the communal position, literary analysis. For Gummere was essentially a literary critic, an armchair scholar whose most valuable weapon was a brilliant and incisive analysis of literary texts. By astute literary analysis he sought to prove that the ballad is not literature at all: it contains elements which are not of literary origin and cannot be referred to any single poet or artist. And on the basis of these elements he makes the clear distinction between "the definition by destination and the definition by origins." As he writes in *The Popular Ballad*, by another test of the ballad "there is nothing but the law of copyright and the personal fame of Mr. Kipling to exclude his 'Danny Deever' from a collection of English popular ballads or to differentiate it from 'Hobie Noble.' " But be it always kept in mind that Gummere advocates no mystery for the making of a ballad, "which was composed originally, as any other poem is composed, by the rhythmic and imaginative efforts of a human mind. The differencing factors lie in the conditions of the process, and not in the process itself."

To support his contention that the ballad is a communal production submitted to oral tradition and therefore a separate genre, Gummere relies chiefly on tests that he terms *organic* (i.e., structural or formal). Convinced that the ballads of the collections are related, if remotely, to conditions of production which are nonartistic (i.e., nonindividual) and clearly recognizing that they cannot themselves be carried back to primitive conditions, he attempts to discover by analysis those basic elements which cannot be explained by any other theory. Not that he refused the support of other evidence. But, recognizing the vulnerability of many of the arguments, he prefers to point out the weaknesses himself and to rely on what he considers fundamental facts, those which would connect the ballad securely with popular poetry and refer it to "ennobled popular improvisation" rather than to "degenerate art."

Among the tests which Gummere considers nonorganic are those regarded as basic by many critics. He agrees that ballads are objective and impersonal narratives found in the tradition of unlettered peoples. But the ballad, at times sharing its story with literature or depending on literature, was not always epic. Nor will the objective quality of the ballad set it off absolutely from the objective narrative of art. The test of impersonality is worth enough that Gummere takes pains to note the "I" of the ballads as a late intrusion, a device of the singer or reciter not affecting the impersonality of the species; but the test is not an absolute. Furthermore, Gummere is not willing to concede the origin of the ballad species to the forces of tradition: the variation of the oral, traditional record will not explain the ballad form.

The communal elements which Gummere finds in the ballad are, as he states in *The Beginnings of Poetry* (p. 172), "repetitions of word and phrase, chorus, refrain, singing, dancing, and traces of general improvisation." But when considering, in *The Popular Ballad*, the narrative songs of the collections, he does not emphasize the direct evidence of two elements: singing and dancing. Gummere is not giving up anything. He still maintains the importance to the ballad of its having been sung, but finds this evidence a weak reed. Nonballad material is also sung, even to tunes reminiscent of the dance step. The evidence for dancing songs in the Middle Ages he still considers important, but not decisive: not all dance songs are ballads. Even the evidence which he has continually presented for the existence of the ballad from early Germanic times to the twelfth century is, though not jettisoned, held open to question. In fact, he asks the same questions as do his opponents, although in a way more favorable to his own conclusion. The only evidence which he insists on is that of Canute's "ballad" from the *Historia Eliensis* of 1166, for it is a record of *form*. Clearly the first record in English of a rhymed stanza in a "ballad metre," it is taken by Gummere to be a ballad fragment, and the chronicler's *in choris publice* is translated as "sung by the people in their dances." Here was the first example of his "organic tests," pointing to certain elements of form which he could claim as unmistakable survivals of communal production. So, accepting neither "the vague test of simplicity nor the false test of imperfect rhythm and rime," Gummere turns to his "fundamental facts" of ballad structure: refrain and repetition.

Critics of Gummere have justly charged him with basing his sweeping characterizations of the ballad on the atypical evidence of a small number of them. Gummere, however, sees the ballads of the collections not as a unit, but as the outline of a process. He believes that the presence of certain elements in an individual ballad varies in relation to the place of that ballad in the curve of evolution from communal song to epic. Therefore his conclusion that the refrain is "organic" is not affected by the lack of refrains in two-thirds of Child's ballads or by the function of the refrain in an individual ballad. The presumption of Child and Svend Grundtvig that the ballads in the two-line stanza are the oldest agreed with Gummere's contention that alternating lines of text and refrain represent a sort of mid-point in the progress from primitive iteration to developed narrative. But the presence of a refrain in a large percentage of the ballads placed first in Child's collection is only contributory evidence, for the presence anywhere of ballads of this type would suit the evolutionary curve. The fact that refrains have a habit of dropping from the record provides flexibility. The presence of narrative ballads without refrain and narrative ballads with refrain, the latter presumably representative of the division between the throng and the artist, is sufficient to permit the postulation of antecedent steps. The refrain, "incontestably sprung from the singing of people at dance, play, work," was once more than the element repeated by the throng between the lines of text sung (earlier improvised) by individuals. Once the text as well belonged to the throng. Gummere realizes, however, that the mere fact of juxtaposition of refrain and text is not conclusive proof of choral origins for the text itself, at least to those not thoroughly convinced in advance of the reality of the evolutionary process. The burden of proof, then, rests upon an analysis of the structure of extant ballads: the main mission of *The Popular Ballad*.

Gummere finds the central fact of ballad structure in that element common to both text and refrain: repetition. And the most important type of repetition is that progressive iteration to which he earlier gave the name *incremental repetition*.

The question is repeated with the answer; each increment in a series of related facts has a stanza for itself, identical save for a new fact, with other stanzas.[13]

This element Gummere takes as basically structural, not ornamental. The fact that it occurs as mere formula or commonplace in some ballads and does not occur in others is no deterrent to the conclusion, for in the varying uses of incremental repetition, even in its very absence, Gummere finds support for his postulation of the epic process.

Behind the earliest ballads Gummere sees a throng gathered to celebrate an event. The result is an immediate, dramatic re-creation of the event in repeated phrases. Because "a group, not one person, is 'telling the story,' concerted action and harmonious words are achieved by only a consent of movement and voice." This sort of unrecorded ballad is but one step removed from extant texts. Certain ballads (or rather, variants of certain ballads) deal only with a situation, recounting it entirely in progressive iteration, largely in dialogue. "Literal repetition yielded, for the sake of progress, to this repetition with increments, developing the situation."

That some variants of a ballad ("The Maid Freed from the Gallows," for example) contain more than the bare situation is explained by the next step in epic progress. The ballad, detached from the immediate occasion in which it took its rise, succumbs to the demand for more facts. A later singer, divorced from the immediate situation, will explain it by the "improvisation of new stanzas, still holding fast to the old formula." Thus "develops, as poetic 'invention,' a higher type of verse." And thus arises the ballad of "split situation," in which the epic or narrative introduction and close may be contrasted with the lingering over the situation in stanzas of incremental repetition. Again and again Gummere introduces "Babylon" as his chief example of this type. In this ballad even the introductory narrative is bereft of essentials: "who the ladies were, why the brother was banished."

From here the road is clear. Prefixed explanations give details; the narrative finally absorbs the situation. The eventual result is the chronicle ballad of the Robin Hood type, but the record is full of examples that mark the way. Incremental repetition, no longer structural, lingers in formula and commonplace. The climax of relatives so necessary in "Babylon" lingers in memory and occurs in new narrative ballads; the legacy becomes traditional and is applied perfunctorily to close many ballads. The old triad of repeated stanzas,[14] necessary to the development of a situation, becomes a senseless repetition of colors, horses, etc. Repetition becomes "a mere manner, by no means inevitable."

Here briefly is the brilliant analysis of extant ballads, which was supported by the mass of historical and ethnological data gathered by Gummere. Not only is the analysis independent of the chronological record, but it can account for or absorb apparently contradictory evidence. The history of a ballad story may be independent of the ballad itself. The ballad form may be the vehicle of tales of literary origin, but the tales do not explain the ballad form. Ballad refrains may, within the historic period of balladry, have been detached and used for various ballads; originally it was not so. The lack of records before the thirteenth century is not surprising; the oral, popular poetry would not have been likely to find a record in the monkish chronicles. The primary iteration of the "primitive ballad" would not commend itself to the record of any time. Because the ballad as a thing of oral tradition depends for its survival on linguistic stability, is it any wonder that our record of ballads extends only to the beginning of linguistic stability in English? And for the Anglo-Saxon period we have what one would expect to be recorded: learned poetry of the warrior class. Be it noted that the problems of stanza and meter are ancillary to the structural analysis. And if he must concede that the septenarius came from Latin hymns, he can immediately suggest that elements which came from the church to the people had previously gone out of the people into the church. Here again is "concession and reaffirmation."

One criterion of the success of ballad theory is its usefulness when applied directly to the individual ballads of the collections. Almost half of *The Popular Ballad* is devoted to a classification and discussion of ballad texts, those of the Child collection with some foreign parallels. The result is not a success. That Gummere's classification of ballads into six major subject-matter types agrees broadly but not quite logically with evolutionary theory is not a major fault. If ballad theorists or editors were judged by their classifications, none would " 'scape whipping," and Gummere's types are as useful as most. It is in the handling of the individual ballads that the method fails significantly.

Gummere's treatment of an individual ballad is limited largely to an outline of the story, with perhaps a slight comment on the history or analogues of the plot, a discussion of the place of the ballad in his evolutionary scheme, and a notice of survivals of custom and belief or commonplaces. At times his capsule summaries give a good deal of insight into the narrative treatment of a ballad and point out precisely the valuable elements. But too often the major thread is: "from the fine, impersonal conclusion . . . one infers the old lament"; or "it is only an echo of the old choral cries; the voice of epic and tradition drowns it almost to extinction." One sees the individual ballad dimly through the accumulation of minutiae, commonplaces, motives, and "elements"; or the place of the item in the world of balladry is so stressed that one cannot see the individual ballad at all. Although Gummere insists that the whole ballad, not any detached portion, "is the thing," the critic is tempted to conclude that, unless Gummere is the complete prisoner of his own theory, he simply is not interested in the ballads themselves.

It is obvious, however, that Gummere *is* interested in individual ballads. Although his main interest does lie in the ballad as survival, its reminiscence of a "cumulative appeal to the emotion of a throng," no reader of his chapter on "The Worth of Ballads" can overlook his appreciation of ballad poetry. But Gummere is not interested in the individual ballad in the same way that later critics have been. In treating "The Lady of Arngosk," he is content to note the source of the "facts," the abduction of about 1736. "Whereupon, of course, the countryside rang with a ballad. . . . So local history found its way into ballads." To leave the problem there, without asking *how* local history finds its way into ballads, is not enough. After noticing several ballads of this type, he concludes:

"In these ballads, disordered though they may be, and favorites as they were in the stalls, there are glimpses of the old choral beginnings." This is adding insult to injury. At least a part of Gummere's willingness to stop short with the observation that "tradition laid hold of a theme" may be seen in a comment on the fidelity of collectors:

> The later group of collectors . . . who took down ballads from singing and recitation, learned fairly well the lesson of fidelity and literal report; but here again was danger, even with such a splendid recorder as Herd, that abbreviation, forgetfulness, distortion, and outright fabrication, on the part of the singer or reciter, should play havoc with the genuine traditional ballad (pp. 315–316).

There is something magic in tradition which one does not see; but the tradition one can see is fabrication. Gummere cannot see the trees for the woods.

Gummere does admit that tradition "made the ballads as we have them." But *ballads* are not *the ballad*. He even approaches the Darwinian theory of communal re-creation in writing of "the process by which a ballad constantly sung in many places, and handed down by oral tradition alone, selects as if by its own will the stanzas and phrases which best suit its public." But tradition is to Gummere a thing of caprice. Although it may run "a fairly straight course in its own way," tradition is outside the sight of the collector and investigator. For Gummere, the study of sources is the study of the *plot*, but not of the *plot in the ballad*; the study of commonplaces, customs, superstitions, and sayings of the folk as they appear in different ballads, but not in different forms of the same ballad; the study of ballads or *the* ballad, but not *a* ballad. There is resignation in his statement that "just where and when [a ballad] was put together is seldom to be known." He points out the possibility of ballad fusions and the other "peculiar qualities of tradition," but implies that these qualities baffle investigation and that one who studies the relationships "undertakes to settle questions . . . by the laws of artistic poetry." To state it bluntly, Gummere advises tracing a ballad to tradition and then renouncing further study. As has already been pointed out, he does not simply recognize that there *is no one text* of a ballad and no original in the ordinary sense; he denies that there can be any such thing as an *original* text:

> The task of the editor is to follow back each of the versions to its particular origin, and to separate from it "improvements" or changes due to interference from whatever hand. But when he has reached the dairymaid or "old man," who got it by natural process in its traditional course, he has done all he can; he has traced it to popular tradition. Of a large group of variant versions, he selects the best, the oldest, those which agree with the kindred ballad in other tongues, and prints them all in the order of preference. This is the only "classical treatment of ballads" (p. 312).

So Gummere finally "rests in a mystery" and ends where modern ballad scholarship begins.

The Paradox of George Lyman Kittredge

Modern ballad scholarship began, at least symbolically, with George Lyman Kittredge, who accepted and supported Gummere's theory, yet fostered much of the investigation which was to undermine the hegemony of the singing-dancing throng. The resolution of the paradox lies perhaps in the qualities of the man. He was not, like Gummere, a scholar with a "curious store of learning" determined to prove a theory; rather, he was a scholar with not only broad learning but broad interests, hoping to contribute to the solution of a riddle by the use of all available means—and genuinely interested in the means. His influence on ballad scholarship is all out of proportion to the amount of criticism he produced. He was directly responsible for producing perhaps more communalists than Gummere, but he contributed at the same time to the shift from literary speculation to field research. Even his introduction to the abridged *English and Scottish Popular Ballads* (1904) testified by its very inconsistencies to that breadth of interest which gave the Harvard Library great collections of detective fiction and broadside ballads, and produced a generation of ballad scholars who were to give the lie to Kittredge's statement that ballad making and ballad singing were lost arts.

In the Introduction, Kittredge accepts Gummere's assumptions and conclusions, at least as working hypotheses. He confines himself to the Child canon, the closed account. Though he later modified his statement on the death of ballad singing, he never admitted that newer songs were true ballads. He accepts the dualism of "poetry of the folk" and "poetry of art." He postulates the homogeneous community of a whole people and reads the minstrel out of court. He even asserts that "there is no difficulty in proving beyond a reasonable doubt" the existence of Anglo-Saxon ballads. But he does not dogmatize. He does not second Gummere's statement in *The Popular Ballad*, that if one considers the ballad "originally a poem, made like any other poem, but submitted by tradition to influences which give it a 'popular' character . . . all boundaries of the subject are obscured, the material is questionable, and a haze at once fills the air" (p. 29).

It is not necessary to point out Kittredge's support of Gummere on many counts, nor even his well-known reconstruction of the composition of "The Hangman's Tree"—a reconstruction so detailed that T. F. Henderson could write sardonically, in *The Ballad in Literature* (p. 75), "One might suppose that Professor Kittredge had seen the ballad factories of the ancient village communities in operation." Nor is it particularly useful to note Kittredge's qualifications and concessions which are in accord with Gummere's. But Kittredge allows tradition and the individual greater importance in ballad production.

While Gummere holds fast to the structural evidence of the ballads themselves, Kittredge hedges considerably. Although he finds in commonplaces and incremental repetition a hint and support of unsophisticated or communal production, he warns that "their occurrence is consistent with several theories of ballad growth" and that "a composing throng is not necessary to explain the phenomenon." Kittredge's stress on the ballads of the collections leads him to examine the composition of an extant ballad more closely than Gummere ever does and to make explicit the concessions which Gummere only hints at. After describing "the characteristic method of ballad authorship as improvisation in the presence of a sympathetic company which may even, at times, participate in the process," and after the familiar stipulation that actual facts are unknown and only conformance to the type is to be expected, Kittredge concedes:

> It makes no difference whether a given ballad was in fact composed in the manner described, or whether it was composed (or even written) in solitude, provided the author belonged to the folk, derived his material from popular sources, made his ballad under the inherited influence of the method described, and gave it to the folk as soon as he had made it,—and provided, moreover, the folk accepted the gift and subjected it to *that course of oral tradition which . . . is essential to the production of a genuine ballad* (p. xxvii; italics supplied).

Henderson was not quite accurate when he wrote (p. 78), "On one page Professor Kittredge says that it matters everything that the ballad should be improvised in the presence of a throng, on another he says it matters nothing." Kittredge is on the one hand defining the ballad in terms of its structure, and on the other explaining the origin of that structure. But Henderson rightly noticed that the importance accorded to oral tradition, "hardly second in importance to the original creative act," conflicts with the weight placed on improvisation in the presence of a sympathetic audience and on inherited form. Here is the important break in the theory.

Kittredge's introduction not only seems to split along these lines, but is actually so divided. At the end of the opening paragraphs he explicitly states that the section was written on the assumption of individual authorship. And here he treats the effects of oral tradition on the ballad, advancing, "for want of a better term, collective composition" to describe the many changes undergone by a ballad in the process of transmission. If this collective composition is not simply a condition of survival, but necessary to the production of a popular ballad, even the improvising village author becomes unimportant. All that remains is to connect the development of the so-called structural elements with the process of transmission. Although Kittredge refers only to losses and gains of stanzas, changes in rhyme, alteration of names, linguistic changes, and fusions, his hint of other explanations for commonplaces and incremental repetition supplies the opening which completely splits the theory. It is possible to reconcile tradition and production within the communal theory by resorting to a postulation of *reversion* or to Gummere's differentiation between origin and transmission as *intension* and *extension*; but Kittredge neither claims the process for the theory nor rejects it. The very contradiction emphasizes his position as an open-minded investigator, not the prisoner of a theory, and incidentally saved his position when the new evidence came in.

The Literary School

Turning to the opposing position—or rather to that section of the opposition which derived the ballad from earlier "literature," one discovers that the division of "communal-individual" is misleading. Although the communalists were not always in complete agreement, they presented a relatively solid front. The individualists, however, were united only by their making common cause against Gummere. Their ranks included proponents of popular as well as literary origins, evolutionists as well as degenerationists. Andrew Lang in his later writings rejects Gummere's theory on many counts and stands as an individualist even on the liberal interpretation of Gummere's use of "origin"; but he supports *popular* origins and is the avowed enemy of the literary school of Courthope, Henderson, Gregory Smith, *et al.* Nor do the members of the literary school always agree among themselves. But they can be treated as a fairly cohesive unit counterbalancing the communalists.

Like the communal position, the literary argument was clearly stated before the completion of *The English and Scottish Popular*

Ballads. The literary school seems to derive more or less directly from W. J. Courthope's chapter on "The Decay of the English Minstrelsy" in the first volume of his *A History of English Poetry* (1895). Courthope, who was extending, correcting, and justifying the conclusions of Bishop Percy in his *Reliques*, engages in no controversy over popular origins. He makes only a passing bow to "philology, comparative mythology, and archaeology," but does clearly enunciate a philosophical position with regard to "the progress of society from the tribal to the civil state," a philosophy clearly antithetical to Gummere's. Courthope derives the "art of metrical composition" from the primitive bard, who was the poet, historian, and philosopher of the tribe. With the advance of civilization, the functions become specialized, and with the art of writing come "the productions of the epic, the dramatic, the lyric poet, of the historian and the philosopher . . . though each retains some traces of the common oral source." Then, like Gummere, he draws an analogy between his hypothesis and the development of medieval poetry. By a somewhat complex and irregular process, to be sure, the Northern scald developed through contact with the remains of Roman tradition into the jongleur, the medieval minstrel. The minstrels "gradually decayed, or were absorbed into higher forms of art." By the middle of the fourteenth century, the earliest date of known English ballads, the upper classes were "occupied either with the prose romances, or with allegorical or other purely literary forms of poetry," and to the lower classes only could the minstrel now appeal. Although the minstrel "would preserve the outline of his primitive art, his handling of the theme would be somewhat degenerate," and this degeneracy is what Courthope finds.

Courthope's telling argument, like Gummere's, is based on the features of the extant ballads, form and matter. He finds three classes of English ballads: those like "Otterburn," reflecting the characteristics of the *chanson de geste*; those, like the Robin Hood ballads, combining the features of the *chanson de geste* and the literary romance; and the romantic ballads, like "Earl Brand," having a purely literary origin in the romance, lay, or fabliau. Courthope does not, of course, argue for anything like a direct derivation of extant ballads from known romances. He conceives that ideas, themes, plots, and types of poems were reproduced in the ballad "in a mould peculiar to itself." In the stronger portion of his examination he traces themes and plots to older "models," and demonstrates by comparisons the "degenerate" handling of elements in the ballads. He finds the ballad tales to be not the legacy of long oral tradition, but changed, combined, and corrupted from literary sources, and "at each stage of their journey" clothed "in new metrical form" by "the art of some nameless poet." Here is the crux of the argument, at least for the communalist. How can the form be shown to be the "art of some nameless poet"? Courthope solves this problem simply and directly. Composing for a crude and vulgar audience, the singer tried "always to present a striking dramatic story in a short form, with rapid transitions and violent contrasts." In borrowing the substance of a romance, the singer chose the outstanding points and exaggerated them to appeal to his audience. This "*précis* of a romance . . . developed certain features of its own . . . abrupt transitions, repetitions of phrases, and conventional formulae." The music was such an important feature that sound sometimes prevailed over sense, with the introduction of "meaningless burdens, and the constant use of the number three, on account of the convenience of the word for rhyming purposes."

Courthope's criticism brings one point clearly to the fore: all the disputants in the early part of the controversy concerned themselves with the same evidence, at least as regards the ballad and its role in recorded European history and literature. Only the interpretation of the evidence varied. Two of the examples cited by Courthope are "Sir Aldingar" and "Mary Hamilton," ballads which figure equally in the arguments of both the communal and the popular theorists. In dealing with the evidence of literary record, the literary school treated it as they would have any other literary evidence. The frame might have been narrow, but the method was clear and conventional. The appearance of the Aldingar story in records previous to the collection of the ballad convinces Courthope that he deals with a literary theme propagated over Europe in Latin texts or vernacular translations, later versified independently by minstrels in Scandinavia and England. Although the story has a long literary history, he dates the ballad not much earlier than its collection, the middle of the seventeenth century, for "the language of the poem in its surviving form does not denote antiquity." As for "Mary Hamilton," Courthope simply points out that the original ballad maker, stirred by the death of a Mary Hamilton in Russia in 1719, "conceived the happy idea of throwing back the incidents of the actual tragedy into the reign of Mary Queen of Scots" (helped, perhaps, by some unknown ballad actually dealing with "the four Maries"), borrowed a little from "Sir Patrick Spens" and "The Two Brothers," and wrote Child's A version. A later maker, with better taste, made some changes. The result is the version in Scott's *Minstrelsy of the Scottish Border.* The changes, however, are not traditional; the people merely "remember and repeat what the minstrel has put together" in the form he "continues to use from age to age." The ballad form is an aid to the minstrel's memory, with its "stereotyped moulds of diction, no less artificial than the stilted phraseology of literary poetry criticised by Wordsworth."

It becomes clear that members of the literary school were as obsessed as the communalists by the literary-popular dualism. Though they might deny its validity, their attempts to demonstrate that the ballad was a literary, not a popular, genre proclaim the tyranny of the dichotomy. The followers of Courthope, forced to answer the communalists directly, countered what they felt to be *a priori* considerations with "antecedent probability," which they went rather to extreme lengths to demonstrate.

Hardheaded men like T. F. Henderson,[15] G. Gregory Smith,[16] and J. H. Millar [17] wanted no truck with the communal origin of *any* poetry. Although for the purpose of argument they were willing to concede a communal "something" as a germ, they looked to the gifted individual for the origin of anything they would term poetry. But they did not argue the case, believing with Millar that it is a waste of time to dispute "the characteristics of productions which no one has ever seen or heard, and whose very existence depends upon bare conjecture." Their chosen arena was the extant ballad; for, says Henderson, the belief in the ballad as a primitive form of poetry "transformed into its present shape by what is vaguely termed the fancy or combined genius of the folk . . . almost necessarily implies that the traditional versions now surviving were originally of communal origin." Yet the problem of emendation in the eighteenth-century collections permitted the literary school to treat the ballads according to their preconceptions, parceling out parts to the "improvers" and parts to the "reciters," according to literary quality.

Assuming that the ballads were simply debased copies of literary poems, members of the literary school had to question the antiquity often assigned to them, in both subject matter and form. The chief argument was a common-sense appeal to the record, seeking to date the origin of extant ballads by internal and external evidence. The literary school was able to demonstrate on the basis of the historical ballads that no copies antedated the fifteenth century and that no ballad could be safely dated earlier by internal evidence. The subject matter of the romantic ballads proved no problem. Andrew Lang's contention that ballads are versified *Märchen* is countered by Millar's argument that a tale's literary expression in verse is no older "than the set poem in which the myth is incorporated." A theme common to a romance and a ballad is taken to mean that the ballad is a derivation. If the ballad is simpler, it represents a "shrinkage in the literary conception." And common or analogous themes in the balladry of Western Europe are but proof of common literary derivation. The school finds no proof that the story came down in an oral ballad side by side with the literary romance, and no difference in form between those ballads derived from a romance and those of supposedly popular origin.

In accounting for the form of the ballads, the literary school experienced no difficulty. None of the members submitted the ballad to a truly rigorous examination, for they did not believe it to be a true genre. Instead, elements were related to analogous "literary" phenomena. Likening conventions of ballads to conventions of literature was practically enough to dispose of them. Thus Gregory Smith finds the ballad treatment of material "the outcome of the same literary mood which produced the aureate speech or Cretinism of the cultured speech of the [transition] period." The metrical form of the ballad was also claimed as a literary derivation, one of the fifteenth-century developments from *rime couée,* and assonance was easily explained as "a pretty name of bad rhyme" or a corruption of "folk fancy."

These literary scholars gave no more serious attention than did Gummere to the process of oral tradition within the sight of the investigator. Their thesis, to which Gummere gave limited assent, that ballads degenerate by oral transmission was never supported by detailed argument; instead they contented themselves with sweeping statements or made wry comments on specific cases. The latter method is perhaps the forte in Henderson's edition of the *Minstrelsy of the Scottish Border.* His method of examining any variation which comes to his attention is to assume derivation of the oral form from whatever printed texts were available, granting the improvements to literary emendation and the degeneration to oral tradition. A traditional copy discovered subsequent to publication in a collection is usually treated, without close examination, as a derivation. His range of material is narrow, and his method involves as much conjecture as that of the "folkists." Instead of a lost traditional version, he conjectures a lost romance.

While agreeing with Courthope on the romance derivation of ballads, his followers extended somewhat his attribution to "degenerate minstrels." They gave the ballads to anonymous fifteenth- or sixteenth-century poets, since, as Gregory Smith writes, "it would almost appear as if anonymity were a leading attribute of the ballad form." Surveying the broader area of Western European literature in the fifteenth century, he finds the ballad "merely a part of the literary debris of the middle ages," a *"rechauffé* . . . of pre-existing literary forms," the "atrophy of romantic tradition," but composed by poets not necessarily minstrels in a restricted sense. Henderson takes issue with Courthope's adjective *degenerate,* pointing out that literary conditions differed in England and Scotland in the fourteenth century and later. And Gregory Smith quite willingly accepts Henderson's contention that the ballad was cultivated "not merely by inferior minstrels, but by a class of poets worthy to be designated 'makeris.'" Although Smith attaches less weight to William Dunbar's reference to "ballat-making," both Smith and Henderson find Robert Henryson's use of ballad technique in "The Bloody Serk" proof of the literary origin of the ballad.

Without specifying what is neglected, one can agree with Gummere that this criticism of the literary school suffers "from the fact that the conclusions are very wide and the range of material very narrow." [18] That they should patiently examine Gummere's material was unthinkable: they treated the communalists as madmen. That there was a dearth of unimpeachable traditional material to guide them is true; but they failed to make adequate and intelligent use of what they had. As literary scholars they confined themselves within a narrow range and failed to see where their methods were no longer an adequate guide. Henderson's statement that Child's work, while "invaluable," is a "sort of library of the different versions—good, indifferent, bad, and worse than bad—" illustrates the attitude that precluded any examination of tradition as an organic process and prevented his seeing the possible value of some of his materials. Millar's comment that the literary school had "the merit of taking the ballads as they are—not as they may have been or ought to have been" misses the point. For, in one sense, the literary school could not take them as they are. These critics, concerned with the problems of faking by eighteenth- and early nineteenth-century ballad editors and imprisoned by their concept of the literary-popular dualism, were too busy searching out emendations to recognize the significance of traditional variation.

Yet the criticism was not totally unproductive. Henderson's knowledge of the Scots vernacular was of great value as applied to

Scottish traditional or supposedly traditional versions. His argument for the Scottish origin of many tunes of Anglo-Scottish broadsides was at least a needed corrective to the conclusions of William Chappell. But more important, the similarities and analogies pointed out by all members of the school (and too hastily adjudged to demonstrate identity) raised questions which could not be ignored or passed off lightly by folklorists and which called attention to the complex relationship of literary and popular genres.

One of the obvious limitations of both the communal and literary schools was their confinement of the problem to ballads selected by older British collectors and scholars. In the words of Philip S. Allen,[19] almost the lone literary voice to speak out early on this point, they were "trying to designate a single historical species of song, carefully walled-in, instead of a dozen differing species." Allen, supporting and extending the arguments of the new German school —men like John Meier and Carl Köhler—took a radical and modernist position by any standard. Attacking the magic use of the term *Volk* as well as the distinction between *Volkslied* and *volkstümliche Lied*, Allen holds that "a *Volkslied* is a song from whatever source, of whatever form, sung for a long time by all kinds and conditions of people." He summarily sweeps aside barriers of origin, time, form, and subject. The status of the author, known or unknown, does not affect the song as long as it "fits the throat of the people." Even alteration in transmission is no criterion, as it does not apply equally to all *Volkslieder*. "For purpose of classification all these things are important, but while scholars are classifying songs, the people are singing them, and the real arbiter after all is said and done is *vox populi*." This attitude had to wait a number of years for acceptance in Great Britain and the United States; it had to wait until indiscriminate collecting was well under way. To be sure, organizations for collection and preservation had been established, the American Folklore Society in 1888 and the Folk-Song Society in 1898; but their early yields were small, and ballad criticism remained Child-ballad criticism, literary and antiquarian.

Communal Disciples

Because of this literary character of criticism, Allen's contention that "if the people sing a silly song long enough, it is a Volkslied" fell on deaf ears for more than a decade. Scholars belonging to the literary school were in apparent agreement with Allen, but they were not interested in *Volkslieder*. And the literary scholars interested in *Volkslieder* derived their conclusions directly from Gummere or from Gummere's sources. The widespread acceptance of the communal theory was foreshadowed in Hamilton Wright Mabie's introduction to the popular *Book of Old English Ballads* (1896). Here Mabie espouses a theory almost identical with that of Gummere and based on the same citations from Herder, Goethe, and ten Brink. An anonymous writer (W. MacNeile Dixon) in the *Quarterly Review* for July, 1898, adds nothing to the evidence but substantially approves the early conclusions of Lang and Gummere. Even E. K. Chambers, despite the fact that his work contains much ammunition for the individualists, must be counted for the communal side. In fact, considering the monumental character of *The Medieval Stage* (1903), Chambers' cautious remarks indicate how strong the communal wind was blowing. He admits that the "ballad, indeed, at least on one side of it, was the *detritus*, as the *lai* had been the germ, of romance," but he concludes that Gummere succeeds in showing that the element of folk poetry is stronger than Courthope, Smith, and Henderson recognize.

The widespread acceptance of the narrow communal view by purely literary scholars, who either ignored growing interest in all types of folksong or simply chose that part of the new evidence which suited their purposes, may be discovered by almost casual reading in the criticism of the first two decades of the century. Although much of this enthusiasm was American, one of the more important cases of conversion was that of the English editor and critic, Frank Sidgwick. In the introduction to his *Popular Ballads of the Olden Time* (1903) he reviews the scholarship in English and German and, although refusing to dismiss the "nebular" theory, concludes that "after weighing the evidence and arguments, the balance of probability would seem to lie with the individualists." Sidgwick, never an extreme individualist, took refuge in Child's qualified language, "though a man and not a people has composed them," and accepted Gummere's distinction between "poetry *of* and poetry *for* the people"; but one may still find his later shift of allegiance significant. In 1903 he refers to Gummere as the "strongest champion of this [communal] theory [who] takes an extreme view"; in *The Ballad* (1914) he accepts the "probable evolution of the narrative ballad from the dancing throng's ecstasies." Sidgwick adds nothing to the evidence beyond slight reference to the work of Cecil Sharp and the Folk-Song Society, and his little volume is but a reworking of Gummere's material.

In America specialized studies were made à la Gummere, such as George Morey Miller's "The Dramatic Element in the Popular Ballad," [20] in which he pleads for greater emphasis on the dramatic qualities of the ballad and for the priority of drama in the development of narrative. (This thesis seems to have influenced Gummere's approach in *The Popular Ballad*.) Using games and the dance drama of children (without examining them closely), using material from Chambers' *Medieval Stage* (with differing interpretation and without Chambers' caution), using the familiar method of literary analysis and classification of "canon" ballads, Miller stresses the *dramatic* ballad dance from which extant ballads supposedly derive. But more important matters were to be considered in studies of "this primitive poetic matter that gives to the ballad its distinguishing characteristics."

Given the conclusion of the communalists that the ballad was not only old but, in form at least, prior to epic, it was inevitable that one of Gummere's students should attempt a detailed justification of the *Liedertheorie*. Walter Morris Hart's *Ballad and Epic* (1907) purports to be the study of a series of types of ballads and epics "made without any *a priori* formula, without any thought as to what the nature of the development may be." This statement is absurd, for Hart selects the method which prejudices the results.

Hart examines separately six types of ballad (Simple Ballads, Border Ballads, Robin Hood Ballads, "Adam Bell," the *Gest of Robin Hood*, and Heroic Ballads) and the epic (represented by *Beowulf* and *Roland*) for the "phase of life," motives, structure, characteristics of narrative method, and undeveloped elements of narration. That he finds "it is possible to trace a development along certain definite lines, through the various types of Ballad to the Epic," is not surprising. He has selected, not arbitrarily, the analytical method which will reveal this tendency; he admits that there are other tendencies in the ballad—toward lyric, drama, and street ballad—but he is not obliged to deal with them. He has selected for analysis only those ballads and ballad versions which "seem to show in some degree the tendency to develop in the direction of epic," claiming that "one is under no obligation to deal with all the evidence." Because the ballad has no canonical form, one version is as authentic as another. This same misunderstanding of folklore method leads him to justify his representation of extant ballads as anterior to the epic by citing study of individual folktales. He fails to realize the difference between setting up a "higher chronology" for literary types and disregarding dates of collection of variants.

Hart can therefore conclude that his examples prove what they were selected to prove, that "in the course of this transition from popular poetry to the poetry of art," the changes are "of the nature to be expected of a transition from communal to individual control." The material—once limited, concrete, common—becomes extended, abstract, and individual. From the Simple Ballad, the poetry develops in length, scope, and characterization by accretion and elaboration until it reaches the epic, the beginning of art. Hart's method is the reverse of that usually associated with the *Liedertheorie*. Resting upon existing *Lieder* "rather than wholly upon an attempt to dismember an epic," the study serves to point out that, in spite of the similarities in kind which Hart can quite deliberately "discover," existing ballads could never be strung together to form an epic; a "poet of remarkable taste and technical skill" is demanded.[21] But in addition to the dampening effect on the extreme *Liedertheorie* provided by such a friendly critic, Hart's study contains quite stimulating, though limited, literary analysis.

Lang and Ker: Lorist and Mature Critic

Amid the growing enthusiasm for the communal theory, the defection of its leading English supporter seems to have been overlooked. In his article on "The Ballads: Scottish and English" in Chambers' *Cyclopaedia*, 1901, Andrew Lang virtually disavowed his adherence to the communal position, but conceded little to the literary school.[22] Lang places in one class the relatively modern historical ballads and the group having somewhat obvious thematic relations with the romances, conceding authorship to "some lowly professional minstrel." To the widely diffused ballads which he feels are clearly related to *Märchen* he assigns the epithet *popular*, but only in the sense that "though there must have been an original author—literary or popular, amateur or professional—of each ballad . . . as they exist they are popular patchwork. . . . It is in this sense that the so-called 'communistic' source of certain ballads is to be understood." Lang insists that in the past, at least, the people did versify and were capable of altering, mingling, and modernizing ballads; he maintains that on the evidence of "Mary Hamilton" the process lasted until at least the end of the seventeenth century. Furthermore, he refuses to concede to the romances the *matter* of many analogous ballads. Observing that the literary school credited the preservation of pagan and primitive elements to the romances, Lang points out that the presence of such elements demonstrates that the matter in the romances themselves was the legacy of oral tradition and that when the ballads in question are not derived from versions which have come down side by side with the romances, they simply represent popular authors retrieving their rightful possessions. "Given the regular stock of the incidents of *Märchen*, and given the primitive ideas and customs on which they rest, any member of the people, illiterate but poetic, could turn these data into rhyme. No professed literary man was needed." A literary man might seize the matter or the rhyme for his own, but popular reciters might alter or corrupt it. Lang not only insists on the ballads as a part of the province of folklore, but refers the ballad problem completely to the folktale problem without serious consideration of "the mould peculiar to itself" wherein the ballad handles its matter.

This problem of poetic form was the concern of W. P. Ker, who managed to remain relatively clear of the intense controversy and to do his important work objectively. He contrived to examine and accept both communal and individual evidence yet avoid extreme conclusions and the hysterical tone too often typical of the controversy. Although his earlier writings allowed more to the popular muse, his position from 1896 to 1912 [23] grew rather than changed. Ker was that rare combination of folklorist and literary critic who could take account of folk dance and song as a universal phenomenon and at the same time view particular types of folk dance and song in cultural context. Concerned with the relation of the popular ballad to the northern epics, he could as late as 1912 refer favorably to the *Liedertheorie* but treat the ballad poetry of Western Europe as "related in a strange way to the older epic poetry, not by derivation, but by sympathy." He admits that refrains were known in the old northern poetry and that the interpolated refrain is found universally in popular poetry, but he can yet point out that the use of the refrain as well as other elements in the Scottish and Danish ballads is "after a French original." Insisting on the validity and necessity of distinguishing between what is popular and what is artistic in medieval poetry, he clearly recognizes that "all popular poetry, in Europe at any rate for the last thousand years, is derived from poetry more or less learned in character, or . . . from more or less learned music." Therefore one looks almost in vain for the epithets "communal" and "individual." When Ker does find it necessary to take cognizance of the communal argument, he moves with dispatch to the heart of the matter without polemic. Elsewhere the opposing arguments are absorbed into a criticism that strives not for finality, but maturity.

Ker does not so much define the ballad as accept the limits of the great collections, referring to them for the "lyrical narrative poem . . . either popular in its origin or using the common forms of popular poetry, and fitted for oral circulation through the whole of a community." For it was the peculiar type of narrative song represented in the volumes of Child, Svend Grundtvig, Constantino Nigra, and Damase Arbaud that interested Ker. Therefore his most trenchant criticism is concerned not so much with analogous forms of literature, popular or otherwise, as with the ballad as a unique form of narrative. And therefore in viewing the balladry of Western Europe he sees not only similarities, but differences, an approach which contributed much to the clarification of the ballad problem.

In absorbing successfully the evidence furnished by outstanding figures of ballad criticism, Ker takes account of the "primitive" features of the ballads, "the old tricks of repetition, found all over the world wherever poets are not too highminded or artificial." But, since these features are so widespread, they cannot account for the special nature of the ballad. He admits that refrains were present in the older poetry, including the Anglo-Saxon: "it would be strange if this common thing were lacking in any age." But he looks for an explanation of the special type of refrain common to many French, Scandinavian, and Scottish ballads. He recognizes the large folklore element in the ballad; but "a ballad is not the same thing as a fairy tale . . . it has a form of its own." As the ballads "are not mere versified folklore," so they "are not merely a limb of the great medieval body of romance. . . . They are not degradations of longer stories, for even when they have the same plot, they make a different thing of it." It is this different thing which Ker attempts to account for.

The unique note Ker finds in ballad poetry is the *lyric*, for the ballad is "a narrative poem lyrical in form, or a lyrical poem with a narrative body in it." Surveying the similarities and differences among the ballads of Europe, he is able to trace the lyric note to France. The northern ballads resemble in some respects the old heroic poems, but "are cut off from them by one of the most decisive revolutions in history—the change from the old alliterative verse to the rhyming measures introduced from France." Ker cannot account for the adoption of the new forms, but "the change is there, whether you can explain it or not." The French fashions in poetry, probably well-established on native grounds before 1100, extended in different degrees through Europe in the twelfth century. The French dancing songs—the caroles with their couplet and refrain—conquered Europe about the beginning of the twelfth century, probably triumphing in Germany first, as is illustrated by the eleventh-century legend of the dancers of Kölbigk. Perhaps the Normans were active agents in the revolution, but the fact of the revolution must be accepted and explains much.[24]

Ker finds that the carole answers the ballad question in terms of origin, form, popularity, and date. The carole was a dance song with a leader and a chorus, alternating in their functions. In both origin and performance it was popular in the widest sense, a favorite entertainment among the noble and rustic alike. The carole became the ballad by the addition of a story. But to relate the ballads—that is, the addition of the narrative substance—to the date of the carole fashion is not so easy. Here Ker leans heavily on the internal evidence of the Danish ballads, as the record of the ballad in Denmark is, if anything, later than in Great Britain. But, dating by event, language (cautiously), and treatment of theme, Ker makes a fair case for dating extant narratives as early as the thirteenth century; but the evidence hardly justifies his dates of 1100–1400. For that matter, he is unable to apply these dates even approximately in other areas, especially in France. The comparative lateness of the French ballads, despite the fact that all the necessary elements of

the ballad form were available in twelfth-century France, is puzzling, a problem which leads to Ker's conjecture of unrecorded
existence. A possible solution to the puzzle is provided by the implication (which Ker might have made more explicit) that the
phenomenon of the ballad form is closely related to the culture
complexes of various areas, as he shows in analyzing the similarities
and differences in the ballads of Western Europe. What was made
of the ballad form in Germany is different from what was made
of it in Denmark, and the difference must certainly be related to
the cultures. Yet, as Ker so clearly shows, what is so astonishing
is not the differences, but the "sort of resemblances which no
amount of analogues in different languages can explain, and that
is the likeness in temper among the ballad poets of different languages, which not only makes them take up the same stories, but
makes them deal with fresh realities in the same way." And to
explain this, Ker must at last take refuge in "a Platonic idea of a
ballad, a type remaining essentially the same, but repeating itself
in various forms in the world of appearance."

As should be clear, Ker's conclusions paralleled those of the
communalists, at least in making the ballad originally a dancing
form, even in England, where the evidence is slight; but his treatment of the share of the people in the making of ballads gives but
little comfort to the popular position. Ker views a story or plot as
more of an individual responsibility and questions the assumption
of the people as distinct from the gentry. His argument that certain
nations, such as Wales, Iceland, and Denmark, had no populace as
a separate caste would seem to support that assumption of homogeneity set forth by the communalists; but the full import of his
argument is that in Denmark, which he maintains "is the key of
the position," the ballad originated among the gentry. He concludes
that the ballad dances of the Faeroe Islanders preserve the favorite
amusement in the old Danish country houses, which first came in
as a fashion among gentlefolk. "The 'popular' features here were
not derived from the Danish 'populace'; or alternately, it may be

argued that 'populace' here includes the whole nation." Even admitting that Denmark, in view of its lack of other literary forms, is rather a special case, the conclusion was of no great comfort to the supporters of folk origins.

Still, Ker belonged to the older generation of ballad scholars, referred to as the armchair group not so much because of their inactivities as because of their attitudes. His statements that "there is a fallacy in arguing from the more recent states of ballad tradition . . . back to the times in which the ballads were flourishing" and that the "beauty of the ballads is uncertain and often corrupted by forgetfulness and the ordinary accidents of popular tradition" are not incompatible with the views of some members of the later generation. But Ker is interested neither in "the more recent states" nor in the "forgetfulness and ordinary accidents." He stands, perhaps, as the last important figure whose interest in the ballad was purely literary.

The impasse reached by such literary researchers is indicated in Frank Egbert Bryant's *History of Balladry* (1913), written in 1910. Championing no theory of origins, Bryant examines practically everything which went under the name of *ballad* or had characteristics similar to those of the Child ballads. He finds that the Child collection represents a family rather than a homogeneous species, but is unable to find a unifying principle, whether tradition, verse form, necessity of communal throng, naïve quality, mode of construction, or even narrative. His objective survey makes clear the paucity of evidence with which the antiquarian literary scholar concerned himself and states the paradox posed by the communal view:

> As a rule, the ballads that got recorded in early epochs are not as good representatives of the qualities that strike us as primitive as are many of the ballads obtained from oral tradition within the last one or two hundred years. . . . Those who try to connect balladry with primitive conditions throw chronology to the winds or at least ignore it (p. 62).

Nor can Bryant find any sure evidence of derivation from another literary type. Clearly the point of diminishing returns had been reached, but a new dimension was already being added by the Emersonian scholars.

THE BALLAD WAR II:
THE EMERSONIANS

The predominant position of the literary critics and the noise of their controversy must not obscure the fact that the completion of *The English and Scottish Popular Ballads* in 1898 marked the end of an era in ballad criticism. There is no denying that Child's work did stimulate the literary controversy and tend to restrict interest in folksong to a narrow sphere. And to this day the collection retains an air of finality and exerts a limiting influence which bears witness to the labors of a great scholar. But there arose a new generation which was not content merely to explain, justify, annotate, or even supplement Child's corpus. The new critics not only refused to admit that the patient was dead, but found that he had living relatives worthy of consideration.

The armchair critics, whether of the communal or individual persuasion, were formalists who viewed the ballad or folksong "as something long ago given and done." The new generation was

Emersonian: the folk *speaketh*, not *spake*. Formalists like Gummere had recognized that "in colonial and remote, undisturbed nooks a degenerate version is now and then to be found," but the Emersonians did more than collect such versions. They looked to all aspects of contemporary folksinging—not all of it colonial or isolated—for developments analogous to those said to have produced the ballad. Interest became so great that even the most academic could not escape recognizing the new dimensions being added to ballad criticism. The ballad, no longer a corpse to be lamented and dissected, was found in tradition side by side with possibly related but noncanonical songs. The ballads refused to die, the folksingers refused to sing what the scholars said they should, and the scholars refused to stay within the limits Gummere had set. The result was confusion, thirty years of acrimonious controversy and the beginning of considered and reasonable study of traditional songs.

Too much importance cannot be attached to the destruction of the theory of the "closed account" by the Emersonians. As long as the ballad was a text in a book or a concept in the mind of a critic, the theory could control the evidence. But when new material came to light, the communalists could not resist asserting that contemporary folksong gave evidence of improvisation and group composition, and therefore proof of a like origin for the English and Scottish popular ballads. Having accepted the challenge of contemporary record, literary evolutionists were charged with using irrelevant evidence and misusing facts. The communal theory became less and less attractive as more and more information was amassed by fieldworkers and contemporary-minded scholars. At last, their ammunition exhausted, the communalists retreated to the safer ground of communal transmission or tradition. In the third decade of the twentieth century an uneasy truce obtained, for the folklorists, weary of the controversy, were more interested in study than in theory.

More interesting than the retreat is the record of the scholars, some of them communalists, who provided the new insights. The collections themselves will be dealt with in a later chapter, but the history of twentieth-century ballad controversy must write large the names of English and American critics who collected, edited, and analyzed the evidence of contemporary folksinging. Whatever their bias—Darwinian, psychological, diffusionist, historiodynamic, or orthodox communal—they turned to the folk themselves for an answer, and a continuing answer, to the problems of folk criticism. For they had, though in varying degrees, interest in and respect for living tradition and the individuals who comprise it. Thus they have been Emersons all. "The sun shines to-day also."

Despite many differences in the approach, emphasis, and interest of their leaders, the new generations in England and the United States coincided in their early development. Collecting of folksong during the latter half of the nineteenth century had been prolific in neither country. The Folk-Lore Society had manifested little interest in living "relics," and its American counterpart at first proved no more productive. Even in the optimistic atmosphere engendered at the establishment of a new society, the attitude of the founder of the American Folklore Society was hopeful but not encouraging. "As respects old ballads," wrote William Wells Newell, "the prospect of obtaining much of value is not flattering. In the seventeenth century, the time for the composition of these had almost passed; and they had, in a measure, been superseded by inferior rhymes of literary origin . . . or by popular doggerels, which may be called ballads, but possess little poetic interest. Still, genuine popular ballads continued to be sung in the colonies . . . and it is possible that something of value may be obtained." [1] During the first decade of the society's existence, the *Journal of American Folklore* published a few scraps of song from Negro and white sources, as well as four texts which were to find their way into Child's collection. But, conveniently enough for the historian, important American criticism based on contemporary collection begins with Newell's article on "Early American Ballads" in 1899, one year after the renascence of English collection signaled by the founding of the Folk-Song Society, May 16, 1898. And again, conveniently enough, Cecil Sharp's call in 1904 for systematic collecting was paralleled in the United States by Henry Marvin Belden's 1905 suggestion for systematic research. Critics on both sides of the ocean were developing a criticism based on contemporary field experience.

These and other parallels cannot obscure certain differences in early editing and criticism in England and the United States. American labors grew up largely under the aegis of Child's work and, predominantly academic, were chiefly concerned with textual and literary problems. But, remarkably enough, practices were less selective and restricted in America than in England. (Scottish practices conformed more closely to American.) The leaders of the Folk-Song Society, primarily interested in the music of the folksong, practiced highly selective collection and publication according to somewhat narrow criteria. Even those American scholars committed to a rather extreme communal view and sheltered by Child's mantle were more liberal.

Cecil J. Sharp and the
English Darwinians

The roots of the modern English school of folksong study reach at least to the Rev. John Broadwood's *Old English Songs*, privately printed in 1843. The interest of this county clergyman in the tunes of his parishioners was not widely shared until later in the century. M. H. Mason published her *Nursery Rhymes and Country Songs* in 1878, and the movement began to take shape in the next two decades with the collections of J. Collingwood Bruce, Heywood Sumner, Sabine Baring-Gould and H. Fleetwood Sheppard, William Alexander Barrett, and Frank Kidson. In 1890 Lucy E. Broadwood issued *Sussex Songs*, a new and expanded edition of her uncle's book; and with J. A. Fuller-Maitland she edited in 1893 *English County Songs*, a selection from collection over a wide area. These collections, by and large, tried to reproduce faithfully the tunes taken down directly from "the mouths of the people." The lesser attention devoted to the text was to be typical of the early work of the English school; but, as Cecil Sharp was to point out, it was time "that the balance, as between the respective claims of words and tunes, should be restored." [2]

The Folk-Song Society, founded under the leadership of Mrs. Kate Lee in 1898, had a nucleus of nonacademic musicians and private scholars, though the professors held the vice-presidencies. But Sir Hubert Parry spoke for the amateurs as well as the professors when in his inaugural address he lamented the influence of "the common popular songs of the day" in driving out "the old folk-music . . . among the purest products of the human mind. It grew in the hearts of the people before they devoted themselves so assiduously to the making of quick returns." He hoped that by immediate and accurate collection members of the society might "save something primitive and genuine from extinction" and "put on record what loveable qualities there are in unsophisticated humanity." [3] There was but the vaguest suggestion of a theory here; nor was much systematic collecting initiated. Sharp complained in 1904 that the Folk-Song Society had published only 109 songs in six years, had received little support, and had become moribund. But largely because of Sharp's collection and criticism the Folk-Song Society gained a new vigor, developed a critical position, and became the dominating force in English folksong study.

As a collector and student of folksong, Sharp came late into the field.[4] At Christmas, 1899, he accidentally saw a Morris dance at Headington and noted the tune the following day, but his first published collection, *A Book of British Song for Home and School* (1902) was made up from other books. His first encounter with live folksong came in September, 1903, when at the home of his friend Charles Marson he heard Marson's gardener sing "The Seeds of Love." This fortunate incident stimulated Sharp to begin his tireless collecting in Somerset. Using as headquarters the home of Marson (curate at Hambridge), Sharp had by August, 1904, collected enough songs to fill an issue of the *Journal of the Folk-Song*

Society (II, 6, 1905); and *Folk Songs from Somerset,* the joint work of Sharp and Marson, appeared from 1904 to 1906.

The immediate result of Sharp's first forays was a strengthening, almost a reactivation, of the Folk-Song Society. At the beginning of 1904 Sharp published a call for an *ad hoc* organization to solicit funds for the urgent collecting of folksongs. Attacking the Musical Association for its complete lack of interest and the Folk-Song Society for its lack of accomplishment, Sharp sought the establishment of a new organization which would take immediate action. The new society did not materialize, but on February 8, 1904, Sharp was made a member of the Committee of Management of the Folk-Song Society, and Lucy E. Broadwood was appointed Hon. Secretary to succeed the ailing Kate Lee. The society began almost immediately to take active steps to stimulate collection, especially among the county clergy.

More important for the crystallization of Sharp's views was the controversy initiated early in 1906 when the Board of Education recommended to teachers the use of "National or Folk-Songs." Sharp took violent exception to this list of fifty songs, all but seven of which he found to be either art songs or artistic reworkings of folksongs. The ensuing argument carried on in the public press should have concerned the distinction between *Volkslied* and *volkstümliche Lied.* Sharp's opponents, however, defined *traditional songs* as those with "a long life in the public ear," thus including songs which would not seem to fall even within the category of *volkstümlich.* Sharp realized that there was more to the issue than the controversy over the use of the song "Tom Bowling" in the schools. For he was by now convinced that there was an intrinsic difference between a folksong and a people's song. "The mere knowledge of the name of the composer has nothing to do with the matter." Although Sharp classified national song as individual and folksong as communal and racial, he denied the belief of which he stood accused, that "folksongs grew like trees in the fields and national songs came out of human brains." He agreed that brains created both, but maintained that folksong "has been evolved by

the brains of countless generations of folk-singers and composers."
Convinced of the rightness of his views and isolated by the Folk-
Song Society's approval of the Board of Education's *Suggestions*
(although without any mention of the offending list), Sharp resolved to present a full justification of his position. On the strength
of the 1,500 songs he had by this time collected, he published in
October, 1907, *English Folk-Song: Some Conclusions.*

The strength of this book lies in Sharp's analysis of the melody
of what he recognized as folksong and in his study of the process
of variation in folk tunes. His technical analysis is not completely
new, but it provides a systematic consideration of English folk
scales, rhythmic forms, and melodic figures. Although the work furnished later students with much material, Sharp makes little of the
relationship between the words and the tune, despite his assurance
that "the two elements of the folk-song, the words and the melody,
should be considered as inseparable." He does not pretend that his
technical analysis is exhaustive or definitive, nor that it provides a
scientific definition of folk music. But he feels that certain conclusions have been reached. In characterizing folk tunes, Sharp rejects
anonymity as a definitive element. Although all folksongs are anonymous, all anonymous songs are not folksongs. "Anonymity is a
condition, not a cause." Modality, however, is a technical peculi-
arity. Modal melodies, set to secular words, are usually of folk
origin, whereas minor tunes are either composed tunes or corrupted
folk tunes. Folk tunes do not modulate and are nonharmonic, as
demonstrated by the use of nonharmonic passing notes, by a certain
vagueness of tonality, by the use of the flatted seventh in the final ca-
dences, and in the difficulty of harmonizing a folk tune. Folk tunes
often contain bars of irregular length, and five and seven time measures are prevalent. These conclusions, largely descriptive, provide
such a feeble reed that Sharp is reduced to writing, "We know a folk-
tune when we hear it;—or we don't."

The subjectivity of Sharp's conclusion serves to remind us that
one of the bases of his criticism is that which underlies Gummere's:
the dichotomy between *art* and *folk*. Sharp, too, believes that folk-

song is the "spontaneous utterance of the people"; he differs from the Gummere-communalists only in his method of accounting for the spontaneity. But Sharp accepts so many arguments advanced by differing theorists that his comments on folk poetry can hardly be taken seriously. He agrees that ballads preceded songs, that the impersonal element preceded the lyric. He accepts as relevant evidence the etymology of the word *ballad*—from *ball* as well as from *ballare*. In spite of his own demonstration that there is little difference between a ballad tune and a song tune, he seems to find no difficulty in maintaining the inseparability of words and music and in accepting such tests of the ballad as repetition and commonplaces. His concept of the history of the ballad is a somewhat undiscriminating compilation of all the older theories. He is willing to trace the subjects of ballads to a common source—the East or the common heritage of the "Arian race." The ballad is originated by the common people, is then appropriated by minstrels, who piece together ballads into epics and romances. After the spread of printing, the minstrels, forced to cater to the tastes of the common people, break up the romances into ballads again. Perhaps his failure to include the popular theory that the ballads have continuity exclusive of the romances is mere oversight. But enough of what Sharp inherited and could not digest. His contributions offset the inheritance.

Though admitting that "folk-song must have had a beginning, and that beginning must have been the work of an individual," Sharp makes not a single concession to those who would derive folksong from earlier art music. Finding in preserved specimens of older music the originals of neither the tunes nor the technical peculiarities distinguishing folksong, Sharp concludes that folksong is "created by the common people . . . is the unaided composition of the unskilled." His contribution to the theory of folksong lies in a different answer to Gummere's question of "how got the apples" of spontaneity in. Sharp's answer, like Gummere's, is evolutionary; but it is a Darwinian, not a Spencerian, evolution.

To Gummere the communal act was initial, and the ballad or

folksong is communal because it contains elements that can be referred to the initial process; the ballad is a sort of halfway point
in a process of evolution from communal to artistic control. But
to Sharp, the communal nature of the folksong results from the
process itself: "the method of oral transmission is not merely one
by which the folk-song lives; it is a process by which it grows and
by which it is created." The various forms of the folksong are not
corruptions, but akin to sports in organisms. Although the productions of individuals, the changes must win the approval of the community. Through this survival of the fittest is evolved a form which
reflects the tastes and feelings of the community as a whole.

It may be observed that this theory at once disagrees with Gummere's and is more radical. The very tradition which Gummere
said "could make no literary form" is responsible for the communality of folksong. Sharp is thus asserting communal origin for
extant folksong, a conclusion Gummere dared not openly avow.
Neither Gummere nor Sharp seemed to realize the nature of their
disagreement, for Sharp accepts many of Gummere's postulates,
and Gummere in a letter to Sharp shows no understanding of the
basic disagreement: "It is the sort of work that you have done
[*English Folk-Song: Some Conclusions*] which really counts. It is
an unspeakable comfort to have a man who knows folk-song at first
hand write such words about it as you have written." [5] Yet the core
of Sharp's theory seems to have been suggested by a criticism rejected by Gummere. Sharp quotes Franz M. Böhme's remark
(*Altdeutches Liederbuch*, 1877, pp. xxii–xxiii) that "one man sings
a song, and then others sing it after him, *changing what they do
not like.*" Observing the structure of folksong and the habits of
folksingers, Sharp develops Böhme's comment into an evolutionary
process of three stages: *continuity, variation,* and *selection.*

Whatever the form of the folksong at its inception, the song
must be persistent. The persistence of the type "must be the rule,
and variation the exception. Otherwise types would be so quickly
changed and multiplied that their relationships one to another
would be obscured." From his own experience Sharp is able to

demonstrate the accurate memory of folksingers which is essential to that continuity necessary for survival. Though essential, continuity is passive rather than active, a condition rather than a cause. Variation "creates the material which renders development possible."

Sharp finds the causes of variation to be largely unconscious, believing that "in most cases, melodic alterations apparently spring subconsciously from out of the heart of the singer." He concludes that the folksinger attaches more importance to the words than to the tune and is therefore more or less unconscious of the melody. Changes proceed "very rarely, if ever, from a conscious desire to improve." Although the causes of variation are certain to be manifold, Sharp can suggest a few of the reasons for melodic change. Love of ornament, faulty memory, adaptation of an old tune to fit new words, change of mode—all are important. The temptation always exists to relieve the monotony of a sustained tone by introducing turns, trills, or passing notes. Corruption of lines will lead to adaptation of tunes to fit irregularities. Singers learning a new set of words from a ballad sheet will adapt a tune to fit them. And a singer who prefers one mode will change a song into it, thus causing a change in melody because of the characteristic idiom of each mode. Although some few singers habitually vary tunes in successive renditions or continually introduce stereotyped variations —and these singers greatly influence the development of folksong— most transmitters make only trivial variations. But "any change, however small, may eventually lead to results all out of proportion to the initial variation."

While variation is individual and may be sterile, Sharp's third principle, selection, is communal and ensures "that variation shall, in certain cases, result in organic growth." Variations attractive only to the individual will die; those appealing to the community will be perpetuated. Whether the appeal be expressive or esthetic depends on racial characteristics. Admitting that racial ideas are "highly speculative," Sharp insists that "it is evident that . . . national peculiarities must ultimately determine the specific characteristics of the folk-songs of the different nations." Communal choice, not communal invention, determines the racial character of a song or ballad.

> The individual, then, invents; the community selects. . . . Every line, every word of the ballad sprang in the first instance from the head of some individual, reciter, minstrel, or peasant; just as every note, every phrase of a folk-tune proceeded originally from the mouth of a solitary singer. Corporate action has originated nothing and can originate nothing. Communal composition is unthinkable. The community plays a part, it is true, but it is at a later stage, after and not before the individual has done his work and manufactured the material (p. 31).

These were brave words. They have so inspired other critics that we tend to forget that for Sharp they represent an end, not a beginning, at least as far as theory is concerned. Sharp never passed beyond this point. His collecting and arranging continued, along with his services in introducing folksong into English middle-class life. He was to make a fruitful exploration into American territory, 1916–1918. He was to make further contributions to the analysis of the music of folksong. But his theory remained constant, became the creed of the Folk-Song Society,[6] and still is breathed through the English Folk Dance and Song Society. The public lectures delivered in 1932 at Bryn Mawr College by Ralph Vaughan Williams might have been given by Sharp, so faithful were they to the virtues and limitations of the latter's credo. In the concluding lecture, Williams indicated the impression he must have left:

> You may think, judging from previous lectures, that I think folksong the one thing needful [for the future of American music], and that conditions in America do not admit of folk-songs because there is no peasant class to make and sing them.[7]

The concessions he makes regarding "the folk songs of the Negro, those of the Indian, those of the English settlers," and those of other immigrant groups fail to modify significantly the limitation common to his and Sharp's conception of folksong. Sharp's belief that folksong was the "unaided composition of the unskilled" extended to the original germ of melody, a rambling and indefinite tune or a string of commonly used phrases—in either case an instinctive, though individual, creation, differing generically from composed music. Thus the source of a folksong is again pushed beyond our sight.

To some extent this limitation gives an added reason for the English collectors' preoccupation with the music of folksong. Certainly the emphasis was a needed corrective. But the neglect or cavalier treatment of texts was justified by comments on "modern doggerel" and "scraps of imperfectly remembered broadside versions" now set to folk tunes. If not dead, the English ballad "is now at its last gasp; its account is well-nigh closed." [8] For indeed the concern of Sharp and his co-workers remained with the *ancient* rather than the *traditional* ballad, with song whose source we cannot see rather than one demonstrably derived from an original. Sharp expressed this "qualified Emersonianism" when he wrote that "no one has ever witnessed the actual creation of a folk-song, and now, of course, no one ever will. All arguments must therefore be inferential, must be based upon collateral evidence obtained by the observation of the folk-song collector when in close contact with the folk-singers, or upon . . . analysis." [9] Sharp's faith in tradition was, after all, limited. He stopped short of admitting that his evolutionary process could transmute the dross of broadside doggerel into the gold of folksong. This admission was to be made by American scholars.

Three American Emersonians: Newell, Barry, and Belden

Prior to 1898 little effort had been expended in the collection and criticism of American folksong. The earliest substantial work had been the collection of *Slave Songs of the United States* (1867) by William Francis Allen, Charles Pickard Ware, and Lucy McKim Garrison. Thomas Wentworth Higginson, David C. Barrow, and George Washington Harris had contributed to the criticism of

Negro song in popular magazine articles, but less attention had been directed to folksongs of the white population. The work of Frank Moore and Alfred Mason Williams was largely antiquarian and held little promise. Significant collection and criticism began under the figurative shadow of Child's collection and under the literal shadow of Harvard University. The leaders of the movement during the first decade of the twentieth century had intimate associations with Harvard, and the first significant comment on American balladry was made by the founder of the American Folklore Society, the Cambridge scholar, William Wells Newell.

Newell brought to the problem experience in American field collecting and a wide knowledge of international folktale scholarship. His *Games and Songs of American Children* (1883) is a pioneer work not yet superseded. He had already made clear his position as an individualist and a diffusionist, an opponent of general theoretical assumptions and of analogies with archeology or language. "Problems of folk-lore diffusion must be considered separately on their own merits." [10] To Newell, the ballad problem was merely one facet of the folktale problem, and the problem was to study individual items in their different forms and to trace the items to their separate and individual origins. Therefore his interest in American balladry was not esthetic, national, or sentimental, but "scientific." Newell's two articles on "Early American Ballads" in the *Journal of American Folklore*, 1899–1900, outline his position and illustrate it with evidence from ballads collected in the United States and presumably originating there.

In his first article Newell distinguishes between old English ballads and later productions mainly on the basis of their literary merit. Admitting that "the history of old English ballads is conjectural," he determines, largely on Danish evidence, that before the end of the fourteenth century, histories were cast in the form of narrative song by persons of literary taste and refinement. Later ballads were written by men of the people, but were no less popular ballads, even though inferior. These later ballads were brought to the New World and others were composed in America. Although now sung chiefly in the Southern mountains, the songs were once well known in the Northern states. Newell adds that the failure to collect them has been no great literary loss, but that they have a value "as illustrating popular taste and folk-life." Printing ten ballads or fragments, including a two-stanza text of "Springfield Mountain," Newell prophetically states that "very likely the publication will bring to light a whole crop."

In his second article he not only prints a part of that crop, but uses seven variant texts of "Springfield Mountain" as evidence for his argument that individual origin and subsequent diffusion explain the traits of ballads. "Springfield Mountain" is "a striking example of a song composed in a particular place, on a definite occasion, with regard to substantial accuracy, and by a person of some literary education, which, nevertheless, almost in our time, has passed into folk-lore and obtained popular currency." The piece is taken to represent the entire ballad literature, to show that any ballad, "no matter how ancient and universal," could have originated like any ordinary piece of literature, but spread and changed so that the variants represent different minds and become "more vaguely human" or take on romantic elements.

> The theory that ballads were born out of a mental state quite independent of any conditions familiar to literature, that they represent an unconscious cerebration, that, to use a phrase which to my mind conveys no distinct meaning, they possessed "communal origins," has no more application to the songs of old England than of new England, no more place in the twelfth century than in the eighteenth (p. 10).

Newell's use of "Springfield Mountain" was in accord with his work in general folklore. "One fact is worth a thousand speculations," he writes in his final statement on the problem, "Individual and Collective Characteristics in Folk-Lore." [11] This essay, though not dealing exclusively with the ballad problem, is a frontal assault on Gummere's theories and provides adequate explanation for Gummere's efforts to separate the ballad and folktale. Newell's strategy ignores any substantial difference between the ballad and folktale, treats the larger outlines and assumptions of the communal theory, and challenges the view of ethnology which underlies Gummere's theory.

Newell's review of folktale scholarship in the introduction to his article is not a particularly effective weapon against Gummere in its support of the diffusion of folktales. Gummere had carefully distinguished between the form and content of at least the late ballads. But Newell, after discrediting earlier folktale theories, demonstrates the similarities between Gummere's arguments and the discarded theories. Making analogy between Max Müller's "myth-making age" and Gummere's "song-making age," Newell places against Gummere's "idea of a primitive simplicity, freedom, and direct contact with nature," the "present-day conception" that "as we recede in time, and in the order of culture, formality, habit, rigid custom, precise ritual, appear to prevail." Further, Newell attacks the reliability of much of Gummere's ethnological evidence by explaining "those collective characteristics which are attributed to folk-lore." The oral nature of folklore provides free growth. The "presumptive inventor" of a narrative rearranges preexisting elements and, depending on the memory of his audience for the perpetuation of his production, can use few personal elements. Even these few disappear in transmission. In so far as the material represents community rather than personal opinion, it may be regarded as belonging to the folk as a whole. While a particular narrative may be old, its ideas are those of the uncultured part of the community and are therefore more conservative and less affected by the changes which influence written literature; and the conservative character of the community explains why new compositions seldom replace the existing stock. These qualities produce the impression that oral literature is collective rather than personal. Therefore, concludes Newell, the oft-cited travelers' reports that all tribal songs of certain primitive peoples are improvised would seem to be the consequence of imperfect record.

Newell contributed substantially to the establishment of the Emersonian school by his denial of Gummere's "closed account" and by his neglect of the esthetic tests of the ballad. While he does not face directly the problem of distinguishing V*olkslied* from *volkstümliche Lied*, he anticipates it in his statement that "between folk-lore and literature exist intermediate territories." He casts suspicion on all general theories of origin, advising the folklorist to "keep himself as far as possible from any speculations which transgress the field of actual experience," and to seek particular reasons for particular elements of style or type, such as the origin of dramatic ballads. He finally defines the gulf between communalists and individualists:

> There never was a time, since mankind emerged from the brute condition, in which literary invention and expression was not individual, as it is today. There never was a time when the prophet and poet did not seek his inspiration in solitude, just as he does today. The question whether early or present man is the more social, makes one of those philosophic theses which can be answered with equal correctness in favor of either alternative (p. 14).

Before Newell's death in 1907, the crop of folksong was slowly being harvested in various sections of the United States, and two major figures had arisen to follow his lead. Not to minimize their differences or to grant them equal status in an assessment of folksong scholars, Phillips Barry and Henry Marvin Belden shared traits which made them leaders in the development of ballad criticism in the United States. Neither seems to have begun his investigations with a theory to justify, neither was willing to limit his interests to a narrow field, and both turned to American tradition for an answer to ballad problems.

Barry was the first Anglo-American scholar to investigate traditional song in all its aspects: text, tune, performance, and transmission. If, as he said, "It is not a one-man job to write a critical history of a popular ballad," [12] Barry had the greatest command of the three requisite fields of research—folklore background, origin of text-tune complex, and re-creation. He combined the experience of the field collector with the erudition, if not always the equanimity, of the academic scholar. His work today is known only to the specialist, for his important criticism remains buried in folklore journals.[13] Although his conclusions developed with his research between 1903 and 1937, he began "with an instinctive sense . . . that it might be proper to go to the folk singers themselves to find such evidence as might lead to the solutions of the many, not the one, problem involved." [14] The evidence for his early conclusions was sometimes insufficient or faulty in detail; but later investigations provided fuller documentation, and the errors in detail affected only the detail. His conclusions may be regarded as reasonably complete by 1914, but must be assembled from the mass of partial statements made in his articles.

Barry's concept of folksong is similar to that of Sharp and was undoubtedly influenced by it. Barry's theory, too, is individualistic and, to some extent, evolutionary, but lacks the obvious Darwinian analogies. It emphasizes psychological factors and is more inclusive. It not only gives to the tune and text some of the treatment promised by Sharp, but makes room for factors of tradition which Sharp ignores or refuses to admit. It moves one more step away from the "mystery" by refusing to make matters of style or origin valid criteria for definition, yet allows origin and style a validity within the larger system.

Barry's theory may be called *modern* in that it is descriptive and inductive. To learn "what is folksong?" he asks, "What are the folk singing?" And he finds that the answers are one. Instead of lamenting with Sharp and others that singers too often furnish the collector with music-hall songs or ballads from the broadside press, Barry notes that the folksinger makes no distinction among the items of his repertory. Barry's conclusion: "Why make a distinction when the folk makes none?" Apparently starting from this definition of a folksong as a song sung from memory, he develops a concept of folksong as a phenomenon rather than an entity, as a process rather than as an event. Matters of structure and style are to be referred to the process, which will account for them. The process or processes are those of tradition: "individual invention plus communal re-creation." [15]

Barry's theory is more than the "definition by destination" which Gummere opposed so bitterly. Establishing folksong as dynamic by definition, Barry can both ignore and admit "the mere accident of origin." He concedes that the words of certain folksongs might be traced to communal composition, but denies that this circumstance makes them folksongs. Indeed, in his early criticism he often seems to take pains to admit wherever possible Gummere's terms and evidence. Of the formula so irritating to many individualists, he writes, " 'Das Volk dichtet' is as true as ever. Yet not of communal composition." He finds the "iterative style" very old and "primitive." But Barry's task was to demonstrate that the primitive iteration is an acquired trait even in the older ballads, that *das Volk dichtet* must be interpreted progressively, and that "the process of balladry has not changed, nor will it change." The steps in this demonstration cannot be shown to have developed chronologically in his articles, for another suggestion of his modernity is the manner in which he adopts a hypothesis and tests it (or illustrates it) in his successive pronouncements.

Barry's first step is to destroy the concept of the closed account. To be sure, the storming of that battlement is the task of the entire theory, since the closed account denies not so much the singing of folksongs as their composition in the approved style. But the first move is to establish folksinging as a living art, to show that what was being found and preserved represented more than "the last fading flowers of popular poetry." Barry does this by publishing versions of the ancient ballads and by pointing out that the variants he collected in New England and those collected elsewhere by others represent a living tradition because of their excellent preservation. He attacks the concept that folksong exists as a survival in isolated communities, showing that "the voice of the folksinger may yet be heard, as well in the heart of the great city as on the lonely hillside." Barry then seeks to demonstrate that ballads are being created as well as preserved, that the despised "vulgar" ballads and native American creations as well, flourishing side by side with the older ballads, have developed the traits used to distinguish popular ballads as a genre.

The marks of the popular ballad as set forth by Barry are three: multiplicity of version, impersonality of authorship, and iterative style—"unfailing characteristics of poetry of the folk and music of the folk, the world over." This analysis parallels Gummere's in isolating certain distinguishing features but pointedly ignores matters of form which can be referred to culture patterns or local usage, specifically: rhyme, meter, and stanzaic structure. Barry might have pointed out that he considered their origin, like that of the archetype, a mere accident. It is the universal popular elements that he explains as a growth, not an original feature.

Barry's evidence for the development of the popular traits consists of studies of variation in texts and tunes of certain ballads. He demonstrates that particular composed tunes in oral circulation do more than change and diversify: they develop traits of melodic structure which he calls "the climactic iteration of partial melodies." In a similar fashion the text is diversified into variants and re-created in different forms. A literary text such as "The Ocean Burial" becomes "The Lone Prairie," just as from the unknown original of the "Lord Randall" tune descends the melody of "Lochaber No More." As the melody of a composed song develops iteration at the hands of a succession of folksingers, so do some literary texts, such as "Fair Charlotte." The variation in traditional versions of broadside or native American ballads is slight as compared with that in older ballads, and the development of iteration is less pronounced. "Communal re-creation is not a rapid process, nor a uniform one." American balladry has been formed not in the "golden age of folk-song," but in a "period of decadence." Diversification and iteration are more pronounced in tunes because of the accessibility of printed copies of the text. Especially is this true of the British vulgar ballads. But the principle of "individual invention plus communal re-creation" remains the same.

This much of Barry's criticism had been generally understood by other critics. It agrees with Sharp's concept of variation, adding the application of the process to composed tunes and to the texts as well. Even print is accepted as a part of the process of transmission, with the stipulation that print is an interruption in tradition, just as is "the caprice of a folk-singer who reserves the right to sing a certain ballad to a melody different from that to which it has been sung hitherto." And, adds Barry, "No ballad . . . ever died of printers' ink." But more is involved than the simple diffusion of an individual invention and its re-creation by a succession of singers with deliberate adaptations or with unconscious changes according to a fixed law "as yet imperfectly understood." The direction in which Barry is moving becomes apparent when one considers his use of *literary atavisms* and *reversion to primitive form*. The psychological elements are becoming dominant, and the theory is more modern than at first suspected.

The extent to which Barry has departed from both evolutionary and diffusionary hypotheses is made more clear when we understand the definition of the term *ballad* which he advances by 1913:

> It refers not to an event, but to a process. . . . The process is one by which a simple event in human experience, of subjective interest, narrated in simple language, set to a simple melody is progressively objectivated.[16]

This means that *the* ballad is an idea; *a* ballad is an illustration of that idea. Barry's conclusion differs from W. P. Ker's because it means that ballads are to be classified according to their themes. Somewhat earlier Barry points out the danger in assuming actual borrowing or direct transmission as the only explanation of correspondence in ballad themes. Observing the appearance in the vulgar ballads of ancient ballad themes, he admits the possibility of coincidence, borrowing, or the reworking of a traditional ballad for the broadside press. But his discovery of a Vermont prose narrative paralleling "The Crafty Farmer" leads him to postulate "a traditional ballad mythology, stereotyped ornamentations and details, suited to certain events." He rather cautiously concludes at this point that "the origin and transmission of ballad themes may not in any two given instances be the same, or due to the same causes." But when he later proposes a classification which would list under one head ballads whose only demonstrable connection is similarity of theme, he adopts a wider conception of ballad tradition than is encompassed in a study of textual filiation.

Whatever the validity of this judgment, Barry's most important contribution to the developing American ballad criticism is his demonstration that both ancient ballads and modern ballads of admittedly individual authorship exist side by side in a living folk tradition and are subject to influences which develop a number of analogous traits in both types. He makes a significant assault on the concept that the style of the "good" ballads "bears witness to any actual difference in origin" and on the right of the critic to establish upon its [the style's] basis a ballad aristocracy . . . to regard the three hundred and six [17] 'popular' ballads as having an exclusive right to the name 'ballad.'" In his demonstration Barry proves the value of individual ballad studies which take into account the relationship of text and tune and their dissemination and change in oral and printed transmission.

While Barry was beginning his work in New England, Henry M. Belden embarked in 1903 upon parallel endeavors in Missouri. Belden, with the help of students and instructors at the University of Missouri, collected in two years eleven Child ballads and numerous other pieces of "authorless popular song." On the basis of this collection and that already made by Newell and Barry, Belden, in a 1905 article on "The Study of Folk-Song in America," [18] called for further collection, justifying the labor and setting forth a plan for systematic and exhaustive investigation. He admitted the lack of literary quality in American folksong but urged its study to gain knowledge of the literary taste and conditions of the people among whom it was found. But he made clear his main interest in American ballads: the light they would throw on ballad problems.

Belden's article is important not so much because of its extreme optimism—that teachers and students could carry on an organized research that in ten years would recover all vestiges of the Child ballad in America, and that questions concerning the New World tradition of the ancient, broadside, and native American ballads, would be shortly answered—rather, the importance lies in the nature of the questions and directions given to collectors, which augurs the course of future American investigation. Belden is interested in the origin of American pieces which seem to parallel ancient balladry and in the traditional history of ancient and modern ballads, especially the part played by print. He suggests a more even distribution of ballads that challenges the communal hypothesis of ballad communities. His advice to collectors suggests the recording of data not previously emphasized: circumstances of recording, family and racial background of singers, and their knowledge of the sources and history of the song. In a sentence broadly representative of future work, he writes, "Inclusion rather than exclusion should be the rule in the work of collection," even to the acceptance of printed matter. Work of this kind was soon to cause Belden to qualify his phrase, "old and vanishing folk-song in America."

The years immediately following Belden's "call" to collectors did not produce what he had hoped. He had to say in 1911, "Seven of the ten years are gone, considerable effort has been expended, and there are still plenty of questions to be answered." But enough had been done to justify his conclusion that balladry, "in the wide sense of the term, is found to be restricted to no part of America." [19] The *Journal of American Folklore* had published materials from such unlikely areas as the Pacific Coast, Wisconsin, and Illinois. Barry, Belden, and Hubert G. Shearin and Josiah H. Combs had published check lists of their collections. John A. Lomax's historic *Cowboy Songs* had been published the previous year; Louise Pound was soon to publish an outline of the Nebraska materials, some of which had already appeared in the *Journal*. And Belden had reached certain tentative conclusions which left him with more questions than he had asked before.

One conclusion of Belden's sets him apart from those members of the Emersonian school who, though maintaining the existence of balladry, expected its death momentarily. Belden believed that "the spirit of balladry . . . is as immortal as romance itself." He urged the collection of living American balladry, but refused to incite collectors with the cry of "Now or never!" This is more than the simple denial of the "closed account." The discovery of ballads dealing with recent events contributed to his belief, but more important was the theory he had developed to account for the ballad style—or styles. His conclusions are important because without a frontal assault on Gummere's work, which he calls "by far the most important contribution to ballad study [excepting Child's collection] . . . made in our time," [20] he manages to undermine the center of the communal front.

The most brilliant analysis of orthodox communal theory to come out of the controversy, however, was Belden's review of Gummere's *The Popular Ballad*,[21] an attack masked as an endeavor ". . . not to confirm or controvert his theory, but to show what his theory is." Belden, explaining the "conditions of the problem," puts his finger on three weaknesses of the communal argument: the confusion of "the origin of the form and style of the ballad and the origin of any particular ballad"; the treatment of "the distinction between the ballad and 'artistic' poetry as impersonal and individual, respectively" as generic rather than relative; and the attempt to draw a definite line between the reproductive and inventive processes in composition. He finds the evident motive of Gummere a desire to secure for the Child ballads "a venerable, if not aristocratic, pedigree" separating them from their "despised neighbors," not merely by structural analysis (which Belden approves), but "by a gulf as wide as civilization and reaching back to the beginnings of human society." Belden notes that Gummere's closed account "would assure a peculiar distinction to the ballads in Child's collection, and at the same time lock the door against any inquisitive experimenter who might wish to test the theory of communal composition of ballads in living society." But to define Gummere's meaning, Belden applies the communal theory to a typical ballad, the oft-used "Mary Hamilton," which Gummere calls "a genuine ballad of tradition, still undeveloped into epic breadth," and which can be given, with some confidence, a date *a quo*. Applying hypotheses of origin (and incidentally exposing Gummere's equivocal use of the word *tradition*), he demonstrates that Gummere means, and can only mean, that later than 1563 a homogeneous community at a festal dance composed "Mary Hamilton," various members of the community improvising it bit by bit. Only this hypothesis, which must reject even the gifted individual recognized by Lang among Australian blacks, will provide Gummere's definition by origins, will make of the ballad "an authorless composition from the start." And Belden "admits" that "it is an extinct method of composition," a method that never, in any recorded European instance, has produced a ballad. With tongue in cheek, he leaves the tenability of the theory to be judged by those "better versed in the social history of northern Britain."

Belden has praise for Gummere because the latter provides aid in definition and classification, without which "there can be no scientific criticism of the ballad." Belden faces "the question of whether we shall classify ballads according to intrinsic qualities of tone, style, and structure, or according to theories (more or less insusceptible of demonstration) as to their origin, or according to their known history and vogue." [22] His own answer is not a simple choice from among the three, as the categories are not mutually exclusive. Although he emphasizes transmission and persistence, Belden takes a position largely in the first category, maintaining that there is more than one sort of product in what have passed for ballads. He accepts the separation of true or popular ballads from vulgar ballads, but denies that either group is the sole concern of the folklorist, or that either is primitive poetry or the product of other than conscious art.

The central point of Belden's theory is provided by his analysis of the vulgar ballad. Even the term applied by Child to the British broadside and street ballad indicated the attitude of the romantic critics. Gummere found it to be poetry *for* the people, to be distinguished by style and marks of artistic making. Belden, trying the ballad by Gummere's explicit tests, finds that although it lacks the stylistic and structural characteristics of the popular ballad, it resists the romantic division into popular and artistic. The vulgar ballad lacks the concentration of situation, the "leaping and lingering," the extensive use of incremental repetition, and the poetic qualities which Belden agrees are tests. The vulgar ballad tells the whole story in a deliberate fashion, with its own stereotyped commonplaces and clumsy repetition. Yet it does not belong to the poetry of art as defined by Gummere because it also lacks the personal note, the consciousness of individual authorship. Even though the author be known, the vulgar ballad as well as the popular ballad has "nothing in thought or style to suggest the conscious poet."

By demonstrating that the type of ballad impossible to refer to primitive conditions meets the tests set up by the communalists to distinguish literary productions, Belden strikes at the core of the communal theory, the assumption that the poet is a solitary genius, isolated from tradition. Belden finds not the dichotomy between the products of *art* and *nature,* but the productions of makers following different "schools." Whatever the origin of either style, the ballads themselves were the creations of individuals impersonally following a tradition. The ballad, like *all poetry,* is a social product and a thing of tradition. Thus Belden concludes, with Ker and Barry, that the ballad is an *idea,* but that the popular ballad and the vulgar ballad are both *ideas.* Both belong to the unlettered and are perpetuated, whether by print or oral tradition. The ballad problem consists of "the processes of transmission, of modification, of transformation into a recognized type." And to Belden it remains a problem to be solved, not a theory to be demonstrated. He accepts neither the evolutionary nor the degenerative hypothesis, writing that the "material of story and song does not work only up, as some evolutionists would have us believe, nor only down, as the dominant theory of folk-tales seems to imply; instead it is a conscious circulation, passing from the region of high art to that of vulgar legend, and thence back again. . . . And who shall say, of any given tale, in which of our cultural strata it originated?"

Belden concludes that even if the collection of American materials may not throw direct light on the basic problem of classification and definition, it can certainly aid in the solution of preliminary problems. The discovery by Belden and others of the great prevalence of ballads in popular print and manuscript, together with W. Roy MacKenzie's observations of the transmission by ballad prints in Nova Scotia,[23] points the way to an investigation of the relationship between print and oral tradition. Although Belden observes that the popular-ballad style tends to disappear in America, he admits that traditional versions of American ballads have more of the style than the printed copies and finds Barry's work valuable —even if the changes represent only unconscious assimilation to the style of the older ballads already in the people's memories, even if "communal re-creation explains not the origin of the ballad *style*, but only why traditional ballads assume that style." Further collection can help solve problems of authorship and social and geographical distribution of ballads. Though he is able to contribute little to the study of ballad tunes, he recognizes its importance and believes cooperative collection including the recording of music will mark a considerable advance.

Thus seven of the ten years Belden originally proposed provide only a better understanding of the problems of balladry. What he proposed is but an expansion of his earlier "call"; what ensued has been characterized by a recent "folk-critic" as "the aimless collection of folksongs, children's rhymes, and so forth, without any comprehension of their significance or ability to sort them out." [24] However this may be, Belden's proposal was lacking in neither aim nor comprehension of the significance of the material: "We shall be able to check, by first-hand, living, verifiable evidence, theories regarding the essential conditions of balladry that have derived in great part from fragmentary, sometimes prejudiced, sometimes ignorant, and in all cases now dead and unverifiable evidence of past centuries."

Four Communal Apostles

The Emersonian school of American collectors and critics was not composed entirely of anticommunalists. To be sure, a percentage of the interest in folksinging in areas such as the Southern Appalachians was "nonpartisan," but numerous collectors and scholars sought the new evidence as support for the theory which had originally denied its relevance. The five years following the publication of *Cowboy Songs* witnessed the formation of seven state folklore societies, largely by Southern ballad scholars of communal leanings. To the roll of state societies, consisting of Missouri (1906) and Texas (1909), were soon added North Carolina (1912), Kentucky (1912), Virginia (1913), Nebraska (1913), West Virginia (1915), and Oklahoma (1915). With few exceptions, these groups had as their aim the collection and preservation of Old World ballads and related material. One might be tempted to call some of them Child Ballad Societies (Communalist Persuasion). Although they did not limit their collecting activities to the canon of 306, many were interested in other songs primarily to support the theory of communal origin. Early leaders were such communalist disciples as E. C. Perrow, C. Alphonso Smith, and Frank C. Brown. But first place among these figures must be accorded to John A. Lomax. To take him seriously as a critic is perhaps neither wise nor fair. It is as a collector and editor that he must be judged. But the pronouncements of such a great and influential field collector cannot escape notice; indeed, they are of great importance.

John A. Lomax was not the first to bring the cowboy songs to notice, nor was he the first to publish a collection of native American folksongs printed with the music. His *Cowboy Songs and Other Frontier Ballads* (1910) is not a model of editorial practice, and fortunately its methods have not been influential. The great stimulus his unflagging efforts gave to others must not be minimized, but Lomax's work in other respects affected the pattern of American folksong study. It placed perhaps an undue emphasis upon occu-

pational songs, particularly those of the Southwest; it called attention to nationalistic qualities in American folksong; and it stimulated
the use of living materials to bolster the communal theory. Although the last is of special interest here, separation of the three
elements is difficult. They all seem to flow from two important
experiences clearly suggested in his *Adventures of a Ballad Hunter*
but earlier pointed out by Barry.[25] A Southwestern farm boy ro-
manticized his cowboy neighbor into a "knight of the plains"; later
contact with the "Harvard school of communalists" fixed his impression "that the cowboys were a homogeneous folk in miniature
and that folk-song was primarily men's song." Herein lies, at least
in part, some explanation for the contradictions in his comments
on American ballads.

It was perhaps natural that a man whose collecting labors had
been inspired and aided by Kittredge and Harvard and whose first
book received the communal blessing (see Barrett Wendell's introduction) should be sympathetic toward a theory of popular and
group origins. His belief that the "indigenous popular songs that
have sprung up as has the grass on the plains" were created by "that
unique figure in American civilization, the cowboy" [26] meant more
than an assumption of cowboy composers; for in the introduction
to *Cowboy Songs* he postulates a perfect equality among the cowboys, a society reduced to its lowest terms: the homogeneous throng
—at least in the sense that whatever "the most gifted man could
produce must bear the criticism of the entire camp, and agree with
the ideas of a group of men . . . any song that came from such a
group would be the joint product of a number of them." If cowboy
songs "can lay no claim to being influenced by motions of the
dance," they may have been influenced by the movement of the
cow pony.[27] Thus the combination of experiences produced an attitude which none of the subsequent discoveries was ever to dispel.
The discovery that such a "palpable result of group inprovisation"
as "The Railroad Corral" had been written and published by J. M.
Hanson less than a decade before Lomax collected it chilled some
enthusiasts. Lomax remained unaffected. His position is made clear

in the address he delivered as retiring president of the American Folklore Society, December, 1913.[28]

Lomax accepts Kittredge's definition of the ballad—that it is a song that tells a story, is of community or group authorship, has no date, is handed down by word of mouth, and is impersonal in tone —and adds that it is "the spontaneous poetic expression of the primitive emotions of a people." Confessing that by such a definition of the ballad, America has none at all, he seeks to show that there is a body of American folksong, "called by courtesy 'ballads,' which in their authorship, in the social conditions under which they were produced, in the spirit which gives them life, resemble the genuine ballads." By his own admission, American ballads are of the folk largely by adoption. The authors are not the "spinners and knitters in the sun," but "the victims of *Wanderlust*, the rovers, who find solace in the wide, silent places of the earth." The songs have been in circulation "not long enough to receive the polish they would get by repetition through two or three centuries." But he makes one point which seems to have more relevance and has had a wide echo. He finds that two "ballads," "The Old Chisholm Trail" and "The Boll Weevil," "are absolutely known to have been composed by groups of persons whose community life made their thinking similar, and present valuable corroborative evidence of the theory advanced by Professor Gummere and Professor Kittredge concerning the origin of the ballads from which came those now in the great Child collection." Thus a new weapon [29] (which critics were to discover had two handles) was added to the armory of the communalists: the evidence of loose improvisations with slight narrative content. On this type of song, rather than on native American narratives, were the chief arguments of the communal disciples to be based.

The first significant published collection of Southern folksong was E. C. Perrow's "Songs and Rhymes from the South" in the *Journal of American Folklore,* 1912–1915. The 270 heterogeneous items, derived from Perrow's memory and from students and friends, are from Tennessee, Kentucky, Mississippi, Missouri, West Virginia, and Alabama; sources include both Negro and white singers. Perrow had spent his childhood in eastern Tennessee and had a mountain background to draw upon. Therefore his judgments can demonstrate clearly how the communalists selected and judged the material they interpreted.

His excellent introduction, dealing with the characteristics of the mountain whites and their social environment, provides a background which aids in the understanding of the songs and justifies his conclusion that "among them there still exist traces of the ancient ballad making facility." But his meaning is restricted when he writes that "apparently the very material out of which the popular ballad is made may be picked up here today." For he refers not to the narrative songs, nor to the banjo minstrel. He chooses dance (play-party) songs, revival songs, and work songs of the Negroes. The choice is based on style and manner of composition. The homogeneous throng with its foresinger is represented by the improvising caller and the participants in the play-party, by the leader and the congregation at a revival. "On such occasions . . . we have the miracle and *das Volk dichtet*, one foresinger after another taking up the hymn, and adding his own contribution to the melting pot." Yet when Perrow points out the sequence of relatives in revival songs and lack of order in dance songs, he unwittingly provides ammunition for the individualists' attack on the ballad as genre.

Perrow's recognition of the repetition and improvisation in Negro songs, which leads him to write that the Negro, more than the white, is "a representative of the ballad-making epoch," is paralleled in the criticism of C. Alphonso Smith and Frank C. Brown.

C. Alphonso Smith was probably the outstanding purist in his generation of American collectors. To him oral tradition was absolute; ballads which could be traced even indirectly to print were to be discarded. He refused to "count" a fragment of "Chevy Chase" which was traditional in the family of a Virginia singer because the fragment was almost identical with a portion of the Percy version and, "though the singer had seen no printed copy . . . the printed page had plainly . . . been one of the relay stations in the journey of the ballad from source to singer." *Ballad* to C. A. Smith meant the Child ballad, for "there *are* three hundred and five English and Scottish ballads, neither more nor less." But Smith's attitude derives more from Kittredge than from Gummere, in that transmission is allowed equal rights with origins. "The first version, if we could catch it hot from the lips of the composing throng, would not through mere priority be one whit more authentic or authoritative than the latest version, provided the latest version was also the product of the people." He accepts the remaking of tunes as well as texts, emphasizes the ballad as song, and presents evidence for collateral rather than lineal relationships between tune variants.[30] Yet in justification of the communal theory he leaves the charmed ballad circle to seek his evidence in Negro revival and camp-meeting songs.

These songs are proof to C. A. Smith of the reality of communal composition of the ballad. Here he finds a leader and a responsive throng creating material containing the ballad elements—refrain, iteration, and sequence of relatives. Simpler than "The Hangman's Tree," these songs require at the most but the singing of two stanzas to set the pattern for the cooperating throng. To be sure, these songs are not "ballads in the restricted sense," but only because of their subjectivity! "They lack the note of impersonality." [31]

The North Carolina collector, Frank C. Brown, differed from C. A. Smith in being more liberal in his collecting practices and in qualifying his affirmation of the communal authorship of ballads, even though finding the Negro song the most important evidence. The ballads themselves, Brown writes, are so changed by tradition as to be untrustworthy evidence, but preserve certain characteristic traits which connect them with modern Negro improvisations. He refuses to believe that such "crude expressions of individuals could ever have united of themselves to form a finished ballad of the most intricate sort." Therefore talented individuals must have reworked the material between meetings of the throng.[32] A momentous concession, perhaps.

Spirited Individualist Attack

Though the communalists had captured the dominant positions and the thoughtful protests of men like Belden and Barry could scarcely be heard above the scholarly clamor, descendants of the literary school had arisen to challenge the spontaneous-combustion theory. Some appeared briefly, and one was to wage ceaseless and unremitting battle with the doctrine of the *Gesammtgeist*. The guiding principles of these critics are, like those of the communalists, largely reducible to *a priori* conviction: a conviction that art is in a strict sense the product of gifted and trained individuals, that popular poetry in the communalists' sense is a contradiction in terms. As T. S. Welby expresses it, "There never has been a poem to which any audience contributed anything worth mention. . . . All the people had to do with the ballad was to vulgarize it." [33] Sir Arthur Quiller-Couch attributed the original *pattern* or *style* of the ballad (not the ballads themselves, as some critics seem to think) to an individual.[34] But before we consider the somewhat intemperate, but important, criticism of John R. Moore and Louise Pound, we must take note of the unheeded resolution of a judicious critic who does not hold an *a priori* position.

Although Arthur Beatty was by no means an armchair critic, his contribution to the origins controversy was not based on American finds. His "Ballad, Tale, and Tradition: A Study in Popular Literary Origins" [35] makes use of the conventional apparatus of the literary student of the ballad, to which he adds the conclusions of other folklore research and of the newer anthropology. Beatty stands between, or above, the contending forces, denouncing the doubting Thomases of the literary school but seriously questioning the methods of the communalists in that the latter failed to deal with other forms of popular art and failed to study the ballad in its cultural context.

Beatty separates form and content of the ballads but considers the relationship between the two. Comparing ballads with prose forms of the same tales, he finds that the latter preserve beliefs, customs, and rituals more clearly and are therefore presumably older: "the body of European folk-tale has a closer affiliation with fundamental primitive beliefs than has the ballad." But as we trace the form back through "lower" stages of culture, the ballad's chief characteristic—narrative—disappears; the primitive poem does not tell a story. For the ballad, the content rather than the form is the constant, and the question of origin of ballads is bound up with the origin and diffusion of popular tales.

As to ballad form, Beatty readily admits three communalist contentions: that communal dancing is a fact among every people in a primitive stage of culture; that Europeans have danced in companies from the earliest times; and that ballad characteristics such as the refrain must be connected with dancing. But he refuses to bridge the gulf between primitive and European dances. He insists instead on the differences; in fact, the only resemblance he finds is in the *idea* of the dance. The dances develop within tribal tradition, and resemblances are to be explained by borrowing. Following the newer anthropological investigations, he suggests that the ballad problem is specific, in that its background is solely the tradition of a given culture, but not unique, in that it must be investigated as a part of the folklore of a given tradition.

Beatty finds inapplicable many of the ballad characteristics supposed to connect it with the dance. Impersonality, anonymity, repetition, and even communality are characteristics of other forms of folklore. Peculiar to the ballad "are only (1) metre of a rather uniform kind (but not wholly so), and (2) *refrain* in various forms." Even making a definite connection of these with European dancing is not easy. Following Ker, the Danish critics, and Alfred Jeanroy, Beatty connects the Scandinavian and Faeroe ballads with the French carole, a relationship of little comfort to the communalists. For the ballads seem to have developed not in France, with the refrains and dances, but in Scandinavia. The older Scandinavian ballads deal with heroic tales or contemporary events and in their content have little relation with France. The Danish ballad with inset refrain is nearer to conditions of the dance than ballads of any other nationality. Ballads of other areas appear to be later and show even less connection with the dance. Thus the most reliable evidence shows that the ballad began "in a definite tradition originating in a borrowed artistic form superimposed on a native form and practice." The ballads of Europe were produced in a complicated tradition from many sources.

The reasoned and temperate conclusion of Beatty is that the ballad as we have it is later than its folklore content and is a distinct phenomenon in time and place, to be explained by borrowing and reborrowing among the peoples of Western Europe. It is to be understood as a part of a specific tradition, with differences in development even in different districts. Had more heed been paid to Beatty's approach, many of the intemperate battles of the next twenty years might have been avoided and more constructive investigation undertaken. But the worst was yet to come.

The confusion engendered by the conflicting arguments is illustrated by the abortive criticism of John Robert Moore. His articles [36] are a peculiar mixture of differing brands of communal and individual argument, a mixture which, in spite of valuable perceptions, had no catalyst.

Moore's major thesis is that the ballad is art and, excepting the "one or two survivals of a very early choral dance" represented by the riddle ballads, is the product of individuals belonging to popular "schools of anonymous poetry." The simple ballad is better art than the gest precisely because of its lack of developed narrative. The best evidence of this is the omission of the central action, a development analogous to the appearance of the intense lyric and the short story—both late forms. One must look to individuals, members of the "schools," for the virtues of the ballads. "It is almost universally true that the most effective of the ballads, and often those which exhibit the most conspicuous characteristics of what is commonly called genuine traditional poetry, are those which have least claim to oral transmission." So far Moore's position is at least intelligible. But his evidence and supporting argument seem

chosen to prove just the opposite or hopelessly to confuse the issue, for he states that it is in the unity of interest manifested in the group composed of a narrator and a listener, "and in the act of transmission within the group that we should seek for an explanation of the peculiarities of our English ballads."

His arguments, drawn from the data of clinical psychology and from his own study of differing ballads and ballad versions, tend to contradict his thesis and each other. A portion of his argument is clear. Ballads tend to degenerate and lose their form because of forgetfulness—normal, induced by linguistic change, or resulting from the disappearance of factors which aid the memory in preservation, e.g., dance, tune, custom of singing, or a sympathetic audience. Even the custom of singing tends, by prolongation of vowels and the resulting loss of consonants, to destroy the intelligible story. But certain psychological factors operating in tradition seem not to function precisely in accord with Moore's concept of degeneration. Citing experiments, he points out that the conventional ballad stanza of four and three would normally result when material is submitted to popular transmission. The pronounced rhythm of the ballad is admittedly primitive, but in the sense that it is inhibited by the "higher brain processes" in any culture. The refrain, itself a part of this universal rhythmic activity, can be explained without an excursion beyond modern times: periodic repetition is necessary to secure rhythm, and nonsensical arrangements of words are rhythmically more effective. The refrain is not a survival, because instead of becoming stereotyped it is the more variable element: new refrains are added to old ballads. Further, the repetition of the tune will cause one stanza to affect the character of the next, just as the repetition of its rhythm forces the conformance of the text, resulting in wrenched accents. Even if assonance were not original, it would develop.

Moore's evidence thus leads us to conclude that marks of the ballad style are due to oral transmission. But it seems it is not so, for he insists that "it is the simple ballads which most often have the fixed refrain and the broadsides which exhibit the most marked use of incremental repetition. Furthermore, when oral transmission adds a refrain to an original broadside, it is only a simple refrain, without the structural device of accretion." This conflicting evidence is relatively innocuous compared with the total abandonment of logic at other points. Moore notes that commonplaces and the numbers three and seven, "considered peculiar to the cabalistic lore of the ballads," are "relatively lacking in the earlier versions, but more and more conspicuous as the ballad is transmitted. . . . The later versions of the ballads are the beggar children of poetry, each dressed in the cast-off finery of a dozen of its superiors." Here he has hopelessly confused his argument for the development of ballad traits in transmission with his argument that the art of the simple ballad, the result of individual composers, degenerates at the hands of a succession of reciters. And after attributing the omission of the central action to the efforts of skilled poets he demonstrates such omission to be the result of corruption in transmission.

Moore's evidence is not as contradictory as he makes it seem, however. The contradiction arises from his refusal to accept both good and ill effects from the same causes. When he observes that a "use of set forms leads to a sort of incremental repetition in the later ballads, which in no way conflicts with our previous statement that true incremental repetition is more common in the broadsides than in the simple ballads," he indicates the element which might unite his evidence. His earlier statement that "all ballads seem to be made, some well and some badly," would, when applied to changes induced by the conscious and unconscious processes of a sucession of singers, explain how the same techniques might result now in a memorable performance, now in the botched versions attributed to Buchan's "wight of Homer's craft" or to the "love of detail" in the unlettered mind. In fact, Moore's conclusion that he has yet to find a clear case in which a ballad can be shown to have improved as a result of oral transmission "except in the way of becoming more lyrical" presents a clear case for improvement if we agree with his judgment that "the most powerful of all ballad devices [is] the omission of the central action." His outline of the process of ballad change from narrative to nursery song, while demonstrating that the forces of transmission "will destroy the whole poem eventually," provides for a period in which the ballad may, by loss of narrative passages and by improvisation of skilled emenders, achieve those versions acclaimed by ballad lovers.

Moore's criticism has not been of great historic significance but it does demonstrate the dangers of the disparate and conflicting evidence used by ballad critics. Perhaps his most telling argument is that which outlines a ballad development opposite to Hart's concept of successive stages of ballads from the simple ballad to the *Gest*. The demonstration is all the more effective because of its own suspicious analogies and insufficient or conflicting evidence. It shows that any theory which seeks to explain all the known facts of ballads by a simple process of evolution or degeneration is doomed to failure. It must either dismiss many matters as irrelevant or destroy itself by its own contradictions.

Moore's work was peripheral compared with the attacks of Louise Pound, who was the nemesis of the communalists from 1913 on. Determined to play Ritson to the communalists' Percy, she leveled her criticism at all aspects of the communal theory and all its proponents. The theorist who marshaled world-wide evidence for support, the literary critic who accepted the theorist's judgment, the anthologist who organized his texts and notes according to the critic, the folksong collector who interpreted his evidence by communal standards, and the teacher who reported the "communal" compositions of her charges—all have suffered from Louise Pound's lash. She challenged the theory, its evidence, and its interpretation. Her view of the matter was not particularly new, nor is most of her evidence. But her attack was loud and long. Articles and notes published between 1913 and 1921 were stitched and expanded to comprise the first book-length refutation of the communal position which met the popular school on its own ground: *Poetic Origins and the Ballad* (1921). And in a summary article of 1924, she sought to deliver the *coup de grâce* by placing the theory in its historical and ideological context, outworn and discredited.

It is as easy to become irritated with Louise Pound's methods as it is difficult to disprove her arguments. In attacking an entrenched position, a bludgeon may be more effective than a rapier. We must not forget that the literary criticism of the second decade of the twentieth century had almost completely accepted the communal theory. If her voice was strident, we must remember that urbane scholars were prone to dismiss any deviation from the communalist line as fatuous. Polite criticism met with stony silence. Only repeated bludgeonings were to have an effect. If Miss Pound's view of the problem is narrow, the broad generalizations of her opponents conditioned it; if her approach is unnecessarily literal, a hard-headed attitude furnishes a needed corrective. Her almost endless repetition of identical points was made necessary by an audience who did not want to hear them. When at the Modern Language Association meeting of 1951 she read a brief report on American folksongs,[37] one tyro murmured that she had learned nothing and had forgotten nothing. But a grizzled veteran of the communal wars reproved him with the wry remark that the performance was rather a moment of triumph. For the admitted special pleading no longer brooked challenge.

Louise Pound's position in *Poetic Origins* is that of the literary school—but with a difference. Whereas such a critic as T. F. Henderson dismisses out of hand the evidence of primitive poetry and traditional recital, she takes all evidence into account and examines it closely. In fact, her honest attempt to meet the communalists on their own ground subjects her argument to criticism that might have been better directed at her opponents; her method forces her to adopt the very approaches she decries. But she takes up point by point the types of evidence adduced by the communalists, primitive, historic, internal, and traditional, and—perhaps more important—calls into question the flexible definition of *ballad* which permitted so much shifty argument. She concludes that the ballad is a late form, a short lyric tale of individual authorship, that the English and Scottish popular ballads are mainly aristocratic compositions surviving among the vulgar and sometimes containing

stylistic elements found in other types of folksong, themselves
gesunkene Kulturgüter.

She first attacks the postulated evolution of the ballad from primitive dance by challenging Gummere's sly introduction of the etymological argument into his own work. Her demonstration of the
ambiguous and contradictory uses of the term *ballad* prior to the
twentieth century is but an echo of Gummere's own comments;
but she adds a consideration of the ambiguous and contradictory
uses of it by Gummere and his followers: "the loose usage which permits scholars to use the word in the sense of dance song and of
lyrical narrative in the same work." She lays bare the contradictions
in the theory that can make an absolute distinction between narrative and lyric but can advance as evidence for origin of a narrative
form the lyric form whose separate nature it has insisted on. But
exposure of logical fallacy is not enough; she deals with the evidence.

In canvassing the records of primitive song, Miss Pound had access to new studies by special scholars and to the "carefully observed facts of scientific record," but her method differs from
Gummere's most strikingly in taking account of all the evidence.
Instead of searching for examples to bolster a theory or using a
critique that can dispose of antithetical usages as irrelevant, she
examines the bulk of the record. She shows that many types of
songs exist among the peoples we label *primitive.* If members of
Gummere's favorite tribe never sing without dancing or dance
without singing, other tribes have songless dances and danceless
songs. Individually *and* in throngs, primitive peoples sing songs
that are traditional and songs that are improvised. If we mean by
the word *ballad* a song story, primitive peoples do not dance to
ballads; in fact, primitive peoples compose not narratives, but lyrics.
Needless to say, Louise Pound's evidence and argument do not settle the problem of poetic origins. They simply show that conditions
of primitive song differ little from the conditions of civilized song.
But she does demonstrate that the communal theory does not rest
on Gummere's "overwhelming evidence"; nor, she adds, does it
rest on probability: "the individual ought to be able to engage

in rhythmic motion, to compose tunes, and then to evolve words to those tunes, at least as early as he is able to do these things with others of his kind."

The primitive evidence countered, Miss Pound examines other evidence advanced for the relation of the ballad to the dance. She shows how meager is the medieval record of the ballad as dance song. Examining specimens of dance songs of the Middle Ages, she finds that they exhibit neither the structure nor tone of the narrative songs of the Child collection. The dance songs are lyric. Their refrains, the repeated elements, are the identifying portions of the songs and persist above all else. And the same characteristics are found in contemporary dance songs. Nor have these latter, surviving under oral and communal conditions, shown any tendency to develop in any sort of epic process! Her argument casts doubt on the supposed dance origins of the English and Scottish ballads (though she does not deny dancing to narrative songs in exceptional cases) and shows that the postulation of ballad evolution, at least as advanced by the communalists, cannot stand the light of evidence. To insist that Miss Pound's conception of dance origin is far too literal, assuming over their protests that the communalists believed in dance origin of extant ballads, does not discredit her evidence. Even if the protests were not merely strategies, they do not alter the communalists' insistence on the special nature of the dance survivals in the ballads. As Miss Pound demonstrates, other types of song show much closer connection with the dance, and the ballad's textual connection is surely no more than that of other forms.

There remained other allegations of the primitive and special character of the ballad, particularly those concerning its style. Louise Pound's examination of the ballad style shows scholarship, ingenuity, and a concern for the literal fact that is, if annoying at times, at least refreshing as compared with the lack of concern manifested by her opponents. Her argument is, as usual, double-barreled. She finds first that there is no ballad style, and secondly that the "ballad style" is neither primitive nor limited to ballads.

The great variation in stanzaic form, use of iteration, and method of narration is, she feels, the reason for Child's fluctuation in judgment. Her attack on the stylistic touchstones—incremental repetition, climax (or sequence) of relatives, and concentration on dialogue and situation—turns on their chronological appearance in ballad texts and in literary history and their diffusion in other types of literature. She establishes that incremental repetition and sequence of relatives occur in forms other than the ballad, e.g., revival hymns. Iteration, at least, belongs to the style of folksong in general and is not a ballad differentia; consequently, urging the ballad especially as a primitive form is questionable.

Louise Pound's attack on the primitive nature of these devices themselves is perhaps less successful, although it suffices to discredit a literal application of communal evolution to the ballad texts. Whereas the communalists cast chronology to the winds, she follows it slavishly, demonstrating that the elements of the ballad style come late in literary history and in the ballad texts themselves. She admits that "the date of recovery of a ballad is no sure indication of the antiquity of a ballad, or the lack of it," but adds that "it should not be left out of the account when other evidence fails." Yet her method produces positive evidence that cannot be overlooked. Following Moore, she finds that incremental repetition, sequence of relatives, and concentration on situation and dialogue are most prominent in texts collected after the fifteenth century, rather than in "Judas," "Inter Diabolis et Virgo," and "the long epic narratives of Robin Hood." Thus the facts (of collection, at least) contradict the communal theory of development. Further, the facts agree with the literary judgment of the situation ballad (e.g., "Lord Randall," "Lizie Wan") as artistic and the Robin Hood pieces as relatively crude and with parallel developments in other literatures which show dialogue as a late form. Again there is contradiction in the communal theory, which holds that "the ballad is the earliest universal form of poetry," but that "the early simple forms only later became ballads by developing complexity and plot."

Miss Pound attacks also the popular theory, which connects ballad origins with the folk, or illiterates. Her ammunition is drawn from a consideration of the sources of the extant texts and from an examination of the internal evidence offered by the ballads themselves when compared with twentieth-century folksongs and with the literary record. Her examination of sources is, as might be expected, quite literal, but is rather less successful than her other arguments. She exemplifies the tendency of the individualists to assume that a text in print or manuscript is earlier than a later-discovered traditional copy, and she is not always accurate in referring to collections on which Child drew. When she points out that a large number of texts in Child's collection, in fact some of the best, do not come from oral sources, she may be making little more than a comment on collecting habits and the accidents of ballad scholarship, but her concern with the recovery of ballads from "special persons" is today assuming more importance. Her argument here, however, is but part of her unsafe analogy with language, that usages move in one direction, from high to low in society.

Her examination of modern folksinging yields the same conclusion. She finds that popular improvisations are crude and structureless, deal with immediate concerns of the class producing them, show no tendency to develop into the Child type of ballads, and are the first to be forgotten; she finds that the memorable pieces surviving in a folk community usually come from elsewhere and are more often composed on a "higher" level, and that narratives composed within a community are based on imported models. The subject matter of the old ballads is aristocratic, not peasant, and proves that they, like the "good" narratives in modern isolated communities, were composed on a higher level. The literal nature of the parallel between the late Middle Ages and twentieth-century society is rather suspect. Her rejection of the communalists' homogeneous society need not imply that the social interests of medieval peasants be identical with those of modern folksingers, or more particularly, of the isolated groups which she presents as the norm of folksong.

In somewhat better case is Miss Pound's consideration of the relations of the ballad with literature, especially as an attack on the distinction between the poetry of art and the poetry of the people. She points to the special vocabulary of fourteenth- and fifteenth-century poets which appears in the ballads. Her recognition of literary devices—the premonitory dream, the *chanson d'aventure* and *reverdi* openings—provides evidence against the postulation of a single source for the ballads and suggests ballad affiliations not congenial with the theory of popular origins. Her insistence that weak rhymes are but the retention of French accent loses force because of her failure to take into account the relation between text and tune or to consider tunes at all. But the mounting evidence provides background for her statement that if "minstrels were the authors of any proportion of the ballads admitted by Professor Child into his collection . . . it is an admission that there is no fundamental distinction plainly differentiating the 'true' ballad, in origin and style, from other types of ballads and songs."

The character of Louise Pound's criticism is determined by the role she has chosen—the dragon-slayer. The apparent irrelevance of portions of her argument may be traced to the protean nature of the communal theory and to her insistence on contradicting it at every turn. Her zeal leads her to present analogies which are convincing only when applied to specific communal claims. But the parallels she urges are the very ones utilized by many communalists. Her policy of attacking the logic of a theory while at the same time working within the logic to contradict the evidence gives her criticism its irrelevant and negative cast, a characteristic which applies even to her attempt at a positive approach.

Miss Pound's affirmation that the older ballads originated in a manner analogous to the "good" narratives which have entered the song repertoires of contemporary folksingers does not explain the precise origin of the older type. But her suggestion of a close relationship between the early ballads and the church is itself somewhat negative in that it is a counsel of despair in which she has little faith. Her position follows logically from her literal approach to the chronological record. Viewing the mass of songs descending from the late Middle Ages, she discovers no ballads of the Child type other than religious narratives. She discards the communalist postulation of "a defect of the record" because of the variety of other material surviving and considers the secular ballad a later development. To explain the form of the ballads recovered in the fifteenth and sixteenth centuries, she suggests that the lyrical qualities of some types of carols were imposed upon the short recited tale or song story which was either created or adapted by clerics to popularize religious materials. More than anything else, the suggestion fits the *absence* of facts. It accounts for the lack of ballads in fourteenth-century manuscripts which contain religious pieces in ballad style. It accounts even for the late appearance of the refrain, for her theory suggests that not until the early Tudor period did the singing of ballads replace recitals.

But the theory raises as many questions as it answers. This addition of lyric to a narrative type takes place under restricted conditions; the new combination is separated from the music and must wait many years for a reunion. If the lyrical quality of the narrative be the prime consideration and "the earliest texts remaining to us seem to have been meant for recital rather than singing," it may well be that the origin of the form has not yet been reached. When Miss Pound acknowledges the poverty of musical evidence, she does not justify a conclusion that ignores the relation of text and tune. Her statement that "the melodies of ballads are more shifting, less dependable, than are the texts," even if true, misses the point. Her dependence on only the literal fact calls to mind Gummere's remark: "In the lack of actual material, any theory can be proved."

The extent to which her attitude blinds her to the essence of the problem is shown in her article on "The Term: 'Communal,' " [38] which may be regarded as the final statement of her position. The article succinctly summarizes her important demonstrations: the connection of the communal theory with the romantic *Gesammt-*

geist; the individual and modern nature of the ownership of primitive song; the paucity of evidence for dance origin of the ballad; the confusion of ballad and folksong by those who urged a special origin for the ballad. But three of her conclusions are *non sequiturs*:

1. "The typical process, for the great majority of ballads, is a process of decay." Miss Pound sees the ballad record as a one-way street, to be judged by the condition of its last few miles. Scanning the partial evidence of collectors, making no detailed studies of individual ballads, and paying insufficient attention to the few studies existing, she never conceives of processes other than evolution or degeneration.

2. "The refrains, salient situations, repetitions, and commonplaces of style appearing in many ballads" have no connection with primitive or communal throngs because these features are shared by pieces other than ballads and because the improvisations of throngs are not narrative and do not develop into ballads. The very points which make her demonstration a telling anticommunal strategy are those which are the most questionable: the confusion of origin and essence, the emphasis on the special character of the Child ballad, and the exclusive concern with the historical problem. That the features of the ballad may be associative, that the ballad may be primitive or even communal for reasons other than the literally historical, Miss Pound seems not to conceive. And, following both Gummere and the literary school, she gives little consideration to other forms of folk literature except as they illustrate her thesis.

3. The term *communal* has no validity, even in reference to the re-creation of ballads in tradition. As late as the publication of her *Poetic Origins and the Ballad*, Louise Pound accepts communal re-creation; but she is finally driven to deny the term altogether on the grounds that the traditional changes occur at the hands of individuals and are therefore not truly communal. Here is perhaps the apogee of the literal-minded approach. Gummere, accepting the communal concept, sees only the woods; Miss Pound, to whom the term is anathema, sees only the trees. Nothing else

demonstrates so clearly the essential similarity of the absolutist forces in the ballad war. If, as Miss Pound insists, the term *communal* must be given up, the reason lies in its absolutist associations that defy reinterpretation. For within the confines of a single article Miss Pound herself moves from a denunciation of the failure to apply the term to "gradual recreation by a succession of singers" to an attack on the term itself in a sentence that, on any but the crudest literal level, destroys itself: "There is no communal text; there are many shifting texts in the mouths of many singers."

Contrary to some opinion, the publication of *Poetic Origins and the Ballad* did not cause the "whole house of cards" to collapse.[39] Reception of the book was, to say the least, mixed. Friendly reviewers regretted the overlappings, repetitions, and polemical tone resulting from Miss Pound's failure to recast completely her articles, and they pointed out the weaknesses of what constructive argument she offered. Avowed opponents took her to task for the lamentable habit—shared by Gummere—of quoting out of context passages favoring her argument, and for her "seeming assumption that in the theory of the communalists the first product of the communal process must be a narrative poem."[40] Gordon Hall Gerould, who discovered her lack of Child's and Gummere's "exquisite literary tact," found her "obviously incapable of orderly thought" and the book "dull, confused, and unconvincing."[41] But more important than reviews is the continuing argument in books, articles, and notes to collections.

Continuing Melee

It is virtually impossible to place the continuing communal-individual criticism in any strict chronological pattern. The truth is that by this time the issues had become so confused that one cannot always be certain what was being debated: the origin of the Child ballads or their form, the origin of folksong in general, or the effect of transmission on ballads and folksongs. But at the risk of oversimplification and with the admission that certain figures belong in more than one category, we can discern a number of tendencies in the decade following Louise Pound's summation. There was continued urging of all sorts of examples of "communal composition," and critics who seem ill informed of the issues and facts continued to claim all sorts of ballads as communal. Nonscholarly editors wrote confused and contradictory introductions to collections. Other critics continued to present evidence for the individual origin of the ballad. And the intelligent and informed supporters of the communal position began to clarify and modify their stand.

Three types of communal composition were urged by writers: nonnarrative improvisations, narrative songs deliberately composed by a number of persons under the immediate stimulation of an event or claimed by informants to be of group composition, and "ballads" composed to order by high-school English classes. Negro religious songs, and work songs as well, continued to be cited regularly, and shanties and soldier improvisations (especially "Hinky Dinky Parlez-Vous") were added to the array of evidence for the improvisation of songs, a point which was not really at issue. American narrative songs which had little resemblance to Child pieces were shown to have resulted from the efforts of a group of individuals, each composing separate stanzas. Some of the reports may have been genuine; others demonstrate the gullibility of collectors.[42] In either case the evidence was irrelevant to the argument that the special characteristics of the Child ballad were the result and relic of poetizing by the communal throng. But the final irrelevancy was produced by the well-meaning teachers who introduced their charges to ballads and the communal theory, then produced the group compositions of the students as evidence.[43]

Yet in 1929 Arthur Kyle Davis, Jr., writes in his introduction to *Traditional Ballads of Virginia*, "With so many satisfactory definitions of the ballad ready to one's hand, it would be platitudinous, or even impertinent, to present a definition of one's own." Thelma James's complaint that Davis "devotes a scant two pages to the matter of definition and is thereby launched upon a five-page dis-

cussion of the theory of origins" [44] would be justified were it not
for the fact that all seven pages deal with definition—the definition
by origins. How unsatisfactory such a definition has been is shown
by the laborious introduction of the irrelevant evidence. And attempts at definition by such curiously ill-informed writers as Robert
Graves only added to the confusion.

Graves's *The English Ballad* (1927) perhaps deserves Dorothy
Everett's epithet of "muddle-headed thinking." [45] Graves seeks to
do more than to define the ballad "merely in terms of subject,
length, metre, language, structure, or to confine it geographically
and between certain dates in history." His "more hopeful approach"
is to relate its development to social psychology. But in one respect
Graves's approach is more geographically confining than that of
the critics he opposes, for he denies the relation of the English
ballad to the dance because of his belief that dancing was not old
as a social custom in England. Therefore he associates the ballad
with "hard group labour." We find it difficult to explain the thinking that must lie behind his apparent confusion of terminology
and origin:

> When the word ballad was adopted by English singers, though
> the association with dancing did not survive, there remained latent in
> it the sense of *rhythmic group action*, whether in work or play. Wher-
> ever this sense of action remains in a ballad, let the ballad be dis-
> tinguished as a ballad-proper. . . . For this ballad-proper is earliest
> in poetic succession; from it derive all the other so-called "ballads"
> . . . indeed it is the common ancestor of all varieties of verse (p. 8).

This ballad-proper seems to belong to a primitive society without
social organization, a society which makes common decisions, as
"constantly happens with herds of deer." Yet the ballad-proper
may be contemporary with civilized society. Here, we fear, are the
main tenets of Gummere's theory without Gummere's considered
qualifications.

There are numerous points of agreement with Gummere's approach, but Graves's theory pushes beyond to the conclusion which
exposes the irrelevancy. Graves understands the ballad-proper not

primarily as a narrative poem or a song. It is "*a song and chorus evolved by the group mind of a community, a group mind which is more than the sum of the individual minds that compose it.*" Although he excepts certain ballads, "Sir Patrick Spens," for example, from such group compositions by postulating a development of individual inspiration somewhat similar to that advanced by Gummere and Kittredge, he recognizes the composition of new ballads in contemporary society. Thus shanties are not simply evidence of communal composition: they are *ballads*. Graves seems most blissfully unaware of contemporary scholarship, most clearly in his acceptance of the cowboy song as an example of his "group mind." His information extends no further than Lomax's introduction to *Cowboy Songs*. His admission that a song of individual authorship may be accepted by the group and become a ballad-proper is balanced by his treatment of "London Bridge" as a ballad.

Should it be surprising that the confusing arguments resulted in highly confused comment by nonscholarly collectors? [46]

An outstanding example is the introduction to John Ord's *The Bothy Songs and Ballads* (1930). To Ord, "folk-song means briefly that form of minstrelsy which circulates among the common people of a country and has originated among them. It is a communal product and not, as a rule, the result of individual effort." He admits exceptions but provides no means of distinguishing between the individual and communal. On one page he refers to a group of songs as "communal"; on another he treats them as representing the "lash of the local poetaster" and the "rural poet." The word *communal* has been divorced from form and theory; it is simply an epithet not even recognized as metaphorical. Such an introduction to a collection which includes without apology "When You and I Were Young" demonstrates how far the dichotomy between art and nature has traveled. And Ord's comments are even more amazing because Alexander Keith, having already examined the evidence from the northeast of Scotland, gives an extremely anti-communalist report.

To Keith fell the task of preparing for the press the Child portion of the Aberdeenshire folksongs collected by Gavin Greig and J. L. Duncan and partially edited by William Walker. Keith's comments on ballad origins are bound up with local collecting and the defense of the much-maligned nineteenth-century editor, Peter Buchan, and his blind collector, James Rankin. Buchan had been denounced as a forger and fabricator by J. W. Ebsworth, F. J. Furnivall, William E. Henley, T. F. Henderson, *et al.* And despite Svend Grundtvig's advice, Child never quite accepted the "extraordinary *vulgarity*" of Buchan's lengthy texts as genuine.[47] The attempt to rehabilitate these worthies is important not simply because it affects the authenticity of a number of ballad texts. The doggerel and "pinch-beck finery" of the Buchan texts had been pointed out as exemplifying the production of the poetaster and not that of unsullied tradition. When Buchan was not viewed as the culprit, the fabrication was laid at the door of his blind beggar-collector (though Rankin seems to have had little to do with the materials printed by Buchan in 1828). Kittredge makes Rankin representative of the professional minstrel-author, whose productions can be distinguished from the better versions of genuine tradition.

Keith's defense of Buchan in the introduction to *Last Leaves of Traditional Ballads and Ballad Airs* (1925) supplements William Walker's *Peter Buchan and Other Papers* (1915). The most important evidence for the authenticity of the Buchan versions is not the manuscript-print relationship, the citing of authorities from Scott to Child, or the information concerning the character of Rankin. Miss Bell Robertson's notes do contribute much in picturing Rankin as a "wight of Homer's craft" only in being a blind beggar singing songs of the countryside and incapable of composition. But most important is the evidence of the texts collected by Dean Christie and especially by Greig in the area gleaned by Buchan and Rankin. Keith points out numerous texts from later tradition which correspond with Buchan's. Influence of Buchan's published versions is unlikely, and some traditional texts correspond with versions which remained in manuscript. The correspondences give point to the conclusion that noncollecting ballad editors, whether of the literary or communalist school, erred because of their failure to understand the processes of oral tradition. "A beautiful version and a despicable version of the same ballad may be recovered from different sources at the same time; yet both are genuine." Keith finds, as does Grundtvig, that the lack of elegance, the mediocrity of Buchan's versions are in fact proof of their authenticity.[48]

Greig himself, at least in 1906, accepted a sort of communal origin for folksong, beginning in the dance with nonsense syllables and subsequently breaking away to "set up on its own account." Reversing Gummere's reasoning, he found that the lyric was social in origin, material, and rendering: the main channel of the emotional utterance of a community. He believed that the general continuity of folksong has remained unbroken, the songs being revised from time to time by "the operation of the communal sense." But the ballad "began with the words." First recited, the ballad passed from chant to rudimentary melody.[49] How much his views had altered by 1914 is not clear, but his remarks in *Folk-Song of the North-East* appear to support individual though popular authorship, applying the term *communal* only to evolution in transmission.

Keith's discussion of the ballad problem in *Last Leaves of Traditional Ballads and Ballad Airs* and in an essay published the following year [50] cannot be said to have furnished new insights. He was admittedly supplementing Miss Pound's strictures, using evidence from a study of older collection and from experience with contemporary Scottish tradition. He quotes the epigram of the Scots professor, "Water that's drumlie is nae aye deep," adding that "no crowd ever created anything but a noise or disturbance." While attacking the impression spread by the communalists, he does not misconstrue the arguments of the leading scholars. He clearly recognizes their argument for the communal nature of the ballad only as a derivation or development from the dancing song. But he points out even more clearly than does Louise Pound the nature of such reasoning:

What would literary critics have to say of an historian of the drama who reasoned that, because both in Greece and in England the first attempts at dramatic construction were bound up with religious observances, the plays of Shakespeare, Congreve, and Shaw were written for the same purpose and are essentially religious in character? (p. 108).

But Keith is Emersonian, drawing his best arguments from contemporary evidence.

The two most important conclusions reached by Keith deal with the lateness of the ballad and the function of such ballad features as refrain, commonplaces, and incremental repetition. He finds that, though the ballad grew over a period of three centuries before 1550, its golden age began only in the middle of the sixteenth century and lasted through the seventeenth century. Though ambitious collectors of the seventeenth and eighteenth centuries recovered only a handful of ballads 200–300 years old, twentieth-century collectors, in a period of decay, find many of that age. The other evidence from Scottish collectors shows that the "constituent features" of the ballad furnish little evidence of communal composition. Repetition, commonplaces, and refrain occur as functions of ballad singing but not as communal productions. They fill out the words to fit the air, fill the needs of the transmitter whose vocabulary is limited, and provide a breathing space for the singer by permitting the audience to join in the remembered or repeated elements. These elements are developed in transmission, and the product is "incremental, cumulative, and hap-hazard, not communal and instantaneous."

Keith is another critic who found the ballads to be, in the first instance, the product of individuals, whether "inglorious, but not mute Miltons of village and field" or "poets either of local or national reputation, or deserving of such fame." But all noncommunalists did not follow Keith's trenchant dictum that "the foundations of all ballad theories are dug in sand."

Martha Warren Beckwith in 1924 [51] valiantly revived Joseph Jacobs' suggestion that from the cante fable developed the ballad form. On the basis of her fieldwork in Jamaica and reports from investigators in other areas, she suggests not an evolution of prose to poetry, but a survival of the dialogue or dancing song apart from the story to which it once belonged. The cante fable supplies a source for most of the characteristics of the ballad style: the simple language, set incidents, and stock phrases are characteristic of the folktale; ballad and folktale are both impersonal and unlocalized; the paucity of connectives in the ballad is the natural result of the loss of the prose; the inset dialogue song furnishes the ballad proper, and the scraps of song the refrain. Beckwith thus provides a folk origin for the ballad form, but avoids the communal stigma. She leaves room for minstrel appropriation of the form and makes no suggestion of other than individual origin at any time. Consequently the theory satisfies no one. It presents enough of the concepts of literary evolution to enrage the individualist while introducing those factors which the communalist considers irrelevant. The metamorphosis of cante fable into ballad cannot be demonstrated by any evidence from northern Europe. In the Americas, ballads have become cante fables in some instances. And the theory poses the nice question of the origin of the cante fable, an art form which presupposes a dual tradition.

But the various individualist attacks had not been without their effect and cracks were appearing in the communalists' armor.

Communalists in Retreat

The criticism of the important communalists in the period 1921–1933 represents a gradual shift of position. We might interpret it as an attempt to get off the hook as gracefully as possible with the least surrender of basic principle. The strategy consisted of a minimizing of the communal-individual issue by a shift of emphasis from origin to transmission. The point of departure had been suggested by Kittredge when he wrote in 1904 that it made no difference whether or not a ballad arose from a communal-improvisatory state "provided the author belonged to the folk, derived his material from popular sources, made his ballad under the inherited influence of the method described, and gave it to the folk as soon as he had made it."

The strategy was clearly announced in Gordon Hall Gerould's 1923 article on "The Making of Ballads" [52] when he wrote, "Why dispute about the origin of ballads if it is what happens to ballads that really matters?" Louise Pound was shortly to remark almost bitterly that the article contains "little that has novelty for the special scholar." [53] Gerould replied that Miss Pound "altogether misses the point." [54] In this exchange lies the key to an understanding of the strategic retreat of the communalists. Miss Pound's reaction must have been partially motivated by the realization that the communalists were appropriating their opponents' conclusions, not always with due acknowledgement. But more important was the statement of the conclusions in language offensive to Miss Pound and calculated to leave an impression not unpalatable to those who believed in the *Gesammtgeist*. Thus references to the "Gerould theory of ballad origins" were doubly offensive.

In his article Gerould pointedly relinquishes any immediate concern with ultimate origins and admits that ballads are of many types and must have originated in different ways. He focuses attention on the different versions, particularly "good" and mutually exclusive versions of the same ballads. Simple oral preservation of a text will not explain all phenomena of textual differences. Other folk poetry has no great merit compared with the ballads such as those collected in Great Britain and Denmark. Therefore the worth of the ballads must result from peculiar circumstances, "a tradition of poetic utterance that enhanced the powers common to most illiterate folk," which made the "good" ballads possible. The tradition being dead, the great days of balladry are now over.

Such a summary points out the justice of Louise Pound's remark that few "among the leading ballad scholars of the present day would have failed to concede his leading positions before his article was written." The air of discovery with which Gerould prefaces his remarks and his failure to give credit to any predecessor except

Sharp is irritating to any serious student of ballad scholarship. The lack of even a bow to Phillips Barry is almost insulting. But the omissions become at least understandable in the light of the true significance of the article, which Miss Pound *did* recognize. Gerould had something "new" to offer, but only as far as his tradition of scholarship was concerned—a new explanation of the unique communal and esthetic qualities of the Child ballad.

First must be noted those elements of classic communal theory he jettisons. He renounces the "definition by origins" in so far as primitive poetry and the dance are concerned. He suddenly finds the matter of no particular importance. Thus his concession that the humble minstrel may have had a part in ballad creation is balanced by his previous declaration that "any ultimate or original text is not only undiscoverable but comparatively unimportant." Also dismissed are any sharp differences between kinds of ballads, since it is the traditional process which determines authenticity. Even the "closed account" vanishes, at least in so far as it denies the existence of American ballads. And, most important, he avoids any direct consideration of structural traits.

To demonstrate what of the communal theory Gerould is able to salvage, it is necessary to quote extensively:

> The variations must have been introduced by actual singers of the ballad. . . . Therefore . . . [the variations] may properly be said to have been the result of communal tradition and communal activity . . . (p. 22).
>
> . . . in certain regions, long before the beginning of popular education, there developed a tradition of poetic utterance that enhanced the powers common to most illiterate folk. . . . Only a people homogeneous in nature, possessing what Child so well called "collective sympathy" and trained by long generations of uninterrupted tradition, could have produced the ballads we recognize as "good." (p. 23).
>
> Can one doubt that artistry of this unconscious sort went into the making and shaping of the ballads? Without it there might have been ballads, but there could not have been good ballads. . . . It was the traditional art that counted, not the artist (p. 24).
>
> . . . let us not be deceived by our enthusiasm over survivals into

thinking that the day of balladry is not past. The new ballads, like most of the versions of the old ballads collected in America, have few of the qualities that we prize in the verse of the folk who for so many centuries clung to their community life. The impulse to create is still present, but the power to create beautiful things has largely perished with the violent change of environment. . . . The sun of balladry has indeed set (p. 28).

The language is, of course, enough to drive the extreme individualist into frenzy. But more important is the almost exclusive concern with the "good" versions and emphasis on the traditional process without examination of the part played in it by the individual. (It is clear why he recognizes Sharp and not Barry.) The Child ballads remain a vestigial group whose good qualities are due to a "collective sympathy" which suffered a sea change and in America produced ballads, but not those with which Gerould wishes to concern himself.

Miss Pound perceived his point. Let there be no mistake about that! But she restated his position in her own terms and reiterated her own interpretation of the evidence. She corrected Gerould's "long before the beginning of popular education" to "the seventeenth, eighteenth, and nineteenth centuries." The illiterate have no special powers; "good" versions are recovered from special persons. The older versions tend to be better because the older singer composed for the ear; all fifteenth- and sixteenth-century popular song was superior to that of later centuries; and the earlier collectors drew on selected people and preserved only the best texts. Some singers improved their texts, but the garrulous versions from Buchan may be better representative of the general popular tendencies. Miss Pound did not mistake Gerould's meaning; the two simply did not speak the same language.

Other communalists-in-retreat followed Gerould's lead, dissociating themselves in one way or another from the "more extreme conception expressed in the phrases 'communal authorship' and 'communal composition.'" [55] They tried to accept the most attractive conclusions of the noncommunalist scholars while clinging to the shreds of the group-mind concept. Some writers, such as Reed Smith in the extensive introduction to his *South Carolina Ballads* (1928), tried unsuccessfully to maintain two positions at once. Smith gives a lengthy review of the arguments, ostensibly objective but with notes highly critical of the individualists. There are curious slips, as when, ignoring the pieces by Martin Parker and Lawrence Price, he writes that "we do not know the author of even a single one of the 305 traditional ballads," then later accepts Scott's composition of "Kinmont Willie," "the one ewe-lamb of individual artistry that can mingle undetected with the communal flock." He assumes that "The Maid Freed from the Gallows" was composed before Chaucer and states that "this ballad has held its original form surprisingly well" when he has not demonstrated what the original form was. But the performance is able. His almost unequivocal acceptance of the demonstrations of such anticommunalists as Barry, J. R. Moore, and Fannie H. Eckstorm, paralleled with passages from Kittredge, C. A. Smith, and Hart, presents a common ground for the disputants. It should perhaps be viewed as a genuine attempt to call a truce in the dispute:

> . . . there is strong presumptive evidence of the communal composition in the case of a few of the simpler and earlier ballads; but the great majority of the traditional ballads are best accounted for on the theory of individual authorship in origin, plus a remolding and making-over through the objectifying and impersonalizing process of communal transmission (p. 53).

But this begs the question because it ignores the fundamental issue: the origin or creation of the ballad form. By accepting the transmissional argument and ignoring the principles involved, Reed Smith defends a watered-down communalism which has sacrificed the basic and significant principles of Gummere's theory. This retreat was the strategy forced on the communalists by the pressure of twentieth-century collection and criticism. But the communal position was not to be surrendered without one last effort, which attempted a synthesis of contemporary evidence within classic theory.

The observation that the communal position was maintained by "a literary theorist in the realm of traditional song, rather than an experienced field worker or a practical folklorist" [56] is nowhere so aptly refuted as in the work of Robert Winslow Gordon, fieldworker and literary theorist who knew intimately and took into account evidence from contemporary singers and their sources. A report of his fieldwork and of his theories was published in a series of articles in the *New York Times Sunday Magazine* during 1927 and 1928.[57] He was well aware of the reciprocal influence of traditional and music-hall materials, and took all factors into account in an approach that, while Emersonian, was at once historic-universal and cultural-dynamic.

The academic communalist tended to accept the material of contemporary folk tradition as mere survival or as evidence for the postulated origin of the ballad, which was, if not the only true folksong, at least the only one worthy of serious study. To Gordon folksong is neither a closed account nor limited to one particular type. The ballad is only one small division of folksong, with its own peculiarities. "To study the ballad is not enough. . . . To approach any true doctrine of origins, to discover the laws of growth, we must include all available material." Thus Gordon makes clear his own use of nonnarrative materials to illustrate the origin of a narrative type.

Gordon's Emersonianism is part of a theory of historic and universal literary growth wherein folk literature was and is the earliest of all types. A "lower rung in the ladder of development that reaches eventually to the ballad and the epic" is represented by the fiddle songs of the Southern Appalachians. These nonnarrative, formless songs are but one step removed from what Gummere called the productions of the horde. Music and rhythm are still more important than words; at this stage music is beginning to call forth words to accompany it. With only the tune and stock stanzas as fixed entities, one singer will start a song and many others will cooperate in its momentary formation: "there is nothing that demands thought or authorship in their [the songs'] composition; they practically compose themselves." In this stage appear the repetitions, sequences, and other traits that persist after the appearance of narrative. The banjo songs occupy higher rungs on the ladder. Some are largely composite, with much repetition. Others, more coherent and more narrative, seem more recent and have more connection with individual authorship. (These rungs Phillips Barry[58] describes wittily as "the communal-improvisatory, agglutinative, and author-narrative stages respectively.") Thus modern songs demonstrate "the process of development which is always the same and is always taking place."

At the same time, Gordon recognizes that the universal process is incremental as well as spontaneous, and that it produces different styles under different circumstances. The old ballads have a special style and are not truly representative. So modern ballads represent only the different circumstances of growth. His recognition of the presence of music-hall material in oral transmission and his comments on the growth of versions would seem to place Gordon in the camp of the supporters of "communal transmission." But his view differs significantly, and the following remarks have a special meaning:

> Folk-song is not the product of an author. An author may have composed it, but it is not his; he is merely an incident, unimportant and soon forgotten. . . . Some author was necessary, but almost any one would have served as well. There would have been little difference in the resulting product (p. 3).

Thus when he concludes that all modern folksongs contain both author and folk elements, he is not defining folksong. He seeks to separate the elements in order to discard those derived from any sort of author, humble or high.

Right or wrong, Gordon's attitude and method are clear. Although he defines folksong in terms of oral transmission among illiterate and isolated singers, he distinguishes true or genuine folksong largely by the presence (retention?) of iteration, repetition, and impersonality. American folksong is thus divided into various categories, depending on the relative amount of folk and author elements. A song "of pure folk composition" is a shapeless, disorganized group of stanzas with refrain, in continual flux; a coherent narrative, lacking impersonality and the approved style, is judged to be "pure 'author,' rather than folk." The doubting Thomases can, of course, point out that Gordon does not demonstrate how any one song moves up the ladder of development, nor—since the categories are coeval—that one type succeeds another. Still the theory is well made; but it fails properly to place and account for the old ballads.

Considered as developed narrative, the end of the universal process, the old ballads should certainly contain more author elements than the banjo songs and be far removed from the lower stages. But the old ballads, he says, are "true folksongs." Though Gordon does not specifically point out the ways in which they do not conform to his standards, he hastens to assure us that they are "of a limited and peculiar type" and "represent the culmination of a long period of growing folk technique and artistry." His explanations of the basis of the special technique clear up the matter not at all. Other folksongs appeal to the ear rather than to the eye. If, as he maintains, music is the source of ballad repetition, all folksongs are so influenced. Other types of ballads are stories meant to be sung. Whatever special factors account for the traits of the old ballads, Gordon fails to find any consonant with his theory.

Such criticism was fast becoming an anachronism. Academics such as Alexander Haggerty Krappe [59] were now in the individualist and re-creative camp. And when the recognized historian of English and Scandinavian ballad criticism came to pass in review the nineteenth-century collectors and collections, he maintained an objectivity which indicated that the communal jig was up. Sigurd Bernhard Hustvedt's *Ballad Books and Ballad Men* (1930) is in part a history of, and in part written in, the classic ballad tradition. Admitting the lack of a definition or canon of popular ballads, Hustvedt is, nevertheless, content to deal with "the sort of verse so-named by Child." But his cautious survey of the problem of origins owes allegiance to no one theory. His suggestions are neither extensive nor precise, but they show the quarter of the wind.

Maintaining that ballad origins must have been plural and complex, Hustvedt separates form and content in a way satisfactory to no adherent of popular origins. He considers the ballads a mingling of popular and nonpopular elements, and suggests—*mirabile dictu*—that the "form may have been mainly nonpopular." The stanzaic and metrical features, which are to determine the age of the ballad, are considered to have a regional origin, probably deriving from France. Implicitly and explicitly he calls for study instead of theorizing, "special inquiries in relatively limited fields," including form, content, music, distribution, and recent tradition. Hustvedt's approach, if classical in its attitude toward the "fountainhead," demonstrates the open-minded appeal for evidence which is only now beginning to make of ballad scholarship a discipline.

Uneasy Truce

Before any special studies could be concluded, there appeared Gerould's thoughtful book, *The Ballad of Tradition* (1932). Although some critics believed Gerould to be warming his hands before the dying fires of communal theory, there can be little doubt that he was making an honest attempt to define and account for the ballad. As a literary scholar who had never heard the ballads sung, he is open to the charge of knowing only half his subject. But the noncollecting scholar may at times maintain greater objectivity, see the matter whole, and not be misled by purely local phenomena. Certainly definitions, distinctions, and analyses are the strong points of Gerould's work. This full-scale study of the ballad problem not only modifies his earlier position but places his discussion of ballad variation in a context which immediately clarifies a number of the issues. Gerould may not have answered satisfactorily all the problems of definition, origin, and diffusion, but he poses the questions so clearly that there is no longer any excuse for confusing the issues.

Gerould clarifies the problem first by framing a formal definition of *ballad* which summarizes the universal-organic features of European ballads, separating the local, inorganic, and indeterminate elements. At the same time he defines the ballad as a dynamic phenomenon, developing through a process not antithetical to that of art. By judicious (though not always acknowledged) use of evidence and conclusions of his many predecessors, he pictures the ballad as a distinct genre produced by a specific tradition of folk art, communal in essence if individual in the stricter sense: "the result neither of blind chance working upon degenerate strays from an ordinary garden of song, nor of a mysterious power somehow resident in the ignorant folk when emotionally stimulated" (p. 165).

"A ballad is a folk-song that tells a story with stress on the crucial situation, tells it by letting the action unfold itself in event and speech, and tells it objectively with little comment or intrusion of personal bias" (p. 11). Such restriction may not seem justified to the critic who deals with narrative folksongs of more recent provenience, but Gerould's definition summarizes succinctly those traits he finds universal in European ballads and peculiar to them. Notably missing from the definition is any reference to incremental repetition, refrain, and metrical form. His clear recognition of the ballad as a narrative form relegates stylistic elements to a subordinate position. Incremental repetition he classifies as a species of parallelism, a rhetoric neither essential nor peculiar to the ballad as genre. Neither does he find the refrain an essential feature. He separates metrical from narrative form, recognizing differences in ballad traditions. His analysis leads him to pose three questions, whose distinctness is Gerould's most important contribution:

(1) What was the origin of the narrative form peculiar to ballads . . . ? (2) What was the origin of the melodic and poetical form found in British ballads as well as in some of their continental relations? (3) What was the origin of the individual ballads that make up our collections? (p. 193).

In accounting for the narrative form, Gerould refuses to carry the origin of the ballad "back to a very remote century," but at the same time makes use of evidence from the poetry of primitive peoples. He does not postulate a continuous development from earliest times; he uses the evidence as analogy only to establish three constants of popular poetry:

(1) that the power or habit of verse-making and music-making, though not universal, is more widely diffused among folk with a simple culture than among folk whom we call civilized; (2) that songs are ordinarily made as the result of some immediate and definite stimulus, which is more often than not concerned with tribal matters and sometimes results in improvisation; and (3) that song is intimately related to the dance (p. 197).

The first two constants buttress his conclusion that the ballad is a popular genre. Although the third constant permits him to connect ballad origins with the eleventh-century dancers of Kölbigk and the song they are reported to have sung (which may or may not be a narrative fragment), he does not insist upon a direct relation between the ballad and the dance. Rather he assigns to the dance tune the important role in the origin of the ballad's narrative form. A story adapted to a recurrent melody will develop "compression, centralization, with the impersonality that results from the dramatic treatment of a theme, and, above all, the swiftly moving action." Gerould seems to feel that the dance may have played a greater role in the formation of the ballad type, but he does not insist that ballads were necessarily danced. Nor is he willing to concede that any sort of communal composition took place before the pattern became fixed: individuals created the ballads which "set the form." Even the professional minstrel is allowed a possible share in the formation of the ballad pattern. Keeping strictly to the evidence—or the lack of it—Gerould places the origin of the ballad form in the eleventh or, more likely, the twelfth century. And he astutely remarks that the early ballads may have had no great virtues.

His account of the origin of the ballad's metrical form is not as convincing. His analysis of the stanzaic forms emphasizes their diversity, and he denies any justification for the assumption that ballads in four-stress couplets are the oldest (yet he implies that the form itself is earlier). He is left with only the alteration of the primary and secondary stresses to explain. These he traces to "some sort of influence from the Latin hymns of the church." His brief discussion of the problem is confused because of his failure to distinguish between the ballad and other types of popular song—or to admit there is no difference in the origin of their metrical form. All popular song would have been subjected to the same influences; therefore his suggestion has no particular point as long as he restricts his consideration to the ballad type. The circular reasoning is revealed in his discussion of the developments in the Latin hymns:

> As soon as accentual rhythms began to replace the earlier quantitative meters, there appeared in the hymns a tendency to alternate primary or heavy stresses with lighter ones: a tendency that must have been due to the musical accompaniment (p. 221).

The problem is obviously a much wider one than Gerould is willing to admit, and he implies as much in a later passage:

> If . . . a people whose ears were attuned to such alliterative poetry began to make secular songs . . . to fit rounded melodies, they would achieve something not too remote from the older verse, yet similar in cadence to the Latin hymns (pp. 222–223).

Certainly Gerould should be concerned with the spread of the carole fashion into northern Europe, but he limits himself to the example of the "Equitabat Bovo" song of the dancers of Kölbigk, quite possibly because he prefers to think of the ballad as developing not from a borrowed form, but from a common impulse in the peasantry. A reference to the carole might clarify his conjecture

> that the people who made stories for singing . . . were responsive to the same influences which were operative throughout the larger part of Europe at the same time. In all cases, musical form would have been the determining factor . . . (p. 223).

The origin of the individual ballads Gerould readily concedes to individuals, although he refuses to deny that, once the pattern was set, some sort of cooperative composition was possible. His main point is to reconcile different types of origin within a "controlling and moulding tradition." This tradition of artistry is that affirmed in his 1923 article, with some modification. He extends the tradition of "good taste" into a more modern period, concedes a reciprocal relation between broadside and folk pieces, and devotes attention to American balladry. He applies the term *ballad* to many pieces and finds that they furnish important evidence that "the habit of singing and power of adaptation persist even after what we may call the communal discipline of taste has gone."

Gerould's treatment of origins may be considered largely a summary and his important arguments may be given the label which Louise Pound applied to his earlier statement: "accepted positions." An eclectic scholar, Gerould does not always give sufficient credit to earlier laborers, particularly those with whom he formerly disagreed. Doubtless the individualists would have been satisfied with nothing less than a public recantation in sackcloth and ashes; but certainly more humility was to be expected from a critic who had attacked the individualists with such heat. He makes quite clear his latter-day disagreement with Gummere and Kittredge, with such "exquisite literary tact" that their reputations emerge hardly damaged. But he is sparing in his acknowledgments to earlier dissenters. He credits Barry with pioneering, but makes the latter's comments seem more cryptic than they were and sometimes he paraphrases Barry's writings without credit. Perhaps because of dependence on Sharp for a discussion of ballad music and because of Sharp's communal leanings, Gerould treats the English scholar more kindly. Louise Pound fares less well. We sympathize with her when she remarks that "his references to me were few, mostly unimportant, though mostly derogatory, and in some instances wrong." [60] Gerould's attitude would be hardly worthy of notice were it not for its probable importance in encouraging sniping in the Ballad War.

There are other reasons why Gerould's summary is not completely satisfying. Even more important than his inadequate treatment of the text-tune relationship and his uncritical acceptance of collected texts is his failure to consider closely enough the re-creative process. As a literary analyst he is more interested in results than in conditions. The individual singer and his relation to the ballad are seldom taken into account. Although Gerould refuses to make incremental repetition a ballad test, he treats it as an important characteristic without explaining adequately its development. His account of the origin of individual ballads and their variation suffers because of the lack of study of individual ballad histories. Considering textual variation in a number of ballads, Gerould relies too much on generalized accounts and fails to distinguish adequately between variation and recomposition. Thus the forms of "The Two Sisters" are to Gerould a "mass of inconsistent detail" impossible to reduce to order. Though he regards the versions of "The Two Sisters" as "a group of related poems," he has only the general "processes of variation" to account for them. Gerould's work, as a treatment of what Barry called the " 'Omeric way of the folk," is premature. But it called the truce in the Ballad War.

Shooting continued, of course, primarily on the part of Louise Pound and Phillips Barry. While Miss Pound continued only to make negative points,[61] Barry continued to work largely on positive grounds, attempting to demonstrate through individual song histories how ballads—texts and tunes—came to be as they are. His one great negative point came too late to be of much service as an anticommunal weapon. "Das Volk Dichtet Nichts" [62] is a gem of scholarly clarification, pointing out concisely that the brothers Grimm neither said nor implied *das Volk dichtet*, and that Gummere lifted from context and misinterpreted the words of Karl Lachmann, Ludwig Uhland, and Heymann Steinthal. Had the note appeared thirty years earlier, it might have cut the roots of the dogma of communal composition. Instead, Barry's words became but a footnote to history. But his more important work was constructive: demonstration and clarification of communal re-creation.

While Barry's method in the last decade of his life continued to follow his earlier pattern, inductive reasoning based on studies of items in current tradition, he enlarged his scope by editing collections and clarified his views in brief articles. His basic technique of using a song history or portion thereof to develop his position had its drawbacks. The *Bulletin of the Folk-Song Society of the Northeast,* his personal monument, is littered with fragments, prolegomena, and conclusions incompletely illustrated. Only after we have absorbed scattered citations does the solidity of Barry's judgment become apparent and the meaning of his summaries clear. For we have but fragments of the great studies of Anglo-American folk music that Barry did not live to complete. As Gerould belatedly writes:

> From his vast store of knowledge he drew general conclusions so penetrating and so sound that they have invariably been accepted when once understood, though some of them had to wait a good while before this came about.[63]

The fragmentary nature of Barry's work is partially explained by his recognition that folksong is a paradox: [64] "It is the possession of a people or *folk,* yet it was not made by the people." Folksong is a living organism—a unity—and must be so understood, while at the same time it is a product of individuals—a diversity—and must be so studied. These two principles, unity and diversity, so pervade all aspects of Barry's writings that only with difficulty can we separate the elements of unity (text and tune, old and new folksong, and ballad styles) from the factors of diversity (the individuals who in all senses created the individual songs). To state it even more paradoxically: folksong is an organism itself composed of organisms which must be studied individually because they are the result of a tradition explicable only in terms of the individuals constituting it. If tradition "makes the folksong what it is, . . . the individualism of the folk-singer, both consciously and unconsciously exerted, makes the tradition what it is." The study of folksong is then the study of "the 'way of the folk' or rather 'ways,' with its traditional songs."

To Barry, folksong is a unity, a living organism, in two aspects. The text and *whole tune* to which it is sung comprise a unit of tradition and of study; the interchange of tunes only makes the organic relationship more clear. Secondly, folksong is one continuous structure; the processes of the past were similar to those of the present, and the "folk knows no ballad aristocracy: unconcerned about origins, it treats alike ballads old and new." But the folk provide also the element of diversity.

Barry's folk are no nebulous entity: "whoever sings a song from memory, let it be Child ballad or Tin Pan Alley ditty, . . . has already become a folk-singer." The folk, the "keepers of a tradition . . . never for a single moment dominated by it," include even the ballad printer. Print has no terrors for Barry, for the re-created text of the printer is itself subject to later change, and in any case does not hamper melodic variation. Nor does Barry bow to the shibboleth of illiteracy. On the basis of his New England collection he pronounces illiteracy a "negative factor in ballad tradition; it distinctly inhibits the chances of survival."

Communal re-creation means then a collective labor *"cumulative through tradition in time and space."* The term *communal* is metaphorical, for the folksong owes its origin and development to individuals. The style of folksong is the result of *zersingen* and re-creation, the unconscious and conscious changes of singers exercising their rights as cocomposers. Ballad styles are adventitious, arising "by gradual development as a by-product of the psychological laws of association and memory."

> No two song histories are necessarily similar, let alone identical; each quest is an investigation by itself, unrelated to any other, except in so far as the psychological laws—imperfectly known—of *zersingen* and re-creation affect everything transmitted by memorial tradition.

Although Barry's convictions led him sometimes rather far afield in the application of Freudian concepts, they stimulated study of individual ballad traditions. By his criticism and by his investigations he helped to give positive character to the truce in the Ballad War. Study, not theory, became the maxim, at least.

The year of Barry's final statement, 1937, produced two symptoms that the truce was uneasy. Sir John Squires and John Goss sparred somewhat ineffectually on the grounds of minstrel versus folk authorship,[65] and Paul G. Brewster was impressed with folk authority for communal composition of an American ballad.[66] But during the next decade echoes of the communal argument persisted only in literary anthologies and popular discussions, as respect for Gummere's theory now lingers largely in the halls of Harvard.[67] Leading scholars were convinced of the individual victory or preferred not to raise troublesome questions. William J. Entwistle's study of *European Balladry* (1939), though dealing with controversial problems of the dating and derivation of the ballad type, predicates individual authorship and cultural independence. The literary scholars H. Monro and N. Kershaw Chadwick relinquish the problem of ballad origin to the historians of music.[68] And E. K. Chambers, once so warm a friend of the communal doctrine, has adopted a position totally bereft of "eighteenth-century Teutonic mysticism." [69]

Thus ended (perhaps) a protracted war which produced more heat than light. The fight may have been inevitable, but it lasted too long. Although the meagerness of the historical and ethnological evidence was early apparent, scholars continued to wrangle over the same material. Even when the new evidence of modern collectors was considered, it was narrowly interpreted by both sides. Scholars tried to settle general issues before individual problems were in focus, let alone solved. Studies of individual ballads lagged or were narrowly conceived. The history of the war therefore produces more caveats than exempla. But the more than forty years of struggle were not barren and produced more than a parade of personalities.

The most important results might be called negative. The dualism between art and nature has been discarded. The ballad is no longer connected directly with primitive poetry, and the concept of a uniform development from the earliest times has vanished. Attempts to trace the ballad to a single source have ceased. No scholar can now treat the ballad as a unique form, a thing apart from other types of popular literature. The restriction of the Child canon no longer troubles the critic, and belief in a "closed account" refuses to meet a challenge. If the war produced no satisfactory definition of the ballad, it destroyed the possibility of defining the ballad in other than narrative terms.

The positive factors are less apparent. No dispute, however unnecessary, fails to stimulate some interest in its subject, and narrowly conceived investigations often produce interesting by-products. Besides tending, ironically enough, to make ballad study more "respectable," the argument gave much support to collecting activities. The first half of the twentieth century was a collectors' age. The Ballad War was but one of the stimuli, but it contributed its share to the growing interest in all sorts of song materials recovered from tradition. If the warring factions neglected studies of individual ballads, there is reason to point out that studies could not begin until more controlled evidence was available. And that is the subject of another chapter.

THREE

FOLKSONG COLLECTIONS
IN GREAT BRITAIN AND
NORTH AMERICA

No scholarship can be better than its materials, and the years since 1898 have yielded a rich legacy of collected folksongs, much of which remains unpublished, even unavailable and unknown to the student. There are a few surveys and syllabi of unpublished American collection,[1] but none of British; consequently the amount or quality of the material cannot be correctly assessed. Our conclusions must therefore be based largely upon examination and comparison of published folksong collections.

Certain British and American collections are parallel in content and approach. But the broad patterns of collection and publication differ greatly because of the attitudes and interests of the students and the conditions of traditional singing in the two areas. Thus we may see the American collections as largely academic, literary, but nondiscriminatory, and the English collections as esthetic, musical, but discriminatory. We may find collections in the United States to be scrupulous, even pedantic, in their fidelity to the recovered text, and discover laxity and cavalier treatment of texts in British collections. We may show how the American collections neglect the prime consideration of the British publications—the tune. Unfortunately none of the easy distinctions serve adequately to define and separate the two traditions. Almost any characteristic found in the collections of one area may be matched in the collections of the other. Nevertheless, the differences are real and cannot be ignored.

Evaluation of collections is full of pitfalls. Though we are often at the mercy of collectors, we dare not always take their material on trust. There are a number of valid purposes that influence or determine the manner of presentation of a collection. And we cannot overlook the difficulties of commercial publication, though we may lament the results. But the student who accepts the half loaf must never mistake it for a whole and must judge and censure, albeit understandingly.

Collections are almost as difficult to classify as folksongs themselves. They can be distinguished as to aim, fidelity, organization, material; but they cannot be placed in categories which do not overlap. Nor can one set apart absolutely those with which the student of folksong has no concern, even in terms of the traditional record. This study is concerned only with primary materials, but the criterion is difficult to apply. The inclusion of a freshly collected song in a popular *réchauffé* is not a problem—unless the item is rare. Similarly the collections filled with "mosaics," i.e., composite songs, or emended material should cause little difficulty were it not that some of them also contain valuable undoctored songs or are based on primary material now inaccessible. Consequently we can set up no rigid lines circumscribing primary collections any more than we can determine, at least at the outset, valid tests for the inclusion of a particular item in a particular collection.

This survey of British and American folksong collections views them against the background in which they developed, but at the same time judges them in terms of the values and needs of folksong scholarship.

British Collections and Collectors

In a study that begins with the publication of Child's final collection, it may seem illogical to consider first the modern tradition of English folksong collection. For English collection antedated the post-Child period and has been primarily concerned with matters to which Child gave slight consideration. Yet these two objections are among the reasons which dictate prior consideration of the English work. Developing outside the shadow of *The English and Scottish Popular Ballads*, the English tradition is concerned with the musical scholarship which complements Child's textual labors. By throwing the musical half of folksong into the scales at the outset we may contribute to a balanced presentation.

The roots of the English folksong renaissance lie in England proper, where national pride played a considerable role in stimulating the new collectors, just as it had in the researches of William Chappell more than half a century earlier. Many collectors wished to demonstrate that England, as well as Scotland, had her traditional songs and that the reason for the absence of folksong in national collections could not be a dearth of English songs. The beginning of the English renaissance can be traced to the Rev. John Broadwood's sixteen songs privately printed in 1843 as *Old English Songs As Now Sung by the Peasantry of the Weald of Surrey and Sussex* (usually referred to as *Sussex Songs*, after the title of the edition of 1890). But the movement did not take shape until the last quarter of the century. Between 1877 and 1895 half a score of folksong collections were published, representing songs still living in "the mouths of the people." Miss M. H. Mason's *Nursery Rhymes and Country Songs* appeared in 1877, followed in 1882 by the collection of J. Collingwood Bruce and John Stokoe, *Northumbrian Minstrelsy* (containing material garnered in the late fifties). A small collection by Heywood Sumner, *The Besom Maker*, came in 1888. The movement began to gather momentum in 1890 with Miss Lucy E. Broadwood's expansion of her uncle's earlier collection and the beginning of *Songs and Ballads of the West* (4 parts, 1889–1892) collected by S. Baring-Gould and H. Fleetwood Sheppard. Frank Kidson's *Traditional Tunes* and William Alexander Barrett's *English Folk-Songs* were published in 1891, and the influential *English County Songs*, edited by Miss Broadwood and J. A. Fuller-Maitland, in 1893. And with the appearance in 1895 of *A Garland of Country Song* by Baring-Gould and Sheppard, approximately 600 tune items had been printed.

Although the collections vary in value and differ to some extent in treatment of the material, they clearly mark the direction to be taken by the main English public collections and, to some extent, scholarly printings.

To begin with, these are largely singing books. The aim seems to have been to provide tunes and texts for performance and appreciation, not for study. Except in *Traditional Tunes* and *Northumbrian Minstrelsy*, the tunes are provided with accompaniments, and in almost all the collections the texts have suffered some emendation or conflation. No editorial dishonesty is involved; the facts are clearly stated. The aim of the collections (and in part of the English folksong renaissance)—to introduce traditional songs into middle-class life—may have been laudable; but from the scholarly viewpoint, the value of the collections was diminished. A few examples will reveal the varying values.

At one extreme are the collections of S. Baring-Gould and H. Fleetwood Sheppard. These collectors alone tinkered with both texts and tunes. Their manner of dealing with tunes was to collect as many variants as possible and either to give "that form of the air which seemed . . . most genuine" or "to discover what was the original form of the air, which deflects this way or that according to the capabilities or idiosyncrasies of the singers." Unfamiliar folk intervals were modified to humor the public. Most of the musical liberties seem to have been corrected by Cecil Sharp in the 1905 edition of *Songs and Ballads of the West*; and fortunately the original materials collected by Baring-Gould, Sheppard, and F. W. Bussell are deposited in the municipal library at Plymouth. The published texts are bowdlerized, emended, shortened, rewritten, extended; they suffer every possible indignity, especially addition by the Rev. Sabine Baring-Gould. This worthy was emulating the Scots more completely than any other of the collectors, seeking to perform for English traditional songs what Burns and Allan Ramsay did for the "stupid and nasty songs of Scotland": take them in hand and rewrite them. Though the good cleric butchers the texts and aids in "restoring" the tunes, he does provide, however, particularly in *Songs and Ballads of the West*, the fullest notes of any of these collectors. His comments give informants, sometimes date of recovery, references to other copies of the songs and to the historical or folklore background, and often rather precise explanations of the method by which the printed versions were arrived at. The editors of the English folksong revival were not of the tribe of Percy: we cannot question their basic honesty.

The other collections, by and large, reproduce texts and tunes with greater fidelity. Miss Broadwood and Fuller-Maitland print the words with almost no emendation, but apparently they selected those versions whose frankness would not offend. Kidson and Barrett substitute asterisks for "undesirable stanzas." Barrett collated texts with broadside copies to "avoid obvious corruptions," and all the collectors combined words and tunes from different sources. Although sources of the songs are often indicated, the information is seldom complete and other notes are scanty. Such is to be expected in the popular collections, but even Kidson's *Traditional Tunes* has little annotation. Kidson alone prints texts not allied to tunes and makes a slight attempt at organization.

In spite of the similarities, two trends may be distinguished. Most of the collections typify the later "public" printings by the English folksong collectors: carefully noted, accompanied tunes, composite or edited texts, cursory notes, and little indication of source. The books were designed to reintroduce versions of folksongs into the esthetic life of the English people. Despite frequent citation by students, few of the public collections are completely trustworthy as a record of tradition.

The other trend, represented largely by *Traditional Tunes,*
Northumbrian Minstrelsy, and some of the notes in other collections, leads to the private scholarship of the Folk-Song Society in
which a somewhat greater fidelity is achieved.

THE FOLK-SONG SOCIETY

The Folk-Song Society, established May 16, 1898, soon became the
greatest force in English folksong study; and its journal, *The Journal*
of the Folk-Song Society beginning in 1899, became the largest
repository of printed folk tunes. The Society had the support of the
principal academic musicians; its Committee of Management was
composed of amateurs who were to become the leading collectors and
scholars; and the membership included practically every worker in the
field. The attitudes and policies of the Society soon crystallized and in
a measure determined the course of English folksong study.

The Society was more nearly a folk music society. In their own
words, the members collected tunes. Not that they totally ignored
half of folksong—eventually learned and ingenious textual studies
were carried on, notably by Lucy E. Broadwood and Anne G. Gilchrist. But the society existed to collect and publish the tunes; texts
were considered secondary and often of slight value.

The Society became committed to a position that folksong is a
distinct genre of folk (i.e., peasant) authorship, to be presented,
studied, and judged in its best examples. This position is apparent
in the comments of pioneer collectors [2] and in early issues of *JFSS.*
Sharp's insistence on these points in the educational controversy
of 1906–1907 (see pp. 58–59) merely forced the Society to accept
the logic of its own practice. Although collectors accepted Sharp's
evolutionary concept, they viewed the product as a *fait accompli*
and refused to apply the process to orally circulated songs with
demonstrable origins.[3] Their descriptive approach to folk music was
apparently based on rigid selection. Collectors were urged to garner
the traditional songs of the countryside, but—as Miss Broadwood
wrote in a leaflet distributed by the Society (1904?)—to "give them

[the singers], if possible, an example of the kind of traditional music and words that the Society wishes to procure." Before publication, a tune was often tested by consulting the large library and vast knowledge of Frank Kidson in order to sift the purely traditional from the once-printed songs. Apparently the only disagreement came from those who argued that under a sixteenth-century printed tune sometimes lay a traditional foundation.[4] Thus contemporary folksong was considered a distant and dying echo, reverberating only in the mouths of the aged.

The methods of the Society also determined the character of *JFSS*. Aside from sponsoring festivals with prizes for folksingers and publicly urging collection, the Society operated as a clearinghouse for collections of its members. The pattern of collecting was local and individual; the publishing was collective and judicial. Songs contributed to the Society remained the property of the collector and were published only with his consent. But the selection of songs worthy of publication rested with a subcommittee appointed by the Committee of Management. Thus the type of material included in *JFSS* clearly reflects the attitude of the Society's leaders.

Disregarding for the moment the few but important critical articles which began to appear about 1910, *JFSS* may be regarded as a collection—or series of collections—representing the Society's ideals of scholarly publication. It is a repository of what the leaders felt was necessary first for appreciation, later for study, of the folksong. Our judgment may be qualified by the realization that a closely knit organization in a relatively small country might not have felt the need to publish its material completely, since unpublished songs could be procured without great difficulty. But selection was quite strict: twenty-nine of Sharp's 500 folksongs from Somerset, for example.

We may pass quickly over the great strength of the collections—the accurately noted tunes, for which *JFSS* is the greatest repository—to consider the manner in which the songs are presented. The relative isolation of the tunes is the most apparent feature. Although the tunes are grouped or labeled according to the locality in which they were procured and informants are listed, there is often a general air of vagueness concerning the source of the song. General comment and example usually substitute for exact information concerning circumstances of recovery. The tune is too often an inadequately labeled laboratory specimen. The notable exceptions—such as Miss Broadwood's "Songs from County Waterford, Ireland" (III, No. 10 [1907]) and Francis Tolmie's "Songs from the Western Isles" (IV, No. 16 [1911]) only emphasize how often, especially in the early numbers, the tune is the thing.

The texts often receive cavalier treatment. Some correspondents neglected to send in the complete text. Words were sometimes "completed from a Fortey ballad sheet." The text to a long and important ballad is sometimes omitted altogether, and a note to the effect that "the words appear on so-and-so's ballad sheets" leaves us unenlightened as to the source of the printed copy. Broadsheet versions were often printed instead of the texts from tradition—assuming that the collector had bothered to record them. Though the words may come from a singer with an "almost Chaucerian pronunciation," they appear in the London dialect. These practices appear at odds with the Society's stress on accuracy in noting tunes *and words*. The treatment of texts underscores the contention of these collectors that the modern words come from ballad sheets and are not therefore to be considered folk—though Miss Broadwood testified to the contrary, insisting on the reciprocal relationship between the ballad singer and the broadsheet.[5] The practice of altering or completing the text can be justified only on the assumption that oral versions are but corruptions of an easily available original.[6] Reckoning time in centuries, these critics found the oral texts modern. What changes the singers made cannot be ascertained from examining many texts published by the Society. Fortunately the practice varied with individual collectors, and as *JFSS* continued, relatively more attention was given to full and accurate texts. By 1907 variant texts were given as well as variant tunes, and broadsides soon began to be viewed more nearly as a part of tradition. The extent to which texts continued to be altered or suppressed on the grounds of delicacy, even in *JFSS*, is indicated in James Reeves's *The Idiom of the People* (1958), edited from Sharp's manuscripts.

The continuing emphasis on tunes, however, avoided the type of selection sometimes encountered in American academic tradition. The Folk-Song Society countenanced no hierarchy of folksong based on the Child canon. All types of folksong were granted equal place, provided of course that the tune met with approval. Such a tune could serve as a vehicle for many types of texts. Although modern poems which had supplanted those from older tradition were sometimes omitted, folk tunes often brought with them words of recent origin, and folk tunes were identified in spite of literary texts which might have been ignored by another type of collector.

Both the serial nature of the collection and the emphasis on tune mitigated against classification. Narratives, lyrics, flitings, and game songs rub shoulders, especially in the earlier numbers. An early attempt at organization includes only Child items in "Conventional Songs," but "The House Carpenter" is placed in "Love Songs" and "The Farmer's Curst Wife" in "Miscellaneous Songs." [7] The editorial divisions finally adopted in 1914 separate narrative songs, carols, game songs, street cries, etc., though not rigidly.

Annotation is understandably sparse in the earlier issues, especially since the Society was then more interested in the esthetic value of the tune. Comment was generally restricted to references to similar tunes or discussion of musical peculiarities. But as early as 1906, with Anne G. Gilchrist's notes to her songs, "scientific" interest comes to the fore. Miss Gilchrist applies a more historical and comparative approach to tune and text alike. As this type of annotation is applied in succeeding issues, one of the values of the Society's method becomes apparent. The notes of the collector-critic are supplemented by further references or judgments by members of the editing committee. The reader receives a cross section of comment rather than a digest or a series of arguments in successive issues. This pooling of resources with retention of individual responsibility gives more valuable as well as more entertaining notes.

The special knowledge and ability of each critic is given play—Kidson on broadsheets, Miss Gilchrist and Miss Broadwood on symbolism, etc. Lacking the scholarly finish of a more academic approach, the method was yet more suited to a publication devoted almost entirely to the continuing publication of relics. But most important, out of the interchanges grows the recognition of genetic types of folk tunes.

The greatest publishing work of the society was done in the period bounded by Francis Tolmie's "Songs from the Western Isles" (1911) and A. M. Freeman's "Irish Songs Noted in Ballyvourney, Co. Cork" (1920–1922). These two collections are landmarks in the printing and study of Anglo-Celtic folk music, and the publication of Miss Tolmie's material was the occasion for Miss Gilchrist's analysis of pentatonic scales. Between these two limits lies most of the comparative publishing of tunes and texts. The printing of an item was made the opportunity for an interchange of historical and comparative notes, particularly those dealing with "Come All You Little Streamers," "The Maid Freed from the Gallows," and "The Bold Fisherman," as well as sea shanties, the Padstow May Day songs, and many others. The last decade of the Society's existence saw the publication of much important material: Miss Gilchrist's selection of traditional Manx tunes from Dr. John Clague's collection, further songs collected by the late H. E. D. Hammond, and selections from the late Cecil J. Sharp's garnerings. But the word *late* tells a part of the story. Hammond died in 1910, Sharp in 1924, Kidson in 1927, and Miss Broadwood in 1929. And, as Margaret Dean-Smith writes, there was no second generation "equal in enthusiasm, learning, and scholarship to that which was finding, publishing, and annotating." [8] Furthermore, until the end of World War II, no new generation arose.

A part of the problem lay in the inflexible attitude of the Society. It is now apparent that England still contained folksong, but little that the Society considered worthy of preservation. Maud Karpeles and others continued to echo the conclusions and restrictions of Sharp. A study of the index to *JFSS* reveals hardly a song which originated in the nineteenth century, and—aside from shanties and street cries—no indication that folksong existed except among the dying peasantry. Thus Frank Howes, urging the amalgamation of the folksong and folk dance societies in 1931, could say that "there are no more folk-songs, only variants, to collect." And to judge from the *Journal of the English Folk Dance and Song Society,* founded in 1932, there were very few variants to collect. Songs published early in the history of the new journal were from earlier collections. Though some of the early collectors had collected with the phonograph, only after World War II did the phonograph and radio seriously affect the pattern of English collection. The work of the British Broadcasting Corporation in seeking recordings of traditional singing uncovered a number of items found worthy of publication in *JEFDSS,* and other collectors were finding youthful traditional singers. But collectors associated with the Society still tend to follow the old formulas and shudder at the singer "totally without modal feeling in his bones." [9] For indications of a different approach to traditional song we must look outside the confines of *JEFDSS.*

OTHER ENGLISH COLLECTIONS

Most separately published collections of English folksongs are by members of the Folk-Song Society—public or school collections of authentic tunes and revised words, designed for performance. The tunes are often esthetically satisfying but not always indicative of trends of folk art. Sharp printed, in all forms, only 500 of the almost 3,000 tunes in his English song collection. The public collections repeat each other but include items not printed in *JFSS.* They often lack necessary annotation, and the texts, when not amended, are often recast. (Even the Sharp manuscripts reveal textual deficiencies.[10]) Of course the textual revisionism of these collections is honest. The texts needed revision to be singable—or so as not to offend public taste—so they were abbreviated, extended, or rewritten. When, for example, in Frank Kidson's *Folk-Songs of the*

North Countrie (1927) texts are written by his niece or supplied by Miss Gilchrist, the reader is informed. But the process breeds distrust of all publications in similar format. The singing books of Alice E. Gillington, *Old Christmas Carols of the Southern Counties* (1910) and *Songs of the Open Road* (1911), contain important primary material from gypsy tradition, but only a number of fragments and corrupt texts suggest authenticity. It is indeed unfortunate that so much of the English material appears only in singing books,[11] whose selection and textual purity is open to question. And it is doubly unfortunate that the one unselected English collection of the early twentieth century is deficient in other ways.

Alone among the major English collectors of his time, Alfred Williams "had no time to obtain tunes" (though he intended to return to collect them), contenting himself in *Folk-Songs of the Upper Thames* (1923) with a "word book" of 346 songs (plus eleven variants) from a collection of 600. And almost alone among the English collectors, Williams seems to have had little knowledge of what a folksong should be or what had passed for folksong in other collections. This latter ignorance (if it was ignorance) gives the collection a special value.

Williams belongs to a group which is much larger in American folksong collecting—the local enthusiasts with a folk background. As an antiquarian of sorts he proceeded to collect "that which amused, cheered, consoled, and so profoundly affected the lives of the people of an age that has forever passed away." He printed the texts largely unemended, not because of a knowledge of the significance of variation, but because of an honest regard for the "musical tastes of the people," and because of lack of time to consult other texts to verify his own. Therefore his unwitting agreement with other English collectors that the texts are largely incorrect copies of broadsides written in large cities bred no disrespect. The lack of arrangement, the almost total lack of enlightening comment on the texts (except for mention of the source and important record of the occasions at which they were sung), even his preoccupation with "good" or complete versions can be overlooked when we realize that the collection gives the only reasonably full illustration of the English folksong repertory at the turn of the century (Williams collected in 1914–1916, 1919–1923). As he remarked later, he did not "attempt to adhere to the accepted canon, which has always seemed to me too rigid as ordinarily applied to folk songs and ballads." [12] The collection includes songs reeking of broadside "elegance," drinking ditties of the flowing-bowl variety, American blackface pieces such as "Blue Tail Fly" and "Old Ann Tucker" (*sic*), and a few literary rhymes, side by side with excellent texts of older ballads. With all its faults, the collection helps to fill the gaps left by the Folk-Song Society, because almost nothing else exists which gives an indication of the full repertory of the English folksinger.[13]

The only other English collections of importance made prior to World War II are of shanties, the one type of song not associated with the peasantry which interested many English collectors. Members of the Folk-Song Society were attracted to shanties to some extent because the tunes were old and largely modal, and because they were considered relics, since the decline of sail had eliminated the function of the work song. Though a number of tunes were printed in *JFSS* (1908, 1914, 1916) and Sharp edited public collections, the Society in general apparently considered them somewhat outside the scope of English folksong proper. (Margaret Dean-Smith omits shanty collections from her *A Guide to English Folk Song Collections*.) And the ladies, gentlemen, and clerics of the Folk-Song Society were even less suited for the task of gathering these songs. As W. B. Whall writes, apparently of Laura A. Smith's *Music of the Waters* (1888):

> If a lady goes round sailors' boarding-houses and attempts to copy down the words and music of Shanties from the men, she is bound to fail. First, sailors are shy with ladies. Secondly, few of the songs have words which a seaman would care to sing to a lady in cold blood. And thirdly, very few sailors were shanty men.[14]

Seamen themselves were the better collectors.

The shanty problem is considered in the next chapter; here reference is made merely to three collections as examples. (We cannot in connection with sea collections separate absolutely the English and Scottish.) All three stem from seamen who knew shanties and their singers, but none of the three are strictly field reports. W. B. Whall's work, the first and best of the three, was printed in *The Nautical Magazine* and *The Yachting Monthly*, 1906–1910, and as *Ships, Sea Songs, and Shanties*, 1910. The twenty-eight songs, by no means all shanties, are those which Whall, a ship's officer with academic and musical training, took down or learned 1861–1872. Most tunes are unharmonized, and, allowing for some expurgation, the work is an excellent report of his own experience. But the simplicity of the tune transcriptions betrays perhaps too much familiarity with the medium. Yet Frank T. Bullen, who had to trust to W. F. Arnold to note and arrange his singing, produced a book—*Songs of Sea Labour* (1914)—full of amateurish harmonies and surely inaccurate transcriptions. Richard Runciman Terry knew his shantying and his music; he used informants to add to his knowledge; but he failed in a complete understanding of traditional art. In the two parts of *The Shanty Book* (1921, 1926) he does camouflage many expressions and combines verses from a number of singers (because of "no connection or relevancy between the different verses of a shanty"), but his lack of insight shows most clearly in his treatment of the tunes—each from an individual sailor. His attitude and performance are made clear in the introduction to Part I of *The Shanty Book*:

> It is doubtless interesting to the folk-songer [the meticulous enthusiast] to see in print shanties taken down from an individual sailor with his individual melodic twirls and twiddles. But since no two sailors ever sing the same shanty quite in the same manner, there must necessarily be some means of getting at the tune, unhampered by these individual idiosyncrasies . . . (p. ix).

Terry therefore uses his "familiarity with the shanty as it was in its palmy days" to get at the tune, not trusting the memory of an old man who would "sing quite glibly a tune which was in reality a *pasticcio* of three separate shanties all known to me." Familiarity does not always breed understanding.

Though they continued to bring back a harvest, collectors within and without the Folk-Song Society had by the end of the third decade practically written off English folksinging. In 1905 Sharp had written that he never considered a singer trustworthy who was under sixty.[15] Alfred Williams wrote that by 1920 all his oldest and best singers, whose ages had ranged from eighty to one hundred years, were dead.[16] In 1925 Christopher Mayson was garnering "quite genuine folk songs" from singers aged forty to seventy and concluded that the decline of folksinging was less rapid than others believed. But even he was convinced that "the old tradition is doomed at last." [17] And so were other collectors, whose waning enthusiasm resulted in slight reward until almost mid-century. But before considering recent collection, we must turn to the record of collection in the north.

SCOTS COLLECTIONS

North of the border, folksong collection was less well organized and proceeded on somewhat different lines. For the English songs of the Lowlanders, we need concern ourselves mainly with the work of three collectors: Robert Ford, Gavin Greig, and John Ord.

Although approximately thirty years separate their published collections, Robert Ford and John Ord, who belonged to the tradition of the local amateur, produced similar works. Both claimed their material as a "species of folklore" collected from oral sources. But neither found anything sacred in an oral version or refused to make use of popular prints. Although their collections are largely textual, a number of tunes are included. Their texts are generally good—too good, in fact, for many are composites or revisions.

Ford approached his collecting and his collections rather casually. His two volumes of *Vagabond Songs and Ballads* (1899, 1901) purport to contain songs "more generally those of the rural population of the Scotland of yesterday than almost any that have heretofore appeared together in book form." Ford had apparently been in the practice of noting down songs as he heard them, and some are referred specifically to oral sources. But for a very good reason he did not limit himself to a presentation of oral versions.

Ford was little interested in oral tradition per se, except to note that the essential identity of texts gathered from many parts of Scotland gives evidence of excellent memory or common taste. Instead, he was interested in preserving good copies of the "songs and ballads that have been the familiar entertainment of the country people of Scotland during three-quarters of the nineteenth century." He often looked for the original or the version sung by a professional entertainer, and used broadsides and chapbooks with no other authority. Although he sometimes indicated changes made in texts (bowdlerization, dropping of stanzas to produce the commonly sung version, etc.), we suspect that a good deal of alteration silently occurred.

Though one can place little credence in his textual accuracy, Ford's volumes are valuable in preserving rare chapbook material, indicating what songs may have been sung generally throughout rural Scotland, and giving insights into the methods of song distribution. The first volume contains ninety-nine texts (in 100 variants) and sixteen tunes; the second contains ninety-seven texts (in ninety-nine variants) and eighteen tunes. The lack of variation testifies to Ford's dependence on print, to his combining of texts, to a selection, to the excellent memory and common taste of the Scots—but which in greater proportion is impossible to determine. The songs themselves comprise a very few of the Child variety, a good selection of eighteenth-century broadsides, and a scattering of the humorous songs of courtship: all types familiar to the American collector. A large proportion are bowdlerized versions of rather free rustic courting songs such as "The Plaidie Awa'," not generally transplanted, to judge from printed collections. Notably lacking are sensational murder ballads, found in both England and the United States, and pure lyrics. As the latter occur in other

Scottish collections, we may set down the lack to a limitation in Ford's taste.

Possibly one of the more important contributions of Ford's volumes is the indication of the number of *poems* of known authorship which had circulated widely in the countryside—these to be distinguished from the vulgar broadside. We may complain of the vagueness of some of his references but must be grateful for the ascriptions of many of the songs to eighteenth-century authors, whether local poetasters or writers of larger reputation.

John Ord's *The Bothy Songs and Ballads* (1930) is largely a companion volume, and much of its material, despite its late publication, was collected early in the century. Like his predecessor, Ord, Superintendent of Glasgow Police, collected from the bothies, from newspaper correspondents, and from prints, but his work was limited to the northeastern counties. Unlike Ford, Ord not only has a confused notion of communal and folk authorship, but seeks to organize his material—with little success. Of the 208 separate songs (plus five variants and fifty-four tunes), thirty-two are by authors known to Ord. Ten of these latter songs are stated or implied to have been in oral circulation; certainly some of the others were not, one having been written especially for the collection. Five texts are reprinted from broadsides or chapbooks and one from a magazine of 1844. The collection thus consists of songs written by, written for, or written about the rustics; but it is sometimes difficult to assign songs to any one of the three categories. How much textual manipulation has occurred is not apparent, as Ord notes alteration in but one case. The suspicious completeness of the texts may testify only to a judicious selection. Yet the few references to informants leads to little trust in the authenticity of the texts. The considerable amount of local or localized material is important but may be better appraised in the work of another collector in the same area.

Both of these popular works bear a strong resemblance to the preliminary labors of the Aberdeen collector, Gavin Greig. His *Folk-Songs of the North-East* (1914) is but a reprint of articles contributed to the Buchan *Observer* from December, 1907 to May, 1911, and only twelve copies of the book were printed. The articles themselves were largely a device to bring his collecting to the attention of readers and to obtain help from them. But since only a seventh of Greig's collection is otherwise in print, the articles must be given consideration.

Greig was schoolmaster at Whitehall, parish of New Deer, Aberdeenshire, from 1878 until his death in 1914. After beginning a personal collection of folk music, in 1903 he accepted a commission from the New Spalding Club to prepare a volume of traditional music for publication. With the aid of the Rev. J. B. Duncan of Lyturk, he undertook extensive collecting activities. Seeking first only the tunes, he soon "found it impossible to dissociate words from the music." [18] By 1917 he had received a grant from the Carnegie Trust Research Scheme for the Universities of Scotland.

The collected articles in *Folk-Songs of the North-East* make quite a respectable collection, containing some 600 songs and ballads. As might be expected, Greig maintains a popular tone and accedes to the requests of his readers, sometimes making the column a sort of exchange, with the publication of local poetry and requested songs. Some of the articles become quite chatty, as his taking time for a temperance lecture (No. V). Yet there are telling comments on the habits of folksingers, the nature of folksong, and the characteristics of folk music. Greig could not, of course, print tunes contributed by his readers, but he often sought out the informants to secure tunes and satisfy himself of their reliability. [19] Because of the aim of the articles, one cannot hazard a secure judgment of his criteria of inclusion. But his material is a valuable cross section of the repertory of at least the older singers.

Even allowing for the popular and local character of the articles, the song material is unusual and differs somewhat from many other English and Scottish collections. There is the usual sprinkling of older, or Child, ballads and a good number of the vulgar ballads. Like other reports of Scottish song, the articles confirm a wide circulation of songs by lesser poets; but many inclusions point to the continuing habit of song composition by humble authors on personal experience and events of local interest. There are a number of plowman's songs dealing with occupational interests of the countrymen. "The Boghead Crew" was on folk authority composed in 1872, and "The Ardlaw Crew" is by internal evidence dated 1880. A number of others, such as "Ellen of Aberdeen" and "The Road to Peterhead," seem to be of nineteenth-century origin (textually speaking, of course). Pieces such as "The Dalmuir Ploughing Match" indicate that the local song-making tradition did not die early in Aberdeenshire, as also it did not in the northeastern United States. (At least one song of American origin is included: "The Jam at Gerry's Rock.") Greig also includes come-all-ye execution ballads such as "Jamie Raeburn" and "Burke's Confession." Regrettably, however, out of the approximately 3,000 texts and tunes in the Greig collection, relatively few have been printed, and those given scholarly treatment are limited to the Child canon.

Last Leaves of Traditional Ballads and Ballad Airs (1925) is unique among British collections in following the Child pattern. Because of the size of Greig's collection, the decision was made to concentrate first on ballads—ballads as exemplified by *The English and Scottish Popular Ballads* of Child. The Rev. J. B. Duncan, before his death in 1917, wrote the textual and musical introduction to seventy-seven of the ballads. William Walker added a few notes and delivered the manuscript to Aberdeen University, where the work was taken up by Alexander Keith. By collation, Keith reduced the number of texts from 400 to 125, eliminated half the tunes "by withholding variants of no importance," revised and expanded the notes, and wrote the introduction. The result is a book that, in a number of respects, is comparable to certain American academic collections.

Last Leaves is a scholarly edition of 107 [20] Child ballads which follows a mean course between the textual scholarship of the American academic tradition and the tune scholarship of the Folk-Song Society. Generally speaking, Keith gives equality of treatment to text and tune, printing more tunes than texts only because of collation of verbal variants in notes. Textual notes are not exhaustive in the manner of American counterparts; they refer to a few of the great collections and some of the work of the Folk-Song Society and slight American investigations (little of which was in book form before 1925). Notes to tunes are somewhat better and the sources of the ballads are scrupulously indicated.

In the face of the achievements of the long-delayed edition, we hesitate to suggest shortcomings. Full publication of even such limited sections of folksong collections is seldom economically feasible, and Keith's practice of collation would probably have been justified in a number of American collections which have printed every scrap of the Child ballads at the expense of other materials. Keith's collation, however, is extreme, far beyond that practiced by Child. For example, of twelve texts of "The Twa Sisters" he prints only Mrs. Bell Robertson's, giving such comments concerning other texts as: "There are more or less detailed accounts of the retrieving of the body by the miller, or more generally 'they.' " But the greatest loss stems from the publication of the Child ballads to the exclusion of others.

The revelation of the mass survival of 107 Child ballads in Aberdeenshire, far more than in any comparable part of the United States even after four more decades of search,[21] is only of slightly less value than the printing of the large number of tunes associated with them. Even granting that "the true ballad is to folk-poetry very much as the heroic poem is to art poetry—a section marked off by discernible characteristics," one realizes what Keith hastens to add: that "the ballad airs are an integral and indistinguishable part of folk music." [22] Consequently, the separation of the Child texts has divided the music, since the tune knows no ballad aristocracy. Perhaps when "the sun and moon set on yonders hill" we shall have an edition of Greig's 3,000 folksongs *in extenso*; but already there are later materials needing publication.

These materials, however, are of recent collection, and the only other collectanea of note appeared in the privately published *Mis-*

cellanea of the Rymour Club of Edinburgh (1906–1928). John Goss was reasonably accurate when he wrote in 1937 that "since the deaths of Cecil Sharp and Gavin Greig, the only work of any consequence on matters connected with British Folk Music has been done in America." [23] Though Goss overlooked some serious study, he did not overlook much collection.

American Collections and Collectors

The pattern of folksong collecting in North America has differed markedly from that in Great Britain. The explanation for the difference lies partly in the size of the area and the difference in folk tradition and culture, but especially in the character of the leadership of the American movement. The mere size of the United States, in which one area rich in folksong—the Southern Appalachians—is larger than England and Scotland combined, was bound to produce problems different from those encountered in Great Britain. The conditions of folk tradition, for which perhaps not the size alone of the United States was responsible, had given rise to what one collector was to call *"la seconde période, peut-être la dernière de la ballade traditionelle, comme à tirer à son declin parmi les nations de langue anglaise."* [24] Although recognition of this new growth could not completely escape even such a purist as Cecil Sharp, the temper of the native collector—itself a product of American conditions—to some extent determined the acceptance of newer folksong. While he was in the United States Sharp collected native American ballads linked musically and to some extent textually with what he regarded as English folksong, but he excluded many types accepted into other American collections and could remark depreciatingly that the cowboy had been "despoiled of his inheritance of traditional song," [25] implying that the cowboy songs were not genuine folksongs. A somewhat different approach was characteristic of the leaders of the dominant American collecting tradition, a tradition often regarded as not only academic, but

narrow. Yet their collections are often partially edited archives, re-
porting material sung, and providing a basis for future study.

Three collecting traditions may be distinguished, somewhat
loosely, in the United States and Canada: the musical-esthetic, the
local-enthusiastic, and the academic. The first, concerned primarily
with folk melody as a distinguishable art form, is certainly the earliest if we concede that it began with the post-Civil War collections
of Negro spirituals. The local-enthusiastic tradition, typified by
those interested in the "quaintness" and pure enjoyment of the
songs of a folk group, is difficult to isolate, though Henry E. Shoemaker's Pennsylvania collection is a fairly clear example. In fact,
it is almost as difficult to find a pure instance of any of the traditions as it is to discover that perhaps mythical scholar who regarded
a non-Child ballad as unclean. And one of the reasons for the interdependence of the traditions is the early dominance of the scholars
accumulating and annotating texts for literary and historical study.
The work of these scholars comprises the academic tradition which
tended to stimulate, utilize, and absorb the others.

THE RISE OF THE
ACADEMIC TRADITION: 1898-1917

Except for the collecting of Negro spirituals and the sporadic activities of a few individuals, there was, prior to the completion of
Child's work, little interest in American folksong or even indication
that it existed. The *Journal of American Folklore* before 1899 published a small number of texts: old ballads, carols, game songs, and
Negro spirituals. Tunes were almost completely unrecorded. Child's
collection contains from American tradition, twenty-seven ballads
in fifty-five variants, and the unpublished Child manuscripts include twenty versions in twenty-six variants.[26] Whether this be
judged a slim promise or a good beginning, the publication of the
final volume of *The English and Scottish Popular Ballads* signaled
the beginning of a collecting era that was to extend beyond the

bounds of the Child canon, but was seldom to escape its lengthened shadow.

The distinguishing traits of American academic collection derive clearly from Child: the treatment of a folksong as a document for study, the emphasis on the text, and the predominant position accorded to the Child canon. Whatever the concessions made to the function and performance of folksong, the emphasis was placed on the record—the *accurate* record—of a text as the subject of literary and comparative analysis. Although interest was certainly not restricted to the Child ballads, they received more emphasis; and other ballads and songs were separated and judged by the standards of the older ballads. In the published collections this attitude resulted in a series of texts, usually without the tunes, but with notation of source and date of collection. Items were provided with headnotes giving lists of analogues and references and comments on the "freakishness of oral tradition." The Child ballads were printed first, and "later" pieces arranged in various attempts at logical order. A separately published Child-and-other collection did not appear until 1922, but the pattern of the collections was early established in *JAF* and in syllabi.

The leadership had much to do with the collecting pattern: George Lyman Kittredge, Harvard professor, Child's disciple and successor; William Wells Newell, private scholar domiciled in the shadow of Harvard; Phillips Barry, Harvard-educated private scholar of Cambridge; C. Alphonso Smith, Reed Smith, Frank C. Brown, E. C. Perrow, English professors all, at various universities. And the roll could be swelled with the addition of English professors who made important contributions to ballad collecting and editing in the first two decades of the century. The names of Henry Marvin Belden, Louise Pound, W. Roy MacKenzie, John Harrington Cox, Albert H. Tolman, and Hubert G. Shearin would not complete the list. Few of these scholars had what is thought of as a "folk" background, although as a group they were closer to the folk in sympathy, understanding, and fact than the majority of English collectors—a condition referable to the American experience, perhaps, rather than to the scholars themselves. But only a few—though an important few—can be considered field collectors. They depended for much of their collection on students, friends, correspondents, and members of the state folklore societies which these scholars established. Although William Wells Newell had already collected and edited a book of children's games and songs, this investigator who announced the era of great American collecting had a largely secondhand acquaintance with his material.

The first expression of the growing academic interest in American folksongs was, though developing out of the communal-individual controversy, not devoted primarily to American copies of Child ballads. W. W. Newell's 1899–1900 articles on "Early American Ballads" [27] emphasize the production and survival of the later or plebeian ballads of English and American origin. The texts printed in the first article are mostly of the late British broadside type from various sources in New England and North Carolina. But the article prints twenty-five stanzas of a moralistic funeral lament from a manuscript at least extremely close to the composer of the poem, and a two-stanza fragment of "Springfield Mountain" from oral tradition. Newell's second article contains six variants of "Springfield Mountain" plus the version from George H. Derby's *Squibob Papers* (1865), seven texts of Child ballads (one of which was not new), and a copy of a local mortuary ballad similar to that printed in the first article. The recovery of the mortuary piece caused Newell to modify his statement that the lament printed in his first article was "of a literary character . . . produced with the pen and designed for reading." The text and tune of the new ballad, "Isaac Orcutt," had been received from the granddaughter of one of the six young ladies who sang it at Orcutt's funeral about 100 years previously.

Newell's articles heralded the general acceptance of all sorts of material, particularly broadside verse recovered from oral tradition and local ballads no matter what their source. The recovered songs pointed out the widespread character of ballad singing, for the twenty-two texts sent in from contemporary tradition represented informants from eleven states and territories, north and south. Whatever Newell's competencies, he, like the collectors to succeed him, was hospitable to tunes which correspondents could provide. He printed two tunes in his second article but made no comment on them. Newell may have had little consciousness of the material awaiting collection, but he accepted all songs eagerly and looked forward to further collection, writing that "as illustrating popular taste and folk-life the ballads have their curiosity."

Newell's pioneer efforts bore fruit in the increasing number of songs sent in by far-flung contributors and in the appearance of individuals who began to lead collection in areas throughout the United States. Barry began his work in New England in 1903. Henry M. Belden embarked on the great Missouri collection in 1904 and encouraged Louise Pound to begin the Nebraska work about the same time. In less than a decade, schoolmen in other areas had taken active interest: W. Roy MacKenzie, Nova Scotia; C. Alphonso Smith, Virginia; Frank C. Brown, North Carolina; Reed Smith, South Carolina; E. C. Perrow, Hubert G. Shearin, and Josiah H. Combs, Kentucky; and L. W. Payne, Jr., Texas. Of course John A. Lomax was inspiring interest throughout the academic world; and behind all these scholars was the active encouragement of George Lyman Kittredge. This academic interest was chiefly reflected in *JAF*, and mainly in its pages are found the attitudes and activities of the academic tradition early displayed.

In viewing the outstanding traits, the strengths and weaknesses of the academic tradition, it is obvious that our distinctions are sometimes relative. Among the academics and their publications are found attitudes and material that resist the main current of the tradition. Treatment of music and attitude toward the function of folksong are cases in point. Barry's according of equal status to ballad music does not place him outside the academic group; it merely points to the deficiencies in the tradition as a whole. And the folksinger himself receives a place, if a subordinate one, in the pages of *JAF*; but the reports of Louise Rand Bascomb, W. Roy Mac-

Kenzie, and E. C. Perrow [28] illustrate how often in the reports of others, "the text is the thing." [29]

Academic interest was by no means restricted to the ballads printed by Child. A wide range of material was reported in *JAF* and in collectors' check lists. Of the 333 items by Hubert G. Shearin and Josiah H. Combs in A *Syllabus of Kentucky Folk-Songs* (1911), only twenty were Child ballads; and of the 270 published by Perrow in *JAF* (1912–1915), only eight were represented in Child. But the collection of Child pieces still received the greater emphasis, as is shown in a number of ways.

The amount of emphasis placed on the collection of one type of material to the exclusion of another is difficult to estimate. One can seldom follow the collector and observe whether he rejected any songs or whether he deliberately sought out certain types of songs or primed the singers in any way. In most instances restrictions seem to have operated unconsciously. It has become axiomatic that a collector finds what he is looking for or is interested in. Possibly students, friends, and informants tended to supply material which the collector recognized and seemed to desire, but the great collections that were later published reflect little restriction. Excepted, of course, must be Reed Smith's *South Carolina Ballads* (1928) and especially the work of the Virginia Folklore Society initiated by C. Alphonso Smith. This latter effort was a deliberate search for Child ballads only, encompassing ten years and the single-minded labors of an enthusiastic society and of the teachers in the common schools of the state. But, for the most part, the emphasis was displayed in other ways.

The relative emphasis is present in the choice of materials for early publication and their treatment in print. During the period when *JAF* was almost the sole medium for folksong publication, the selections from various collections almost always give priority to ballads recognized by Child. When space curtails full printing of texts, the Child ballads are seldom slighted. And—what has irritated some critics—Child ballads are usually given precedence, a procedure worthy of some explanation.

The practice of separating Child ballads and printing them first was not universal in academic publication. Perrow, for example, placed them last, scattered among a section of "Songs of Love," [30] but the Child-and-other arrangement, firmly established in Kittredge's editing of Katherine Pettit's Kentucky collection of 1907,[31] became the standard. This arrangement certainly represents the history of academic interest, but the use of the Child canon as a method of departure has another significance, for not all editors who so arranged their collections had any special reverence for Child or even admitted the special nature of his collection. But, in the words of Belden, "in the absence of any scientific classification of ballads, Child's great collection forms a convenient starting-ground." [32] The academic scholar found a familiar pattern within which to compare texts and to note variations and relationships. It permitted a statistical approach, beginning in Reed Smith's ballad lists in *JAF*, 1914. The Child ballad was at least a known quantity, and the greater ease of measuring and comparing Child recoveries gives the academic tradition an air of snobbishness that is somewhat deceptive until one considers the entire scope of the ballads recovered.

There is as yet no adequate classification of folksongs against which to measure. By 1914 variants of seventy-three Child ballads had been recovered,[33] but the recovery of other ballads and songs can be indicated only in lists or examples. Even the statistics of Child-ballad recoveries may be deceptive. Many collectors were eager to claim a new discovery at the least provocation, not only reclaiming material from transients and from the disordered recollections of elderly informants, but classifying as Child texts almost any material remotely related. Floating stanzas or commonplaces such as the "who will shoe" lines from (?) "Lass of Roch Royal" were considered to constitute a Child piece. A ballad printed in an appendix was at least *next* to the canon. Further, collection and study revealed that a number of noncanon ballads related stories similar to those in the ballads Child accepted. Thus arose the concept of the secondary ballad, one textually unrelated to a Child ballad but telling the same story.[34] In ballad lists there is confusion over the counting of "The Bold Soldier" as a form of Child #8, "The Blaeberry Courtship" as a form of Child #226, or "The Yorkshire Bite" as a form of Child #283, to mention only a few. But this stretching of the Child canon leaves still a vast amount of material to assess.

The classification of the collectanea of the American song collector is difficult, even for our immediate purpose. But the fact that the difficulty existed in the early period of academic collection makes, at the outset, the major point of our assessment: the wide scope of the material. Following for convenience the general pattern of an American folksong editor, the following loose categories can be discerned: imported narratives, native or reshaped narratives, lyrics, parlor songs, Negro songs, game songs, instrumental music.

Of these categories, the first calls for the least comment. The acceptance of the vulgar balladry as found in American oral tradition was immediate. Comments were at times condescending, but the pieces were welcomed regardless of age or theme. The collectors had not the interest in tunes which justified acceptance of broadside material among English collectors and motivated the latter's cavalier treatment of the words. One might conclude that because American scholars were widely separated from Seven Dials and because the colonial has often an immediate respect for the imported, the songs received a deference that would otherwise have been withheld. But the distribution of the vulgar ballads by American broadsides and songsters was acknowledged. The acceptance of this material is more likely the first symptom of the growing respect for oral currency as the test of folksong.

The mere acceptance of American narrative songs, on the other hand, is not as surprising as the amount and variety of the material. The two post-Child decades did not quite establish the canon of American balladry, but they outlined its sections and brought to notice most of the important narratives. "Bury Me Not on the Lone Prairie" was printed in *JAF* in 1901, and by 1909 texts of "Young Charlotte," "John Henry" (fragment), "John Hardy," "Jesse James," "Omie Wise," "The Silver Dagger," "The Jealous

Lover," "The White Captive," "The Dying Cowboy," "Lonesome Scenes of Winter," "The Shanty Boy on the Big Eau Claire," and others of lesser note had been published. Notice of recovery of many others was made publicly and privately. As check lists of collections were printed, the chief themes of American balladry were clearly presented: domestic tragedies, outlaws, murdered lovers, disasters, incidents of American wars, occupational pursuits. And what is equally important, the chief occupational groups contributing ballads or themes had come into notice. The cowboy was most widely represented, but items dealing with other occupations foreshadowed later discoveries among shantyboys, railroad workers, and hoboes. Unpublished collections seem to have contained ballads from all groups, including ocean sailors.

These academic collectors did not limit themselves to ballads, even in the sense of songs with explicit narrative content, although published texts were usually narratives. A few survivals of English carols had been printed in *JAF* beginning in 1891, and a few moralistic, religious, and patriotic songs had appeared in 1901; but lyrics did not appear in any great number until a variety of texts from the South were printed, the first in 1907. Then came not only such imported texts as "Loving Nancy" and "The Wagoner's Lad," but American ditties like "Bonnie Blue Eyes" and "Sourwood Mountain." The first large collection to be printed, that of E. C. Perrow, contains a preponderance of the lyric. The check lists of Belden and of Shearin and Combs indicated the diversity of nonnarrative folksong swimming into the nets of these early scholars. Although the proportion in early reports is not accurate, it indicated a divergence in American folksong tradition: the relative paucity in the North of lyric materials other than nursery or game songs.

The inclusiveness of the collecting habits is proved by the acceptance of what are termed *parlor songs*, late nineteenth- and early twentieth-century music-hall or popular songs. These were seldom published during this period, although such sentimental pieces as "The Blind Child" and "Rosewood Casket" appeared in Perrow's collection. But consider the following titles in Shearin and Combs's

Syllabus: "On the Banks of the Wabash," "Will You Love Me When I'm Old?" "Mollie Darling," "After the Ball," "The Broken Engagement," and in Louise Pound's: "The Pardon Came Too Late," "I'll Be All Smiles Tonight," "Old Dog Tray," "The Two Drummers," "Father, Dear Father." The liberality of collectors is clarified by Shearin's note:

> Amid the flotsam and jetsam of popular parlor-songs everywhere current the following have come to hand. They are hardly worth preserving, even by title, save for the fact that in spite of their pseudo-literary tang they are fellow travelers by oral tradition with the true folk-songs and song-ballads.[35]

Thus it may be seen that the attitude rather than the collecting practices of the academic tradition has given cause for the ire of more liberal critics.

The collectors already discussed dealt largely with white informants, receiving Negro tradition at second hand; but scattered through the early numbers of *JAF* are songs reported directly from Negroes, beginning in 1891 with the contributions of Mrs. Fanny D. Bergen, who noted the thin line between religious and secular songs. Texts began to appear in numbers only with the work of Howard W. Odum. He printed about 100 religious songs in the *American Journal of Religious Psychology and Education* in 1906[36] and 115 secular songs in *JAF* in 1911. These collections were supplemented by Anna Kranz Odum's materials in the 1914 *JAF*. Odum's collections are part of *an* academic tradition, though not quite *the* academic tradition considered here. His collections arose from sociological rather than literary interests and are regarded more as means than ends. To be more precise, Odum treats the songs as a part of the background for a cultural study, whereas the academic folksong tradition treats the culture as a part of the background for folksong study. Yet certain similarities are apparent.

The collections of the Odums are also inclusive, containing any songs in the possession of the folk. Odum found Negro songs to be of three types: modern "coon" songs and popular songs of the day; such songs greatly modified and adapted; and songs originating with Negroes or adapted so completely that they "become common folk-songs." [37] In spite of references to the music, he prints no tunes and makes no extended musical analysis. But for him the text is not quite "the thing" and is not separated from the singer and his culture.

Excepting the collections of the Odums and a similar one of Henry C. Davis in the 1914 *JAF*, only one academic collection of the early period contains a great deal of Negro tradition. Of the 270 items in E. C. Perrow's "Songs and Rhymes from the South" (*JAF*, 1912–1915), 118 seem to be Negro. Perrow's interest in Negro song was, like that of C. Alphonso Smith and Frank C. Brown, due to his belief that the Negro, more than the white, was "a representative of the ballad-making epoch." Otherwise, most of the songs reported by academic collectors seem to have come from white informants, although the facts are not always clearly stated.

A final illustration of the inclusiveness of the early academic collectors concerns game songs. It is perhaps significant that the first academic collection of American folksongs from oral tradition was Newell's *Games and Songs of American Children* (1883) and that the first song text published in *JAF* was "My Pretty Little Pink" (1889). Early interest was stimulated by the understanding that children's games are often survivals of ancient practices. Collectors found texts among elderly reciters who remembered the songs as "current and popular . . . in the days of their youth," [38] and they soon discovered the play-party, first as a memory, then as a live custom among adults.[39] Of more moment, most of the syllabi and *JAF* selections already referred to contain liberal amounts of game songs as well as all sorts of rhymes.

In fact, rhymes were the main subject of collection. Not only were academic collectors generally incompetent to deal with the music of folksong; they virtually ignored instrumental folk music whether as accompaniment to song or as an end in itself. The one interested and qualified collector, Phillips Barry, worked in the Northeast, where the folksong and instrumental music traditions seem to have been in some respects separate. Those working in the rich and more unified tradition of the South seldom even comment on instrumental music. Were it not for Louise Bascomb and a few others, nothing would be known of the banjo minstrel squatting by the roadside with his unfretted, homemade banjo and his French harp fastened to his head by wire, nothing of the fiddlers' and pickers' conventions.[40]

Ignorance of instrumental tradition resulted partially from methods of collection and the social status of collectors. The educator reached his informants through students or community leaders. He most often met "respectable" informants and met them in "respectable" situations in the home. He was himself somewhat in the position of the English cleric-collector—"respectable." Therefore he seldom surprised the folksong; he had it recalled for him by self-conscious informants on their best behavior and without their instruments of the devil. He collected not just half the folksong, as often charged, but sometimes only a third of it.

The academic collector, thus personally divorced from the full stream of tradition, struggled valiantly to collect all the scraps he could. However he interpreted what he found, he accepted and preserved it (excepting the music), and succeeded in opening up more approaches than could possibly be followed and engendering some confusions in the process. One of these particular approaches is that of manuscript and print. The importance of these had been demonstrated by Child and prior students, and American broadsides were known. But the early twentieth-century collector stumbled on manuscripts and local broadsides among his informants. It is to the credit of the academic tradition that it accepted and even published these versions. But the inclusion of such materials may be partly responsible for some of the present-day confusion between broadside and folk. The early academic collector clearly saw the materials in their proper value:

> Inclusion rather than exclusion should be the rule in the work of collection. . . . Printed matter is by no means to be refused; both because the investigation is ideally a study of popular taste, in which print certainly nowadays plays a most important role, and because

the relation of print to oral tradition is precisely one of the chief problems to be solved.[41]

But the presence in a folklore journal of supposedly original ballads from the printed sheets distributed by a traveling minstrel may be one of the seeds of the latter-day adulation of songs made by a member of some "folk." In point of fact, many more of the broadsides should have been collected and correctly appraised.

Although this was but the first phase of the academic drama— not a single separate collection being in print by 1917—Belden, ever optimistic, hoped in 1911 [42] that a way might be found to publish not check lists, but a gathering of ballads in a single volume— all the traditional balladry known in America. The university presses had not yet begun to issue the formal volumes of academic collecting, and even today some of the great collections remain published only in part. But the principles of collection had been established by 1917 and were either to control or to influence most collecting and publishing henceforth.

The textual scholarship of George Lyman Kittredge set the ultimate model, as may be seen in his edition of a large number of songs grouped in *JAF* in 1917.[43] The texts (and such tunes as had been forwarded) are arranged in imitation of the Child pattern; the full headnotes are textual, bibliographical, and comparative. The imported ballads and those which had appeared in American broadsides have annotations that are still standard. For good or ill, the textual scholar had laid hold of the entire folksong tradition from Child ballad to "Down in the Valley."

A final glance at the main area of collection indicates the work initiated by academic collectors in this period. Barry's work in the Northeast had uncovered eighty-four items by 1906, continued to grow, and was soon to enter into the fruitful period of the Folk-Song Society of the Northeast. To the north, MacKenzie had reported from his Nova Scotia collecting in *JAF*, 1909 and 1910, and was to produce a valuable report on ballad singing and one of the standard academic collections. The South, particularly the Appalachian area, held great promise. The Virginia Folklore Society was busily amassing the material for a monumental publication of Child ballads and—without the support of its leader—a great unpublished collection. Reed Smith was stimulating South Carolina workers to perform a lesser task. In 1913 John Harrington Cox had begun his West Virginia collection, and Frank C. Brown's North Carolina collection, of which he gave a partial list in 1915,[44] continued to grow, though lying unpublished until issued at mid-century as the largest single American collection. The material of Shearin and Combs had thus far seen the light only partially in Combs's two small volumes. Farther to the west, Belden had virtually completed his collection by 1917, though it remained in manuscript until 1940; and the Texas Folklore Society had begun in 1916 a series of annual *Publications* which were to contain notable contributions to collected American folksongs. The picture in the Midwest was not as bright, although those laboring in the field furnished stimulus for later collectors. Albert H. Tolman was gathering songs in Illinois and elsewhere,[45] and a portion of Louise Pound's Nebraska material was soon to be issued in *American Ballads and Songs* (1921). Though Bertrand L. Jones's list of Michigan collectanea [46] was to produce no direct result, it stimulated the beginning of a later collection. No mean achievement this, in the first two decades of the noble sport of American ballad hunting.

THE LOCAL-ENTHUSIASTIC TRADITION

Folksong collection in the United States probably owes as much to the pure enthusiasts as to any other group. Behind the achievements of the academic tradition lie the labors of the inadequately known individuals who devoted themselves freely to collecting or paving the way for collectors. In spite of the acknowledgments of the academics, individual workers have received insufficient recognition. But in themselves they do not constitute the local-enthusiastic tradition, because they were often associated with state folklore groups and their work was garnered and issued under academic control. On the other hand, there are publications that qualify as local-enthusiastic. The editors were not necessarily lacking in learning, or even ballad learning; their attitude toward their material and their treatment of it places them in a particular classification.

The local enthusiast directed his material to the general public. He was less interested in classification and study than in perpetuation and enjoyment. His attitude toward the folk and the song was more openly primitivistic, and he stressed the quaint and unusual in the song and in the singer. The published collections were in the nature of poetic miscellanies, lacking organization and significant or accurate notes; nor were informants fully credited. The editing principles of the local enthusiast ranged from attempts at accurate reproduction to methods reminiscent of Scott and Percy. And he found space for much vaguely popular material, local or "folksy" poetry.

There are strengths in these collections, not to speak of naïve charm. The warmth and interest of the local enthusiast kept him close to his sources. He often knew much of the local background, whether of the singer or of the song. If he naïvely accepted folk authority, he recorded it. He sometimes knew more of local culture than the vaunted expert. Although he tended to accept uncritically a romantic definition of a folksong as one which "just growed," he had as little discrimination as the most liberal academic collector and no trace of snobbery. Unfortunately his attitude is not conducive to trust in the accuracy of his texts. And too often he shares the musical incompetencies of the academic tradition.

The first important post-Child collection separately published, *Cowboy Songs and Other Frontier Ballads* (1910), belongs to the local-enthusiastic tradition despite the fact that its editor was a sometime academic who was to become the greatest popularizer and one of the greatest field collectors of American folksong. Already noted have been the background, the academic support, and the communal ties of John Avery Lomax. Of interest here are his collecting methods and his early editorial practice.

The elder Lomax certainly used almost every known collecting method. He reached informants indirectly through newspapers and magazines; he rummaged through songsters and collected the "flying leaves" of broadsides; he made contacts through his Texas college students. And—most important—he went where the singing was and seems to have been the first American fieldworker to collect songs in English with the phonograph.[47] All these methods went into the amassing of material for the first edition of *Cowboy Songs*, as Lomax indicates in his book of reminiscences, *Adventures of a Ballad Hunter* (1947). But the critic is often left in doubt as to which methods obtained which songs.

Values and shortcomings of *Cowboy Songs* were trenchantly indicated by Robert W. Gordon when he wrote that Lomax's 1910 collection is "still by far the best."

> But this, as its compiler states, was intended to be "frankly popular." Hence he does not indicate the sources from which he obtained the individual texts. . . . In several cases the texts as printed are composites, put together from a number of versions obtained at different times and from different places. The book gives a marvelous panorama of cowboy song that no future collector is likely ever to surpass or even equal. But it is not accompanied by certain facts needed for final interpretation of the precise relation between the songs and the folk.[48]

Unfortunately, Gordon's statements must stand almost uncorrected, for even with the help of the Lomax manuscripts it is not possible to reconstruct all the links between the folk versions and the printed texts.

Investigating John Lomax's volumes is, as Bliss Perry said of Longfellow criticism, "like carrying a rifle into a national park." A critic, possibly Phillips Barry, once suggested that *Cowboy Songs* was modeled on Percy's *Reliques*. Certainly the book is miscellaneous and popular enough, though the editing methods and the color of the volumes remind us more of Scott's *Minstrelsy*. But the analogy with the *Reliques* is apt in another way, for modern criticism of the good Bishop is tempered by recognition of his great service as a popularizer and of the fact that without his "improvements" there would have been no *Reliques*. We must make

the same apologies for *Cowboy Songs.* Yet Lomax cannot be excused
from the rigorous examination such as Percy has undergone. Nor
can we forget that Percy was at least unaware of the scholarly convention he was violating.

The 1910 edition of *Cowboy Songs* contains 122 texts and eighteen tunes, which might have been 100 or more had the publishers
been willing to include them. The songs are arranged haphazardly,
and in only a few instances are the texts supplemented by notes or
explanations as to source, origin, currency, or history. (Certainly the
publishers would have balked at extensive notes. Two other houses
had rejected the book.) Lomax's introductory statement that "the
volume is meant to be popular" refers to more than his violation
of the "ethics of ballad collectors, in a few instances, by selecting
and putting together what seemed to be the best lines from different versions, all telling the same story." The selection of the material emphasizes the romantic concept of the cowboy that was
growing in the minds of the public. One suspects that a number
of the items are nontraditional, but because of Lomax's reticence
concerning sources, judgment is difficult. In his introduction he
expresses the hope that "enough interest will be aroused to justify
printing all the variants of these songs and such explanatory notes
as may be useful." That interest was never aroused—or at any rate,
never rewarded. The 1916 edition merely adds forty texts, and the
revised edition of 1938 raises as many questions as it answers.

Of the 152 songs in the 1916 edition, eighty are included in the
1938 revision unchanged or virtually unchanged, thirty-three are
omitted, and thirty-nine appear with significant alteration. Of the
eighty virtually unchanged texts, sources of twenty-four are indicated exactly (one being the repetition of an earlier acknowledgment). In almost every instance the source is another collector or
a correspondent; thus this information is in the nature of a past-due
acknowledgment to a person, a book, or a newspaper. Attribution
of authorship of six other songs is given, and one of these is reproduced from the earlier edition. Finally two notes give incomplete
and inexact information concerning sources. Forty-two songs remain

totally unannotated. The thirty-nine songs reprinted in altered form present an even more confusing problem, for there is no way to tell whether we deal with altered copies or versions collected later. A variety of annotations, like those accorded the previous group, are given for these songs. All in all, the inconsistent annotation makes one even more dubious of the traditional status of some of the songs. Something more can be seen by an examination of the thirty-three songs omitted in the revision. Two omissions result from the elimination of variants: "The Kansas Line" is omitted and its title given to "The Dreary, Dreary Life"; "The Cowgirl" is combined with "The Bucking Broncho." Two other songs omitted are fragments. Fourteen or fifteen exclusions are not strictly cowboy songs, e.g., "The Old Man under the Hill" and "Foreman Monroe." The remaining fourteen might be considered pieces of local verse included in the earlier editions for color, e.g., "By Markentura's Flowery Marge" and "The Campfire Has Gone Out" (though the latter was certainly circulating anonymously at the time Lomax was collecting for *Cowboy Songs*). But if these omissions are taken as a tacit attempt to "purify" the volume, some inclusions need explanation.

Seeking to explain and document *Cowboy Songs*, one turns to the Lomax manuscripts, recalling that Kittredge said to Lomax in 1908, "Go and get this material while it can be found—the words and the tunes. Set down the dates of your recordings, the name of the singer and where he got the song. . . . Preserve the words and music. That's your job." Unfortunately, the advice was apparently not followed exactly. The most charitable conclusion is that the elder Lomax was extremely careless and inefficient in documenting and preserving his field material. For example, of probably 250 cylinder recordings made in Texas and Oklahoma in 1908–1910, while he held a Sheldon Fellowship from Harvard, only forty-seven are now in the Library of Congress. The remainder are lost or broken and no transcriptions have been discovered. Lomax's collection of texts, now in the Eugene C. Barker Texas History Center of the University of Texas Library, was once well organized and indexed. Whether its present state is due to the work of writing *Adventures* or to the rifling of a careless researcher is not clear. There is some evidence to support both conjectures. But the fact is that the papers do *not* contain complete documentation of the texts of *Cowboy Songs*. There are many texts without dates or sources, or both. The changes in an overwritten base text cannot always be accounted for by other texts available; nor does the revised text always agree with the text in *Cowboy Songs*. But the papers do provide a picture, hazy and incomplete, of the background of *Cowboy Songs*—unless verbatim texts of most of the songs were on the 200 lost cylinders.

In the first place, the amount of material from correspondents, manuscript, and print is surprising. The sources are legitimate, though they should have been acknowledged. But the material does not seem quite to justify Lomax's, "The songs of this collection, never before in print, as a rule have been taken down from oral recitation." "The California Stage Company" and "The Happy Miner" were among a group sent by W. J. Handy from songsters and *Out West Magazine* (1907–1908). The base text of "The Buffalo Skinners" seems to have been an undated clipping from a Dallas newspaper. Lomax was then, as later, the recipient of material from other collectors, which he did not properly document, even in manuscript. His editing ranges from exact transcription to extensive collation with personal "improvement." A few examples will indicate the range of the editing.

There are a number of accurate transcriptions in *Cowboy Songs*, often, though not always, of songs not known in many variants. "New National Anthem" (1916–1938) is given as sent by W. P. MacLaughlin, Clovis, New Mexico, March 14, 1911. "Poor Lonesome Cowboy" agrees exactly with the "copy taken from the scrapbook of E. B. Frazer, Henrietta, Texas. Copied from manuscript." But we find changes even in apparently unique copies. A ballet copy of "S M S Range" (an actual brand) headed, "Composed and written by G. W. Barr of Stamford Tex Coppy Right applyed for," appears with a few other emendations as "U-S-U Range" (1910–1938).

The handling of more widely known songs is more complex. There is more to a Lomax composite than an assembling of stanzas or even lines from variant copies. "Jesse James" (1910–1938) is represented by nine copies in the Lomax papers. The published text is largely that sent by H. M. Belden, who collected it in 1906.[49] Stanzas three and nine are from J. P. Arnold, Meser, Texas. Not only did Lomax have to change Belden's *Glenville* to agree with Arnold's *Glendale,* but he made a number of unjustified changes in Belden's text. For example, line two of the chorus can be found in none of the manuscript versions, though of course it might have come from the source of the tune, now lost. All one can say is that its printed form could have come neither from the "old blind negro at Hearne, Texas," nor from Mrs. Tramtham, the gypsy fortuneteller at the Fort Worth cattleman's convention of 1910. In the 1938 edition Lomax indicates that "The Jolly Cowboy" is from "eight fragments found in Arizona and Texas." Actually only three of the eight texts are fragments, and one text is from Mary J. Jacques *Texan Ranch Life* (1894), which furnished the base text of "The Dying Cowboy." The printed version of "The Jolly Cowboy" was based on a composite text made by D. L. Browning, Garner, Texas, but it was combined, collated, and "improved." Stanza three is varied from the first stanza of a version from W. W. Bogel, Texas Agricultural and Mechanical College. Stanza four is not exactly represented in any of the variants, but is pieced out. Stanzas five, six, and seven occur in a number of the variants, but not *exactly* in any. And there are slight changes that can be traced to none of the variants. The text is, therefore, not representative of folk tradition. It is more or less a free composition based on variant texts, not all of which are adequately documented. And apparently Lomax sometimes went even further in usurping the prerogative of the folk. According to evidence in the manuscripts, "My horses ain't hungry" entered "Old Paint" (1916) via John A. Lomax from a three-stanza fragment of "The Wagoner's Lad."

The making of composite or even emended texts is sometimes justified, and in many instances Lomax was forced either to alter or omit texts. The changes in "The Range Riders" (1910–1938) are those necessary to turn an informant's manuscript into readable form; they involve spelling, punctuation, restoration of stanzaic form, and the change in the number of a pronoun. Though on the basis of the manuscript Lomax perhaps overemphasized the salty character of his collection, a number of texts are still such that "as yet polite society is quite unwilling to hear." The base text of "The Bull Whacker" (1910–1938), from Tom Hight of Oklahoma City, could not today pass muster for a learned journal. Collation was in this instance impossible, and Lomax chose the not altogether wise course of emending freely and producing an unrepresentative text. (We of course do not know how much expurgation has gone on silently behind the façades of other collections.) Yet it is difficult to censure Lomax for some of his emendation. Even as polished for publication, his "crude songs" were not appreciated by his colleagues and the good people of Texas. The songs were later made the lever to pry him from his position in the University. He may have gone too far in collation and "creation," but the basic error was his failure to publish anywhere "both the extent and sources of editorial changes and restorations," and to leave unpublished a full accounting of his stewardship. Folksong collections must often be taken on trust, but Lomax's editing inspires distrust. In the Lomax papers is a text, apparently in the handwriting of a Mrs. Henson, of "Dona Gal." In 1938 these stanzas with two slight changes and the addition of three stanzas and a tune are printed as "Doney Gal," "from the singing of Mrs. Louise Henson." The 1938 copy actually represents a rendition recorded for the Library of Congress, but without evidence one is hardly disposed to accept it blindly. And then there is the case of the Thorp songs.

Thereby hangs a tale of the little-known collector and editor of the first collection of cowboy songs. Nathan Howard (Jack) Thorp, a young easterner turned cowboy, became interested in the songs sung on the range. According to his account,[50] he decided in March, 1889, to drift about and collect the songs. In March, 1890, having ridden over 1,500 miles of New Mexico and Texas, he was back on his home range, with a "handful of songs" in his notebook. His interest continued, and he not only collected firsthand, but obtained material from correspondents in other states. And his work resembled Lomax's in other ways. He discovered on his collecting trip that "none of the cowboys who could sing ever remembered a complete song." He collected verses here and there until he had something like a complete song. He "dry cleaned" his composites, but found no publisher interested. Finally in 1908 he "made a dicker" with a printer in Estancia, New Mexico, and printed 2,000 copies of a red paper-bound pamphlet of fifty pages, twenty-three songs—the first edition of *Songs of the Cowboys*.

Cowboy Songs is the first collection with music, but *Songs of the Cowboys* stands in somewhat the same relation to it as *A Collection of Old Ballads* does to Percy's *Reliques*. Thorp's *Songs of the Cowboys* is a true collection and is important as such; but it must also have functioned as a *broadside*. How many were sold at the price of fifty cents is not clear; but even 1,000 copies, sold in cow camps and at roundups and cattle fairs, and distributed at least as far as Kansas, certainly had an effect on oral tradition.

Thorp was more than a collector and editor; he was a singer and composer; and five of the pieces in *Songs of the Cowboys* are his own. On this fact turns his quarrel with Lomax. "Little Joe the Wrangler" appeared in the 1910 edition of *Cowboy Songs*, and the other four—"Chopo," "The Pecos River Queen," "Speckles," and "Whose Old Cow?"—in the edition of 1916. Appropriation of published folksongs is hard to prove, but Thorp has rather clear evidence.

> I closed my first little paper-covered book with a ballad I wrote myself, called "Speckles." There were eight verses as I wrote it, but the printer lost part of the copy and printed only six. Some time later a very learned professor brought out a big book of cowboy songs which he claimed to have collected with great labor, and he printed my abbreviated "Speckles" (without credit), but changed the name to "Freckles" and called it a fragment he had picked up.[51]

In a note to "Little Joe the Wrangler" in the 1938 edition of *Cowboy Songs*—after Thorp had set forth his claims in the 1921 edition of *Songs of the Cowboys*—Lomax writes:

> During 1907–1910 I found in Texas several versions of this song, and printed it anonymously in 1910. Later I discovered the song in a small collection of cowboy verse published in Estancia, New Mexico, by N. Howard (Jack) Thorp. Mr. Thorp says he wrote the song in 1898.

The Lomax manuscripts and one of the cylinders in the Library of Congress support the statement. But the note seems to tell us something more. The other songs in question were added "later," presumably after he had seen Thorpe's first collection. Lomax omitted "Chopo," "The Pecos River Queen," and "Speckles" from the 1938 edition, but printed "Whose Old Cow?" and credited it to Thorp's volume of 1921! The Lomax papers contain no texts of the four songs added in 1916. In fact there is but a list of the songs "Thorpe claims to have written" and the following in a letter to J. W. Jones, Beloit, Wisconsin, November 26, 1923:

> Thorpe's book . . . is largely cribbed from mine with a lot of so-called songs to which he signs himself as author. I . . . find that he has no really good cowboy song that has not hitherto been published in my collection.

The weight of the evidence lies with Thorp. Though he did not then claim authorship, he had printed and *copyrighted* the texts in 1908. Though copyright does not deter the folk, it should be respected by the collector.

We could multiply the examples of obfuscation in *Cowboy Songs* [52] without destroying the importance of the book. But we may always doubt that all the means were necessary to achieve the end.

Lomax's work was perhaps more enthusiastic than local, but such collections as those by Henry W. Shoemaker fully illustrate the local side of this tradition. In 1919 Colonel Shoemaker published a group of texts as *North Pennsylvania Minstrelsy*, with blank leaves at the end of the volume to be filled from later collection. He published instead two later editions, one with the same title in 1923 and *Mountain Minstrelsy of Pennsylvania* in 1931, but with no alteration in method or approach. The 1919 edition reveals many of the values and weaknesses of the local enthusiast.

The book contains a potpourri of 104 texts and fragments in no discernible order. The range of material is comparable to that of the most inclusive academic collection—Child ballads, widespread American ballads, popular and school songs, and local poetry—but we cannot be sure that any standard was applied in judgment. Unlike Lomax's first volume, *North Pennsylvania Minstrelsy* includes information concerning the source and provenance of some texts— just enough information to madden the critic and cause him to distrust the accuracy of every recording. Shoemaker received much of his material from local correspondents and old-timers in the Pennsylvania woods, and many of his notes may be the comments of his informants. Remarks under a text state, "The above is about right"; stanzas are appended to a text and marked only "later"; and songs are credited to both an author and an informant with no other explanation. Whether the comments come from Shoemaker or a correspondent is not clear; the correspondents, however, must have shared Shoemaker's belief that he dealt with "more or less inaccurate reciters" and that a "correct" version should be sought. Yet there is no evidence that the Colonel ever willfully altered a text. Three texts noted as being "sung by" an informant agree exactly with those printed in Springer's *Forest Life and Forest Trees* (1851).[53] The texts might have been secured from print by the informant or by the correspondent. But in such a case, unless the editor has given the full facts of recovery and has no other suspicious entries, he is likely to be charged with dishonesty.

Values as well as weaknesses stem from indifference to academic concerns. The inclusion of the "authorless" "O Susannah" or "Darling Nelly Gray," even from a newspaper clipping is valuable. A school song from a copybook is not to be despised. Pieces like

"Friendship on Indian River," which seems to be local poetry, may have a place; unfortunately that place is not made clear. The local collector may know the author of a neighborhood ballad when he is in ignorance of the provenance of a popular song. But a correspondent who admits changing one word to make a rhyme invites suspicion of other changes, especially when the editor of the collection requests "corrections and suggestions." The great comfort to the critic is that changes made by a local enthusiast are more likely to be folk corrections than editorial "improvements"—unless the lure of monetary profit turns the enthusiast into a half-read charlatan.

THE MUSICAL-ESTHETIC TRADITION

The third important tradition manifested in early American collection concerned itself largely with the esthetic values of the music of folksong. There are two strains of the tradition. One, which may be called the *singing-book strain* and is represented by the collections of Josephine McGill and Loraine Wyman and Howard Brockway, seeks to provide versions of songs for performance. The other strain, represented by the work of Cecil Sharp and Maud Karpeles, is more scholarly but is still largely concerned with esthetic qualities. Both strains are closely associated with the concept of the unique qualities of the "mountain whites . . . [who are] not to be confounded with the 'poor white trash' of the South!" [54]

Folk Songs of the Kentucky Mountains (1917) by Josephine McGill and *Lonesome Tunes* (1916) by Loraine Wyman and Howard Brockway were collected at approximately the same time in approximately the same area by the same methods and have the same traits. Both collections are the results of "expeditions." Miss McGill's collecting was done in the autumn of 1914 in Knott and Letcher Counties, Kentucky, with the Hindman Settlement School as her headquarters. Miss Wyman and Mr. Brockway's journey in 1916 of 300 miles "through the Kentucky wilds" covered seven mountain counties, including the areas under the sway of both Hindman and Pine Mountain settlement schools, and yielded seventy-seven variants of fifty-nine songs (including one collected in North Carolina, apparently "on the way").

The presentation of the material is in the standard method of art music intended for performance. Thus a full transcription of the music indicates not the variation of the singer but an aid to the performer. The musical settings fall below the British standard, particularly the modern harmonies of Brockway. The exact sources of individual items are not noted, and both volumes merely give credit in the prefaces to a number of informants. One is left to wonder if the full texts set to good tunes resulted from improvement, conflation, or judicious selection. Miss McGill's manuscripts cannot be located, but Miss Wyman's texts and a few of her tunes were sent to Kittredge for possible publication in *JAF* (where a few did appear in 1917), and are now in the Houghton Library.

Comparing the texts and the few tunes in the manuscript with *Lonesome Tunes* and a later publication, *Twenty Kentucky Mountain Songs* (1920), one can determine the apparent accuracy of these singing books, which may serve as an indication of the fidelity of similar collections. Examination of the few tunes available (all would have been supplied had Kittredge requested them) indicates the melodic accuracy of those printed. Twenty of the forty-five texts are accurately printed; six suffer slight emendation. Two are simple collations. One has the addition of a second-version ending not in the manuscript; since the text is attributed to two informants, we might guess that it is a conflated text. In one case a text from one informant is set to a tune from another. Fifteen of the published texts suffer serious addition, emendation, omission, or all three. Whether this is a good or bad record depends on the point of view. But the examination will not support the statement in the preface to *Lonesome Tunes* that the songs are "reproduced as nearly as possible as we heard them sung by the people." Assuming that the fidelity of other singing books is comparable, one cannot accept such publications blindly as source material for scholarly text study. Of course they were not intended for such a purpose. But they are *primary* collections. The books represent pioneer work in the collection and printing of tunes. They also illustrate one of the prime difficulties of early folksong collection in the United States. As it was once phrased: the scholars were not musicians and the musicians were not scholars. It is too bad that the singing books were not documented and that the collected materials were not made generally available for scholarly study.

The publication in *Lonesome Tunes* and *Folk Songs of the Kentucky Mountains* of forty-six tunes would have been an event of considerable magnitude in American folksong collecting had it not been for the almost providential appearance of Cecil J. Sharp in the mountains at about the same time. The type of material collected by these musicians agrees, as we shall see, with that of Sharp, and will label them "purists," though not of the academic sort. Miss McGill's volume is, of course, "Child-heavy"—thirteen of twenty texts; whether or not it is representative of her whole collection we cannot judge. The publications of Miss Wyman and Mr. Brockway are thoroughly representative of the songs they collected, which include not only Child ballads, English broadside texts, lyrics, nursery, nonsense, and religious songs, but even some native American ballads. But there is an esthetic common denominator in that crude or sentimental pieces then current in mountain tradition are generally lacking. We do not *know* that these collectors restricted their notations and publications to what was esthetically satisfying to urban sophisticates; we do know that this sort of selection seems typical of most publications associated with the settlement schools, which encouraged collectors but had something at stake in the kind of picture painted for outsiders.

The other strain of the musical-esthetic tradition has had more academic influence than have the singing books. The volumes printed from the collection made by Cecil Sharp in the Southern Appalachians have never been imitated, but they have been accepted not only as invaluable, but as "the best *regional* collection we shall ever get." [55] Sharp himself has been the subject of a kind of blind hero worship, not all of it English. His contribution to the collection and publication of American folksong is immense, perhaps indispensable. But one cannot assent to the myth that an English collector discovered American folksongs and interested America in their collection, that he initiated directly the musical portion of ballad study, and that his work published in the two volumes of *English Folk Songs from the Southern Appalachians* (1932) is a model folksong collection. The facts belie the myth, which is a disservice to the essential modesty and deference of the great English collector.

Although Sharp's presence in America in 1915 may seem providential, his collecting trips to the mountains were not. They were the product of the labors and interest of Mrs. Olive Dame Campbell, whose husband was Director of the Southern Highland Division of the Russell Sage Foundation. She had begun collecting texts and tunes in 1908, and, convinced of the necessity of immediate collection by a trained musician, she made a special trip to Cambridge, Massachusetts, to interest Sharp, who was then on his second visit to the United States. As a result Sharp and Miss Maud Karpeles spent twelve months in the Southern Appalachians, 1916–1918. The harvest of two months' work plus Mrs. Campbell's collection was issued in 1917 as *English Folk Songs from the Southern Appalachians* under both names. The chronicle of Sharp's three collecting trips has been related by Maud Karpeles,[56] but a few comments are necessary.

In relation to the amount of time expended, the amount of material Sharp collected is impressive. Sharp's forty-six weeks of collecting yielded 1,612 tunes, about thirty-five a week. In a period of less than a week at Hindman, Kentucky, he noted sixty-one tunes from twelve informants. The harvest testifies to the strength of mountain tradition in the second decade of the twentieth century. It also testifies not only to Sharp's skill and speed, but to his ingratiating manner with both singers and collectors. He was ever careful to make contact with regional collectors and to avoid "poaching on their preserves." Their favorable reaction and aid is a tribute to Sharp, but to the other collectors as well. They were as anxious as Sharp that tunes be secured and sometimes more than a little flattered to be able to give every aid to the famous collector. Sharp's success then seems admirable, but a little short of miraculous. Without ignoring the energy Sharp displayed and the hardships he encountered, we can see that he skimmed the cream of Appalachian folksong. An experienced field collector devoting full time to the task, he spent about three and a half months in North Carolina, Virginia, and Kentucky, a month in Tennessee, and a few days in West Virginia. To be exact, he spent but two collecting days in West Virginia and left because songs "did not lie so ready to hand as in the other states." [57] Sharp ranged widely but not deeply.

Of late Miss Karpeles' edition of Sharp's collection has received the extravagant praise of a group we might call the "latter-day purists." It has been called "the most significant contribution that has been made to the study and collection of American folksong with the exception of Child's own volumes." [58] The meaning of this praise is made manifest in Evelyn Wells's ranking of Sharp as "the 'Child' of the ballad tune." [59] For Sharp was a selective collector, too, "spending hours perhaps listening to inferior songs in the hope that a real gem will be extracted from the singer's memory." [60]

Edited from the Sharp manuscripts and published posthumously in 1932, *English Folk Songs from the Southern Appalachians* is a rich collection of 274 items in almost 1,000 variants, including a wide range of material, even a few jigs and play-party games. There are a goodly number of American texts, such as "John Hardy," "Poor Omie," "The Battle of Shiloh," and "The Lonesome Prairie." But almost totally lacking are the nineteenth-century sentimental songs. To judge from this collection, such songs were not prevalent in the mountains during Sharp's visits. But we know otherwise from prior collection and from Miss Karpeles' own testimony concerning one such song, "The Little Rosewood Casket": "It is not a folk song; it is not good music. When I was in the mountains forty years ago, it was being sung, but I did not bother to record it." [61] The esthetic bias is obvious. It is musical purism—

though in this instance it represents the application in America of the standards of the English folksong collector. We note that Sharp collected *English* folksongs and can apparently justify an inclusion by remarking that when, "by chance, a modern street-song succeeds in penetrating into the mountains, it is at once mated to a traditional tune" (I, xxvi). Strangely enough, his example of the "modern street-song" is "Wild Bill Jones," which cannot be traced at all, let alone to broadsides, and has not the characteristics of the vulgar ballad. But it *is* in a newer folksong style. When Sharp writes that the only secular music which the hillman "has an opportunity of learning is that which his British forefathers brought with them from their native country" (I, xvi), he must refer only to some singers or to the songs he was willing to notice.

What Sharp did notice is painstakingly recorded and fully represented—or half of it is. For Sharp was still the English collector who writes in terms of *tunes* collected and published. The reader of the two-volume collection would guess that something over 400 texts have been sacrificed in some manner. An examination of the more than 500 songs Sharp collected in Kentucky yields interesting results. Of the 298 published in Miss Karpeles' edition, 155 contain only one stanza of text. Were 155 texts sacrificed to make room for musical examples? Hardly. For 120 of the one-stanza texts are complete as Sharp collected them. In fact, slightly more than 300 of the Kentucky songs have no more than one stanza, and this ratio is representative of the entire unpublished collection. A number of the texts may represent all that the singer remembered, but the manuscript evidence is convincing that Sharp and Miss Karpeles often failed to record all the singer knew. Certainly musical emphasis was needed to redress the balance, but here it goes too far.

In many ways the Sharp-Karpeles volume is troublesome. Texts are usually accurate, though there are a few unexplained collations and emendations. Almost never is the reader told that textual material is omitted. For practical reasons, full publication of collected material is seldom possible, and selection is often a matter of personal judgment. But one might be willing to sacrifice a few of the thirty-one printed copies of "Lord Thomas and Fair Ellinor" for a sight of "Frankfort Train," "Once I Had a Sweetheart," or "Colonel Sharpe," which were not printed at all. The sacrifice of a single tune should have made room for the full text of the only printed copy of "The Fateful Blow." Sharp noted all too little information concerning the singers, the songs, and the performance; and what little he recorded is largely omitted. But, eschewing the myth that Sharp alone is all we need, we must be grateful for what we have: the largest and finest collection of American folk tunes yet published and a mine of unprinted material.

Although no other book quite like the Sharp-Karpeles collection has appeared, the general plan of the 1917 edition foreshadowed the Child-and-other collections of the academics, and the inadequately explained division between ballads and songs has been followed by at least one editor. *English Folk Songs from the Southern Appalachians* has provided a refuge for the purist who has finally recognized the folk status of non-Child material but who cannot bring himself to consider the entire repertoire of the folksinger. It has interested the musician as well as the musicologist, but it has overemphasized a portion of American folksong.

TYPES OF AMERICAN COLLECTORS

One of the outstanding characteristics of American folksong collections is their heterogeneity, which is in a measure due to the differing men and women who compiled them. There has been no central training, support, or control. Within each of the various areas of collection, workers have varied in interest, attitude, knowledge, and skill. If the results have been uneven, at least there is no uncritical monolithic structure. A system of checks and balances is perhaps preferable to the possibility of a unified but narrow approach. Though no more than the collections themselves do the collectors lend themselves to the classifications of the sub-sublibrarian, we can discern several categories.

The most important single fact of American collection has been its close relationship to educational institutions. The institutions themselves have not always officially approved and supported folk-song collection; but academic folklore interest encouraged teachers to take advantage of the American emphasis on universal educa-tion, which brought into the classroom informants and contacts with traditional culture. In the early years of the century the work of Professors Child and Kittredge had made Harvard University an unofficial center of folksong study, thereby setting in motion a pattern which operated on all levels of the educational system: the teacher interested in ballads and ballad lore "discovered" in his classroom or community the songs which were the subject of scholarly study or literary appreciation. And the pattern is roughly the same, whether it is Kittredge encouraging and aiding Lomax or Paul G. Brewster making a collecting assignment in an Indiana high-school literature class. The direct and indirect influence of Harvard University produced results which, when archives and col-lege theses are eventually surveyed, will be truly staggering. One of the effects of the teacher-collector has been to extend the influence of the academic tradition, the collection of folklore for scholarly study. The teacher's interest in the folk has been largely peripheral, arising from the fact that among them was found the object of academic study. But the teacher's interest in folksong itself had to be somewhat peripheral, for he was almost invariably a teacher of literature, not folklore. Though he might manage to obtain offi-cial sanction and even support for his activities, though on occasion his labors might result in professional preferment, his collecting time had to be stolen from his professional duties and his off-duty hours. Whatever professional rewards there were were in no way equal to his labors.

Not all teacher-collectors have belonged to the academic tra-dition, nor have all academic collectors been teachers. But one of the early developments of academic influence was the regional archivist, a college professor stimulating, controlling, and preserving the findings of a number of subordinates. To picture the regional archivists as detached scholars analyzing the folk material which their workers furnished them is not completely accurate. They were often field collectors as well. But they were primarily leaders of the collecting efforts in various areas and custodians, and sometimes editors, of the results. They were not always great organizers, and some folklore societies seem to have withered because of their failure. But they managed to stimulate other individuals to pursue the quest. The number was small, but they produced some of the great collections. Recalling a few of the names—Henry Marvin Belden, Louise Pound, C. Alphonso Smith, Arthur Kyle Davis, Jr., Frank C. Brown, John Harrington Cox, Arthur Palmer Hudson, Reed Smith, and Harold W. Thompson—we see that they differ among themselves, but that their methods have much in common. Usually drawn to balladry by Child's work, they chanced upon a local version of an old English ballad (as did Belden in 1903 and Hudson in 1923) or an American ballad (as did Cox in 1913). They interested educators in other areas to begin collection. Belden encouraged Miss Pound, about 1904, to begin to collect in Nebraska. C. Alphonso Smith, by his lectures at West Virginia University in 1915, helped Cox gain the necessary interest to form the West Virginia Folklore Society. Some became permanent leaders—secretaries or archivists—of local societies; they recruited help from their students, reared new generations of collectors. They worked through public school teachers, some of them former students instructed in ballad lore. They publicized the work through educational bulletins and magazines. So much was in general agreement.

But the archivists were not all seeking quite the same kind of material. Despite their respect for the Child ballad, most of these leaders urged the collection of all kinds of folksong, and some, like Frank C. Brown, Arthur Palmer Hudson, and Harold W. Thompson, sought and preserved all kinds of popular tradition. But C. Alphonso Smith resisted all efforts to make the Virginia Folklore Society "merely an agency for the loose record of all sorts of popular stuff" and kept the effort "pointed steadily to the collection of these old world songs" [62]—the Child ballads. Virginia was scoured by a few energetic collectors until each of its 100 counties had supplied at least one Child variant. Not until 1924 were the Society's archives opened to "all sorts of popular stuff." Fortunately many members had collected and withheld materials which, together with the results of able collection since that date, have made the Society's archives rich in folksong, at least. The South Carolina Folklore Society, although its activities were not extensive, seems to have been directed by Reed Smith on a somewhat similar course.

The academic archivists were separated from the folk by their position and by their attitude toward the material. Lacking close ties with the folk, they depended upon the reports of their students and active subordinate collectors. The amount of direct contact with traditional singers varied. Whether, like C. Alphonso Smith and John Harrington Cox, they met singers only after introduction by a student or local collector, or whether, like Frank C. Brown, they toiled the muddy roads of the back country in search of informants, the archivists, by the very nature of their interest, saw the singer from a distance. The fact is not always to their discredit. The distance in some instances may have given them a clearer vision, while their aides prevented the distance from becoming a barrier. In any case, the services of the academic archivists have been indispensable.

Phillips Barry belongs in this group as the important exception. Barry was a private scholar with no official academic connections; and though his Folk-Song Society of the Northeast numbered collectors among its members, it functioned largely as his own publishing device and collapsed at his death. Alone among the early collectors, he dealt with folksong as a unit, a marriage of text and tune. True, he approached folksong as an academic, but he may seem a lone academic rather than a center of collection. Barry stands somewhat between the lone academic and the archivist, partaking of the qualities of both, but belonging with neither. Though he began work as an individual laborer, he became in later years the leader of folksong collecting in New England. He stands in lieu of an official regional archivist, and when an official state archive was established in Vermont, he contributed his material collected there. Just as did the true academic archivist, he controlled to some extent the work of the enthusiastic amateurs, but he lacked the educational and class-room devices of other archivists. Thus independent workers such as Mrs. Fannie Hardy Eckstorm and Mary Winslow Smyth (not amateurs in folksong by any means) came under his wing. The work of Mrs. Helen Hartness Flanders benefited greatly from Barry's aid. In setting the tone for area collection, he performed the most im-portant function of an academic archivist. Unfortunately, because of his failure to establish a stable society with a continuing reposi-tory, he did not provide for the future, as did C. Alphonso Smith and Frank C. Brown.

Closest to the archivists are the teachers who, introduced to folk-song through academic work, made subsequent investigations in the areas of their teaching assignments or in neighboring areas, some-times as research for higher degrees. Often these collectors were but links in the chain forged by the archivists; sometimes, as is shown in Alton C. Morris's state search of Florida, they were archivists with all the facilities but a state society. But their work was usually less extensive and covered a shorter period, as is illustrated by Earl J. Stout's collection in Iowa in 1931 and Emelyn Elizabeth Gard-ner's work in the Schoharie Hills, New York, in the summers of 1912–1914. Although these area collectors were occasionally natives of their collecting regions, that fact was not crucial in their work. Their relationship with the folk was usually developed after aca-demic influence. Unusual experiences sometimes made collectors out of teachers. Elizabeth Bristol Greenleaf followed the pattern of being introduced to folksong through schoolteaching. But she was a volunteer teacher in Newfoundland when she encountered tra-ditional song in 1920, and she returned with Mrs. Grace Yarrow Mansfield as the "Vassar College Folk-Lore Expedition to New-foundland, 1929." Similarly, Mellinger Edward Henry's hikes and vacations in the Southern Appalachians began in 1927 to turn into folksong expeditions which eventually produced two volumes of folksongs.

A few American academic collectors have had a folk background which they have successfully exploited. One of the earliest academics, E. C. Perrow (though he later collected extensively from students and friends) belongs to the group of native collectors, as does W. Roy MacKenzie. MacKenzie was not only a native of Pictou County, Nova Scotia, but had—in his own words—enjoyed "low associates" and was fitted to push the tankard to the old salt in exchange for a ballad. It is significant that after six or seven years of sporadic collection, his first book was *The Quest of the Ballad* (1919), which was largely an account of traditional singers and singing rather than a folksong collection. But in spite of his ability to communicate on equal terms with his informants, Mac-Kenzie lacked the folk background of Josiah H. Combs, who made his way from a Kentucky mountain settlement school to the University of Paris. His doctoral dissertation published there was a study and collection of *Folk Songs du Midi des États-Unis* (1925), collected from his family and other singers in eastern Kentucky and from Appalachian informants reached during his teaching at West Virginia University. Combs's work is a valuable combination of the academic approach and an American folk background (though once away from his home area he functioned as a typical teacher-collector). It is regrettable that his other interests called him not only to Texas and Virginia, but away from serious folksong scholarship, for perhaps the only other important academic collector who drew largely on a folk background has been Louis W. Chappell. The songs he printed in *Folk-Songs of Roanoke and the Albemarle* (1939) are drawn from his home community in eastern North Carolina, and his intimate knowledge is reflected in the quality of his collected materials. Unfortunately, he fails to supply the background, other than announcing a combative defense of the "tide-water whites."

Certain academic collectors became interested in more specialized projects than area collection, though usually because of opportunities in their teaching localities. Outstanding among academics searching specialized occupational groups were those questing for lumbering songs. All three of these collectors worked with elderly veterans of the shanties, but Roland Palmer Gray, the earliest in the field, seems to have had the least contact with the singers themselves. A large proportion of his collection is derived from students and local amateur collectors in Maine. Franz Rickaby, however, dealt more extensively with his Minnesota singers. But Earl Clifton Beck has devoted many more years to the quest, tramping the woods in search of informants and touring the country with a semiprofessional group called the Michigan Lumberjacks.

Other specialized academic work includes two contrasting collections of Negro songs. Newman Ivey White was a typical teacher-collector. He began collecting Negro songs, largely from white students, in 1915. He collected from manuscripts and memories of friends, as well as from some few Negro informants and published his findings as a part of his study of Negro song origins in 1928. White was academic in this sense, but Howard W. Odum and Guy B. Johnson were primarily sociologists. Their interest in Negro song was but a part of their "story of the Negro." Their material came largely from fieldwork among Negroes of Mississippi, Tennessee, Georgia, and the nearby Sea Islands. George Pullen Jackson differed from the sociologists—and from the other academics, for the most part—in approaching the folksong through its music, and through religious music at that. He was a transplanted New Englander who learned by chance of the Southern singing conventions and followed his leads into the field and into rare books. He was not the first to notice the religious folksongs of the whites, but he produced the first competent work in the field (*White Spirituals in the Southern Uplands*, 1933) and became their most important student. Although other collectors did not spurn print, Jackson added a new dimension to ballad collections by his garnerings from the shape-note hymn books.

The academics were thus field collectors, lone workers more frequently and intensively than the archivists. Their fieldwork and their interests were limited by area or by some other definition of a manageable scope. Area collectors pursued all traditional song within boundaries as often political as cultural or geographical. Specialized collectors sought one type of song wherever found, but they, too, were usually limited to their surrounding areas. But one academic played the field. Though John A. Lomax is the prototype of the roving American field collector, Robert Winslow Gordon was the first to undertake an expedition to track down many types of traditional song over large sections of the country. After building up a nationwide group of over 2,000 correspondents through his column "Old Songs That Men Have Sung" in *Adventure Magazine*, 1923–1927,[63] Gordon began in 1927 the most extensive field trip undertaken up to that time. Under the sponsorship of Harvard University and armed with recording apparatus, Gordon set out to cover the Southern Appalachians, the Southeastern seacoast, the interior of Georgia, the area northward along the Mississippi to Minnesota and the Dakotas, and eastward on the Canadian side of the Great Lakes into New Brunswick, Nova Scotia, and Newfoundland. The resulting 1,000 cylinder recordings have thus far produced only a group of texts published in the *New York Times Sunday Magazine*, 1927–1928. As a collector—even as a publisher—Gordon stands as the exception among the academics, among almost all American pursuers of the folksong.

To distinguish a group of folksong collectors from the academics by calling them *amateurs* is to imply neither that the academics were professional collectors nor that the interested amateurs were necessarily unscholarly. Usually the academic was, like Child, "doing a work he liked in a fashion that competent judges might be expected to approve," [64] and he was concerned primarily with the larger values of disinterested scholarship. The amateur was less disinterested, and he sometimes had an ax to grind. But he was also doing a job he liked in a fashion he believed acceptable. His chief interest was more often in the quaint or esthetic values of the songs, or in the folk themselves; his work was more personal than that of the academics, and sometimes closer to sources. In some instances his special knowledge and contacts made of him a scholar in a sense that the academic could seldom achieve. Like the collector of buttons or of bottlecaps, he would spare no pains to master the lore of a narrow field and had to justify his labors to no one. Though the motives and productions of certain of the amateurs (those who, paradoxically, made their collecting pay) are suspect, the high caliber of most amateur collections is a credit to the influence of the academic tradition and to the honest aims of most of the amateurs themselves.

The amateurs have been of three general types. Some drew on their personal background; some became interested in their native area as a source of folksong and developed into area or special collectors; others developed their interest as visitors or immigrants to a section. As a whole, they were more sentimental and romantic in their attitude, but no generalization will adequately enclose their work. Some were close to, even members of, the singing group from whom they collected; others seem to have been farther removed than many academics. But their work has more often enriched than confused the record of American folksong. Myriad amateurs have contributed selflessly to the great collections, but we can notice only some of those who contributed in their own right.

The enthusiasts who drew on their own personal background range from collectors who were their own informants to travelers who brushed against songs and later published them from records and memories. In between lie the great majority who drew on the repertory of their friends and neighbors. The first post-Child collection of American folksong was the *Family Songs* (1899) of Rosa F. and Joseph H. Allen: twelve texts and tunes intended apparently to perpetuate these songs among later generations of the family. Not all amateur collectors were able to preserve tunes, as is shown in the large collection from the memory of Michael C. Dean, retired woodsman of Virginia, Minnesota, who later served as an informant of Franz Rickaby. Likewise, only the texts remain from the musical experiences of the seafaring officer, David W.

Bone. But the wider picture is preserved in the two small volumes from the memories and *ballets* of Lucian L. and Flora Lassiter McDowell and their friends in middle Tennessee.

Such direct relationship to the folk is rare among American collectors, and most amateurs have been a bit farther removed. Although Jean Thomas, the promoter of the American Folk Song Festival in Ashland, Kentucky, had a mountain background, most of her collection was gathered from friends and acquaintances, many encountered during her experience as a court stenographer attached to a mountain circuit court. Friends and neighbors have been the sources for many of these local amateurs. They contributed to the collections of Henry H. Fuson of Harlan, Kentucky, and of Mary O. Eddy of Perrysville, Ohio. The Louisiana Negro informants of R. Emmet Kennedy might also be considered friends and neighbors. Certainly to be included here is the work of a New England sea captain's daughter, Joanna C. Colcord, whose collection came from memories of voyages with her father, 1890–1892, and later from old shanty singers. Similarly, much of Fannie Hardy Eckstorm's work stems from her family's connection with the Maine lumber industry and from her many local contacts. Although the collections are of varying value, a good deal of their importance comes from the intimate relationship of collector and singer. A local background adds much even to such a small collection as Ethel Park Richardson's. But towering above them all are the achievements of a lone Ozark collector, Vance Randolph. Beset by failing health and financial distress, persistently refused grants from foundations because he was an "amateur," he persisted in the collection of Ozark folksongs as a part of his study of the entire lore of the region—an interest which stemmed not from interest in folklore per se, but from the love and understanding of a region and its people.

Similar in function have been the collecting activities of the travelers, men who have touched folksinging in various areas, especially among groups least often encountered by the orthodox collector. Such a rolling stone as Charles J. Finger garnered many of his items from gold hunters, beachcombers, jailbirds, sealers, and smugglers. An even more varied group contributed to the song-bag of the poet-performer Carl Sandburg. Though Sandburg and Finger had more than the usual contact with drifters, one collector made the songs of the outcast and the migrant his special concern. Most of our knowledge of the American tramp and hobo muse comes from George Milburn, who collected in jungles and boxcars many of the songs in *The Hobo's Hornbook* (1930).

To be differentiated from these background collectors are those amateurs who, like most of the academics, *discovered* the folk and the folksong. The occasion for their interest varied greatly. Helen Creighton, searching for literary material, followed the suggestion of the Superintendent of Education for the province of Nova Scotia and began looking for ballads in 1929. Although she had never before heard a ballad sung, she discovered a rich and important vein across Halifax Bay from her home in Dartmouth and became a serious and important collector. In May, 1930, the Committee on Traditions and Ideals of the Vermont Commission on Country Life decided that one season of their work might be devoted to the attempt to discover folksongs in the state. The eight months of correspondence and of field work were only the beginning of an effort which, under the leadership of Helen Hartness Flanders, resulted in the large collection at Middlebury College, only a portion of which has been published. Similarly the interest of the Daughters of Utah Pioneers grew into a lesser collection. In this group of local-interest collectors belong those connected with the Negro institutions of the South: Fisk, Tuskegee, and others. The amateur interest in Negro song began considerably before our period of investigation, but is represented in the twentieth century by such collectors as S. Coleridge Taylor, Natalie Curtis Burlin, and R. Nathan Dett. Interest in locality and race alike led to important and significant contributions.

The experience of many amateurs was more individual, often growing out of visits or assignments to areas rich in folksong. Much of the general interest in the folksong of the Southern Appalachians developed from the mission workers attached to the settlement schools. John and Olive Dame Campbell were responsible for more collections than their own, and teachers such as Katherine Pettit of Pine Mountain and Hindman, Kentucky, not only made small contributions of their own but maintained collecting headquarters for traveling enthusiasts. During his few years (1931–1933) as head of the foreign-language department of Lincoln Memorial University, Harrogate, Tennessee, Celestin Pierre Cambiaire somehow gathered a small collection. Elmer Griffith Sulzer, while director of publicity and radio work at the University of Kentucky, had occasion to visit "remote regions in all parts of Eastern Kentucky," where he made hundreds of transcriptions. And eight years' residence in western North Carolina enabled Susannah Wetmore to gather a small collection.

Of the occasion and background of many amateur collections, such as Eloise Hubbard Linscott's New England work, we know too little, but George G. Korson has given full particulars of his work among the coal miners. Whereas most amateurs became collectors because they had discovered folksongs, Korson began a quest because he had not. As a newspaper reporter in the Schuylkill Valley in 1924, he had established for himself a place in the daily and festal life of the anthracite miners. Hearing no songs about the miners' life, he inquired for a collection at numerous local libraries. Finding none, he set out to remedy the lack. His anthracite miners' collection was the result of a true quest, in which he obtained songs no longer sung but once a part of the industry. Yet his labor in pursuit of the vanishing anthracite song was slight compared to the survey of bituminous miners' folklore which he undertook in 1938. Instead of a portion of one state, he had more than twenty states to search. With the full cooperation of the United Mine Workers and with the aid of recording apparatus, Korson made as nearly complete a collection from one industry as one is ever likely to find.

The number and types of collectors—academic and amateur— passed in review (and the selection has been typical rather than exhaustive) should help explain the rich but somewhat uneven and chaotic record of American folksong in the collections themselves. But first it is necessary to review the collecting pattern which has given some measure of centrality to American labors: that established by the Lomaxes and the Archive of American Folk Song.

John A. Lomax's part in the establishment of the local-enthusiastic publishing tradition has already been examined. But collectors and their published collections cannot always be placed in the same category. As an editor, John A. Lomax is associated with the composite and inadequately documented text; as a collector, he symbolizes the deliberate expedition and the objective field recording. Although he did not initiate the Library of Congress Archive of American Folk Song, he was largely responsible for its development and for stimulating much of the institutional support for the collection of American folksong.

After the publication of *Cowboy Songs*, John A. Lomax gave little indication of becoming a great collector. He was active in the Texas Folklore Society and the American Folklore Society. While president of the latter (1913), he encouraged the formation of many state societies. He further contributed to the growing interest in American folksong by lectures in colleges throughout the nation. But these activities were ancillary to a busy life alternately in the academic and financial worlds. Between 1910 and 1931 his collecting was sporadic and limited. He had apparently settled into the role of part-time enthusiast when a financial crisis in 1931, illness, and family tragedy conspired to launch his career as a great American folksong collector.

At the close of a none too successful lecture and collecting tour, John A. Lomax reached New York and, in his own words, "drifted into the offices of the Macmillan Company . . . desperate." [65] Within two days he had a contract for a book of American folksong and within six months had returned to the road to "fill the gaps" in his collection. Aided by the Library of Congress and the American Council of Learned Societies, he acquired an inefficient electric recording machine and with his son Alan set out on a historic four-month field trip that covered 16,000 miles.

Although the Lomaxes visited other types of community, the chief object of this trip was to record authentic Negro songs, those least open to the influence of white songs and Negro jazz. Deep in the Black Belt back country and more especially in Southern prisons, they found perhaps the richest field yet unearthed. They proved the theory that Negro prisoners still sang the old Negro work songs. But more important than their book of *American Ballads and Folk Songs* (1934), was the development of the Library of Congress Archive of American Folk Song into a central repository of traditional American song.

The Archive had been established in 1928 by the interest of Carl Engel, Chief of the Music Division, who looked forward to the growth of a "great centralized collection."[66] As its nucleus, the Archive had the private collection of Robert W. Gordon, its first Archivist. The Archive was financed in its early years by a fund established by private individuals. In 1933 John A. Lomax offered, in return for the loan of recording equipment, the records he would make in the Southern prison camps. With the aid of funds provided by the American Council of Learned Societies, equipment was furnished the Lomaxes for their fieldwork in the summer of 1933. The elder Lomax was made Honorary Consultant and Curator of the Archive. In 1934 the Rockefeller Foundation furnished a portable recording machine, and the Carnegie Corporation financed another year of collection for the Lomaxes.

Thus began an important period of national collecting. The years of financial depression were serving to interest Americans in their own culture, and the WPA provided new opportunities and workers. The elder Lomax, serving without salary, enriched the Archive through his privately financed expeditions. In 1937 he undertook the evaluation of the folklore material of the Federal Writers' Project, continuing to collect folksongs on his travels. The same year, the Congress of the United States made a small appropriation for the support of the Archive,[67] which could now for the first time purchase a recording machine from its own funds. Alan, returning from a field trip to Haiti in April of that year, became Assistant-in-Charge, the first Archive worker paid from Library funds. And with the help of the Federal Writers' Project, a *Provisional Check List of Disks* of folksongs was prepared. The Archive was beginning to function.

During the years following, the Archive was enriched by Alan's collecting in Kentucky, Ohio, Michigan, Indiana, and Vermont, by John's collecting in the South, by Herbert Halpert's extended trip across the South sponsored by the Joint Committee on Folk Arts of the WPA in 1939, by other individual efforts, and by the duplication of other collections. In 1940 the Recording Laboratory was established by a grant from the Carnegie Corporation; field equipment was made available for loan to private collectors; and WPA and NYA aid made possible cataloguing and the publication of the three-volume *Check List of Recorded Songs in the English Language in the Archive of American Folk Song to July, 1940,* indexing 4,000 records. Duplication service was available, and in 1943 the Archive began the public issuance of albums of recorded folksong.

By 1945 the Archive, with B. A. Botkin as Chief, had doubled the number of its recordings. Then, under the direction of Duncan B. M. Emrich, it blossomed for a brief period into the Folklore Section. Though continuing its same functions, it is now the Archive of Folk Song, headed by Mrs. Rae Korson. Unfortunately, it is still understaffed and underfinanced. But great strides are being made in cataloguing and duplicating original recordings so that they may be more readily available to serious scholars. The more than 60,000 songs or performances in the Archive represent the work of 130 collectors and include, in addition to folksongs in English from America and abroad, material ranging from American Indian song to Greek heroic poetry. This basic material is adequately safeguarded and is becoming more and more a fundamental tool for the folklorist.

The work of the Archive has been advanced by a number of

groups and individuals. The support of the Carnegie Corporation, the Rockefeller Foundation, and the American Council of Learned Societies has been vital; and the labors of individuals too many to name have created the Archive of Folk Song. But the fact remains that the Archive is with reason associated with John and Alan Lomax, whose activities contributed even more than the necessary drama and publicity at an opportune time. Whatever their faults in other respects, the Lomaxes have been great field collectors. Their ability to gain the confidence and thereby the repertory of a singer, their boundless enthusiasm for the native, the common, the low, and their showmanship: all have added immeasurably to the noble sport of ballad hunting.

SOME RESTRICTIONS IN AMERICAN COLLECTIONS

Folksong books made from American field collection reflect in some respects the characteristics of the song collectors but are more diverse and offer more resistance to simple classification. It is convenient to discuss the books, on the basis of their aims and their editing principles, as academic collections, running-comment collections, random-text collections, singing books, and productions of the Lomaxes. Because certain restrictions which have governed the contents of these collections often merely reflect the collecting patterns already examined, these limitations can be considered first.

The great majority of the published collections are concerned with a local, political, or geographical area, or with an occupational group. The local or political-unit limitation of many collections is seldom meaningful. The selection of a political unit, usually a state, has been only a convenience. The editors for the most part gave some consideration to the culture of the area while noting that political boundaries have little cultural significance. Local pride was naturally involved and was sometimes of considerable aid. But the line of restriction was by no means held. The editors often granted space to a valuable song or to an interesting variant, even if it came across the country by correspondence, and the editors were not purists who were restricted by an "imaginary line."

In the books growing out of area collection, selection was made on various grounds. Child ballads were selected less frequently than might be expected (that is, in separately published collections), only three collections being devoted almost exclusively to canon ballads. Reed Smith's *South Carolina Ballads* (1928) and Davis's *Traditional Ballads from Virginia* (1929) were the result of restricted collection, but the contents of *British Ballads from Maine* (1929) were chosen from a more general collection to support a thesis. From a large collection, Dorothy Scarborough selected only songs of apparent English origin for her *A Song Catcher in the Southern Mountains* (1937). While not strictly area collectors, John and Alan Lomax stressed native American material. Mrs. Eckstorm and Mrs. Smyth sought, unsuccessfully, to restrict the contents of *Minstrelsy of Maine* (1927) to local ballads, "the pioneer's creative expression." A few books were limited to play-party songs,[68] instrumental music,[69] and religious folksong,[70] but many collections emphasized the songs of occupational and ethnic groups.

The restriction of collections to a particular occupation presents a rather difficult problem. The discovery of such songs was of great importance, especially in the study of origin and function of folksongs. But the editors of collections limited to songs of cowboys, lumbermen, miners, and hobos (if the latter are rightly included here) were not always able to determine just what their restriction meant and to follow it successfully. Songs in such collections are usually those current among, composed by, or written about members of a group; distinguishing the categories is difficult. A portion of the confusion is due to the general inclusive tendencies of American collectors, evidenced especially in *Cowboy Songs* (though the *Other Frontier Ballads* of the title is somewhat indicative of the contents). Gray in his *Songs and Ballads of the Maine Lumberjacks* (1924) includes other Maine songs, but carefully distinguishes them. Rickaby was unable to limit his collection of *Ballads and*

Songs of the Shanty-Boy (1926) to those that "belonged body and soul to the shanty-boy"; he included songs on the basis of their recovery from men who had worked in the lumber camps. Milburn admittedly included in *The Hobo's Hornbook* (1930) "home guard" material as well as the minstrelsy of the migrant. Korson perhaps held the line most successfully, for the miners' songs in his collections are almost exclusively theirs. Even more restrictive is James Taylor Adams's *Death in the Dark: A Collection of Factual Ballads of American Mine Disasters* (1941). But the habits of the folksinger caused continual difficulty to the restrictive collection. The sailor persisted in roaring out sentimental ditties, and the miner adopted vaudeville songs dealing with his occupation. The problem was initially complicated by the collector's ignorance of the provenance of the songs he collected. But his preconceptions seem seldom to have influenced his collections, though we have no way of knowing whether he ignored songs he did not think significant. To judge from the variety of the songs, he seems to have collected and published most of what he found; and subsequent knowledge tended to broaden his definitions rather than to narrow his collection.

Perhaps only in books of Negro songs does restriction assume serious proportions. While songs of occupation are only a subdivision in an ethnic area, the Negro song may be an ethnic type itself. There the distinction between origin and currency demanded clarification and erupted into argument.[71] But whatever the claims of collectors and editors, the pattern did not differ significantly from that observed elsewhere: collect first and argue later. The significant difference was that collections of Negro songs were often edited by those ignorant of Anglo-American folksong.

ACADEMIC COLLECTIONS

The function and purpose of the books and the editing methods employed suggest useful and significant distinctions. Here again is discovered the academic pattern to place against other methods. Although not the first in the field, the academic approach asserted its dominance and pulled into its orbit many collections of the amateurs.

As we have observed, the academic tradition first expressed itself in the *Journal of American Folklore*. Separate publications prior to 1922 were only check lists. Soon from the great university presses, with Harvard in the lead, began to come the academic collections. Louise Pound's *American Ballads and Songs* (1922) is clearly a forerunner, for the volume sets forth the typical organization and approach; but the collection, while drawn largely from Miss Pound's Nebraska material, contains items from other areas and seeks to be representative rather than exhaustive. Gray's *Songs and Ballads of the Maine Lumberjacks* (1924) is clearly academic, but represents more specialization than is usual. John Harrington Cox's West Virginia collection, *Folk-Songs of the South* (1925), is therefore the first typical academic collection.

Folk-Songs of the South presents the material collected by the West Virginia Folklore Society during a little more than a decade. Exhaustive in printing or noting all texts collected, it contains 185 ballads and songs in 446 variants, all but ninety-seven of which are printed *in extenso*. As in other collections of this type, some of the texts had been previously printed in journals. Completeness is the aim, even to standards of admission. Cox fails to discuss his criteria, and the only one which is clearly implied is that of oral currency through a fair period of time. Such a standard does not mean that all texts come directly from oral sources, as material from local broadsides, ballets, and diaries is included. There is good authority for these inclusions: Child had accepted comparable material.

The collection is Child-centered in many ways. It is a Child-and-other collection: it prints first thirty-three Child ballads in 154 variants, followed by 152 other pieces in 292 variants. Granting that the older songs may have a wider currency, the figures indicate the collecting emphasis. And the presentation of the material follows Child's example.

Cox's *Folk-Songs of the South* is a succession of numbered song

texts with letters assigned to the variants, either printed or summarized. At the head of each numbered entry is a note identifying
the item and giving references. Child pieces are compared with
various Child versions, and materials which originated or appeared
on English or American broadsides are so identified. Information
concerning the origin of other songs is given, be it folk authority
or the result of research. There are references to other published
texts, particularly American. Each variant is preceded by the local
title, the name and address of the informant, the date of collection,
and sometimes information concerning the informant's source (see
Figure 1).

The organization and approach are textual. The 446 texts have
but twenty-nine tunes, and these, rather like poor relations, find a
place at the close of the volume. Concerning their accuracy we are
left in doubt, for they are noted by amateurs—even informants.
Lydia I. Hinkel, who edited the music, writes, "Many of the tunes
were sent in without indication of time, with queer and incorrect
note values, and without any key signature" (p. 520). But no
effort seems to have been made to force them into conventional
modes.

The background for the collection is provided in a brief introduction which relates the history of the West Virginia Folklore Society
and gives characterizations of a few folksingers, drawn from visits
of the editor and from letters of informants. As another concession
to the living nature of the material, a few photographs of singers
and their homes are included.

The collection has its defects, but its values are worth noting first.
The volume seems to give a full record of what was collected. If the
Child pieces receive the first station, "The Soldier's Poor Little
Boy" and "Poor Little Joe" do gain entrance, however. The material is apparently presented accurately as found,[72] with no additions, no emendations, no combining of texts. Full recording of
source and date of collection establishes trust and has value to
the student. The headnotes are often more than literary references.
They are usually résumés of knowledge at the time of writing.

4

LORD RANDAL

(CHILD, No. 12)

TWELVE variants have been recovered in West Virginia, under the titles "Lord Randal," "Johnny Randolph," "Johnny Randal," "Johnny Ramsey," and "Johnny Reeler." A, B, C, D, and E, are all fine vigorous ballads, telling practically the same story, except in E, where the hero has been to visit his sister. In A the lover has been to the greenwood, spent the night with his true-love, and had for supper fried eels and fresh butter. In form and content, it is most like Child A, but verbal similarities and the refrain connect it with Child B, D, E, and F. B resembles most closely Child B, but shows other relations. The refrain is similar to that of Child H. The title is no doubt due to the fame of John Randolph of Virginia. C is so similar in arrangement and diction to B that further comment is unnecessary. D, while not so complete as B and C, belongs to the same group. E shows many variations from the preceding ballads. The name "Henry" suggests the "King Henry" of Child C. The red, black, and yellow poison may be an echo from Child B. "Ropes to hang her" suggests Child B and I. The statement that he had been to his sister's may be a corruption for grandmother's or stepmother's. Cf. Child I, J, K, L, M, N, and O. The remaining variants are more or less incomplete and need no special comment. C was printed by Cox, XLV, 266.

Scores of variants have been collected in this country, and new copies keep coming in from various states: see references in *Journal*, XXIX, 157; XXX, 289; XXXV, 339. Add Shoemaker, p. 123; Pound, No. 1; *Bulletin*, Nos. 7–10.

A

"Lord Randal." Contributed by Miss Polly McKinney, Sophia, Randolph County, February 2, 1916, who writes: "I am sending it to you as I learned it from my aunt. My grandmother says Lord Randal's name was William V and that the song is sometimes sung 'O William, my son,' instead of 'Lord Randal.'"

1 "O where have you been, Lord Randal, my son?
   O where have you been, my handsome young man?"
  "I ha' been to the greenwood; mother, make my bed soon,
   For I'm wearied wi' hunting, and would freely lie down."

2 "Where did you stay last night, Lord Randal, my son?
   Where did you stay last night, my handsome young man?"
  "I stayed wi' my true-love; mother, make my bed soon,
   For I'm wearied wi' hunting, and would freely lie down."

3 "What did you eat for your supper, Lord Randal, my son?
   What did you eat for your supper, my handsome young man?"
  "Fried eels and fresh butter; mother, make my bed soon,
   For I'm sick to my heart, and would freely lie down."

Figure 1

Some provide new, especially local, information; the headnote to "John Hardy," though involving erroneous conclusions, approaches a small study. From the standpoint of historical text study, the method is admirable.

The outstanding fault of the book is the disregard of the musical half of folksong. On behalf of this and similar volumes a few points need to be made. We must keep in mind that tunes were printed when available. Though appearing in the back, as in *The English and Scottish Popular Ballads*, the tunes are not so much musical illustrations as they are the full record of all that the collectors could salvage. We may regret the deficiencies of collectors; we may regret the textual emphasis of academic collectors; we may feel that they could have made greater effort to obtain accurate record of the tunes. But musical critics must answer the question: where were the competent musicians when the collecting was taking place? Had the academics waited for the musicians, the songs might never have been collected. And the collections by the musicians contain faults of their own.

But there is another important shortcoming of Cox's textual approach. Despite the accurate record of sources, the notes contain too little information concerning the function of the songs. There is little indication of the age and social status of the informants, no appendix listing and discussing informants. Were the songs wheedled from doddering octogenarians, or were the songs a part of living tradition? What was the singer's attitude toward his material? Excepting a few notes in the introduction, there are only texts with names, places, and dates attached. An important dimension is lacking.

The emphasis on the Child canon has angered liberal critics. The placing of Child items first is perhaps justifiable on the grounds that since no other classification had been accepted, it was best to accept the convenient and familiar. But the action was symbolic of the value accorded to Child pieces, as are the number of variants printed *in extenso*. The ideal would be to print *all* variants of *all* folksongs. But no scholarly or esthetic aim is served by not employing scholarly collation. More economical methods might have facilitated the appearance of still unpublished collections.

In the arrangement of its texts, *Folk-Songs of the South* is not quite typical of academic collections. Cox makes no formal divisions, printing after the Child ballads a noncanonical Robin Hood piece and then a few important native American ballads. The rest of the collection is in no discernible order, although songs of similar theme or origin are sometimes grouped. The standard came to be, in a sort of descending order of value, Child ballads, other imported ballads and songs, assorted types of American ballads and songs (cowboy, outlaw, etc.), perhaps a category of nursery or Negro (often pseudo-Negro) songs, and then local ballads hidden at the end. Alton C. Morris's arrangement in *Folksongs of Florida* (1950)—"Songs of the New World" first—is perhaps a sop to those who find the Child-first organization an affront. But within Morris's section of "Songs of the Old World," the canon ballads again precede all others. A more serious change was made, however, in Gardner and Chickering's *Ballads and Songs of Southern Michigan* (1939). Miss Gardner organizes her material into subject-matter divisions, breaking the Child-and-other pattern for the first time (in an academic collection). Within the nine sections, however, she gives first place to what she considers "ballads, the oldest ones first, and second place to songs of a similar character in which the narrative and impersonal elements are not so prominent as they are in ballads" (p. 21). So the canon ballads are still printed first. But the organization is a step toward a reconsideration not only of arrangement, but of classification as well.

The pattern established by *Folk-Songs of the South* became standard for most editors with any sort of academic interest in folksong. The regional archivists and the lone academics naturally followed Cox's lead, their aim being to present their collected materials fully and accurately, to be approved and studied by other academics. We should expect the collections edited by Arthur Kyle Davis, Jr., Henry Marvin Belden, and W. Roy MacKenzie to be academic; but the material of such amateurs as Helen Creighton and Mary O. Eddy was also drawn into the pattern (though not as far as treatment of the music is concerned). The huge collections of the archivists and the smaller sheaves of many local workers have tended to fall into the same shape, a trend not to be applauded if it resulted in the suppression of insights gained by local collectors.

The general aim of full presentation of the material can be seen by glancing at six important academic collections published between 1928 and 1950. MacKenzie's *Ballads and Sea Songs from Nova Scotia* (1928) is his personal collection from a single county, 1912–1926. Davis's *Traditional Ballads of Virginia* (1929) contains the results of the state folklore society's quest for Child ballads. *Ballads and Songs of Southern Michigan* (1939) is largely the result of a collection in the thirties by its editors, Emelyn Elizabeth Gardner and Geraldine Jencks Chickering, although some songs were recovered as early as 1912. *Ballads and Songs Collected by the Missouri Folklore Society* (1940), edited by H. M. Belden, had its beginnings in 1903 but was virtually complete in 1917. Vance Randolph's *Ozark Folksongs* (1946–1950) grew from the efforts of an amateur, but is academically edited. Volumes 2 and 3 [73] of *The Frank C. Brown Collection of North Carolina Folklore* contain texts representing the labor of many workers since 1912. Most of the figures in Table 1 will be found to disagree slightly with the counts of the various editors. In the interest of uniformity, portions of numbered entries have been separated or combined.

TABLE 1

| COLLECTION | SONG ITEMS | ADDITIONAL VARIANTS | APPENDIX LIST | | TOTAL | |
			SONGS	VARIANTS	SONGS	TEXTS
MacKenzie	161	35			161	196
Davis *	51	390		203	51	644
Gardner and Chickering	201	126	130	55	331	512
Belden	287	318			287	605
Randolph	891	744			891	1,635
Brown	972	1,231			972	2,203

* Child ballads only.

All variants are not printed in full (609 are printed in part or summarized in the *Brown Collection*), but the amount of material made available for study is impressive. With the additional items and variants being provided by the publication of the music in volumes 4 and 5, the *Brown Collection* will probably surpass that unprinted in the archive of the Virginia Folklore Society, which Arthur Kyle Davis, Jr., in *Folk-Songs of Virginia: A Descriptive Index and Classification* (1949) lists as 974 songs in 2,454 variants, with an estimated seventy-four items not yet classified.

All collection in the academic pattern did not or could not aim at such complete publication. Combs's *Folk-Songs du Midi des États-Unis* (1925) presents but sixty texts from his collection of about 200. Mary O. Eddy's *Ballads and Songs from Ohio* (1939), 160 songs and 98 variants, does not contain all the material in the manuscript originally prepared for publication and possibly not all otherwise available to her.[74] The fortunes and difficulties of publication are illustrated by the appearances of Arthur Palmer Hudson's Mississippi collection. In 1927 Hudson printed eighty-eight songs in *JAF* (XXXIX [1926], 93–194), and the following year published the mimeographed *Specimens of Mississippi Folk-Lore* containing texts of 113 songs. A manuscript accepted by the University of North Carolina Press in 1930 was delayed by the economic depression and appeared in 1936 as *Folksongs of Mississippi and Their Background*. Many variants were suppressed, and, except for Child ballads, Hudson merely states the number of variants recovered. The most serious casualty was the omission of twenty-seven tunes. In 1937 forty-five tunes were published in mimeographed form by the Folk Song Research Department of the Federal Theatre Project: *Folktunes from Mississippi*, edited by George Herzog, assisted by Herbert Halpert. Sixteen of the texts were published for the first time, either as variants or as new to Hudson's collection. Therefore none of Hudson's publications are complete or mutually exclusive. One can appreciate the value of the *Brown Collection*, which contains an entry for all songs originally in the collection, even for those published elsewhere and not reprinted.

Even when they do not print or notice all variants, the collections (with the exception of the Child-only collections) usually include almost all types of songs current in tradition, embracing all sorts of waifs and strays. Leafing through the volumes one discovers "The Fellow Who Looks Like Me," "Darling Nelly Gray," "The Baggage Coach Ahead," "Grandfather's Clock," "The Little Rosewood Casket," and even "Why Did They Dig Ma's Grave So Deep?" Such a selective collection as that of Josiah Combs includes "The Black Mustache," from *un vieux manuscrit* at that. In addition to these nineteenth-century ditties, many of known authorship, space is found for local materials, songs composed about local events, sometimes by known and living persons. Even age is not a criterion. Miss Creighton prints in her first collection a poem by a known author published in a local paper in 1914. Songs from the latest type of broadside, the hillbilly recording or radio show, have been garnered, though their source was unknown to most collectors. We find such songs as "Floyd Collins," "Twenty-One Years," and "Lee Bible" in various collections. The volumes are academic but seldom purist.

The attitude toward the material remains relatively stable, but the treatment of the music shows a growth, which may be seen in numbers alone. One must remember that most of these collections aim at completeness: texts come from ballets and popular prints; many have been sent in by correspondents. Consequently the presentation of a tune for each text cannot be expected. A recovery and printing of 50 per cent of the tunes may be considered excellent. (Although this figure is somewhat arbitrary, it represents the approximate proportion printed in *British Ballads from Maine,* whose editors bewail the neglect of other editors.) Table 2 on page 199 lists the percentage of tunes to texts in representative academic collections.

The percentage of tunes recorded tends to increase in the later collections. The growth of interest in music can be seen by comparing the poor record of Cox's first collection with the excellent showing of his late publications. (The mimeographed form may

TABLE 2

Tune Text Percentages in Representative Academic Collections

COLLECTION	TEXTS	TUNES	PER CENT
Gray: *Songs and Ballads of the Maine Lumber-jacks*, 1924	60	0	0
Combs: *Folk-Songs du Midi des États-Unis*, 1925	60	0	0
Cox: *Folk-Songs of the South*, 1925 *	446	29	6.5
Neely: *Tales and Songs of Southern Illinois*, 1938	96	8	8.3
Belden: *Ballads and Songs Collected by the Missouri Folklore Society*, 1940 †	605	67	11
Brewster: *Ballads and Songs of Indiana*, 1940	261	36	13.8
MacKenzie: *Ballads and Sea Songs of Nova Scotia*, 1928 *	196	42	21.4
Davis: *Traditional Ballads of Virginia*, 1929 *	644	149	23.1
Gardner: *Folklore from the Schoharie Hills, New York*, 1937 ‡	29	9	31
Gardner and Chickering: *Ballads and Songs of Southern Michigan*, 1939 §	327	117	35.8
Randolph: *Ozark Folksongs*, 1946–1950	1,635	811	49.5
Greenleaf and Mansfield: *Ballads and Sea Songs of Newfoundland*, 1933	209	113	54
Morris: *Folksongs of Florida*, 1950	306	170	55.5
Eddy: *Ballads and Songs from Ohio*, 1939	258	144	55.8
Creighton: *Traditional Songs from Nova Scotia*, 1950	258	180	69.8
Rickaby: *Ballads and Songs of the Shanty-Boy*, 1926	75	55	73
Cox: *Traditional Ballads Mainly from West Virginia*, 1939 ———: *Folk-Songs Mainly from West Virginia*, 1939	101	83	82
Creighton: *Songs and Ballads from Nova Scotia*, 1933	149	149	100

* Tunes printed in an appendix.
† Most collection done 1903–1917.
‡ Collecting done 1912–1914.
§ Songs listed in the appendix not included, as editors fail to indicate whether or not a tune was collected.

account for the appearance, but not for the availability, of the material.) The abilities and fortunes of the collector must be taken into account. *Traditional Ballads of Virginia* benefited from the musical interest of C. Alphonso Smith, the first archivist, and from the work of John Stone, Juliet Fauntleroy, Cecil Sharp, and Margaret M. Davis (who contributed twenty-nine, thirty-two, twenty-three, and nineteen tunes respectively). Mrs. Greenleaf, who collected the texts for *Ballads and Sea Songs of Newfoundland*, fortunately secured the musical assistance of Mrs. Mansfield. The academically edited collections of the amateurs Miss Eddy and Miss Creighton have an excellent record, although selective editing certainly played a role in Miss Creighton's first volume. The most heartening fact is the growing attention to music in large regional collections, such as *Folksongs of Florida*, in which more than half the tunes are preserved. And the tunes are no longer in an appendix: they rest with their texts.

Some of the musical problems of large collections are illustrated by the editing of the great collection of Frank C. Brown, who did not live to publish it. The six-volume edition of Brown's entire folklore collection required the services of a number of editors (two of whom have died—and the edition is not yet completed). The folksongs required three editors. Henry Marvin Belden and Arthur Palmer Hudson edited the texts, which appeared separately in volumes 2 and 3. The editorship of the tunes was accepted by Jan P. Schinhan. In terms of early publication of the texts, the decision to publish separately was wise: the two volumes of texts appeared in 1952; the first volume of tunes was published in 1957, and the remainder will probably appear by the time this is in print. The delay in the appearance of volume 4 was due to very real difficulties encountered by Schinhan; but some of the difficulties encountered in the use of volume 4 may be due to the separation of function and lack of cooperation among the editors.

Brown tried, almost from the beginning of his collecting in 1912, to preserve tunes as well as texts. In addition to manuscript scores, the collection contained untranscribed recordings of over 1,000 songs. Brown had played many of the wax cylinders frequently without even changing needles, thus greatly reducing their limited fidelity. During World War II, the cylinders were shipped to the Library of Congress to be duplicated by the Archive of American Folk Song. Some were destroyed in shipment; others were cracked. In dubbing the cylinders on discs, inexpert technicians reproduced the surface noises and often carelessly omitted the beginnings of songs. Schinhan's job was difficult at best, and only his skill and dedication insured its completion. In a number of instances he sought out the original informants to verify or recapture the tunes. The edition of the music is providing additional texts, but how many variants are being provided is difficult to ascertain.

The problem is not the scholarly transcription, annotation, and analysis of the tunes—excellently carried out—but the matching of tunes and texts. In many instances the source of a tune in volume 4 does not agree with the source of the corresponding text in volume 2, for reasons one can only guess at. Additional tunes are added to a lettered entry (e.g., 40A[1], 40A[2]), possibly demonstrating a different concept of version or variant than that employed by the editors of the texts. A combination of the skills and knowledge of Belden, Hudson, and Schinhan in a single editor is not easily obtained. The joint editing that seems to be the practical answer apparently requires more cooperation than obtained here. The student is now left in doubt as to whether the discrepancies in documentation are due to the condition of the collection or to the vagaries of the editors—not to speak of the difficulties of having to refer to two volumes for a complete record of a ballad. Again we are thankful for well-edited tunes (517 in volume 4) and texts; but admitting that the two items may be conveniently studied separately, one finds their separate publication unsuccessful.

RUNNING-COMMENT COLLECTIONS

There is no sharp line of demarcation between the strictly academic and the running-comment collections. The latter differ primarily in printing the texts (and sometimes tunes) not as annotated specimens, but as part of essays which discuss the background of the songs or the singers. The running-comment collections seldom aim for completeness, striving rather to illustrate and explain song types. Most of them deal with more specialized material than the academic collections and arrange it for special purposes. One collection, however, seems to contain many characteristics of both types.

British Ballads from Maine (1929), edited by Phillips Barry, Fannie Hardy Eckstorm, and Mary Winslow Smyth, is clearly an academic collection, in fact a Child-only collection. Excepting for the consideration of ballad music, the editors accept the restrictions of Professor Child. The items are presented in the Child order, variants are lettered in the approved manner, and headnotes give sources and dates of recovery. But variants are used to illustrate critical discussion of the history of individual texts and tunes. Many texts from popular prints are reproduced, not only to make them accessible for future study but as a part of the study at hand. And jury texts are constructed to show what may exist uncollected. The main aims of the volume seem to be three: (1) to demonstrate the richness of New England as a ballad area, particularly as compared with the Southern Appalachians; (2) to prove that many American texts are old compared with Child's copies; and (3) to provide a handbook for fieldworkers, showing how ballads should be collected and suggesting what ballads might yet be found in New England.

The second point, the age of ballad texts, is not the immediate concern. It is asserted (and sometimes demonstrated) on almost every page. The other demonstrations deserve examination here.

Most of the material is the result of about four and a half years of collecting in restricted areas of Maine and New Brunswick by Mrs. Eckstorm and Mrs. Smyth. To these 132 texts and/or tunes are added twenty-two from earlier collection in New England by Barry. (Copies from manuscript, prints in scrapbooks, etc, are included in this count; texts printed for comparative purposes are not.) Represented are copies of fifty-six Child ballads and eight judged to be derivative or secondary. The results are certainly more than respectable. They would seem phenomenal if we were not provided with insights into the manner in which some of the copies were obtained.

Collectors have used various methods to prod the memories of singers, including lists of titles and commonplaces. Few, however, have encouraged their singers to scrutinize ballad texts, as these workers did. (Something of the sort probably went on in the similar project in Virginia.) We do not question the traditional status of the ballad recoveries (though certain readings from Mrs. McGill are doubtful). Many variants demonstrate their independence by internal evidence. But one is certainly not impressed by a flourishing tradition. In fact, the emphasis placed on the familial nature of ballad tradition might seem to indicate by the very discovery of that truth that the springs of Northern ballad tradition were drying up, were it not for ample publication by later collectors. The method of investigation yields important evidence for the student of ballad history, even though it must be used with caution, particularly the "Traces and Jury-Texts." Here we learn that certain singers "recognized" a story or certain stanzas from a ballad collection. Although the editors carefully segregate the material, they seem to attach more importance to it than is warranted. The purpose of the section—to indicate avenues of future investigation—is justifiable and important, for ballads are often found as a result of a specific search. But "recognition" by informants is untrustworthy.

As a handbook for collectors the book is important in its presentation of so many tunes so carefully noted. But we owe many of the notations to the financial assistance of an interested person. How many collectors can discover an angel who will finance the summoning of George Herzog from an Indian reservation in North Dakota? We can be thankful to those who can provide and charitable to those who cannot.

The earlier collection edited by Mrs. Eckstorm and Mrs. Smyth appeared before they found their angel. *Minstrelsy of Maine* (1927) also has a special purpose: to show by a group of coast and woods songs "the Maine man, particularly in his role of pioneer . . . working to make something of esthetic interest to himself" (p. viii). The 138 texts of 111 songs are not all from oral tradition, and many were certainly never sung in Maine or elsewhere. But even "The Later Woods Songs" and the mortuary verse from "The Back Side of Mount Desert" aptly illustrate a song-making tradition. The work is organized for that specific purpose.

Within the broader organization, the texts are presented in conventional academic fashion, with separate variants (there are a few composites) and carefully noted sources. But the editors furnish, instead of elaborate headnotes, short discussions of the song and its history. The songs have been classified, with varying degrees of success, in an attempt to indicate their historical or functional place in the communities. In the first and better half of the volume, Mrs. Eckstorm divides the woods songs into three historical periods, with some justification. The "Songs of the Sea and the Shore," collected by Mrs. Smyth, are grouped by subject or function. Sandwiched between various groupings are essays (probably all from the pen of Mrs. Eckstorm) dealing with the history of the songs and the "way of the folk" with their songs. "The Pursuit of a Ballad Myth" remains the standard study of "The Jam at Gerry's Rock."

The collection not only is a departure from the strict academic lines to meet a need, but it demonstrates the excellent work of the learned local enthusiast, particularly Mrs. Eckstorm. Although her sex was a handicap in collecting—which she recognizes—her background and knowledge enable her to integrate rather successfully the local and universal. The local collector with requisite ballad scholarship is rare. Rarer still is an editor skillful enough to prepare a book "popular enough for the general reader, yet precise enough for the student of folksong."

With few exceptions, these four qualities mark the running-comment collections: special purposes and types of material, proximity to sources, emphasis on the native or homemade song, and popular slant. George Korson's collection of miners' songs (*Songs and Ballads of the Anthracite Miner* [1927], *Minstrels of the Mine Patch* [1938], and *Coal Dust on the Fiddle* [1943]) illustrate all four qualities. Almost all the songs, in their present form, are peculiar to the mining industry and stem from the workers themselves. Collected from singers, from local broadsides, and from the files of the *United Mine Workers' Journal*, the crude songs are arranged by subject matter and form the nucleus of essays on the life of mine workers. Like the editors of *Minstrelsy of Maine*, Korson is able to trace items to their authors, even to record songs as sung by their composers. The earlier volumes, dealing with the smaller anthracite industry, presented a few variants, but the richer lore of the bituminous miners resulted in the printing of only one text of each song in *Coal Dust on the Fiddle*.[75] Both *Minstrels of the Mine Patch* and *Coal Dust* are collections of lore as well as songs, however, giving a wider coverage of the background.

A somewhat similar book is Mrs. Jean Thomas's *Ballad Makin' in the Mountains of Kentucky* (1939). That is, the songs are largely the products of native minstrels, many known to the collector, or to the singers at least; but many of the attributions of authorship are made on purely folk authority and can be given only limited credence. The texts and tunes included may be authentic, although we could not easily discover their singers, for the songs are set against a background that is highly colored. A number of informants are referred to by invented titles. James W. Day, a blind street singer, is built into the romantic figure of Jilson Setters, the mountain minstrel. The J. W. Day of Morehead who composed "The Rowan County Troubles" is more important than "The Singin' Fiddler of Lost Hope Hollow"; the role of the blind street singer in the composition and distribution of native American balladry is really more interesting than Mrs. Thomas's romantic fiction. Had she not been interested in charming the "furriners" and creating a picture she thought they would buy, her work might have been of great value. Mrs. Thomas is a mountain woman herself and certainly knows better; but each year at her Singin' Gatherin' the picture she described in her book, *The Traipsin' Woman* (1933) is carefully recreated, even though the little "mountain children" must be hauled by station wagon from the industrial city of Ashland! One can only hope the songs are more authentic than the background.

Other collections of this type, such as Charles J. Finger's *Frontier Ballads* (1927) and R. Emmet Kennedy's *Black Cameos* (1924), *Mellows* (1925), and *More Mellows* (1931) can be barely mentioned. Edward D. Andrews' *The Gift to Be Simple* (1940) is a collection *and* study of the songs and dances of the Shakers, especially valuable to the history of the American folk hymn. Of even greater importance are other volumes which present collected material against a background which explains it. Joanna C. Colcord's two editions of sailor songs, *Roll and Go* (1924) and *Songs of American Sailormen* (1938), have the virtues of the amateur, the private approach to folksong scholarship. The personal knowledge and zeal of Miss Colcord make her commentary indispensable. Though her treatment of texts falls short of the academic ideal, the texts and tunes are adequately representative of folk tradition. But attention must be given to another type of running-comment collection, the sociological study.

Perhaps all the collections of this type might be called *sociological*; but the emphasis is on the song. The background merely explains the song. In the collections of the sociologists Howard W. Odum and Guy B. Johnson, *The Negro and His Songs* (1925) and *Negro Workaday Songs* (1926), the songs are used to explain the singer. These Negro songs, some collected and printed in journals of 1906–1914 (see p. 152) and some collected in North and South Carolina, Tennessee, and Georgia, during 1924–1925, are presented largely for their sociological implications, as a part of "the story of the Negro"; but they are organized by song types. The running comment on the Negro singers and the sources of the songs is as important to the study of the songs as the songs are to the study of the singers. Though the authenticity of the songs is unquestionable, the editors should have given the sources of individual texts. The greatest lack is the music. *The Negro and His Songs* contains no tunes and *Negro Workaday Songs* but fifteen, although the latter includes a preliminary report of the phonophotographic studies of Carl E. Seashore and Milton Metfessel. Although the authors apparently depend too much on the internal evidence of the texts, the collections demonstrate how valuable a running comment can be in presenting the milieu and function of folksong.

Skillfully used, the running comment permits the collector to escape the formal and rigid academic pattern to follow a new pattern he perceives in his material and to relate closely the background information to the songs themselves. But the mere substitution of running commentary for headnotes is no guarantee of success, popular or otherwise. The compiler must be so conversant with his material that he can not only see its pattern but relate the individual songs with meaningful comment. Or he must know the milieu of the songs intimately and be able to blend skillfully the song and the background. The problem can be illustrated by a brief examination of a few important collections.

The chief complaint against William Main Doerflinger's *Shantymen and Shantyboys* (1951) is that the title tends to encourage confusion of the worksongs of sailors and lumbering songs, though the text distinguishes clearly enough. The book itself is a scholarly collection in unforbidding guise. The songs, largely recorded by Doerflinger and printed with tunes carefully transcribed and edited by Hally Wood among others, are organized in terms of either function or subject matter—thus various types of shanties, "Deep-Water Songs," etc., "The Shantyboys' Life," "Satirists of the Sawdust Country," "Minstrelsy of Murder," etc. The commentary connects the songs with necessary but informally presented background dealing with the singers, the function, the history, and historicity of the songs. The information necessary to the understanding of the songs is painlessly presented; if the reader does not learn to rig a ship, he is at least not lost in the shrouds. Included is an excellent essay on "The Rise of Shantying." Appendices provide more formal annotation of each song and a list and discussion of the informants. Such a successful presentation may be contrasted with that of *Ballads Migrant in New England* (1953), collected by Helen Hartness Flanders and Marguerite Olney. The ballads are supposedly "described as a collector remembers finding them . . . with backward thoughts into their origins." The statement seems an apt reference to the organization or lack of it, if one realizes that Mrs. Flanders seems to have no orderly memory of finding them. Her commentary introduces groups of songs selected not by area, time of collection, type of song or informant. If there is a consistent principle of arrangement, it is certainly difficult to discover. Variants of the same song are widely separated for no apparent reason. Though the comment is not consistently relevant and valuable, it sometimes contains useful information, but buried so far from the song itself as to be practically useless. The account of a collector's experiences may be both interesting and revealing; Mrs. Flanders' notes are too often merely chatty. One feels impelled to reorganize the songs and to select and place the relevant information with the songs themselves. The rest could go into an introduction or into the dustbin. Yet the collection itself is an important segment of the Flanders folk-music material at Middlebury College.

Another contrast is furnished by the books of Dorothy Scarborough and Jean Ritchie. Unlike her earlier volume dealing with Negro songs, Miss Scarborough's *A Song Catcher in the Southern Mountains* (1937) is almost entirely her own, a collection made in the mountains of Virginia and North Carolina during the summer of 1930. The work was fruitful, for the eighty-nine songs in 225 variants represent only that part of her collection which she judged to be imported; because of her untimely death, prior to the appearance of this volume, the native songs have not yet been published. *A Song Catcher* is an apparent compromise between the academic and the popular. The arrangement, "more like the mountain 'hit or miss' quilt pattern," is beyond criticism; within the hodgepodge order, she letters her variants and prints her tunes in an appendix (the 121 tunes transcribed from dictaphone recordings are a great service). Her notes on song histories are seldom original or informative. Although she does more than merely list the informants, too much of the running comment is mere color, adding little to the understanding of the songs' function. The reader gets neither the viewpoint of the informed native nor the observation of the careful student; at best he catches the impressions of the sympathetic summer visitor. It may not be fair, but it is enlightening to contrast the work of Dorothy Scarborough with that of Jean Ritchie, the "least un" in a branch of the "singing Ritchie family" of eastern Kentucky. Miss Ritchie (now Mrs. George Pickow) has been getting a good deal of "mileage" from her family songs in concerts, on phonograph records, and in two singing books, *The Swapping Song Book* (1952) and *A Garland of Mountain Song* (1953). But there is also a third book, *Singing Family of the Cumberlands* (1955), which cannot rightly be considered a collection, containing only forty-four songs in 278 pages of commentary. The book is a highly selective autobiography built around the songs. The scope of the comment is not broad, and the experiences in which the songs function and the songs themselves are not necessarily typical even of Knott and Perry counties. But the experiences are deep and true. The songs are revealed as part of a life and of a family. This is one of the rare revelations of folksongs' function and meaning to those who sing them—seen as people, not informants.

RANDOM-TEXT COLLECTIONS

The random-text collections are often one more step removed from the academic tradition, although they differ among themselves enough to make generalization difficult. Their archetype is the printed collection of a folksinger, a random collection of the songs he knew, loved, and wished to preserve. *The Green Mountain Songster*, compiled by the "Unknown Soldier of Sandgate," Vermont, in 1823, is therefore the first American random-text collection. But within the present period of investigation, priority must be granted to M. C. Dean of Virginia, Minnesota.[76]

Dean's *Flying Cloud* (1922) is a wretchedly printed pamphlet containing 163 texts of well-known popular songs of the turn of the century: Irish stage and broadside pieces, Anglo-Irish ballads, native American ballads, English and Scottish popular ballads—a nondescript, unorganized mass. The texts are suspiciously complete, and one suspects that Dean was not always depending on memory alone. But the book certainly seems to be a slice of the repertoire of the Northern folksinger. The purist may be shocked to find a book containing "My Old Kentucky Home," "There's a Girl in the Heart of Maryland," "My Dad's Dinner Pail," and "The Day I Played Baseball" treated as a folksong collection. Yet the contents conform exactly to Barry's test of folksong: "a song which 'most people—or most *folks*—are fond of singing.' " [77] And in their way, the editors of random-text collections have consciously and unconsciously followed the organization and tests of the *Flying Cloud*.

Three collections of similar format, all from the Mitre Press, might be companion volumes of the *Flying Cloud* had they not been issued as folksong collections, with introductions, notes of sources, and some slight attempt at organization. Yet the three collections, all from the Southern Appalachians, are edited by persons of differing backgrounds, knowledge, and interests. Harvey H. Fuson, collector of *Ballads of the Kentucky Highlands* (1931), was a native of the mountains, a quondam academic, a coalman, a local poetaster of Harlan, Kentucky, an officer of the Kentucky Folklore Society, 1926–1931. *Songs Sung in the Southern Appalachians* (1933) is from the collection of Mellinger Edward Henry, a New Jersey schoolman whose vacation enthusiasms brought him in contact with Appalachian folksingers and local collectors profitably first in 1927. *East Tennessee and Western Virginia Mountain Ballads* (1934) came from Celestin Pierre Cambiaire, Poe scholar and *officier d'Academie*, who spent three years (1931–1933) as head of the Foreign Language Department of Lincoln Memorial University, Harrogate, Tennessee, where he somehow fell heir to seventy-two folksong texts and a chauvinistic attachment to the "principles of conservative Anglo-Norman civilization" (p. xxxviii). He also believed that Mammoth Cave was located "in these mountains."

These editors vary a bit in their citations of sources, Henry religiously giving source and date, Fuson noting the informant in most cases, and Cambiaire being somewhat cavalier about the matter. None includes headnotes or bibliographical references. Both Henry and Fuson make some attempt at folksong scholarship; Fuson champions Percy's minstrel theory and questions the somewhat romantic conclusions of Cecil Sharp; Henry rather apologetically embraces the re-creation theory. Cambiaire displays openly his combination of sentimental primitivism and American white chauvinism, extolling the beauties of a poetry which displays the "inner soul of a race."

In content, these tuneless collections offer few significant differences (excepting that Cambiaire concludes his volume with a section of his own poetry). The slight organization is scarcely more than a folksinger might casually use. We have confidence in the collectors' lack of discrimination, and the fragments, scraps, and rhymes testify to completeness. The casual approach of the collecting and editing makes the contents a valuable cross section of the Southern Appalachian repertoire, 1927–1934. Had the music been collected, the value would have been extreme. We may therefore note the small number of Child ballads, the few songs of American history, the larger number of songs with sensational themes, and the preponderance of sentimental pieces. Henry and Cambiaire include far more items intimately related to radio and phonograph versions current during the period,[78] possibly because Fuson's collection may be somewhat earlier and his knowledge a bit deeper. The difference is noticeable only to the expert in a narrow field and indicates no difference in taste.

This judgment is partially confirmed by another random collection, which, however, includes tunes. Lucian L. and Flora Lassiter McDowell's *Memory Melodies* (1947) consists largely of the memories and ballets of Mrs. McDowell, supplemented by those of her friends. The repertoire is largely that of the 1890s in the Caney Fork region of middle Tennessee. Lacking many late pieces, the collection includes a large number of the sentimental hillbilly songs: "Blind Child," "Sweet Fern," and "Blue Eyes." Missing are the sensational ballads of murder and tragedy, represented only by "Jealous Lover" and a local ballad, "The Braswell Boys."

In passing we might note such a random collection as *Vermont Folk Songs and Ballads* (1931) edited by Helen Hartness Flanders and George Brown. The random method here seems deliberate and selective, the aim being to give a somewhat popular report of the work of the Committee on Traditions and Ideals of the Vermont Commission on Country Life. But from the work done by this group comes a collection edited in conscious imitation of the archetypal volume.

Perhaps we should say that *The* New *Green Mountain Songster* pretends to be an imitation of the work of the "Unknown Soldier of Sandgate." There are a few examples of local or book songs and a few unions of text with unconnected air, but the collection is basically a selection from Mrs. Flanders' extensive Vermont collection, enriched by the critical notes of Phillips Barry. Tunes from dictaphone recordings are carefully transcribed, sometimes with variations indicating the music to which the whole song was sung. But with all its virtues, the collection lacks one of the values of those we have just observed. It is random in organization, but possibly quite selective in content. Certainly no canon of literary values has been employed, but there is no definite assurance that the collection is adequately representative of the Vermont folk repertoire. The selection may also be unrepresentative in that it presents the complete and "good" versions. But, considering the aim of the volume, one could not ask for more careful or honest work.

SINGING BOOKS

As interest in American folksong continued to grow, there developed a need and market for what Phillips Barry called practical works "for people who like to sing," editions made "both singable and understandable." [79] Works of this sort, however, were usually devised, not by editing already published material but by arranging new material. Some of the volumes were the initial publications of collectors, others represented the first opportunity of collectors to publish their tunes, and still others were merely another form for established tune-text collectors. These books, many of which are part of the G. Shirmer folksong series, contain as few as seven and as many as forty-nine songs, the average being about twenty.

There are two basic ways in which such practical works can be constructed. One can select satisfactory versions as received from informants; or one can produce such versions by combining or emending the texts and setting them to suitable tunes, possibly from other informants. When the latter method is employed, the readers "have a right . . . to know both the extent and sources of editorial changes and restorations." [80] Even more basic than this, they have a right to know which method was employed. If the material is represented as primary, they are entitled to expect some sort of documentation. Unfortunately, the singing books too often follow the early examples of Josephine McGill and Loraine Wyman and Howard Brockway (see pp. 167–169). For example, Mary Wheeler's *Kentucky Mountain Folk Songs* (1937) contains fourteen songs obtained from "the children of the Hindman Settlement School, others from older singers, who graciously sang them at the request of the stranger visiting their homes." The most precise documentation is an occasional mention of the county in which the song was collected. The condition of some of the texts indicates collation of some sort. A collection like *Smoky Mountain Ballads* (1949) by Adelaide Van Wey and Donald Lee Moore contains songs apparently unknown to other collectors and leaves the reader to wonder if they are also unknown to the folk. The collector-performer-composer John Jacob Niles in a long series of singing books has occasionally documented his sources. But such documentation is no guarantee of authenticity, for Niles has been unable to separate his three roles. In recent program and album notes he has confessed personal interference ranging from tune alteration to complete composition. A number of editors, like Elmer Griffith Sulzer in *Twenty-Five Kentucky Folk-Ballads* (1936), simply give the material, with neither incriminating nor substantiating comments.

One of the more unfortunate features of this type of publishing is that significant material appearing here has not seen collateral publication. The lack of full information is not particularly important in books like Melvin LeMon and George Korson's *The Miner Sings* (1936), which merely supplement other publications. But a number of the singing books are unique reports. It is regrettable that the efforts of such a sympathetic collector-performer as Bascom Lamar Lunsford have seen print in such an abbreviated, conflated, and undocumented form (*30 and 1 Folk Songs [from the Southern Mountains]*, 1929), even though the music received careful transcription. Superior in some ways is Ethel Park Richardson's *American Mountain Songs* (1927). Her scanty notes pass on important information, but fuller documentation is needed. Some of her informants are also recorded on commercial phonograph records, and her transcriptions of the same songs are of great value. Also among the works not providing all essential information are the volumes of Margaret Larkin and Maud Karpeles. Miss Larkin's *Singing Cowboy* (1931), one of the more important additions to the Lomax canon, gives many cryptic notes and little precise documentation. We fear that at times the professional singer may overpower the collector. Miss Karpeles' *Folk Songs from Newfoundland* (1934),[81] however, gives the tune documentation we might expect from the English collector; we are told when something has been done to a text, but not what. And to the "almost acceptable" category might be added *Mountain Songs of North Carolina* (1926) by Susannah Wetmore. Even in such an excellent report as Edith B. Sturgis and Robert Hughes' *Songs from the Hills of Vermont* (1919), a few changes made in the texts are not fully indicated.

Not all the singing books are open to such criticism. The best come from the Northeast. *Country Songs of Vermont* (1937) by Helen Hartness Flanders and Helen Norfleet is a selection of singable versions, unemended and fully documented. When the same editors employ composites, as in *A Garland of Green Mountain Song* (1934), they fully explain the method employed, as does Barry in *The Maine Woods Songster* (1939). A comparable publication has been made from Appalachian tradition by Maurice Matteson and Mellenger Edward Henry: *Beech Mountain Folk-Songs and Ballads* (1936). Josiah Combs's *Folk-Songs from the Kentucky Highlands* (1939) is also trustworthy, although the documentation should have been fuller.

Little need be said of the contents of these collections. For the most part they represent the larger collections in abbreviated form. The pattern of selection of the early esthetic collectors did not bind later editors. Those who had published other books made fairly representative collections; therefore we find in the singing books of Combs and Henry such songs as "The Little Rosewood Casket," "Broken Engagement," and "On the Banks of a Lonely River," as well as more "respectable" songs. Ethel Park Richardson's *American Mountain Songs* is even more liberal, including "The Child of the Railroad Engineer" and "Howdy Bill." Perhaps only Miss Karpeles continues to remind us that though "the folk-singer does not, of course, distinguish between traditional and composed songs," [82] the collector must reject what does not fit his definitions and his tastes.

THE LOMAXES AGAIN

All collections cannot be forced into these categories, but to those already discussed might be added another type, the portmanteau, a sort of valise stuffed with all sorts of goodies, often chosen with the tastes of a large public in mind. Most of the collections of this type either select their contents from other publications or are on other grounds not worthy of serious consideration.[83] Carl Sandburg's *American Songbag* (1927) is just that sort of book; it might be valuable as a cross section of American tradition if one but knew the extent to which Sandburg's "constructive memory" [84] is involved. And of course we should like better documentation and indication of the songs borrowed from other collectors, such as Edwin Ford Piper. But the "cute" divisions into which Sandburg classifies his collection may have influenced the organization of Lomax's *American Ballads and Folk Songs*.

This second Lomax collection (1934) is almost as important as the first edition of *Cowboy Songs*, and for about the same reasons. Whatever its faults, *American Ballads and Folk Songs* dramatized its subject just at the moment when the United States, in the throes of economic disaster, was turning to its own history and culture for values. The Lomax composite photograph of "music straight from the heart of the people" was eagerly accepted and perhaps still furnishes to the general mind the picture of American folksong. For this reason the volume deserves examination here, although it differs somewhat from the collections being considered.

American Ballads and Folk Songs pretends to be at once personal and typical: the "best examples of the most noteworthy types . . . the personal choice of the compilers from a large mass of material." The large mass included more than the personal collection of John and Alan Lomax. The songs are chosen not only from John Lomax's older field collection, from the records amassed in the field trip of 1934, and from old newspaper clippings, but from commercial phonograph records and other collections, published and unpublished. In fact, almost a fourth of the songs are reprinted from the published work of other collectors. The secondary material is certainly included because of the desire to produce a "typical" collection, but it is difficult to see why a field collector should have to borrow a variant of "The Little Mohea."

That the collection is typical is open to doubt. "Lack of space forces the exclusion" of certain Spanish ballads, but "the beautiful English ballads" are omitted because they are not indigenous. Although material clearly of English provenance is included because the compilers felt it had developed indigenous traits, one need not quibble with this decision. More important are the types that are included. Carl Engel has written that the Lomaxes

. . . hit upon the ingenious idea that, since the radio and other mechanical devices were rapidly destroying the initiative of folk-singers by necessarily obviating the need of music-making among the people, the places to pick up unadulterated folk-songs were those where natural or enforced isolation kept the tradition pure . . .

and that perhaps

. . . as a result of this novel procedure, the book of Messrs. Lomax gives one at first the impression that America depends for its folk-song literature chiefly on "Niggah" convicts and white "bums." [85]

Even in 1934 there was nothing novel in the beliefs and practices of the Lomaxes, excepting perhaps their unparalleled decision to visit the Negro prisons of the South. There may be justice in the conservative critic's doubt "that it was essential or felicitous to allot so prominent a place to the Morbid Muse," but the elder Lomax had indicated his position as early as 1913 [86] in his discussion of the seven types of so-called American ballads: miner, lumberman, inland sailor, soldier, railroader, Negro, down-and-out classes—outcast girl, dope fiend, convict, jailbird, and tramp. And he had also emphasized the coarseness of their songs and their connection with out-of-doors, physical endeavor. *American Ballads and Folk Songs* is not limited to such songs, but it certainly stresses them. In calling special attention to the "folk-made" song, the Lomaxes not only pioneer the functional approach, but stress one function—protest.

The twenty-five sections of the volume are not meant as serious classification. The principles of function, subject matter, and source are used almost indiscriminately. The divisions are neither better nor worse than those of other collections. More important is the editing method applied to the texts and tunes themselves.

Perhaps it would suffice to say that *American Ballads and Folk Songs* is slightly better than *Cowboy Songs* in emendation and documentation. The Lomaxes defend their use of the composite text on popular grounds. They forego "the satisfaction of knowing that we had followed a very ancient scholarly convention" because "only a few persons would be interested in comparing these variants," forgetting perhaps that the point involved was not so much the use of composites as the accurate indication of the source and amount of changes. A general note that stanzas have been rearranged or borrowed from specific collections is not quite enough. Furthermore, to select from "the jumbled and disconnected stanzas of Negro work songs and Blues . . . a group that presents . . . some connected theme" is certainly not a valid procedure in a book which purports to present the typical in American folksong. The editors seem to be usurping the function of the folk artist. Completely undocumented texts are quite puzzling. In 1957 E. C. Perrow sent to the editor of the *Kentucky Folklore Record* a text of "Braddock's Defeat" which agreed exactly, even to punctuation, with the copy printed in *American Ballads and Folk Songs*. The Perrow copy came from a University of Louisville student about 1915. Perrow recalls no contact with John Lomax after their student days at Harvard and is certain he sent Lomax no material and has not seen any Lomax books. The printed source common to both copies will eventually be discovered, but one line of type could have saved much search and speculation.

The fact that few texts are without a tune is a credit to the compilers and editors. The tunes are quite possibly the most reliable items in the volume, although Phillips Barry pointed out that even one reprinted tune is a composite, pieced together from unrelated airs.[87] The musical transcription, for which the Lomaxes depended upon others, received some criticism, even in the light of the editors' aim of producing a singing book.[88] Their later works were to be better in this respect.

Negro Folk Songs as Sung by Lead Belly (1934) is the first book-length report of a folksinger's repertoire and one of the great documents of Negro sinful songs. It is a reasonably clear picture of one folk artist. We may not like the picture; we may deny that it is necessarily true of all folk art. But the Lomaxes found in this criminal and murderer a seminal figure in one folk tradition and drew a full-length portrait. Fortunately the inescapable deficiencies in musical transcription of Negro song are met with all the skills of George Herzog. But the biographical approach here adopted is put to different use in the Lomaxes' second book of American ballads and folksongs.

Our Singing Country (1941) is a superior second volume. Despite the popular aim, the musical transcriptions are better than those in many books of pure scholarship. Ruth Crawford Seeger's attempt *"to include as many characteristics of singing style as is possible, yet to keep most of the notations simple enough to be sight-read by the average amateur"* (p. xix) seems successful. Almost all the material is taken from recordings in the Library of Congress Archive of American Folk Song. The tune documentation includes the Library of Congress record number as well as notation of informant and date. Even the texts are more accurately presented, though there have been some silent emendations. There are fewer composites, and the documentation is improved, though not perfect. The coverage of geographical areas and song types is also improved. That the preponderance of the material comes from the South can be explained by the activities of the Lomaxes and by their principles, as well as by the fact that folksinging is certainly more active in this area. The principles, however, must be examined.

Our Singing Country crystallizes an important trend in American folksong collection and study, for the dominant point of view here is not historical, but functional. Old songs are not excluded, even shanties from the memories of aged sailors. But the collection emphasizes contemporary (1934–1939) and relatively active singing. Other collectors had already demonstrated that folksong was still being sung and even created. *Our Singing Country* gives more emphasis to the new and the living song, but focuses on the singer, his attitude toward the songs, their function in his life, and their contemporary meaning. The value of this approach is indisputable, but objectivity is necessary. The picture painted by the Lomaxes is clear; we doubt that it is complete or unbiased.

The functional approach is best applied intensively in a community. But the chief objection to the Lomaxes' methods is not their scope but their selectivity. "Most of these singers are poor people, farmers, laborers, convicts, old-age pensioners, relief workers, housewives, wandering guitar pickers" (p. ix). One cannot quarrel with the conclusion that these people preserve the most active folksong tradition in America. But one would like more assurance that the attitude of the editors is the attitude of all or a significant portion of the singers. Much of the sporadic continuity that largely replaces historical notes is drawn from a single informant, Aunt Molly Jackson of Clay County, Kentucky. It is doubtful that her experiences and her class consciousness reflect American folksingers as a whole. This imbalance vitiates an important collection, a collection which, like its predecessor, even dares to transcribe from hillbilly records, though it fails to indicate their exact place in folk tradition.

The final Lomax printed volume, *Folk Song: U.S.A.* (1947), is a popular selection of arranged and composite songs which might be considered outside our scope did it not make explicit the Lomaxes' attitude toward sources. The arrangement of the tunes by Charles and Ruth Seeger is certainly a model for the popular presentation of folksong; the documentation certainly is not. The notes "acknowledge fully the sources of the melody, the stanzas or continuity material of every song, *unless the song and the note come from our personal collections*" (p. 379). Documentation is thus considered more a legal necessity or a polite gesture than a scholarly responsibility.

PATTERNS OF INCLUSION

Besides the perennial attack on the "mere accumulation" of texts and tunes, adverse criticism of American folksong collections has been directed at the sources of the material and the type of material itself. Most critics have found published collections too eclectic and lacking in academic and purist values; but one early critic found them too academic.

Writing in 1926, Edmund Wilson declared that "there are disadvantages in having ballad collecting become an established branch of academic study." Distressed because "folk-lore has become a science—running to the same narrow specialization and the same unintelligent amassment of data as the other sciences," he lamented the lack of esthetic values among the collectors, their exclusive concern with the illiterate, and their respect for "folk-etymological changes" and the "blurred or garbled" texts, which tends to make them "shy of such particularly witty or coherent versions of their ballads as can be found in print." He suggested that the collectors look in old college song books and cultivate "the educated people in every community who have a private local reputation for singing entertaining songs: these people, like the illiterate, transmit songs orally from generation to generation and they usually remember them better." To these sources he added the "professional ballad-singers of the bars and cabarets." Further, he pointedly approved the Percy-Scott method of emendation.[89] At first glance one might conclude that Wilson's ideal folklore journal would be *Captain Billy's Whizbang*, and his ideal collection, Charles O'Brien Kennedy's *American Ballads: Naughty, Ribald, and Classic* (1952).

Although Wilson had inadequate knowledge of materials in print at that time, the fact is that certain of his significant objections were to be answered by later collectors. Certain volumes fit his formula perhaps all too well. John Jacob Niles' *Singing Soldiers* (1927) is not notable for its documentation, but the volume he edited with Douglas Moore, *The Songs My Mother Never Taught Me* (1929), is—for all the good material that may have gone into the compounding—hardly useful to the student of American folksong, unless he wishes the source of that piece beloved of contemporary "folksongers," "Venezuela." Similarly the collections of Frank Shay, *My Pious Friends and Drunken Companions* (1927) and *More Pious Friends and Drunken Companions* (1928), are highly indicative of a literate tradition, but the reader is not enlightened as to the "curious sources" of the material. It is significant that later in 1926 Wilson confessed himself pleased with Franz Rickaby's *Ballads and Songs of the Shanty-Boy* and W. C. Handy's *Blues: An Anthology* (edited by Abbe Niles), even though the former followed "the formula of traditional ballad scholarship." [90] Wilson must have been overjoyed at the appearance of *The American Song-bag* and *American Ballads and Folk Songs*. But his serious criticism (although he certainly did not see it so) concerned the relation of print to oral tradition, the re-creation of songs by gifted singers, and the function of literacy in ballad tradition. His praise of Rickaby for including printed copies of W. N. Allen's logger ballads could be applied to later collectors who included prints for Rickaby's reasons, not Wilson's. And Phillips Barry's conclusions as to the negative factor of illiteracy should have pleased Wilson, had it not been that the setting was still academic. In fact, though nonacademic collections appeared to satisfy Wilson's demand for an esthetic anthology, the academic tradition managed to answer his valid criticisms without departing from its "scientific" aim.

More serious criticism, however, has attacked American collections from an almost opposite point of view, questioning their inclusiveness. One of the more recent critics states his conclusion pungently:

> The authors and editors seem to have no idea what "folk" literature or lore or song is, where its boundaries lie, or who belongs to the "folk" under what circumstances.[91]

Stanley Edgar Hyman was reviewing a number of what he termed "bankrupt treasuries," some of which deserve highly critical examination. But he elsewhere makes clear his opinion of

> the poor quality of American collecting, which is largely in the hands of men with little learning or imaginative breadth. The gap between Professor Francis James Child, the learned and polylingual scholar who organized the study of the ancient ballad, and a man like John Lomax, the late dean of American folk-song collectors, represents a steady deterioration of personnel in the field over the past half century. . . .[92]

Obviously Hyman has little love for the noble sport of ballad hunting, preferring the ignoble sport of shooting fish in a barrel. He compares a great literary scholar who sorted and annotated written materials in the light of his immense but imperfect knowledge, with a great field collector who gathered the songs of a people and, whatever his errors in publication, saw to their preservation. Such a comparison can be made only by one who believes that proper scholarship is library scholarship and that one conjecture is worth a thousand facts. And so Hyman seems to believe, for he suggests that "a folk song is a song of anonymous collective folk origin, and a folk singer is a person who learns these songs through an unbroken line of oral transmission and sings them." [93] It is folly to demand that Hyman produce such a folksong. From one who has resurrected the surviving-elements method of folklore research, we would receive only those answers which Gummere wore thin. Hyman proposes that we adopt the label *volkstümliche Lied* to refer to "songs that are not works of collective folk origin, but are patterned after them by a song writer, however anonymous, in modern times, and are then sung by people we can legitimately call a folk . . . ," [94] reserving the word *folksong* for those ancient and obscure songs about which we can freely conjecture—preferably concerning their ritual origin. But in spite of his parochial vision, Hyman touches a sensitive area: definition. More informed critics have written on this point.

Quite instructive is the attitude of leaders of the English Folk Dance and Song Society toward American collections. English criticism has been leveled at the paucity and incorrectness of the tunes, haphazard methods of publication, and duplication in printing variants and songs. Much of the criticism is insular and reflects the inability to conceive "special circumstances apparently not duplicated in the British Isles." [95] These English critics have viewed the printing of folksong as a highly selective process whereby only the "best" songs and variants are chosen by preconceived standards and published only when a similar variant is not in print. The American habit of collecting and printing as much as possible in any way that is possible in the hope that some value may be found is foreign to these critics.

Writing of *Ballads and Sea Songs of Newfoundland,* Miss Karpeles deplores the failure to separate the "folk" from the "non-folk," admitting that such classification is not easy.

> There are many songs which are on the borderline: there are the composed songs, which have taken on something of the folk idiom, and those which have been composed definitely on a folk-basis. Then again, there are the songs in which composed words have been wedded to a traditional tune.[96]

Miss Gilchrist, reviewing *Ballads and Songs of Southern Michigan,* insists that "it should have been sifted before publication," noting that "many American collectors . . . have a much more inclusive definition of this word *folk* than is generally accepted in this country," and confirming our suspicions about omissions from English collections.

> Many English collectors in their hunting grounds must have come across various old-fashioned published songs—comic and sentimental ditties treasured by the lower middle classes of an earlier era.

As an example of the "particular type of sentimentality which seems distinctly American, and which in England would be barred by its sophistication from being classed as folk-song," she chooses "The Dying Cowboy," contrasting it with "the simple, tragic narrative of 'Frozen Charlotte,' which is in the genuine tradition, though born in America of a real event." [97] Miss Gilchrist could scarcely have chosen less congenial examples, for "The Dying Cowboy" is a traditional re-creation of a British folksong, whereas "Frozen Charlotte" is an "author-song" of wide circulation but limited variation. The esthetic criteria of the English critic are somewhat less than Olympian, as may be seen in Miss Gilchrist's comment on *Folk-Songs of Roanoke and the Albemarle.* After declaring that "Sandy and Mary" is not a folksong, she turns to "the other end of the 'literary' scale" to question the inclusion of

> the American doggerel ballads of murders and gangsters, bristling with pearl-handled "44" guns; bartenders, sheriffs, someone addressed as "baby," and rubber-tyered hearses in connection with the

"man who done her wrong." I have found no suitable labels for these. Our common English street-ballads are garden flowers in comparison with these rank weeds of a newer soil.[98]

Marks of a ballad style seem lost on Miss Gilchrist. We must, however, try to draw from American collections their criteria or definition of folksong.

Most American collectors seem to have accepted at least tacitly Louise Pound's four tests of folksongs:

1. They are transmitted orally.
2. They have no fixed form, but are continually changing.
3. They "have retained their vitality through a fair period of time."
4. They have lost all sense of authorship and provenance.[99]

The collectors have not had the information to apply the third principle, and perhaps have not always taken account of the fourth. Although there have been protests that "songs sung by the folk . . . are not necessarily folksongs," [100] the American collector has generally acted as if they are, with the distinction that while he has defined *folk* as "common people" or "the unsophisticated," he has collected on many levels of society, songs which meet Miss Pound's third and fourth tests. It is not fair to say exactly that the collectors accepted songs sung by the folk and folksongs sung by the nonfolk. Rather, they have followed a policy which approaches Barry's conclusion that whoever sings a song from memory is a folksinger.[101] Basing their attitudes on experience rather than theory, they

> learned what every ballad collector must learn if he is to continue his work without discouragement, namely, that no popular version of any sort of ballad, ancient or modern, can be regarded as common or unclean.[102]

Their collections may be partially edited archives to be used and judged by future scholars. The collections may even reflect a faith that folksong is not a closed account and that questionable songs of today may become the folksongs of the future. Therefore documentation of the stages in the process is of vital importance. This sort of collection has led to almost endless expansion and little exclusion. There are other trends of expansion not so limited to American collection. Though differences can still be noted, the remaining discussion of Anglo-American collection will be more unified.

Recent Trends in Anglo-American Collection

Discovery of industrial folksongs, as distinguished from occupational songs such as shanties and perhaps shearing and plowman's songs, can be largely credited to American collectors, though mining songs had been known from Northumbrian tradition, particularly in John Stokoe and Samuel Reay's *Songs and Ballads of Northern England* (1892?) and before that in John Bell's *Rhymes of the Northern Bards* (1812). But serious interest in British industrial and protest songs grew largely after World War II and with the emergence in the folksong field of what some writers might term *working-class intellectuals*—a term useful to describe their outlook —though in terms of collection they correspond to the American collector with a folk background. Men like A. L. Lloyd, Hamish Henderson, and Ewan MacColl have taken a somewhat broader outlook than that maintained by the staid English Folk Dance and Song Society.

The first collection of British industrial song was not published until 1952, A. L. Lloyd's compilation, *Come All Ye Bold Miners*, on which is based his singing book, *Coal Dust Ballads* (1952). MacColl's *The Shuttle and the Cage* (1954) includes some of the material previously printed by Lloyd but adds songs from other industries, some from early collections but mostly of MacColl's own collection. MacColl, himself the author of industrial and protest songs now in oral circulation, is somewhat less orthodox than Lloyd, who not only apologizes for the crudeness of the songs in *Come All Ye Bold Miners*, but excludes "parlour ballads of the type of

Don't Go Down in the Mine, Daddy" as not "what we understood
as folk-songs" (p. 9). But the contents of the volume roughly parallel Korson's American collections (some of the songs were first
published there), including songs from the late eighteenth century
to 1934, the productions of local poets and songs circulated by
broadsides and sheet music, and songs "barely kept alive in the
mouths of a solitary singer here and there." Such inclusions and
Lloyd's statement, "Aesthetics isn't everything," seem to indicate
the British acceptance of an earlier American trend. But the newer
trend is shown not only by Lloyd's emphasis on the functional
quality of the songs, but by his hope for "the pit-songs of the future. If this humble collection can encourage one miner to make
up one ballad out of his working life, it will have achieved its aim"
(p. 17).

Gummere's dictum that folksong is made by the people was only
a part of his theory of communal origin. His opponents attacked
both the communal and popular origin of ballads, with the result
that the criterion of folksong, in America at least, became largely
that of oral circulation, and folk authorship was judged to be after
the fact. The concept of communal authorship died hard. Folk
authorship slumbered, to awaken in an individual but still somewhat magical form.

If a goodly proportion of the American songbag is stuffed with
gesunkene Kulturgüter, preserved or recomposed by the singers, a
significant portion is the production of individuals on the same
cultural level as the singers. The criterion of persistence, which
ignores authorship, will not explain the presence of all the material,
for investigations have shown that songs have been obtained at or
near the source. Consequently it has been rediscovered that song is
folk in composition as well as circulation. The resurrected principle
has grown from the work of investigators who, searching for the
background of songs or questioning singers, have found themselves
in the presence of the bard himself. The first step has shown that
traditional songs have been composed by folksingers. The next step

is to shear the song of its traditional history: a folksong is a song composed by a member of the folk.

Emelyn Elizabeth Gardner approaches this position when, believing she is echoing Barry, she contends that such songs as "Floyd Collins," "Harry Bail," and "Little Mary Phagan" "were folk songs as soon as they were composed by someone close to the principals of the tragedies and accepted by those who sang them." [103] A crucial point involves the status of those who composed the songs (including their methods) and "those who sang them." *Those* has generally meant dwellers in an isolated region or persons engaged in a common occupation who, lacking the appurtenances of mass culture, have followed the traditional practice of composing their own material or recomposing traditional material: thus the lumberjack bards and the "minstrels of the mine patch." The problem could have been better understood and more reasonably dealt with had it not been for a recent extension of the magic of the word *folk*. The acceptance of the homemade song of the isolated community is one thing; the creation of an artificial folk is another.

The investigation of folk culture may convince the investigator that his role "is that of the advocate of the folk." [104] But it may also result in confusion between the value of the song and the song itself. Thus the discovery of democratic elements in folksong has led to the conclusion that American folksong itself is democratic.[105] The recognition that "singing has a direct and reciprocal relation to social, economic, and political issues" [106] has led to an equation of the "cry for justice" and folksong. The discovery of folksongs of social protest has led some to the conclusion that a protest song is *ipso facto* a folksong, and to the postulation of "a new folk community composed of progressives, anti-fascists, and union members." [107]

Such thinking lies behind *The People's Song Book* (1948), which contains tune-text units from oral tradition, new texts to traditional tunes, and fresh texts and tunes, copyrighted. The use of folksong for political purposes is an old device; what is new is the use of the folk concept, the magic term *folk*. The misapplication of the term *folksong* to the copyrighted "Investigator's Song" has less justification than the application of the term by purveyors of commercial popular music to the new songs of country-western singers. But *The People's Song Book* is vouched for by two eminent folklorists, one of whom helped compose one of the texts. In part the group of "People's Artists" is merely a political aberrant of recent emphasis on performance and distribution of folk or folkish song, which includes the anticipation of the folk in composing and distributing "folksongs" of protest. As one wag put it,

> *Their motives are pure, their material is corny,*
> *But their spirit will never be broke.*
> *And they go right on in their great noble crusade—*
> *Of teaching folk-songs to the folk.*[108]

It is rather unfortunate that some of the questionable activities of this group have been associated with a more serious consideration of the problem.

In his *American Folksongs of Protest* (1953) John Greenway squarely faces the problem and, though illustrating the extension of the term *folksong* typical of American collectors, is unwilling to stretch the boundaries without considering the issues. Greenway recognizes that American collectors have clung to the term *traditional* as the distinguishing mark of folksong; he recognizes just as clearly that his contemporary material "will have vanished by the time the next generation composes its songs of protest" (pp. 3–4). Faced with a conflict between restrictive definition and his collected material, he makes the choice typical of American collectors.

> If there is a choice to be made between rejecting a definition which excludes so great a body of material and rejecting the songs, there can be no hesitation in deciding which must go. But rejecting an established definition simply because it will not work with a particular class of songs is indefensible. The definition must be demonstrably fallacious (pp. 6–7).

Therein lies the difference between the American collectors' expansiveness and Greenway's redefinition. Greenway is not simply garnering and publishing material for future study. He declares the requirement of persistence invalid because it fails to take into account the unconscious art of the folk composer.

Greenway's new definition is simple: *das Volk dichtet* individually:

> . . . if an individual is the sole author of a folksong he must speak not for himself but for the folk community as a whole, and in the folk idiom. His function is not that of a consciously creative artist, but that of a spokesman of a community. . . . It is the impersonality of authorship, not anonymity of authorship, that is a requisite of genuine folksong. . . . A folksong, therefore, is a song concerned with the interests of the folk and in the complete possession of the folk (pp. 8–9).

In the first place, Greenway's *folk* is a highly restricted term, an economic term. Recognizing the disappearance of the agricultural folk, he finds a new folk in the industrial community (CIO, not AFL). But he seems to find them the only folk.

> When the college boy changed the nonsense refrain of "Sweet Betsy from Pike" from "hoodle dang fol de di do, hoddle dang fol de day," to "Sing tangent cotangent cosecant cosine," he made an adaptation outside the folk domain (p. 9).

Why are members of a college community necessarily any less a folk than members of the industrial community? Possibly because they don't sing about the right things, for one of Greenway's folk composers is a college graduate turned trade-union leader. Greenway is apparently willing that his folk composer "make an imitation ballad about kings and queens and lords and ladies," but thinks "he has much more business writing about" other things, such as "a mean mistreatin' railroad daddy."

But in writing that the "requirement of persistence" of a song "is a gauge of popularity, not of authenticity" (p. 7), Greenway has made an important point. Unfortunately, he chooses to remain on his opponents' ground, to retain the narrow sense of *traditional* and, though this might seem strange to his ears, a narrow concept of *folksong*. So his only recourse is the romantic concept of the un-

conscious art of the folk composer. The folk composer is not unconscious that he is an artist, only that he is a *folk artist*. His composition may be traditional without surviving for generations. There
is tradition in space, or "horizontal tradition"—which Greenway
may be referring to in the phrase "in complete possession of the
folk." Then there are the tradition of form and even the tradition
of composition itself. If "The Kentucky Miner's Dreadful Fight"
became (as Greenway maintains) a folksong "the minute Aunt
Molly Jackson scribbled it on a piece of paper" (p. 7), the explanation cannot be found in its "unconscious art": Gummere's dichotomy of art and nature which Belden so carefully destroyed.

Finally, there is the concept of *folksong*. It is noteworthy that in
spite of his title and his extended justification of his inclusions,
Greenway admits that much of his material—"most of the broadsides, the more turgid IWW songs, the productions of the more
cultured unions" (p. 9n)—are not folksong. And it does not seem
that a new definition is needed to include "hillbilly songs like Jimmie
Rodgers' blue yodels which the folk have accepted, sentimental
pieces like 'The Fatal Wedding.'" If the folk accept them, they are
folksongs *de facto*. If not, they are broadsides. It may be that Greenway does not see all the implications in the fact that his material
often lies outside both the category of broadside and the narrow
definition of folksong. Could it be that not merely the scope but
the character of the definition is at fault? Greenway merely substitutes another definition of the same kind, one which focuses on
the song as substance rather than as phenomenon. Folklorists have
long written of the process of folksong; only recently have they
been faced with determining at what precise point in its physical
history the *song* becomes *folk*. And in such a frame of reference
there may be no answer. We know that a song is "concerned with
the interests of the folk" by the fact that the folk are interested in it.
And when is a song in the *complete* possession of the folk? But
even should he cling to a formal definition of *folksong*, the folklorist cannot reject and refuse to study material which has the

function of folksong. And the *song-making function* of a folk certainly comes within the purview of the folklorist.

In addition to raising important theoretical questions, Greenway's anthology (for it is not completely a primary collection) is important in bringing together such an interesting group of protest songs, together with important comment. That many may be judged nontraditional is not a criticism. On any grounds, the broadside is a legitimate study of the folklorist, and Greenway is able to throw much light on the origin and history of traditional songs. Much adverse critical reception of the book may have been motivated by its very value, its bringing to light ephemeral material usually ignored by complacent academics.

Perhaps the most important recent trend in Anglo-American folksong collecting involves mechanical methods of collection and presentation. At the beginning of the twentieth century the field collector had the choice of noting by hand or using primitive cylinder recording machines. Though Cecil Sharp disdained the machines because he believed they made singers self-conscious, collectors such as Percy Grainger, John A. Lomax, Frank C. Brown, Robert W. Gordon, and Dorothy Scarborough used them to advantage. But these collectors aimed simply to record the material for future transcription. Not until the Lomax field trips of the thirties did the disc recording become a collecting tool of the folklorist and later a means of presenting his collected songs.

The disc belonged to the commercial recording industry which, however, began early—and at first unwittingly—to exploit folksong.[109] One method of this popular presentation developed from the "natural" appropriation by commercial entertainers of such folksongs as "Casey Jones" and "The Bully of the Town." Minstrel singers such as Collins and Harlan had a repertory that was at least folk-influenced, and such singers were to influence the folksinger. Plantation songs represent a conscious use of arranged folk material, and in 1910 the Victor Recording Company issued some pseudo-cowboy songs. Rube monologuists such as Cal Stewart ("Uncle Josh") and Charles Ross Taggart introduced snatches of folk music into their performances. In fact, a number of folk entertainers had relations with the recording industry in the first two decades of the twentieth century. In 1919 Columbia Records made an attempt to present American folksong to the record-buying public by issuing a series of five recordings of various types of American folksongs. Bentley Ball (probably a pseudonym) sang concert versions of American Indian songs, mountain ballads, cowboy songs, Negro spirituals, and Negro minstrel songs.[110] But the recording industry's most important contribution to the preservation and presentation of American folksong was not in the concert field. In 1919 recording companies began to become aware of a folk market and the existence of artists who could satisfy it. To the Negro folk, the blues singer was not unknown as a professional artist, but the first recording of a Negro blues singer was released in 1920. By 1923 scouts with portable recording apparatus were touring the South and Midwest in search of folk artists whose renditions could be sold back to the folk. And in 1923 the white folk entertainer, already appearing on radio, made his debut on phonograph records. Thus began the parallel broadside traditions of race and hillbilly. These releases were directed at the folk and were to exert a tremendous and as yet unmeasured influence. But they attracted little attention among the sophisticated public or the folklorists. Some students of folksong, such as Odum and Johnson,[111] noted the importance of the blues releases, but the hillbilly items were ignored or reviled. Of course a commercial—or commercialized—tradition was being established; and not all the recording artists were folksingers, nor was all the material from folk tradition. But in many instances the talent scout was actually a folksong collector, recording folk performers and performances which might otherwise have been completely lost—to name a few: Blind Lemon Jefferson, Jesse James, Buell Kazee, Doc Boggs, and Henry Whitter. And the parallel broadside traditions launched artists who affected the style and repertoire of the American folksinger.

By 1938 race and hillbilly records were a good deal farther removed from their folk roots. To be sure, country singers were still bringing new folksongs and fresh versions of old ones into the hill-billy field; and though the race record business was highly urban-ized, it could still make temporary room for a folksinger like Lead Belly. But a market for folksong was developing among the general public, and radio broadcasts such as those by Alan Lomax on the "School of the Air" seem as much symptoms as causes. In earlier years sporadic attempts, such as those made by Carl Sandburg and "Pierre La Dieu," to interest the record-buying public in folksong as such had not been successful. But times were chang-ing. John Jacob Niles, who had been giving folk-music concerts since 1927, made his first recordings for RCA-Victor in 1938. Moses Asch, the greatest single producer of folk recordings, founded his first company in 1939, and Asch Records began the release of re-cordings by Lead Belly, Woody Guthrie, and others. The trend was gathering force, and on major and minor labels began to appear the performances of such diverse singers as Josh White, Burl Ives, Carl Sandburg, and Richard Dyer-Bennet. Commercial issues from the Library of Congress Archive of Folksong appeared in 1943, and the reissue of hillbilly material under a folk label was beginning.

The recording activities immediately prior to World War II were, however, only the prelude. The postwar development of the mag-netic tape recorder and the LP (33⅓ r.p.m.) high-fidelity recording affected significantly the collection and presentation of folksong. The tape recorder has greatly simplified the task of the collector; even the rank amateur who is lucky enough to stumble on a good informant can faithfully record and preserve his material. And the tape recording is now developing into a medium of presentation as well. Beginning in 1948, the LP recording became first a medium for more effective presentation of serious music and soon stimulated listening to all types of music. The new technique simplified and improved the presentation of albums of folksong and has resulted in the availability of a wide variety of folk and folk-based song.

It would of course be a mistake to credit the trend solely to im-proved technical devices. Though the techniques were more crude, the approaches which seem to be innovations have been known and used for a long time. The release of folk performances began as early as 1920, though they were not then recognized as such. The collector who garners material that he can sing himself to another audience seems to be a new development. But Loraine Wyman was using that method in 1917, and it entered the recording field somewhat later in the work of such differing artists as Carl Sandburg and Bradley Kincaid. A broad public interest in folksongs is as much the cause as the result of presentation of songs in schools and night clubs, on radio, television, and recordings. One suspects that the great collections by the BBC, by Hamish Henderson for the School of Scottish Studies in Edinburgh, and by others would have proceeded without certain of the technical innovations which, however, improved and facilitated the work and its presentation.

Admittedly much of the material now labeled folksong on the commercial media is highly arranged, restyled, or even vulgarized. Yet these popularized presentations have aided in creating a market for and have made financially possible the more authentic releases. (See Appendix Two for a selected listing of folksong recordings.) A great deal has happened since a trade journal favorably reviewed Alan Lomax's 1947 edition of *Listen to Our Story* (Brunswick B-1024) but asked, "Where is the market?" It is not completely true to note that major recording labels produce the popular material, while the more authentic releases are distributed by small, specialized companies and private issues. The important *World Library of Primitive and Folk Music* is edited by Alan Lomax for Columbia Records. And the smaller companies often depend on restyled material aimed at a general audience to finance releases of more pristine material. Thus artists and collectors, once known to hundreds, are now familiar to thousands of listeners. The performance of singers like Jean Ritchie of Kentucky, Margaret Barry of Ireland, and Jeannie Robertson of Scotland is now not only preserved but introduced into the classroom and the living room. Collectors like Helen Creighton, Frederick Ramsey, Jr., and Hamish Henderson are no longer limited by the printed page. The sound of folkmusic can be generally heard.

It is not completely fair to single out only a few figures in a broad movement, but three men have made highly significant contributions to the commercial distribution of folksong. Important contributions of Alan Lomax to the popular presentation of authentic folk music have already been mentioned. Without detracting from the fine work of Brian George and others associated with the BBC, it must be recognized that in recent years Lomax's boundless interest and enthusiasm have greatly stimulated collection and the presentation of folksongs on radio and recordings in Europe and particularly in the British Isles. The American influence of Moses Asch has been extremely important. His Folkways label has succeeded his Asch and Disc ventures. Once a purely ethnic label, Folkways now has a catalogue of over 400 albums of ethnic, folk, jazz, and literary offerings. With difficulty and struggle Asch demonstrated a market for folk recordings, and his lead has been followed by many other small companies. The scholar examining the recorded folksong can judge aurally the stylistic authenticity of rendition, but he is often dubious of the sources and editing of the material.

A good deal of the recent improvement in editing and annotation of recorded folksong is due to the efforts of Kenneth S. Goldstein, to whom is also owed much of the credit for the 1956 reprint of Child's *The English and Scottish Popular Ballads*. Beginning modestly in 1952 with supervising the reissue on LP of many of Stinson's earlier albums, he has become a major force in the development of scholarly responsibility in the production of folksong albums. A Goldstein production almost invariably provides, whether in "liner" notes or the more extensive booklets provided by Folkways, not only bibliographical references and brief discussion of the songs themselves, but often necessary information concerning the source of the text and tune and an indication of any alteration necessary to produce a more singable version. Thus even when the style of presentation is not authentic, the student may derive some value from the text and even the skeleton of the tune. Though Goldstein has produced and edited for eight record companies, his most important work is the Riverside Folk-lore Series, which includes not only a number of field collections and traditional-sounding artists from America and Great Britain, but the important four-volume set of *The English and Scottish Popular Ballads* (RLP 12–621–8) and a companion album of *Great British Ballads* (RLP 12–629) sung by Ewan MacColl and A. L. Lloyd. These are not field recordings but competently edited ballads sung in traditional style to provide a basic tool for the teacher as well as a demonstration for the ordinary listener.

One conspicuous lack in collections of Anglo-American folksong has been pointed out on several occasions, most recently by G. Legman,[112] who excoriates Child and "all his progeny almost without exception" for their omission or expurgation of the bawdy ballad. Although Legman is not completely fair to the editors, the situation may be worse than he presents it—granting, of course, that the bawdy material is worthy of preservation and study. The general impression has been that folksong collectors, when they did not expurgate the songs as Legman charges, have retained quantities of unprintable material. The John A. Lomax papers do contain a number of bawdy songs of great importance, and Vance Randolph deposited a magnificent collection in the Library of Congress. But reports of vast holdings by many collectors seem exaggerated. A fact that makes the bawdy ballad even more important for study is that it tends to remain the oral possession of even the collector.

The problem is old, for, as Legman—who knows the field as well as anyone—points out, publicly issued collections of unexpurgated songs ended early in the eighteenth century, after which came "professional silence and amateur irresponsibility." Scholars and editors have often shared the attitudes of their culture, and it is not surprising that David Laing advised Peter Buchan to consign the effusions of his "high-kilted muse" to the flames.[113] It is difficult to prove that sexual references alone determined Child's exclusion of certain ballads, but collectors such as Cecil J. Sharp did not, and could not, publish the songs they collected without expurgating even mild sexual references. The problem covers more than the law, the reticences of the collector-editor, and the reaction of the reading public, as is pointed out by a ballad editor who had at least the courage to discuss the issues.

In 1928 [114] Arthur Kyle Davis, Jr., noted that "the ballad is one of the last strongholds of ribaldry," a fact which "no one would suspect from recent publications." Davis traces the "lily-white" character of collections not only to restrictions placed on the editors by "sanctimonious intolerance," but also to "the ballad-singer's quite natural unwillingness to sing bawdy songs to collectors, who are generally strangers to him and who are not infrequently women." Davis's point is underscored by the fact that unexpurgated folk material, printed or in archives, usually comes from native or skilled collectors who deliberately ask for the material. With regard to publication of the hard-to-collect songs, it does "seem that scholarship should enjoy some immunity" and that folksong scholars should have been more courageous in seeking it. Yet one recalls the anecdote of the Mississippian who, asked if he were Catholic, replied that "down here it's hard enough to be a Nigger." Then too, the scholar often fears that the inclusion of bawdy material will compromise the serious character of his work, that the printing of ribald songs will be taken as an end in itself (a conclusion which seems to have been drawn about Hamish Henderson's *Ballads of World War II*). Thus even today when material which is, to say the least, highly suggestive is dispensed at the corner drugstore, the folklore journal must pussyfoot. Ironically, songs in lusty versions seldom printed may now be heard on folksong recordings.

We do know that particular areas of folksong have been poorly represented because of the ban on ribald song. In *The Idiom of the People* (1958), James Reeves has printed a large number of the forthright, though not bawdy, songs from the Sharp Manuscripts. Only John Brophy and Eric Partridge in *Songs and Slang of the British Soldier, 1914–1918* (1930) give much indication of the type of material generally favored by fighting men, and their songs are expurgated. The repertoire of the sailor, the cowboy, the logger, the hobo is but partially represented, and the blues and ballads of the Negro are seldom recorded full strength. The part ribaldry has played in the song repertoire of American rural folksingers is difficult to determine, but a few unpublished collections indicate its strength. And the bawdy repertoire of the student—which is comparatively easy to garner—is rich not only in amount but in age.

Fortunately Legman promises a scholarly edition of the bawdy song in English, based on privately printed volumes and unpublished collections made available to him. Legman's rebuffs and difficulties in gaining access to the material and permission to print indicate the strength of forces still denying a full and honest picture of folksong and hampering the study of a tradition less affected by print than any in our time. Legman's collection will not make good all past losses, but it will be a great aid to the student of oral tradition and will indicate what might have been available if editors could have worked in Great Britain and the United States instead of waiting for one who of necessity works in France.

THE STUDY OF ANGLO-AMERICAN FOLKSONG

Twentieth-century folksong scholarship in Great Britain and the United States has been concerned primarily with the communal-individual controversy and with collecting. A chapter which attempts to treat other investigations might seem to rival the famous consideration of Irish reptilia. Archer Taylor wrote in 1932, particularly of American scholarship:

> Significant achievement has been regrettably small and, worse than that, it has preferred to remain in narrow ruts—the collection of texts and the endless dispute over ballad origins—without looking to the right or left. . . . Can any of the three main branches of investigation, ballad origins, ballad dissemination, or ballad technique, be pursued on a narrow basis which limits the materials used to a single language? Can we safely discuss the origin of the ballad without previously establishing as well as may be the origin and history of many individual ballads? [1]

No one can dispute the justice of these words, especially in their bearing on the Ballad War. But there is another aspect to the picture. First, the emphasis on collection is both understandable and salutary. The discovery that folksong was not dead naturally focused attention on the recovery of contemporary material. Is it possible that there has been too much collection? If collection was necessarily achieved by the postponement of other labors, must one do more than lament the necessity? It may be regrettable that even more energy was *not* diverted into the narrow rut of collecting. Secondly, Taylor's conception of "investigation in the grand style" is narrow in its own way. He does not point out that folk music, "in the Occidental world, is regional and even local in character." [2] His praise of Grundtvig's and Child's "catholic interest in the ballad texts and all the subsidiary matters, historical, folkloristic, and critical, necessary to understand the texts" ignores music and function, as well as noncanon material in contemporary circulation. An understanding of the problems of the ancient ballad requires some reference to the practices of modern folksinging. But in so far as Taylor's criticism applies to the garnering of mere song texts, it is valid.

Scholarship must collect, catalogue, and study its materials, roughly in that order. For Anglo-American folksong scholarship, the second step is only now under way. Ideally the work should begin with the local and national before crossing the "linguistic and nationalistic barriers" which Taylor decried, but this ideal is qualified by the recognition that even in cataloguing, a knowledge of international ballad forms may reveal unsuspected relationships among items. Practically, scholarship moves by fits and starts and must deal with various aspects of the problem concurrently. Consequently, one discovers that there are snakes in Ireland. Folksong scholarship has been varied, if not as prolific as the critic might desire.

Anglo-American scholarship has been local, incidental, and preoccupied with details, largely because this has been an era of discovery and collection. But there has also been a reaction against the type of generalization which characterized the Ballad War. Investigators have learned that

> the general and fundamental problems of origin and derivation are extremely elusive and can be approached only with a great mass of comparative data; that it is more fruitful at the moment . . . to work toward those long-range goals with a short-range approach.[3]

This preoccupation with detail has meant also a certain broadening of approach. The study of folksong is becoming no longer a comparison of ballad texts, but a study of what people sing in their daily lives, a study including the singer as well as the song.

Therefore when Barry stated that it was no longer "a one-man job to write a critical history of a popular ballad," [4] he spoke conservatively. Barry's three fields of research—"the folk-lore background, including the factual basis, if any, of the plot of the ballad-drama; the origin of the ballad as the artistic expression of a particular folk-complex; the re-creation of the ballad, both psychologically and in relation to the evolving multiplicity of versions of texts and sets of air"—involve all sorts of problems. They involve the study of both elements and processes that must not and cannot be separated. A song, the unstable union of text and air, bears a relation to all the other items in the traditions of which it is and has been a part. It is related as a unit and in its parts to all that it has met. A study of music involves the study of texts, and the study of one tune involves the study of many texts. A study of such an element as place names involves the processes of variation and diffusion. At the same time, each element and process demands specialized study. Even the "critical history of a popular ballad" is not an absolute. For if from such case histories are built up generalizations of origin, diffusion, variation, and the like, generalizations are required to support the case histories. Consequently, folksong studies must proceed slowly on the basis of carefully accumulated detail and interdependent, complementary investigations before the scholar can work confidently in "the grand style."

Incidental Scholarship

Folksong study incidental to collection has been largely comparative. The standard pattern in America has produced headnotes to a formally organized collection. The notes have been often limited to a mere list of other texts, or at least to purely bibliographical references. Some of the academic notes are seminal, particularly those of Kittredge (*JAF*, XX [1908], 251ff. as an example). Cox (*Folk-Songs of the South*), and MacKenzie (*Ballads and Sea Songs from Nova Scotia*). But editors have too frequently only copied the notes of their predecessors. Notes to Child ballads have, in addition to listing appearances in post-Child collections and in broadsides, for the most part done little more than record similarities to Child versions and comment on a few interesting variations. Excepting Brewster (*Ballads and Songs of Indiana*), editors have limited their comparative notes almost entirely to American and, at the most, British materials. Non-Child songs have had somewhat better treatment, although again there are but few seminal headnotes. Belden's comments in *Ballads and Songs Collected by the Missouri Folklore Society* have been especially valuable in analyzing geographical distribution in song texts. Much of the study of the provenance of native American songs has made its appearance in these headnotes, representing the luck, specialized knowledge, or particular research of the local collector.

Exception must be made for the Barry, Eckstorm, Smyth volume of *British Ballads from Maine* in which almost every entry is an important study of text and tune, even to the inclusion of comparative examples. Here, the printing of songs seems almost incidental to the scholarship.

Notes accompanying materials published by the Folk-Song Society were similar to those in the American academic pattern, though less formal. The comments were also largely analytical and comparative, though dealing usually with the folksong as music. Comments by members of the editing committee dealt with esthetic and structural features of the tunes and often cited similar tunes, whether published or in the private collections of the annotators.

A prominent feature of American study has been the headnote article, in which one or more fresh texts are printed as a springboard for a discussion of origin or variation.[5] This method was typical of Phillips Barry's work, especially in the *Bulletin of the Folk-Song Society of the Northeast*. Here each published song was the occasion for a miniature study of origin, re-creation, textual pattern, or singing style.

Not all incidental scholarship has been comparative and bibliographical. As already shown, the regional collector had some contact with and interest in the functional aspect of folksong: its delivery and its relation to the singer and his culture. This interest was particularly true of the American collectors of occupational songs. In a sense, the very collection of such songs involves a functional study. Any sort of historical notes on particular songs is bound to touch on the workaday lives of the singers. American collections devoted to the songs of miners, lumbermen, and cowboys gave attention to the cultural background of the material, and even the staid English collectors were drawn to study the functional aspect of sailors' songs, though their interest was largely historical and analytical.[6]

To summarize, incidental scholarship has been rich and varied but scattered and uneven. Among the notes of various collectors and editors are information and leads for all sorts of investigations, the mere tabulation of which is a separate study. At the same time there are noteworthy gaps. These may be seen more clearly in the following study of folksong investigations, dealing more particularly with separate studies. In approaching the various aspects of folksong study it will be necessary to adopt a nonhistorical organization. In fact, first consideration must be given to the cataloguing of folksongs, an activity only now assuming serious proportions. Then will come studies of details, of individual texts, of music, and of function.

Catalogues and Assessments

Nothing indicates so clearly the close of an era of folksong scholarship as the appearance at mid-century of volumes which attempt to index and/or assess collected songs. Such volumes indicate that, at least in the minds of the editors, the collected materials are complete and final enough to justify tabulation and classification.

If one can insist that a useful index or syllabus should completely cover a significant area and be organized in a meaningful and convenient fashion, at least one of the attempts to catalogue English collected materials will be found deficient. *An Index to English Songs Contributed to "The Journal of the Folk-Song Society" and its Continuation "The Journal of the English Folk Dance and Song Society"* (1951) by the Rev. E. A. White and Margaret Dean-Smith does no more than justify its title. In the first place, the area selected is significant only in that the journals are the greatest single repository of twentieth-century English collection. And any sort of index to such a repository is valuable. But one might question the simple choice of one medium of publication as a significant area. Fortunately, the volume is complemented by Margaret Dean-Smith's *A Guide to English Folk Song Collections: 1822–1952* (1954). A guide to unpublished collections is still wanting.

The White and Dean-Smith volume is an index in the narrow sense, an alphabetical list of titles and first lines. The only attempt at meaningful organization lies in a number of special listings, including cante fables, carols, shanties, game songs, May Day songs, street cries, and wassails. Otherwise the index does little to assemble related material separated by variant titles and first lines. As originally projected, the index was to include the opening bars of the tune of each song. While the dropping of this material by a society which collected tunes, not texts, is surprising, it is doubtful that the planned publication would have been worth the expense. For the investigator would have been provided with melodic clichés instead of the essential form of the tune. Even in its complete form, the *Index* has a limited value.

Although Margaret Dean-Smith's *Guide* retains the alphabetical approach, it eliminates many problems arising in the use of the earlier volume and is a work of scholarship. The *Guide* is an analysis of English folksong collections beginning with Davies Gilbert's *Some Ancient Christmas Carols* (1822). The annotated bibliography of these works is itself a significant contribution. Almost fully indexed are collections "made wholly, or in their greater part from oral communication, or derived from collections made in this way," but comparative reference is made to the *Journal of the Folk-Song Society* and the works of Child, Chappell, and others. Miss Dean-Smith indexed titles not only of tunes but of texts, omitting the latter "only after examination of all collections with music disclosed no associated tune, or where, so far as judgment could decide, by the standards of the Folk-Song Society the item must be deemed 'composed'" (p. 23). Instead of presenting the maze of variant titles and first lines that comprise the *Index*, the *Guide* establishes, largely on the basis of Sharp's Appalachian collections, standard titles, to which variants are cross-indexed. Although the work is anomalous in being neither a full index to texts nor a key to tune families, it seems the best compromise possible from those associated with the English Folk Dance and Song Society. Not the least of its virtues are the historical notes provided for many of the entries. The work is a step toward a syllabus of Anglo-American folksong.

The first American attempt at cataloguing was conceived on lines comparable to but more inclusive than those just examined. In 1937 Archer Taylor [7] announced work on a finding list of American song, alphabetical by title, cross-indexed and annotated, based on most published and a few unpublished collections. The list did not "aim to provide a critical standard of any kind," but was intended as "only a tool for reference." Well-advanced at one time but never completed, it was shipped twice almost across the United States, and it passed through the hands of two other scholars (who added nothing) before reaching Edward Cray, who has undertaken to complete it. Because the completeness of the work of Taylor's clerical assistants is open to doubt, Cray has almost had to begin again. And he has expanded the scope of the list to include all published and unpublished collections and some songsters, hymnals, and newspapers. The result of this ambitious undertaking should provide a firm basis for special syllabi. But in the meantime other types of catalogue have appeared.

Recent American attempts at cataloguing have been interested in just that "critical standard" which Taylor eschewed. Critical work is needed and almost any attempt provides some insight. But in so far as the work has respected earlier limitations or merely erected new canons on the principles of the old, it has been unsatisfactory. For the approach not only has been (of necessity) textual, but represents at least the temporary triumph of the Child-and-other pattern of the academic collections. Tristram P. Coffin's *The British Traditional Ballad in North America* (1950) and G. Malcolm Laws' *Native American Balladry* (1950) and *American Balladry from British Broadsides* (1957) are summaries of scholarship and critical studies as well as bibliographical syllabi. It is the last aspect that is considered here.

From one standpoint, Coffin's volume is an end rather than a beginning. It rests securely in the tradition of Child-ballad scholarship in America and succeeds the reports of Reed Smith which were begun in the *Journal of American Folklore*, XXVII (1914), 55ff Coffin accepts without defense the Child canon, at least as an area of investigation. Certainly the area is significant, the following of the Child organization is convenient, and a survey of the occurrence of these ballads in North American collections is valuable. But the book is another rivet in the bulkhead sealing off the sacred 305 ballads and encouraging the erection of other barriers.

Even in its narrowest aspect, *The British Traditional Ballad in North America* is more than a check list. Coffin's first service is to locate most texts, with the exception of broadside and songster material, printed in American collections. Although most unpublished material and Library of Congress and commercial recordings are not included, the volume is first an organized bibliography of greater value than a mere statistical count. In fact, Coffin avoids a statistical presentation. For these somewhat interesting facts, however, consult the Reed Smith check lists and Branford P. Millar's supplement, "The American Ballad List—1952." [8]

Reed Smith's periodic check lists of American recoveries emphasized the South, but included over-all statistics. Despite his obeisance to "Child's final and authoritative work," his lists demonstrated at the outset an extension of the Child canon. The first list included not only American variants printed by Child, but those he retained in manuscript because he thought they were derived from print or because he suspected their genuineness. And Kittredge expressed the clear opinion that many American texts would have been so judged by Child.[9] Kittredge's part in the first list points out the extent to which Smith was merely a tabulator who had to rely on the judgments and claims of others.

Smith cannot be held completely responsible for all the discrepancies between the check lists and texts which can now be located, yet he certainly welcomed secondary versions into his count. The question of counting as Child recoveries versions textually unrelated to canon numbers (and sometimes rejected by Child) is not the immediate concern. The fact of their acceptance illustrates the expansion of the Child canon as well as the zeal of American scholars in tracking down anything remotely related to the sacred 305. The list of different ballads collected and identified grew rather rapidly, seventy-three in 1914, seventy-six in 1915, eighty-seven in 1925, ninety-five in 1928, 109 in 1934, and 117 in 1937.[10] But because of statistical error, overoptimistic reports, and subsequent failure of certain texts to materialize, the 1937 count must be reduced to 113.[11]

This overoptimistic counting is only one side of the "Child in America" zeal. Counted as American recoveries were variants learned abroad or taken down from transients. Texts have been split or re-evaluated to gain another recovery. And then there are the "traces," recollections (often stimulated) of ballads by informants. Millar furnishes a revealing summary.[12]

Reports have been made concerning 144 Child ballads. Two texts listed by Smith cannot be found, and one report has turned out to be a case of mistaken identity. Seventeen are "traces." Of the 125 remaining, six exist only in secondary or derived versions. Of the 118 canon texts only 106 are reasonably complete. Of the fuller texts two are unpublished. As an index to interest in the Child ballad in America, the lists are valuable. As a means of comparison with overseas tradition, they are hampered by the lack of any comparable list from Great Britain. Such lists have served to stimulate scholarship, although not furnishing enough bibliographical information for thorough study. And in spite of qualifying comments by the compilers, they may be downright misleading, for the appearance of a ballad in the list is no indication of the strength of its tradition.

The Coffin assessment, however, is a good deal more than a ballad list. *The British Traditional Ballad in North America* is a virtually complete bibliography of American scholarship devoted to individual Child ballads. More than a mere summary or even evaluation of study, it contributes its own analysis of the story types of each ballad. This approach, along with Coffin's essays on variation and borrowing, will be evaluated later. The present concern is the value of the work as a convenient locator of texts, a handbook of scholarship, and a guide for future study.

The limitations of Coffin's book are for the most part consistent and valid. As a guide to published texts it is almost completely adequate. Other volumes are needed to chart the Archive of American Folksong and private collections (though the completion of Cray's finding list would do the job). Coffin's limitation of his work to American tradition might have been extremely misleading had he not checked his story types with Child's English and Scottish versions; even so, comparison with texts collected from later British (including Irish) tradition may reveal that certain story types did not "happen in America." Coffin's limitations are natural in reflecting the very scholarship he is summarizing. One in particular reflects a defect in American scholarship: the almost total disregard of ballad music. Not that one could expect Coffin to index tunes or even to discuss them seriously within his imposed limits. Tunes must eventually have their own index; and certainly Samuel P. Bayard is correct in pointing out that folk tunes can and must first be studied exclusive of their texts.[13] But Coffin's index should have indicated at least which texts are accompanied by a record of their music. Precisely because subsequent study of Child texts will have to begin with this summary, it should have insisted on the value of the tune as a part of the ballad record.

As a summary of historical-comparative study of ballad texts, *The British Traditional Ballad in North America* breaks no new trails in classification and arrangement of ballads. But even if there is in one sense no such thing as a "Child ballad," a summary and index to the collections and scholarship associated with ballads so labeled is useful and necessary. But it is disconcerting to note that the Child pattern is still casting its shadow over all ballad scholarship.

The influence is, of course, inescapable. As long as the Child ballads are set apart, classification and arrangement of other ballads will perforce follow the Child-and-other pattern. Therefore many of the difficulties in Laws' *Native American Balladry* and *American Balladry from British Broadsides* result from their limitation of "other" ballads and the separation in terms of geographical origin, which lead to problems in the placement of adapted and recomposed ballads. Like Coffin's, Laws' work has gone beyond the construction of syllabi and bibliographies. In fact, the classified and annotated listings are appendices to chapters surveying problems and summarizing knowledge. In so far as the appendices merely represent illustrations of ballads in the two fields, which are justifiable areas of investigation, the lists present few problems. And at least in *Native American Balladry* Laws seems to take such a view, since he offers this list "somewhat apologetically," admits that it will "undoubtedly . . . have to be expanded," and recognizes other "perfectly legitimate ideas concerning what should be included"

(p. 11). Unfortunately, because of the labor involved in such studies, even arbitrary limitations tend to become standards. A student in a college ballad class recently asked if Laws were the "American Child." John Greenway's characterization of Laws as "the most carefully restrictive classifier since Child" [14] helps to complete the picture. The temper of American scholars will certainly not permit a closed canon, but Branford P. Millar's hope that Laws will "occasionally review the possibilities of additions to his canon and revisions of it *according to his system of classification*" [15] indicates a danger. Addition "according to his system" may be a bit difficult. And we now face three canons based on confusion of origin, style, and subject matter.

Laws' first problem naturally involves the definition of *ballad*, to which he devotes an entire chapter of *Native American Balladry*. He had to face the issue not so much because of restrictive use of the term by collectors, but because critics had not provided a suitable definition of the collected material. Entwistle's "any short traditional narrative poem sung, with or without accompaniment or dance, in assemblies of the people," Gerould's "a folk-song that tells a story," and Kittredge's "song that tells a story" are each qualified by a description that tends to exclude many of the songs which Laws chose to study. He might have insisted on a simple definition of *ballad* as a narrative folksong (as he claims to do on p. 10), but he adds his own restrictions in defining a ballad as a "narrative folksong which dramatizes a memorable event" (p. 2).

The additions that this definition makes to the narrative limitation serve two purposes. By omission they evade restrictions such as impersonality, incremental repetition, and other elements of style or structure. Otherwise Laws would have had no book. But his own restrictions enable him to draw a somewhat shadowy line between ballad and song. On the basis of his definition he sets up four rules of exclusion:

1. Songs weak or disunified in narrative action.
2. Folksongs and chanteys in which the lyric element is dominant.
3. Satirical and fanciful pieces having little basis in reality.

4. Melodramatic and sentimental pieces, usually of professional origin (p. 263).

The first two seem noncontroversial, for there is now general agreement on the narrative quality of the ballad. Application of the rules is, unfortunately, subjective. Few would care to argue that "Down in the Valley," excluded by rule 2, is a ballad. But it is not clear that "The Great *Titanic,*" also excluded, is weaker or more disunified in narrative action than the "The Bucking Broncho" or "The Boll Weevil." Rule 3 is itself subjective. "The Hell-Bound Train" is apparently less real to Laws than to its singers. And why cannot a ballad be fanciful? The recognition that most American ballads have a "basis in reality" is not the same thing as setting up a restrictive definition. Rule 4 can at least be applied more objectively. It is designed, of course, to exclude "The Little Rosewood Casket," "The Blind Child," "The Gypsy's Warning," and the like. The exclusion is no surprise, as these stepchildren often have to fight for their rights as folksongs, let alone ballads. But one suspects that their exclusion depends upon Laws' concept of a proper folk style:

> It seems wisest to reserve the designation folksong for those pieces which exhibit that forthright and unaffected style which is characteristic of unsophisticated people . . . it makes little difference whether this style was originally present in the composition or has come about as the result of folk variation (p. 9).

Otherwise a number of these sentimental songs meet every test.

Just how this restriction or any others involving the concept of a ballad are applied in *American Balladry from British Broadsides* is difficult to determine, because in this book Laws provides no list of "Ballads of Doubtful Currency in Tradition" or "Ballad-Like Pieces." One therefore is not sure of the reason a particular piece was excluded. It is difficult to find any significant difference between "Erin's Flowery Vale" (O 29) and "Betsy of Dramoor," [16] yet the latter is excluded. And one wonders how the lines of "Erin's Flowery Vale" "exhibit that forthright and unaffected style . . . characteristic of unsophisticated people."

One evening fair when Venus bright her radiant beams displayed
And Flora in her verdant gale those fragrant hills arrayed. . . .

There are many exclusions which do not seem to fall in the categories Laws sets up: "play party songs, nonsense songs, sea chanties, religious folksongs, temperance songs, sentimental parlor songs, and songs of various occupational groups, as well as a number of primarily lyrical folksongs." Laws is surely not confusing form and function by excluding as nursery songs the ancient and honorable "Frog's Courtship" and "The Fox"—especially since he admits "Father Grumble" (Q1). Because the songs have as much plotted action as a number of inclusions, one can only assume that the animal characters cause the ballads to be "fanciful pieces having little basis in reality."

Laws' treatment of the ballads which he does accept raises other problems, some due to the ramifications of the Child-and-other approach and some to the very chronology of the studies. *Native American Balladry* includes in its primary list ballads composed or "thoroughly reworked" in America, current in tradition since 1920 but not known to have been composed after 1930. *American Balladry from British Broadsides*, despite its title, covers ballads in the other-imported category—British ballads not included by Child but current in American tradition since about 1900. Within the two lists the ballads are arranged in lettered sections. Whatever the aptness of the sections and their contents for purposes of each study, their use as a permanent arrangement of ballads—or as a convenient tool for the archivist—is questionable.

For critical purposes, *classification* must be distinguished from *arrangement*. *Classification* means the placing of ballad texts with their relatives; *arrangement*, the ordering of these groups of texts. There are two fundamental relationships between ballad texts: narrative and textual. The time-honored principle of classification has been by origin and textual filiation. This is Laws' chief guide, for a classification based on narrative theme requires the destruction of the Child canon. But problems of arrangement and ballad adaptations cause some inconsistency in Laws' application of the principle. Consider first the divisions of his two lists:

Native American Balladry	*American Ballads from British Broadsides*
A. War Ballads	J. War Ballads
B. Ballads of Cowboys and Pioneers	
C. Ballads of Lumberjacks	
D. Ballads of Sailors	K. Ballads of Sailors and the Sea
E. Ballads about Criminals and Outlaws	L. Ballads of Crime and Criminals
F. Murder Ballads	
	M. Ballads of Family Opposition to Lovers
	N. Ballads of Lovers' Disguises and Tricks
	O. Ballads of Faithful Lovers
	P. Ballads of Unfaithful Lovers
G. Ballads of Tragedies and Disasters	
H. Ballads on Various Topics	Q. Humorous and Miscellaneous Ballads
I. Ballads of the Negro	

A number of points are obvious. Laws discovered that the divisions useful in the study of one group of ballads would not apply conveniently to the other group. Consequently the placement of a ballad depends upon the determination of its national origin. The divisions themselves are somewhat illogically based on subject matter or origin or both. In addition, decisions relative to reworking have further complicated the problem.

A few examples will illustrate the difficulties. An American criminal ballad such as "John Hardy" (I 2) or "Brady" (I 9) is omitted from Section E because of its presumably Negro origin.

But the Negro section seems largely based on style, for, in spite of its origin, "Casey Jones" (G 1) is omitted because some versions have been recomposed in a somewhat different style (or because the protagonist is white?). But on the basis of style, "Wild Bill Jones" (E 10) could be placed in the Negro section. Treatment of Anglo-American ballads is even more disturbing. Ballads like "A-Growing" (O 35) are included in Laws only because of the accident that they were not included by Child. And Laws clearly shows that "The Crafty Farmer" (Child 283), "The Yorkshire Bite" (L 1), and "The Highwayman Outwitted" (L 2) belong together, whether in or out of Child's canon.

American ballads on the murdered girl theme, such as "Poor Omie" (F 4), are "Murder Ballads"; but parallel ballads of British origin, such as "The Cruel Ship's Carpenter" (P 36), are "Ballads of Unfaithful Lovers." If "The Miner's Doom" (Q 36) and "The High Blantyre Explosion" (Q 35) had been of American origin, they would have been "Ballads of Tragedies and Disasters." The Anglo-Irish street ballad of "The Unfortunate Rake" gains entry as "The Bad Girl's Lament" (Q 26), which seems to include the derivatives "St. James Infirmary Blues" and "Gambler's Blues." But "The Cowboy's Lament" (B 1) gets separate treatment. How one should handle such a derivative as "Jack Combs" [17] is impossible to determine; but reworking causes "The Buffalo Skinners" (B 10) to be separated from its parent "Canaday-I-O" (C 17). The problem is not so much the subjectivity of the decisions, but the principle that makes such decisions necessary. For the crux of the matter lies in Laws' acceptance of the Child-and-other organization and his understanding of what constitutes a ballad for purposes of classification.

Laws is concerned mainly with textual identification and with the final product. As he writes in *American Balladry from British Broadsides,* two texts belong to the same ballad when they *"not only tell the same story, but tell it in the same stanzaic pattern with essentially the same phraseology"* (p. 102). Even an admitted recomposition, if "the new author has changed the stanzaic pattern or major details of the plot" should be separately classified. Laws thus rejects completely the concept of the secondary ballad in so far as it bears upon ballad classification, quite possibly because of his belief that recompositions and derivative ballads stem from activities not a part of folk tradition. In fact, by his standards, Child's A and B texts of "Lady Isabel and the Elf Knight" must be treated as separate ballads.[18] For these reasons Laws treats "The Old Woman of Slapsadam" and "Johnny Sands" as different ballads. Even in examples less extreme, his classifications separate instead of unify, confuse instead of clarify. His system makes additions to his canons difficult because a ballad must be added at the end of a section and therefore seldom with a ballad of similar theme.

Perhaps a system cannot be developed that will logically classify and arrange ballads to indicate all their relationships. But the possible improvements offered by a narrative-types index seem to have received little consideration apart from Barry's suggestion in 1913 [19] that ballads be classified by their narrative themes. Child's own difficulty in separating ballads should have provided food for thought. Independent studies have pointed out the relationships between ballads and the difficulty of separation. Walter R. Nelles in 1909 [20] suggested a clear connection between "Hind Horn" and "The Kitchie Boy" without indicating that the filiation bore on ballad classification. The investigations of Barbara M. Cra'ster and Samuel P. Bayard have demonstrated that "Lady Alice" and "Clerk Colvill" were once textually the same ballad.[21] Even though American interest in the secondary ballad strained the bonds of textual filiation, there was little disposition to follow Barry's suggestion that there was another way to classify ballads. Recently Anne G. Gilchrist and Ruth Harvey [22] have studied ballad themes in a way that suggests the need and value of a different type of classification.

Such a classification would pose and answer differently the question: what is a ballad? It would place under a single head those traditional songs which converge in telling a single narrative but differentiate between forms of that narrative. The style and form in which a theme is presented and the national origin of the text would not obscure the narrative itself. One ballad age may prefer the confession style, another the impersonal. The fact that the forms arose at different times, in different places, and even independently [23] at the hands of Grub Street hacks is no barrier to a thematic classification. The approach can be justified on the ground that *a* ballad is an idea, of which the various textual forms are manifestations with varying relations to each other. But no such Platonic concept is necessary for the recognition of a convenient method.

An extremely simple and simplified entry in such a system might be arranged something like this:

No. 28.   Lover stolen from family in a skirmish
   28.1   "Earl Brand" (Child 7)
   28.2   "Erlinton" (Child 8)
   28.3   "The Lady and the Dragoon" (including Laws M 27)
   28.4   "New River Shore" (Laws M 26)
   28.5   "The Constant Wife"
   28.5.1 "Locks and Bolts" (Laws M 13)

In such an entry additions of other forms can easily be made and any amount of subdivision is possible. Rather than ignoring textual forms of a theme, this type of classification emphasizes them while relating items in which textual crossing might be expected. Of course, it does not indicate all possible textual relationships. Texts split as well as coalesce, and crossings and recompositions are not limited to ballads of similar theme. But an orderly arrangement of such classifications should provide a more convenient organization for published and unpublished texts, regardless of origin, style, or incidence.

It would seem that the valuable and much-needed syllabi of Coffin and Laws are in some senses premature. But they have been extremely helpful in dramatizing problems. The ideal syllabus—if such a thing is possible—which will arrange materials for study, provide classification, standard titles, etc., cannot come immediately. Local or regional syllabi might be helpful and productive of tentative titles, classifications, and arrangements. Such reports could tap more unpublished sources, procure local support, and experiment with classification and arrangement. That such syllabi should include more than the narrative folksong goes without saying. A brief look at the few attempts which have already been made will illustrate some of the problems.

Most indices of song types, unpublished materials, or regional collections have been little more than alphabetical title lists, useful as these may be. And there have been too few of them. The *Check-List of Recorded Songs in the English Language in the Archive of American Folk Song to July, 1940* (1942) is but a mimeographed alphabetical list with a geographical index to the 10,000 songs then on deposit. E. C. Kirkland's "A Check List of the Titles of Tennessee Folksongs" [24] is another illustration of the alphabetical approach which, helpful as it is, gives too little aid in song identification. Though there are other listings,[25] only Arthur Kyle Davis has made a serious attempt at classification and organization of an unpublished regional collection. *Folksongs of Virginia: A Descriptive Index and Classification* (1949) goes far in identifying texts but is based on orthodox academic lines and offers no new insights.

Little attention has been paid to the classification of songs other than ballads, and there are only a few works like Althea Lea McLenden's "A Finding List of Play-Party Games." [26] Possibly because of lack of study, as well as inherent difficulty, little attention has been devoted to the organization of the folk-lyric, beyond the suggestive remarks of Belden.[27]

Moving beyond the assessment and organization of primary collections, there is need of indices to ballad prints and broadsides. Most of the bibliographical reports are preliminary and more pertinent to the important study of the broadside ballad itself than to the broadside-folk relationship.[28] A classified index to traditional materials or analogues in broadsides and songsters seems not to be projected, though the *Check List of California Songs* (1940) includes such material and Cray plans to include a large number of songsters in the bibliography of his finding list. The modern broadside—largely represented by phonograph recordings of the hillbilly and race type and by the song folios distributed by performers, radio stations, and somewhat specialized music-publishing houses —is only now being recognized. Discographies devoted to issues of particular performers or recording companies have appeared in specialized collectors' magazines, but little has been done in the way of indexing traditional materials. In 1940 Alan Lomax made a brief sampling of the material,[29] and Ben Gray Lumpkin's *Folksongs on Records* (1950) includes a very small amount of such material. D. K. Wilgus has promised bibliodiscographies of a number of native American ballads in hillbilly tradition, and a few students have become interested in compiling more complete discographies of traditional material.

Ballad Anatomy

Nothing demonstrates so clearly the primary position of collection in the twentieth century as the paucity of analytical studies of the Child ballads. The years following the appearance of such a "definitive" collection should have been marked by tabulation and classification of ballad elements. To be sure, such study did occur, but usually as a part of the communal-individual controversy, the other drain on scholarly energy. For information on ballad devices, style, and themes, we look to summary or argumentative work of such scholars as Louise Pound and Gordon Hall Gerould—if not to the scattered remarks of collectors and to esthetic evaluations of literary critics [30]—rather than to austere articles or monographs. Whatever the values of creative and integrated study, we miss the purer source and find its absence symptomatic. For collecting activities at the height of the Ballad War not only drained off activity that might otherwise have been spent in pure scholarship, but questioned the reliability of the canon and advanced new candidates for inclusion. Whatever the canon ballads are called—Child, ancient, medieval, traditional; however we question their exclusive right to the name *ballad*, their right to be separated from other types—their study has been so central and, in a sense, separate, that it must be considered first.

Child's "kind of instinct" for "the genuine ballad tone" [31] provided, without explanation, a corpus immediately claimed as a definition of balladry. Had the matter not been complicated by the Ballad War and the collection of other narratives, the Child ballads might have been characterized with less difficulty. Even so, Child's apparent combination of "scientific" and stylistic tests would have troubled students. His attempt at completeness seems to have dictated the inclusion of pieces lacking the "ballad note," and, as Laws has suggested, a few pieces may have been included merely as examples of a type not meriting full consideration.[32] Still, certain pieces might have been excluded if all the facts had been at his disposal. Considering the range of the ballads included and also the large number of traditional narratives omitted, the canon has preserved its unity surprisingly well.

Because of tendencies already examined, there have been few attempts to strip the canon of individual items, and these few have mainly attacked the popularity of certain pieces, such as "Musselburgh Field," [33] asserted anew the charge that Scott is responsible for the whole of "Kinmont Willie," [34] or questioned the propriety of admitting ecclesiastical pieces like "Judas" and "St. Stephen and Herod." [35] (Revaluations of individual versions have been made, but they do not question the canon itself or even its principles.) Although most attempts to expand the canon have been based on subsequent collection, Louise Pound suggested, however seriously, that certain early ecclesiastic pieces might be classed as ballads.[36] Miss Pound was engaged in special pleading for a theory of clerical origins, but her plea has gained independent support. Subsequent collection, however, seems chiefly responsible for the claims made for "The Bitter Withy," "Corpus Christi," "The

Seven Virgins," and "The Bold Fisherman." [37] That on the basis of subsequent evidence Child would have made space for these carols is moot, but it is significant that most of the other suggested additions, such as "Six Dukes Went A-Fishing" and "Still Growing" involve either new discoveries or new and "better" versions. "Molly Bawn" and "The Lake of Cool Finn" pass Child's test of folklore background; whether their predominantly Irish background would have affected Child's judgment is not to be determined.

Critics who pressed the claims of certain songs have had, therefore, a perception, however rationalized, of the "peculiar ballad note" in narrative folksong. We are reminded of Sharp's "We know a folk-tune when we hear it—or we don't," and of W. P. Ker's "Platonic idea" of ballad form. Obviously such a conception failed to satisfy the "scientific" critic who demanded a clear definition, particularly in view of the canonizing tendency of Child's followers. Nor did it satisfy the followers, who needed to explain to themselves why scholars in various countries "somehow always recognize that they are dealing with the same thing." [38] Even one who considers the ballad "an artistic form, not a scientific category," [39] must needs at least describe the form in the face of critics who find the "mass of materials so nearly indefinable." [40]

The outlines of ballad form in Child's volumes might have been more readily perceived, but critics were too busy emphasizing one aspect or another, tracing the alleged origin of characteristics, or relating them to other genres, to place them in perspective. Gummere, in spite of his perception of much that is fundamental in the ballad genre, failed to distinguish what is distinctive of the ballad from what is characteristic of it. Therefore, studies of various ballad elements during the first third of the twentieth century were, when not special pleading, often tangential, enriching our knowledge without always deepening it. At least partially as a result of that enrichment, Gerould's summary and clarification of ballad outlines avoided the narrow view even though remaining in the vicinity of the popular ballad. It is necessary, then, to return to

The Ballad of Tradition (1932) to review the conception which has become standard for the ballads with which it deals.

Gerould's greatest contribution is his recognition that the sole distinguishing feature of the traditional ballad is its narrative method, the threefold technique of "compressed and centralized episode . . . dramatic presentation of action . . . and . . . impersonality of approach" (pp. 10–11). (Perhaps we need not point out that even this description is strained when applied to certain of the minstrel items in the canon.) By keeping his conception of the narrative method clear of any theory of development and separated from elements of form or rhetoric shared with other types of folksong, he manages to account for the "ballad note" in productions as distinct as "Riddles Wisely Expounded," "Robin Hood and Guy of Gisborne," and "Katherine Jaffray." The fact that his judgment is based on international evidence strengthens his defense of the ballad as genre, as does even his admission that any canon is arbitrary and that the ballad "borderline . . . is a wavering one" (p. 30). Gerould's emphasis on narrative method as ballad criterion has been observed tacitly or expressly in later criticism, particularly in the two recent handbooks, Evelyn K. Wells's *The Ballad Tree* (1950) and M. J. C. Hodgart's *The Ballads* (1950). In his survey of *European Balladry* (1939), William J. Entwistle assuredly confirms Gerould's careful limitations; and even E. K. Chambers, who finds so much to disagree with in ballad investigation, quotes Gerould approvingly in *English Literature at the Close of the Middle Ages* (1945).

Gerould's reduction of Gummere's test elements—incremental repetition, refrains, and commonplaces—to characteristics has also been accepted by later critics. His treatment of incremental repetition and other types of "parallelism in phrase and idea" as part of that ballad rhetoric which included ellipsis, hyperbole, and commonplace, cleared the air for the perceptive appreciations of Hodgart and Miss Wells. Similarly Gerould's treatment of the refrain as a highly variable element in ballad structure marked the end of acrimonious argument. The refrain is considered with the ballad stanza and meter, elements even less fundamental to the ballad genre, and Gerould's contribution to their study will be shown later. The point here is that he separated these formal elements from the definition of the genre itself.

Gerould, then, delineated the ballad genre so that meaningful studies of ballad elements could be made. One of his greatest contributions is his emphasis on the music of the ballads. He not only defined the ballad as a type of folksong but related the narrative form to the influence of the melody which accompanies it. And his relation of the music to the stanza, meter, and formulas of the ballads, though he was not the first to point it out, also made way for profitable study.

THE CHILD BALLAD:
THEMATIC ELEMENTS

Study devoted to the themes of the ballads in Child's corpus has had a number of shortcomings. When the commentators have not, for the purpose of attacking the canon, merely stressed the lack of homogeneity, they either have devised categories to fit their theories of origin or have become mired in a mass of detail. Some critics, by emphasizing a single type of theme have thus sought to justify a theory of origins. Gummere devised six classifications to illustrate roughly a progress from the interests of a local clan to epic considerations. Courthope, Henderson, and Millar emphasized thematic parallels with medieval romance. Miss Pound stressed the themes of upper-class life, but singled out the few religious ballads to develop her own theory of origins. Gerould's survey, emphasizing the adventure ballads, is more balanced, but by failing to distinguish between motives and broad thematic patterns he loses himself and the reader in details of ballad story. Perhaps nothing so well illustrates the preoccupation of critics with their special concepts of the ballad as their failure to take up Gummere's challenge: "Count all the ballads and tragedy is well to the fore." [41] Almost half a century passed before Warren E. Roberts did count them to discover the preponderance of comic elements.[42]

Classification of ballad themes took a turn for the better with Entwistle's simple division, in *European Balladry*, of all European ballad themes into three types: (1) historical themes; (2) those dependent upon previous oral or written literary tradition; and (3) adventure themes (pp. 56ff.). There is oversimplification here as well as overlapping, but the divisions are helpful. In *The Ballads*, Hodgart has made a more detailed division of the Child canon:

1. Ballads belonging to the common stock of international folksong:
     (a) Ballads of magic
     (b) Romantic and tragic ballads
2. Ballads from the repertoire of late medieval minstrelsy
3. Ballads of yeoman minstrelsy
4. Historical ballads:
     (a) Fully historical, dealing with real national events
     (b) Semihistorical, dealing more vaguely with minor and local events
5. Comic songs (p. 14)

That these classifications "approximate to Child's divisions" can be accepted only with a considerable stretching of the meaning of *approximate*, as Hodgart's own discussion shows. But they cause one to speculate that instead of Child following Grundtvig's metrical divisions "with some modifications," [43] Grundtvig's suggestion modified Child's plan. Whatever their relation to the problem faced by "the master" in organizing his material, Hodgart's divisions are a convenient guide to the corpus and the most accurate yet established. Like all proposed classifications, the divisions confuse pure subject matter with origin, but less so than most.

Studies of thematic elements in the ballads, as opposed to ballad themes, have been few. Excepting for that provided in general handbooks, the analytical approach has been largely the province of Lowry C. Wimberly. His *Minstrelsy, Music, and the Dance in the English and Scottish Popular Ballads* (1921) does indicate the separation of dance and song, in so far as the ballads indicate the life of their period, but Wimberly does not always take into account the force of the ballad commonplace. *Death and Burial Lore in the English and Scottish Popular Ballads* (1927) provides a somewhat more meaningful catalogue, but Wimberly's *Folklore in the English and Scottish Ballads* (1928) yields valuable results and is the basis of all subsequent treatments of the subject.

The term *folklore* in Wimberly's sense (i.e., religio-magical custom and belief) had drawn a good deal of comment from previous ballad critics. Although in disagreement as to its relation to the problem of ballad origins, writers had stressed the appearance and importance of the primitive substance. Wimberly makes clear his position—in opposition to that of Henderson and G. Gregory Smith—that the lore of ballads is more popular than literary, that it mirrors the beliefs and customs of the people rather than preserves the incidents of older literary romance; nevertheless, he sets out not "to show how the remains of paganism came to be recorded in balladry, but to show simply that such remains are there recorded" (p. 10), not to prove the age of ballads, but to demonstrate the age of the beliefs therein. He thus escapes Alexander Haggerty Krappe's later criticism that on the evidence of survivals the ballad might have originated in the twentieth century.[44]

Almost every editor and critic had contributed something to the recognition and study of ballad folklore, and a part of Wimberly's task was to assemble and organize these scattered comments, not the least valuable of which are Child's own. The clear exposition of these latter alone is a valuable study. Organizing his discussion in "The Pagan Otherworld," "Pagan Otherworld Beings," "The Otherworld Spell," and "The Christian Otherworld," Wimberly contributes a good deal of study and interpretation without advancing any single solution to such vexing problems as the origin of the fairy faith. In fact, one of the values of his comprehensive survey is the clear demonstration of the complex and contradictory nature of the evidence and of the various levels of culture represented. On the other hand, the study solidly supports conclusions such as the nonmetaphorical character of ballad poetry and the almost completely pagan nature of the ballads. While primarily a tool which, if we include notes on oaths, formulas, and the like, refers to rather more than half the ballads, the book establishes beyond question its few theses.

Study of these elements has continued. Excepting Anne G. Gilchrist's notes on herb refrains,[45] Scott Elliott's study of "Pulling the Heather Green," [46] and, of course, the chapters in the handbooks of Gerould, Hodgart, and Miss Wells, comments have arisen in connection with newly discovered texts or studies of individual ballads. Much of value, such as the revelation that "The Grey Cock" is a revenant ballad instead of an *aube*,[47] has been accomplished in this manner, but cannot be considered purely analytical study. We might, however, call attention to the tendency of a few critics to treat folklore or similar imagery in the ballads as symbolic, religious, social, or Freudian-Jungian (see p. 322).

Too often discussions of thematic elements treat only a self-contained "ballad world" [48] or make Frazerlike references to customs and beliefs of other times and cultures. It is consequently refreshing to find in William E. Sellers' recent studies of kinship in the ballads [49] a careful concern with the social background of the period, wide as it is, in which the ballads can have originated. Sellers shows that the postulation of a totemic clan or a matrilineal society as a background for the ballads is untenable. He finds only the nuclear family and the remnants of feudalism, modified in terms of the environment of English and Scottish ballad singers. He makes room for folklore motifs not as evolutionary survivals, but as mergers with the realism of the ballad-makers.

Studies of thematic elements have, then, turned generally from concern with vaguely popular or primitive elements to a consideration of the available record. Thus William Powell Jones, though supporting in *The Pastourelle* (1931) a popular origin for the type, finds in "The Baffled Knight" and other British examples indications of descent from courtly forms.

THE CHILD BALLAD:
FORMULAIC ELEMENTS

Continual recognition of the "primitive poetic formulae" [50] of the ballads produced at first no special study because of the emphasis on *primitive*. Otherwise the appearance of Child's volumes might have occasioned much analysis. Surprising, however, is the continuing lack of comprehensive study. Much exists by way of generalization or casual comment, yet only color, proverbs, and place names seem to have been studied extensively. [51]

A portion of the neglect may be due to the lack of full recognition of the extent and nature of the ballad formula, the traditional commonplace. Gerould seems to have some conception of the problem in treating the phrasal commonplace as "another illustration of the conventional rhetoric which permeates all the ballads"; [52] and Entwistle appears to have come even closer with the statement that while "ballad language is formula," "the form is singularly free." [53] The ballad commonplace involves more than the phrasal clichés of "red gold" and "tirling the pin," more than the use of identical stanzas to command horses; it involves, potentially at least, all material common to more than one ballad.

A necessary and important technique of ballad study, the search for or reconstruction of the ur-form, has therefore mitigated against the full recognition and study of the ballad commonplace. The tendency (Child furnishes a precedent) to parcel out pieces of one ballad to another continues. Coffin recognizes that the "shoe your foot" stanzas may not be necessarily a part of "The Lass of Roch Royal"; nevertheless, in his valuable "Index to Borrowing in the Traditional Ballads of America," he treats the exchanges as corruptions. [54] May it not be possible that instead of "The Twa Brothers" being corrupted by "Edward," the entire "Edward" ballad was or became a commonplace appropriate to stories of fratricide and/or incest? To entertain such a possibility does not necessarily conflict with Antti Aarne's judgment that we "must not imagine incidents and episodes floating about in a vacuum awaiting a chance to attach themselves to a story": a statement which Taylor has capably defended.[55] Every cliché must, in the long run, have originated somewhere. The exchange of material among ballads seems one of the aspects of the growth of a ballad style, and it must be investigated in more than one way.

Whiting's report of the paucity of proverbs in the ballads [56] furnishes food for thought in this connection. Whiting concludes that the folk avoid proverbs in their ballads because the sententious elements interfere with the narrative and because the folk separate their poetry from their ordinary lives. Granting that, though independent support could be cited, these conclusions are still open to question, they do suggest the development of style *within* the ballads. Studies of commonplaces in terms of both variation and stylization are obviously needed. The ballad refrain needs study, too, both as a commonplace and as a stanzaic element. The commonplaces must be studied not in "zebra-counting" dissertations like that of Meta C. Borregaard,[57] but with the perceptive scholarship Milman Parry [58] and others have devoted to epic songs.

THE CHILD BALLAD:
STANZAIC AND METRICAL ELEMENTS

A detailed account of contributions to our understanding of the ballad stanza and meters should at the same time be a record of the study of ballad music. The puzzling problems of stanzaic form became understandable if not completely soluble only when the music and its relation to the text was considered. In Chapter 7 of *English Folk-Song: Some Conclusions*, Cecil Sharp called attention to the relationship while Phillips Barry was beginning his war for the rights of ballad music, dropping incisive comments in various articles and notes. When Gerould wrote his summary of 1932, the problems were in focus.

Gerould recognizes that ballad meters are not, as Gummere had said, "almost uniform," [59] but diverse. He indicates a number of forms without connecting them precisely with musical form. But his argument for the couplet as the standard ballad stanza, though erroneous, is based on the music.[60] Further, he explains the peculiar alternation of primary and secondary stresses in ballad verse by reference to the rhythm of the tunes. His discussion of the refrain is based to an extent on the facts of contemporary ballad singing, but hardly takes the tunes into account. Of more importance is Gerould's stimulation of J. W. Hendren's analysis, *A Study of Ballad Rhythm with Special Reference to Ballad Music* (1936).

When Hendren embarked on this study he had the evidence of the traditional tunes collected in Great Britain and the United States and the background researches of Sharp and Barry, particularly the latter's "The Music of the Ballads" in *British Ballads from Maine*. Hendren completely justifies Barry's insistence on the union of words and music, fully establishing the interdependence of the two halves of folksong. (He uses a little non-Child material in his analysis.) Though Hendren failed to perceive fundamental tune relationships, his work has a value beyond its immediate conclusions, as a reservoir for future study. A detailed account of his conclusions is beyond the scope of this discussion, but certain major points must be noted, concerning stanza, refrain, and stress.

Hendren relates the stanza form (he finds eleven types plus combinations thereof) to the phrasal pattern of ballad melody, giving the latter precedence in the evolution of the former: language, continuous by nature, was adapted to melody, not by nature continuous. He finds the common-meter ballad stanza usually rightly printed as a quatrain; this agrees with the division of the normal ballad tune into short phrases. Refrain, whether alternating or end, he finds a component part of the stanza, and, like the stanza, accounted for in terms of the tune.

His comments on stress involve at least two important matters: alternation of strong and weak stresses and wrenched accent. George R. Stewart, Jr., had noted the strong-weak alternation in 1925,[61] applying a complex dipodic analysis but connecting the phenomenon with music. Gerould also pointed out the alternation of stress and related it to the ballad tune. Hendren treats the alternation as at least analogous to compound time in ballad melody. But because simple time is not uncommon in melody, though unknown to ballad verse, he attaches more importance to the nature of the metrical language. Since we do not know the nature of the tunes with which the ballad stanza originally arose, no other conclusion seems possible. His treatment of wrenched accent is more sure. He lays the ghosts of pitch accent and retention of Norman pronunciation,[62] maintaining that accentuation at variance with the natural stresses of language is a "natural and inevitable consequence of the development of verses in musical form by generations of people who had never heard of wrenched accent . . . and who had no reason in the world to guard against it" (p. 142).

As more study is devoted to ballad music, more will be learned about the ballad stanza. Bertrand Bronson's complete study of the Child ballad tunes is revealing much about the Child texts. Bronson has shown, for example, that short couplet ballads like "Gil Brenton" must have had a refrain, but not long couplet ballads like "Bonnie Annie." Had Child considered ballad music, and therefore paid more attention to refrains, he might have altered his arrangement. Bronson further points out that a shift in the formal type of refrain implies not an evolution, but a sudden, conscious shift in the tradition of a ballad.[63]

THE NON-CHILD BALLAD: ANALYSIS

Little analytical study has been given to ballads not closely related to those in the Child volumes, and that little by American scholars. The neglect is understandable. Although some have attempted to deny the term *ballad* to narrative songs not resembling those in the canon, the majority of critics have, in practice, admitted that there is more than one type of ballad. The other narratives were of interest to collectors and to critics manning particular positions in the Ballad War, but they held little interest to the analyst. In the first place, there was no canon, no recognized body with which to deal. The material was not quite respectable and had little literary attraction. It was the *vulgar ballad*.

As Gummere wrote in *The Beginnings of Poetry*, the "terminology of the whole subject is notoriously bad" (p. 175*n*). Child's reference in Johnson's *Universal Cyclopædia* to "the vulgar ballads of our day" was unfortunate; for the unpleasant connotation has mitigated against the general use of the term *vulgar*, and no better term has been devised. *Broadside* will not do; meaning a type of circulation, it applies to some ballads in the Child collection, but not to all vulgar ballads. Those who, like Coffin, restrict the term *traditional* to material in the canon, would call other narrative folksongs *nontraditional*. This term seems less fortunate than *vulgar*. And to refer to non-Child narratives as "later balladry" may not be necessarily accurate. The critic must distinguish as best he can without making matters worse.

The only fruitful applications of the word *vulgar* have been made by Belden and Barry. Belden pointed out [64] that the vulgar ballad uses verse forms rarely found in Child's volumes; makes little use of the refrain, formulas of question and answer, series, incremental repetition, and familiar ballad commonplaces; contains no gaps in the action, each step being duly related in the chronological order and the sequence of events duly explained. Barry avoided a mass of detail in a brief description which serves to distinguish the material from most Child ballads while offering hints for future study. The adjective *vulgar*, he writes, signifies "a kind of ballad showing something of the technique of the short story—a complex plot, suitable for a 'three-decker novel,' reduced to the compass of a few stanzas." [65] Though comments bearing on the characteristics of non-Child narratives are scattered through the writings of Barry and other American critics, and though the British black-letter ballad as a journalistic form has been capably outlined by Hyder Edward Rollins,[66] for extended treatment of these traditional narratives we must turn to the two volumes of Malcolm Laws.

Some of the defects of Laws' studies considered as indices emerge as virtues when the books are considered as surveys of ballad types. Matters of form, style, origin, incidence, and method of diffusion, which must not confuse the indexer, are his legitimate concerns in the extensive but careful coverage of the non-Child ballad in America. It is well to remember that *American Balladry from British Broadsides* and *Native American Balladry* overlap to some extent, not only because they are concerned with the same national tradition, but because "ballads of much the same type have been produced by English-speaking people on both sides of the Atlantic." [67] On the other hand, neither volume is limited to ballads in a single, easily recognizable style. In spite of his canon building, Laws accepts the well-established conclusion of Thelma G. James that in a literal sense, "a 'Child ballad' means little more than one collected and approved by Professor Child." [68] But admitting that "one type merges with the other, and on the basis of style alone, ballads in the middle position could be placed in either category," he is still able to make "a distinction between the two classes of balladry." [69]

Laws is perhaps too insistent in treating all English traditional non-Child ballads as broadsides. The problem is largely terminological, because he readily concedes that all the ballads did not take their rise from broadsheets. But it is a pity that the term *broadside* could not be reserved for a method of distribution. A comparison of the broadside types with Child ballads and of the native American ballads with both is necessary and inevitable. Fortunately, Laws' approach is sympathetic enough to avoid the unnecessarily disparaging remarks which have marked many considerations of the non-Child ballads, while at the same time objective enough to refrain from overextravagant praise, particularly of American ballads. And he never forgets that the singers themselves are the final arbiters.

In treating ballad themes, Laws emphasizes, perhaps justifiably, the difference between Child ballads and other types. He recognizes that "human passions remained the same" and that "war and lesser human conflicts, crime and punishment, violence and death, love and sex, humor and trickery, hatred and revenge, dangerous adventures and calamities" are universals; but he concentrates on the "different world" of the later ballads and the different treatment of themes. In commenting on the replacement of nobles by characters of lesser rank, the conventionalization of romantic love, the disappearance or weakening of the supernatural, the "trivialization" of the events, he is careful to point out that this is a *decline* to the sophisticated rather than to the contemporary folk, who "respond to the familiar and . . . are little concerned with aesthetic appeals or with the sophisticated cult of romanticism." [70] Even a glance at the categories into which he divides the ballads in his two studies (see p. 254) indicates the general thematic resemblances between the other imported and native American ballads. Differences are more apparent than real. Ballads of disasters and local conditions are present in British balladry, but do not transplant well. The British murder ballads are prevalent enough, but their imported examples are scattered in other categories. The most important differences in the popular themes of the two ballad groups are shown in the larger amount of romantic tales in Laws M-P groups of British ballads. Laws supplies two reasons: (1) the popularity of the themes in imported balladry preempted the field and additions were unnecessary; (2) American ballad makers usually deal realistically with factual situations, whereas the writers of British broadsides were more often spinning "fanciful yarns for money." [71] A third point might be added: the native American fanciful yarns are what he calls "melodramatic and sentimental pieces, usually of professional origin," [72] and are therefore excluded from Laws' consideration.

In the treatment of themes, Laws can point out significant differences between the Child ballads and most of the other ballads. He finds typical of British broadsides and of native American white balladry in general a sensational, sentimental, and moralized treatment of events; and especially characteristic of American balladry and American versions of British broadsides is a "watered-down sensationalism" marked by "sincere tenderness" and high moral tone.[73] The Negro balladry, of course, constitutes a special case in that, no less sensational, its themes are largely restricted to crime and sex and lack sentimentality and moralization. Laws' conclusions as to the extent of sexual restriction and tabu in American balladry are certainly valid generalizations, but his comments are apparently limited by material available to him. Even in published versions of Negro ballads, tabus seem to be operating. Ballads in general American tradition *do* mince words. But many ballads "created for male audiences" do not get printed unless they are expurgated. Laws gives no evidence of having seen an unexpurgated version of "The Bucking Broncho," and he fails to mention such classics as "The Red Light Saloon" and "Christopher Columbo." But the fact that these ballads are so difficult to procure may strengthen his conclusions about the public tradition.

Although Laws generally agrees with Albert B. Friedman that "as poetry, the broadsides . . . are trash," [74] that fact does not prevent his making a rather full summary of their techniques, including versification. He demonstrates a surprising variety of stanzaic forms within the usual limits of three- or four-stress iambic or anapestic lines. American ballads he finds similar but cruder and, except for a few professional pieces, more limited within the same range. The metrics of ballads should be closely related to associated tunes, as Laws himself realizes. Though one cannot question the value of his discussion of "broadside texts as metrical poems," his justification that "the original broadsides were composed as verses to be printed usually without any indication of a tune" [75] is somewhat questionable, involving as it does a supposition about the writers or revisers of ballads for the broadside press. And Laws uses the word *broadside* to refer to all Anglo-American ballads outside Child's volumes, many of which were composed *to* tunes.

Laws gives most attention to the style and techniques of the broadside type which we have referred to as the *vulgar ballad*. He recognizes other styles in the British material—a folk style akin to that of the better Child pieces, a music-hall style showing "smooth professional competence," and an artistic handling suggesting the work of minor poets in the Scots vernacular tradition. And he finds more in native American balladry than the "hallmarks of street ballads." But he provides a competent analysis of broadside style, including the types of incipits: come all ye, identification of character and time, first-person observer, and confession—which are further classified as summary or merely enticing. He follows Gummere in associating the incipits with only the minstrel ballads of the Child collection but wisely adds that the other ballads may have lost introductory exposition. And it is, of course, exposition that Laws finds typical of the narrative method, the equal emphasis on all parts of the story, the insertion of personal comment, and the moralistic close. American balladry he judges to be a bit cruder but more factually detailed and more moving. Although he refrains from discovering clichés and commonplaces in native American ballads, he does refer to a number in the British ballads, noting their lack of emotional impact as compared with those of older balladry. As some of the broadside clichés and others are also found in native American ballads, it is hoped that further study will be initiated. In fact, the virtue of Laws' analyses, which include other matters as well, is that they should stimulate more intensive and detailed work.

Another style which Laws fortunately emphasizes is that of Negro balladry. The Negro ballad differs sufficiently from the journalistic ballads common in later British and American tradition to warrant the special treatment which Laws gives it in a chapter of *Native American Balladry*. Whatever the influence of white folksong, the Negro has created a style of his own, at once less cohesive and, though compounded of uncouth material and language, more poetic than most other ballads outside the Child canon. The loose, emotional, suggestive narratives, emphasizing character and situation, deserve further study.[76] At the same time, the relation between Negro and white songs, both in form and cliché, cannot be overlooked. Laws writes in *Native American Balladry*:

> White ballad singers characteristically reproduce ballads as they have learned them, even repeating words and phrases which time or misapprehension have rendered meaningless. Thus most native ballads

exist in a fairly definite form and are identifiable even as fragments by certain phrases or stanzas. The same is not true of Negro balladry. In fact Negro folksongs are full of stanzas or phrases which can be compared to the clichés of English traditional balladry (p. 91).

The form of some ballads apparently of white origin seem to have been influenced or dictated by Negro style, possibly through the intermediary of the tune or the banjo (which seems to have carried tune and style with it) or both. It is also possible that there is a common origin. As Laws certainly recognizes, the line between ballad and lyric is even more shadowy in Negro material than in white. A comparison of lyric songs in Southern white tradition with Negro ballads reveals likenesses in form and style. It may be that the Negro has taken material from white song and made a new thing of it. But we cannot be sure. We cannot always tell the provenance of entire songs, let alone commonplaces. Lines like "On Monday I was arrested" and "I'm a po' boy long way from home" occur in songs credited to both subcultures. In the narrative "Julia Waters" [77] appear three stanzas of "Ten Thousand Miles from Home" (Laws H 2) introduced by two stanzas of undoubted Negro origin. Obviously a study of narrative commonplaces will necessarily have to consider material in various types of songs.

Textual Variation

The importance of textual variation was clearly understood and clearly set forth by George Lyman Kittredge in 1904. His summary of the process of oral tradition is now classic:

> Old stanzas are dropped and new ones are added; rhymes are altered; the names of the characters are varied; portions of other ballads work their way in; the catastrophe may be transformed completely. . . . Taken collectively, these processes of oral tradition amount to a second act of composition, of an inextricably complicated character, in which many persons share (some consciously, others without knowing it). . . . It would be a great mistake to regard the results

of what we may call, for want of a better term, collective composition, as identical with the corruptions of scribes and editors in the case of a classical text.[78]

Later study has attempted to detail the process, explaining both how and why ballads change.

Both the Ballad War and the discovery of living folksong emphasized the importance of variation studies and contributed to them. The place of ballad variation in the dispute over ballad origins has already been examined. Although the argument stimulated the study of oral transmission, the intensity of the dispute hampered careful study. Further collecting, itself stimulated by the growing emphasis on variation, occupied the time of the relatively few ballad scholars. Consideration of ballad variation was therefore scattered or summary, most attention being devoted to alteration in words and phrases. Although the comments have appeared chiefly in American collections and criticism, some few valuable notes may be found in the *Journal of the Folk-Song Society*. Fortunately, the scattered American criticism has been admirably summarized by Tristram P. Coffin in "A Description of Variation in the Traditional Ballad of America." [79] Because Coffin's work is concerned with more than mere verbal changes, the review of a few significant developments in American criticism is necessary.

The orthodox approach to variation study has considered the why as well as the what of ballad variation, but, when not theorizing about "a tradition of artistry," it has applied rather simple concepts of linguistic change or corruption. This sort of study examines variant words and phrases, seeking to explain how faulty hearing, forgetting, cultural change, and the like induce corruption and substitution. Thus Edwin Shepard Miller records and discusses mutations in eighty variants of "Lord Thomas and Fair Annet." [80] Paper analysis of this kind is especially valuable when supplemented by collateral investigations, as it is in the work of W. Edson Richmond, who has thrown light on the creation and change of ballad place names [81] and has also demonstrated that textual corruption is not always the result of folk error.[82] But such studies, concentrating narrowly on minutiae, attack only a portion of the problem because they seldom consider the full background and effect of variation. That is, they fail to examine the narrative as a whole and the personality of the singer at all.

The place of the singer is clearly indicated by Barry:

> That folk-singers forget verses and stanzas is known to every tyro in the field, but *only a tyro* is content to admit a fact without the attempt to account for it. Folk-singers are not mere animated dictaphone records: the best of them participate emotionally in the action of a ballad-drama.[83]

Closer proximity to the folk and greater interest in the singers themselves have brought the problem to the fore. But seldom have collectors been able to obtain clear data. How much conscious variation takes place is unknown. Rarely can a collector surprise a text in the process of variation,[84] and even less frequently does a collector find such an articulate informant as did Coffin (see pp. 280–281). Apparently on slender authority most critics have assumed that variation is almost completely unconscious. Most commonly cited are the remarks of Cecil Sharp, who referred primarily to folk tunes,[85] and of W. Roy MacKenzie.[86] They agree at least on the unconscious nature of change. Other collectors have offered conflicting opinions,[87] and a little reflection on the amount of moralizing and euphemism in late versions of old ballads clearly reveals the presence of conscious and deliberate alteration. The legacy of the cult of spontaneity seems difficult to escape, and in the absence of controlled evidence, generalizations are hazardous.

The effect of textual changes on ballad stories was not completely ignored, but it has remained for Coffin to indicate clearly the difference between purely textual variation and story change:

> The former . . . involves those changes that do not affect the story either as to plot or mood, but rather create the minor differences that distinguish the variants, and often the versions of individual ballads.
> Story change . . . is the alteration of the actual plot or basic mood of the ballad.[88]

Coffin has been able to demonstrate his point clearly by his discovery of a singer who was able to indicate how, by a process of misunderstanding and reinterpretation, the story of a ballad changed (see pp. 280–281). His concept of story variation within oral tradition may be seen by examining his description of variation in the Child ballad in North America, in part a summary and in part the result of individual investigation.

Coffin finds three forces at work in both types of variation: personal factors, general trends of folk art, and print. The personal factors, which have received the most critical attention, he lists as forgetting, substitutions of clichés, desire for dramatic effects, rationalization, localization, invention of new story material, misunderstanding, and adaptation of old words to a new or modified tune. Trends in folk art have been less often noted. Here Coffin lists as constants the central situation, the outline of the plot, vivid passages, figures of speech, and embedded clichés. But the tendency to concentrate on a single part of a single situation and a desire to universalize the material sometimes override these constants. Following Belden and Barry especially, Coffin recognizes the effect of print on oral tradition, particularly the rebirth of texts from print and the influence of print on oral renditions. His treatment of the relationship of these forces to textual changes is generally adequate within the compass of his brief space. Only the relationship of music and text is slighted. Except for citing Barry's comments on the relation between the form of the ballad stanza and ballad melody, he virtually ignores the problem. In justification of Coffin's omission, we must note that little attention has elsewhere been given to the problem.[89] Nevertheless, Coffin might have noticed at least such important forces as the influence of similar tunes on *crossings* among ballads. The relation of tune to text is important, not only in purely verbal changes but in alteration of ballad story, particularly in facilitating mergers.

Coffin's concept of story change is, in its extensive application, his most important contribution. That variation affects ballad stories has been recognized, but Coffin's is the first full examination of the problem. His inadvertent statement that changes "effect" stories [90] is indeed accurate and is at least a part of what Barry meant by the psychological re-creation of a ballad.[91] This is not the place to discuss fully the effect of the various forces of variation on the ballad story. The important thing is the recognition that a textual change may alter a story and thus set up the basis for future alteration. Thus the loss of detail may so affect the singer's understanding of the plot that the ballad will be recomposed to fit the new concept. His change thus involves both conscious and unconscious factors. Coffin's careful delineation of the various forces involved —elimination of action, development toward lyric, loss of detail through forgetting, fragmentation, convention and cliché, localization, the effect of literalness, rationalization, sentimentalization, moralization, manner of use, secondary growth, new ballads which arise from the old, mergers—illustrates this combination.

In *The British Traditional Ballad in North America*, Coffin is extremely cautious in drawing conclusions, particularly in regard to the problem of ballad evolution which vexed scholars at the beginning of the century.

> From the facts few, very few, conclusions can be drawn, because any attempt to go beyond extreme generalities is bound to cause trouble. Every word, line, phrase, stanza, and story that circulates creates its own individual history (p. 21).

He demonstrates the value of his approach in his analysis of American variants in the syllabus which forms the major portion of his book. His division of each ballad into story types is more a method than a conclusion. Perhaps some of his divisions are overzealous, being based on details of slight significance. They can be tested only by individual ballad studies which the analyses will facilitate. But Coffin has continued his studies and has reached important conclusions.

Coffin discovered Eugene Haun and his version of "The Drowsy Sleeper" after developing the concept of story variation. The experience presented a concrete instance and a behind-the-scenes glimpse of narrative development. By means of Haun's comments, Coffin was able to perceive how a version of "The Drowsy Sleeper-Silver Dagger" ballad was developing from a story of the suicide of disappointed lovers to a family-fixation tale through the misunderstanding, forgetting, and reinterpretation of one singer. Coffin tentatively proposes four points as the sequence of ballad-story variation:

> . . . (1) some sort of misunderstanding of the events of the narrative behind the song; (2) an adaptation of the original narrative material to fit the new conception of the story that arises from the misunderstanding; (3) omission, and so the forgetting, of the seemingly superfluous remains of the original narrative; (4) minor modifications and associations encouraged by new meanings introduced into the text.[92]

Taken with Coffin's reservations as to other forces of variation which might alter the sequence, the generalization seems to provide an adequate close-up of story change. But Coffin has since provided a longer view of the process.

In a recent article [93] developing a portion of the argument of John Robert Moore (see pp. 86–89), Coffin has outlined *the* trend of folk art in balladry. The folk, not much interested in unified action, tend to disregard plot in favor of an emotional core. Thus a poem with "an emotional core, details of action, frills of a poetic style that are too 'sophisticated' for the folk" enters oral tradition, becomes a ballad with the loss of the frills and some of the details of the action, and finally either becomes a lyric by retaining only the emotional core or degenerates into nonsense by losing all essential details. This is a highly significant generalization which, however, must be ever tempered by Coffin's earlier caution that "every word, line, phrase, stanza, and story that circulates creates its own individual history." As Coffin writes, "Every text of every ballad is in a different stage of development and derives from a different artistic environment." Thus when ballads "stumble into art" they do so through the efforts of trained or untrained geniuses, living often decades apart. Coffin's generalization makes room for both Gerould's "tradition of artistry" and Hodgart's "talented and anonymous

poets" of eighteenth-century Scotland who "transformed folk-tradi-
tion into literature, and gave the ballads their final form as far as
literary criticism is concerned." [94] Neither statement gives an adequate explanation of all the phenomena.

Coffin's discussion of story change is one indication of the shift
in emphasis from a general concept of tradition to the gifted individual as an explanation for major alteration in ballads. This
attitude has, like many conclusions of modern folksong scholarship,
grown out of or been anticipated by the remarks of Phillips Barry.
It parallels, of course, developments in the study of the folktale,[95]
but has been based as well on American field experience. American
collectors are no longer receptive to the romantic concept that
folk communities were once (always at least a generation removed
from the collector's sight) a nest of singing birds. It is to the folk
artist that they turn for full and well-performed versions; and it is
to the alterations of the folk artist rather than to the taste of the
community operating on the unconscious changes of a succession
of singers that they look for the creation of distinct versions of
ballads. And the conclusions have been strengthened by the study
of more recent material, which sometimes provides the investigator
with better documentation of the process.

Laws, however, in his discussion of variation in American ballads,
treats variation largely in terms of faulty memory and minor additions. He concludes that "good texts of most native ballads do not
vary much except in length," and notices the absence of the "sharply
defined narrative types which, over the centuries, have developed,
apparently as a slow evolutionary process, in British traditional balladry." [96] But when he turns to the examination of American versions of the other imported ballads, in which variation seems more
significant, his attitude toward the slow evolutionary process alters.

Though Laws discusses "casual omissions, substitutions, and mis-
understandings," he emphasizes recomposition, which he refers to
rather frequently as "rewriting." Considering his subject, his emphasis on the broadside is natural, but he seeks "conclusions which
may be applicable to all folk balladry." [97] His conclusion that "the

function of the average folk singer . . . is simply to repeat what he has learned" is well documented; his attribution of major changes in a ballad to conscious recomposition is in agreement with the evidence and conclusions of a number of recent students; [98] and his contention that the establishment of a "revised text" needs the help of a broadside or phonograph record has other supporters.[99] But more arresting is his tendency to "give the credit for recomposition to ballad printers and their employees rather than to members of the folk." Although he does not deny that a revision of a ballad "may have first come to the printer by way of a folk composer or even directly from tradition" and admits that the broadside "may have been issued by a rural or itinerant printer," his contention is that, "in their attempt to keep their customers well supplied, the ballad printers apparently ransacked the old ballad sheets for anything that was usable."

The difficulty with Laws' conclusion is that his evidence is based on distribution rather than on any knowledge of the identity of revisers of the ballads. His assumption seems to be that the revisers were usually rhymesters working with older printed texts. On the basis of the evidence it might seem as logical to postulate that many revisions stem from folk artists, whether or not in the employ of the ballad printer. His mention of phonograph recording as a means of distribution introduces an analogy which might be profitable if more information were available. A knowledge of hillbilly and race records, in fact of the entire business of commercial music for the folk (an acceptable characterization of the broadside), supports only partially Laws' major contention. Early recordings (1923–1930) were usually of the performances of folk artists or of those who had learned from the folk artists, and seem to represent only the broadside distribution of local songs or local versions. The influence of commercial management on recomposition and the composition of new songs is hardly clear. "Floyd Collins" seems to have been composed in 1925 at the request of Polk C. Brockman, scout for Okeh records. But the composer was the late Rev. Andrew Jenkins, a "blind newsboy evangelist" of Atlanta, Georgia,[100] who was little less a folk composer and folksinger than John Snead, the minstrel of the Great Smokies, whose unusual version of "Barbara Allen" never achieved wide circulation.[101] On the other hand, the hillbilly version of the Cajun folksong, "Jolie Blon," had the active collaboration of a recording executive. Warming up for a 1947 recording session in Fort Worth, Texas, Moon Mullican and his Showboys were rendering a garbled version of the Louisiana-French lyrics with "knocked-out ad-libbing." In the control booth, Sid Nathan, president of King Records, began scribbling lyrics. In "a matter of minutes" the new version was rehearsed and recorded.[102]

The meager information suggests that the relation between the broadside and the folk artist is complex but real. Evidence from broadside and traditional variants does call into question the view that distinct versions are "the evolutionary result of many contributions from folk singers." As Laws points out, "If the evolutionary theory were correct, we should expect to find the variant in tradition in all its stages and not in the final one alone." But the evidence in no way invalidates the concept of communal re-creation. In the words of its deviser, "It should be understood that *communal re-creation* must include not merely the cumulative effect of accidental and partly conscious change made by many folk singers over a long period of time, but also sudden, marked and perfectly intentional changes by folk singers who are also folk composers, and have, when they might list, retold an old ballad story in more or less new wording of their own." And Barry added that the folk, "the keepers of a tradition," include even the ballad printer.[103] A full understanding of the process not only requires more extensive knowledge of the English and American broadside traditions, but must be developed as well in the core of ballad scholarship, the study of individual ballads.

The Study of Individual Ballads

It goes almost without saying that studies of individual items must occupy a central position in folksong study. Since the most vociferous adherents of the Gummere-communal school disappeared from the scene, Anglo-American scholars have tacitly accepted the central thesis of the historic-geographic method, which Barry phrased:

No two song histories are necessarily similar: each quest is an investigation by itself, unrelated to any other. . . .[104]

Stith Thompson has summarized the chief interest of the investigator (of the folktale) as:

. . . (a) establishing an approximation to an original form which will sufficiently account for all the available variants; (b) determining as nearly as may be the age and place of origin; (c) tracing the vicissitudes of the story through time and place, the course of its wanderings, and the modifications it has undergone.[105]

Following are Barry's three fields of research requisite to the writing of the critical history of a popular ballad:

. . . the folklore background, including the factual basis, if any, of the plot of the ballad-drama; the origin of the ballad as the artistic expression, through words and music, of a particular folk-complex; the re-creation of the ballad, both psychologically and in relation to the evolving multiplicity of versions of texts and sets of air.[106]

One may safely say that Anglo-American scholarship has yet to produce a single study satisfying these requirements. Barry himself declared that the writing of a critical history is no longer a one-man job. But the job has been begun. Like the Great American Novel, critical studies are being written in installments. Collectors and critics have been contributing pieces of the evidence, and portions of critical histories have been written. The recent guides of Coffin, Laws, and Miss Dean-Smith have done much to order the previous work and facilitate the appearance of true critical histories.

In surveying studies of individual ballads, it is more useful to deal first with native American ballads. No one can maintain that the origin and tradition of these ballads are completely analogous to those of older ballads. Nevertheless, in the absence of proof to the contrary, the evidence furnished by indigenous (or apparently indigenous) American ballads offers suggestions for the study of older balladry.

NATIVE AMERICAN BALLADS

Because American ballads seem relatively close in time and space to their origins, and because historicity is the first concern in dealing with any narrative, possibly the greatest amount of effort has been devoted to Barry's first field of research, ascertaining the factual basis of the plots. A good deal of work has been done by collector-editors to provide notes for their volumes, and scholars have made separate reports of their investigations, the first one in 1914.[107] Significant examples will point out the problems involved, the methods employed, and the results achieved.

Investigators generally assume American ballads to be based on fact for largely the same reason that folksingers believe in the truth of their songs: analogy with songs chronicling known events.[108] But, as Laws has pointed out, American narratives are of four types: those containing accurate details of known events, those apparently telling a factual story which cannot be satisfactorily traced, those telling a timeless and placeless story impossible to connect with facts, and those containing fiction masked as fact.[109] Ballads deal with local and national events known to the authors directly and by hearsay. Although "in the typical American ballad factual detail takes precedence over both drama and artistry," [110] certain ballad makers have shown a "disregard for the facts when a dramatic situation beckons." [111] Variation and localization further complicate the work of the investigator. The amount of knowledge we now have of the background of many ballads testifies to the extensive work of a number of contributors.

The factual basis of American ballads has been established by three types of evidence: historical documents, testimony of witnesses, and memorial tradition. Granting that some of them are adaptations, journalistic ballads—particularly those chronicling disasters, battles, and murders—have sent their investigators to newspapers, court records, and local histories. When these means fail, scholars must fall back on the testimony of witnesses and memorial tradition and must try to differentiate between the two. The investigator receives reports such as the following:

> We had in our company during the Civil War . . . a fellow named Marshall Johnson from Waco, who was the greatest hand to make songs and speeches that I have ever known. Poor fellow, he got killed in a stampede one fall early in the seventies, up on the Bosque River, and the well known cowboy ditty, "When Work Is Done This Fall," was made on the occasion.[112]

The unreliability of such evidence has been demonstrated in Mrs. Eckstorm's inconclusive but almost exhaustive study of "The Jam at Gerry's Rock." [113] But reports of witnesses are sometimes creditable and furnish conclusive information, as Geraldine J. Chickering's discovery of the fact and fiction behind "Jack Haggerty" reveals.[114] But when the origin of a ballad has been traced, its factual basis has not always been resolved. We sometimes have the word of the author or his notes; the facts may be elusive. We know, for example, that "Young Charlotte" was written by Seba Smith, apparently on the basis of a newspaper account; [115] the truth of the story has yet to be determined.

All in all, the results of such investigations do not give much promise of a general method for determining the background of older ballads which seem to be based on facts. Investigators reasonably close in time and space to the origins of ballads have found evidence contradictory and unreliable, answers elusive and conjectural. The more widespread and popular the ballad and the more it resembles older balladry (as "Frankie and Albert" and "John Henry"), the more difficult the problems. Despite much investigation and many reports, the historicity of "Frankie and Albert" is almost as conjectural as that of "Lord Randall." The problem of "John Henry" involves merged ballads, lack of documentary evidence, and widespread but conflicting popular reports. Louis W. Chappell's investigation of the factual basis of the John Henry tradition [116] has demonstrated that: (1) popular report can confuse scholars more than internal evidence of ballad texts; (2) in the absence of documentary information the investigator can separate testimonial data from popular report, but only if he has extensive and intensive knowledge of the subject matter treated in the ballad and of the community investigated; and (3) evidence which might seem conclusive enough to identify a character in older balladry cannot be credited.[117]

Investigations of the "timeless and placeless ballads" offer more analogy with the study of older balladry. Laws says of ballads such as "The Jealous Lover," "Unless they can be found in early broadside or manuscript form, they must remain almost as mysterious in origin as some of the older Child pieces." [118] Perhaps so. But investigations into the background of "The Jealous Lover" can furnish insights into the problems of the Child ballads. Laws objects to Barry's derivation of "The Jealous Lover" from the early nineteenth-century English street ballad, "The Murder of Betsy Smith" because no "demonstrable process of oral tradition could within a few decades transform so poor a ballad into one of such relatively high quality." [119] Yet all that is required is one folk composer! Laws' judgment stems, of course, from his views on ballad identification, classification, and recomposition, which have already been examined. But this instance helps to show how a narrow approach may prevent insight. We grant that Barry's study is not conclusive enough for Laws to determine "whether or not 'The Jealous Lover' is based on fact." Actually Barry calls into question the relation of fact to the ballad as idea. To Barry, "The Jealous Lover" was re-created from "Betsy Smith" just as "Poor Omie" was re-created from "The Wexford Girl." One may extend Barry's reasoning and discover that "The Jealous Lover," "The Murder of Betsy Smith," "The Wexford Girl," "Poor Omie," "On the Banks of the Ohio" (which is even closer to "The Wexford Girl"), "Rose Connoley," "The Cruel Ship's Carpenter," and others form a complex which, given enough time, enough singers, and enough recomposers, might develop into a group of versions which an orthodox scholar would classify as a single ballad. Here are, perhaps, early stages of that process, and we see that different types of composition, re-creation, and adaptation are taking place. Barry's study tends to show the re-creation of a factual ballad (if the British broadside *is* a factual ballad) into a timeless and placeless ballad. "Pearl Bryan," "Nell Cropsey," and other forms of "The Jealous Lover" show how it can become a factual ballad again.

The investigation of the factual background of a ballad is not the same thing as tracing a ballad to its source, though the two studies overlap. And neither investigation can overlook problems of re-creation. The events related in a ballad story may not always give a clue to the time and place of its origin. Re-created forms of a ballad not only hamper one type of investigation but prevent a simple interpretation of "the origin of a ballad." It is difficult to determine the difference between a variation, an adaptation, and a composition. Taking the restricted view of authorship, Laws neatly summarizes, in *Native American Balladry*, some of the problems involved in seeking the composers of American ballads.

> Considering the relatively short history of native balladry, it is rather surprising to find that only a few ballads can be traced to specific authors. Investigators have found that statements made by singers are frequently so misleading that further searching has almost always been necessary before a conclusion can be reached. Even at that, scholars have on occasion revised their original opinions about authorship. We cannot even assert with confidence that first-person ballads of the confessional type were actually written by the convicts themselves (p. 44).

Evidence for the authorship of a ballad may be internal or external to the ballad in all its forms. External evidence consists of claims and attributions of authorship, whether oral or printed. The internal evidence is the style or signature of the text, and the currency of the ballad. Students of American balladry have depended largely on the external evidence and have learned a good deal of "the way of the folk."

Claims and attributions of authorship are often more interesting and valuable than true. They sometimes help to identify the author of a ballad, but even when they do not, they may provide insights into folk concepts of authorship and ownership. A folksinger may simply claim authorship of any song that is anonymous and popular,[120] or he may have known the song so long that he believes he created it. A song may be attributed to a singer for various reasons. He may have introduced it into the community or have sung it for so long that it is considered his song.[121] A composer and singer like the woods poet, Lawrence Gorman, may have had the authorship of other songs thrust upon him.[122] And "in the realm of folk song, 'made up' frequently means 'made over.' "[123] A folksinger "would claim 'Hamlet' if he had added four doggerel lines to the Soliloquy."[124] Claims and attributions in print sometimes differ little from oral reports. Barry's inclusion of ballad printers in "the keepers of the tradition" seems true in a wide sense. Without supporting evidence, a claim in print has the same authority as popular report and may have arisen on similar grounds.

As noted above, an informant of J. Frank Dobie reported that "When the Work's All Done This Fall" was composed "in the seventies, up on the Bosque River." But D. J. O'Malley claimed that he composed the poem in Montana about twenty years later and supported his claim with a clipping of the text, signed D. J. White (he used his stepfather's name at the time), from the Miles City *Stock Growers' Journal*, October 6, 1893. O'Malley's text of "After the Roundup" is clearly early and uses as its refrain line "When work is done this fall" or "When work's done this fall," agreeing with the report cited by Dobie. And O'Malley seems to have been a cowboy poet in that he claimed authorship of not only widespread items like "The D-2 Horse Wrangler" and "The Cowboy's Dream," but poems otherwise unknown, such as "Cowboy Reverie" and "A Busted Cowboy's Christmas." Assuming the validity of O'Malley's claims, his publishing practices pose another problem for the investigator. In the *Stock Growers' Journal* of February 3, 1894, "The D-2 Horse Wrangler" is signed R. J. Stovall. O'Malley explained "that he himself wrote the lines but because an acquaintance who was the subject of the yarn wished to surprise his wife in Denver by blossoming out as a poet, the latter was allowed to sign his name. There was one consideration, a $5 hat, which incidentally was the most Mr. O'Malley ever got for a poem." ("A Busted Cowboy's Christmas" appeared in the *Stock Growers' Journal*, December 23, 1893, over the name of Iyam B. Usted.) [125]

The commercialization of American folksongs has given claims to authorship interest and value beyond the curiosity of the folklorist. Folk entertainers are on record as composers of songs they could not possibly have written, though the claims may possibly represent "only a necessary legal step in issuing records and clearing them for radio." [126] Versions of "The Gypsie Laddie" are credited to at least three separate "composers"—A. P. Carter, T. Texas Tyler, and Warren Smith. These rival claims seem to have passed without challenge, but other claims have resulted in suits involving large sums of money. Because Jimmie Rodgers recorded as his own a Marks-Stern song still under copyright, the Victor Recording Company was made liable for large royalties.[127] Suits involving the authorship of "The Wreck of Old 97" and "Home on the Range" [128] have benefited the folklorist by providing examples of folk "authorship" and unearthing information he could not afford to secure.

Because the form of folksong tends to be traditional and the text subject to continuing variation, the style of a ballad has been of little help in determining authorship, though it has been used on occasion. Barry employed stylistic evidence to aid in tracing the authorship of "The White Captive," [129] though the evidence is hardly conclusive. The best evidence of style is negative, as in William Main Doerflinger's point that Larry Gorman, "with his satirical sense of humor and his love of rapid metres and internal rhyming, would never have composed so grave and mournful a ballad as 'Peter Emberly'" (though this judgment seems really hindsight). On the other hand, Doerflinger's argument that the style of "The History of Prince Edward Island" supports attribution to Larry Gorman [130] is countered by Edward D. Ives's rejection because he finds Gorman's satire "usually personal, occasionally social, but never political." [131] Before stylistic evidence can be of much help, the scholar must reconstruct or discover an original text and determine that the stylistic points are in no way traditional, whether of the folk or of the nineteenth-century poetaster. The reverse process, the study of how a ballad acquires a traditional style, is more rewarding.

The study of signature in ballads involves similar problems. Signature has been defined by Robert C. Stephenson as the "awkward intrusion of the ballad singer, or . . . of the ballad singer as ballad maker." The definition indicates the difficulty of using signature as an aid in discovering the author (in the narrow sense), for one cannot simply determine that the signature is a part of the original form of the ballad or even if the original form of the signature is preserved. The signature itself is often a traditional formula, and "these pathetic claims to authorship," [132] do not always furnish explicit information. Ballad signature ranges from the use of the first person to the addition of an elaborate author tag. As Laws has pointed out, the "first person may be merely a conventional device to add the appearance of veracity to the ballad story." [133] The confession ballad is a traditional form, but nothing prevents the criminal from composing his own song in the tradition. We know that

> *My name is Charles Giteau,*
> *My name I'll never deny,*

is a hoary convention. Popular report ascribes to the malefactors themselves such first-person songs as "Tom Dula's Lament," "Ellen Smith," and "Frankie Silver," but one cannot be sure that the reports did not take rise in the signatures themselves. Yet there is strong evidence that some criminals have written their own "good-nights,"—Bonnie Parker, for example; [134] but no widespread confession ballad has been traced to an author subject. Author tags, sometimes quite specific, have likewise been of little help. "Jesse James" may have been "made by Billy Gashade," but some later singer may have added the stanza. No one has yet discovered the playful author of "The Burning of Henry K. Robinson's Camp," though his claim seems far from "pathetic":

> *And now that camp is finished and we have settled down again,*
> *I will give you the initials that you may guess my name.*
> *There is "H" for hard, and "N" for none, and "R" for royal role.*
> *Just add "YE" and you will see my Christian name is told.*
>
> *Then there is "T" to take each letter and place it where it belongs,*
> *And then proceed to "OMP" for "H" will not go wrong;*
> *Then spell the sun that rules the day, gives forth its silvery light,*
> *These letters told, my name unfold, if you will just place them*
>   *right.*[135]

The more reticent author of the following remains unknown:

> *This song was composed in the flowery west*
> *By a man you may never have seen.*
> *Oh, I tell you the name, but it is not in full:*
> *His initials are J. R. D.*[136]

A ballad tag prophetically explains the situation:

> *You may forget the singer,*
> *But don't forget this song.*

Ballad signature offers much opportunity for study, but it has proved of little direct aid in ferreting out authors.

The currency and geographical distribution of American ballads have played no great part in their study, although the most important ballad studies have taken account of such evidence as existed. Because collecting did not begin until the twentieth century and because sufficient reports are only now becoming available, few conclusions can be drawn. Laws' brief survey in *Native American Balladry* (pp. 56ff.) of the distribution of a number of ballads indicates only a spread in all directions; that there have been many jumps instead of a fanning out is certain, but more evidence and intensive study of individual ballads are required. Investigators have too often had to depend on the memories of informants for reports of earlier currency of such ballads as "Frankie and Albert." Barry cited the known distribution of "Young Charlotte" as supporting evidence of its composition and spread by "William Carter, the Bensontown Homer." Since Barry's later identification of Seba Smith as the author,[137] and since the recovery of more variants, no reexamination of the ballad's distribution has been made. Distribution and dates of currency seem more valuable in disproving than in establishing authorship.

The most thorough and important studies of American ballads have been perhaps the most disappointing. The twenty years Mrs. Eckstorm devoted to "The Jam at Gerry's Rock" settled "nothing except that it did not occur at all the places where it has been located." [138] Barry's extensive treatment of "Springfield Mountain" (significantly subtitled "Materials for a Critical Study") [139] uncovers the facts of the plot in an accident of 1761; but Barry can trace the domestic versions of the ballad no earlier than 1849 and the stage versions no earlier than 1836. He therefore finds "no evidence that the ballad is of earlier date than the second quarter of the last century." If we agree with Laws that the "Springfield Mountain" ballad, "like many others, was locally composed soon after the tragedy it recounts," [140] it is only because it should have been.

Since it is becoming clear that the problems of the widespread and popular American ballads (like those of older balladry) will never be solved by documentary evidence, more thorough study must be given to less popular and perhaps less interesting material that can be adequately documented. In *Death in the Dark* (1941), James Taylor Adams prints twenty-three ballads of mine disasters and identifies the authors of seventeen. Perhaps not all attributions are accurate, but the number is certainly significant. A full examination of the tradition of every ballad that can be traced to a source may provide knowledge of the multiple variables in other ballads. It is not enough to identify the singer who launched the ballad or to demonstrate that the song is *gesunkenes Kulturgut*. The investigator must learn not only the *possible*, but the *actual* behavior of songs and singers. Barry himself illustrated the requisite type of conclusion when he wrote:

> We flatly disagree, as far as American folk music is concerned[,] with Béla Bartók, who, speaking for Hungarian tradition, has grave doubts about the ability of a folk singer to compose a *new* tune. All that we can say is that to the best of our knowledge and belief the compositions by American ballad makers of new tunes is something which is not done.[141]

But it must be remembered that the action of the forces which determine the history of a song "is never the same in kind or in degree in any two instances," [142] and we should anticipate the tragedy epitomized in Barry's study of "Young Charlotte": a theory done to death by a fact.

OTHER NON-CHILD NARRATIVES

Considering their number, the British non-Child ballads have received little individual study. The ballads are, as a group, a good deal older than native American items, a fact which restricts the use of popular report and even documentary evidence. British scholars have as a rule not been interested in textual study and histories of late ballads, and American students have been somewhat cut off from sources of information. Therefore, with notable exceptions, particularly among the older ballads, scholarship has been largely confined to bibliographical headnotes, which usually note the ballad's appearance on broadsides, infrequently identify the factual basis, and rarely (usually by Scots editors) note an individual author.

To judge by the comments of British writers, the study of late ballads must deal largely with oral versions of printed originals. Whether this condition is the cause or the result of the atrophy of song making by folk composers we are not certain. There are, in fact, indications that members of the British folk did not completely relinquish their creative powers to urban professionals. This seems more true of Northern tradition, though the difference may be primarily the result of differing attitudes among the collectors.[143] The plowman and poacher songs, for example, deserve careful scrutiny both as song types and as individual ballads. To what degree broadsides distributed the efforts of local composers as well as the products of hacks of the penny press remains to be determined, although internal evidence points strongly to Grub Street and its equivalents in smaller cities. Laws in *American Balladry from British Broadsides* has had to assume professional authorship for most of his material, from which, however, many local British pieces are excluded because of their failure to migrate to America or to survive under changed conditions.

The dating of British ballads is often conjectural because of lack of knowledge of the events which they concern. A large proportion of British ballads, especially those current in America, seem to be fictional; yet we have seen how a factual ballad takes on the air of fiction and then becomes factual again. Laws is forced to use internal evidence—conventional names, stereotyped or contrived plots, lack of circumstantial detail, etc.—in most instances to determine whether or not a ballad is factual; and he must resort to style or broadside appearance to date the ballads. Investigations of the factual background of a number of individual ballads, though admittedly quite difficult, might be of great value.

One of the problems of American editors has been to separate the imported from the indigenous, especially since a number of Old World ballads may have escaped the nets of British collectors or may have been rejected as "composed." Internal evidence or the discovery of a British copy from print or tradition has usually been enough to settle the matter, though there have been exceptions. Barry's argument that "The Indian Lass" was derived from the American "The Little Mohea" [144] is not quite convincing, though the matter bears further investigation. Laws treats "The Flying Cloud" as British, but Horace P. Beck believes it to be of American composition, or at least of American re-creation.[145]

Though they are but few, there are some significant studies of a few individual ballads. (The attention paid by British students to a number of religious narratives will be referred to later.) Most attractive to American scholars have been those ballads containing old or universal themes or ballads related in some way to Child ballads, such as "The Bramble Briar," returned-lover ballads, and "The Bold Soldier." Belden's early study, "Boccaccio, Hans Sachs, and the *Bramble Briar*," [146] is in some ways a document in the Ballad War, a battle for the rights of the traditional vulgar ballad. His conclusion that, although "The Constant Farmer's Son" is a hack rewriting of "The Bramble Briar," the latter was more or less directly derived in the early eighteenth century by an itinerant entertainer from an English translation of the *Decameron* and distributed only orally or by local broadsides is based on a careful and detailed examination of the ten English and American ballad variants known to him. Derivation from the *Decameron* is still open to question, and since the discovery of an American broadside and a large number of traditional copies, no full reexamination of the ballad has been made. Though Belden contributed stimulating notes on the modification of such ballad themes as the returned lover,[147] his work in separating "The Bramble Briar" not only from "The Constant Farmer's Son" but from the Yarrow ballads (Child 214 and 215) seems to have been one of the influences on contemporary students' carefully separating textual treatments of themes and tracing them to independent or rewritten broadside forms.

An example of such recent work and of the careful study now beginning to be devoted to other imported ballads by American students is David Mason Greene's recent article on "The Bold Soldier." [148] The method is a close textual comparison of British and American oral and broadside texts. The resulting picture is that of a late seventeenth-century broadside ("The Seaman's Renown") unrelated textually or in detailed plot to "Earl Brand," reworked by a later seventeenth-century hack (who may have been acquainted with the "Earl Brand" tradition) into a form ("The Masterpiece of Love Songs") which was later remodeled into a lost eighteenth-century broadside, and from which in turn derive the English traditional version and a post-Revolutionary American reworking with additions by the reviser ("The Bold Soldier"). This last (together with slightly differing but unknown printings) is responsible for all American oral variants. This is undoubtedly a "correct" study, and its conclusions add more weight to the belief that relations between older ballads and so-called secondary forms are the "result of conscious imitation and not . . . of traditional variation" and that widely differing forms of the same ballad are due to purposeful reshaping and not to more or less random variation. But a lack in this sort of study, excellent as far as it goes, can be seen in an "incorrect" study of the ballad.

Norman Cazden's earlier article on "The Bold Soldier of Yarrow" [149] seems faulty in rejecting any thematic relations between "Earl Brand" and "The Bold Soldier" while maintaining that the latter ballad is a later parallel of the Yarrow ballads; and it is obviously "incorrect" in relying upon "the analytic concept of the *image*" and "social meanings" rather than on strictly textual comparisons.[150] But Cazden admits at the outset that between old and new treatments of his theme, "no direct relationship or genealogy" can be drawn, that "The Bold Soldier" is not a "simple and mechanical alteration of the original text to fit new social settings," and that "the lines of the later song were surely written by an unknown penny-sheet writer of small talent, and are not the result of a process of popular creative accretion." He even implies the availability of printed texts establishing that stability in oral tradition which Greene documents. To these points he adds his conclusion that "The Bold Soldier" is "a direct transfer of the imagery, the content, the social theme of the Yarrow ballads into later conditions, which happen to affect also the making of songs." It matters not so much at this juncture that his judgment of the thematic relationships may be in error, partially because of his earlier unconvincing reconstruction of "The Braes o' Yarrow" (see pp. 311–312), which, in avoiding the mechanical approach of the more orthodox student, seems arbitrarily to produce the original story Cazden wished. Nor is it of immediate concern that his indictment of the attitudes of orthodox ballad scholarship, while containing much truth, is overdrawn. What is important is that, however erroneous his application, he suggests an approach which might be fruitful as an *addition* to exacting textual study.

The *facts* of creation, variation, adaptation, and recomposition must always be carefully established through a strict methodology. But the student should not stop without a consideration of the method and meaning of the processes. One of the important factors is the social framework of the ballad, the variant, the singer, the composer, the adapter. Thus Cazden pictures the broadside writer as typical of the popular poetic process of his time, reflecting "not only the desires but also the traditions" of his audience, using and re-using traditional themes, turning into his phrases the popular images, existing "only on the basis of a popular tradition." The concept needs more adequate documentation, but Cazden demonstrates that it can be useful in ballad study. Too often writers interested in social meanings have made only general forays on ballads or have simply chosen examples to illustrate a thesis. Cazden demonstrates that social meaning and social context can be used in studying histories of individual ballads and ballad themes. Cazden's work lights up a weakness in Greene's comment on "The Seaman's Renown" and "The Masterpiece of Love Songs":

> . . . they have little of the timeless or classless appeal of traditional ballad stories, but seem expressly designed to open the purses of a worldly servant class which might well be titillated by seeing its own daydreams of wealth, position, and equality fulfilled in such quasi-realistic tales of somewhat brutally achieved social climbing.[151]

That the older ballads were unrelated to the social realities of their time seems as inconceivable as that later ballads employing the same themes should employ the earlier style. The point is, by this time, generally recognized. But Cazden's conclusions are somewhat new in demonstrating that ballad images seen in their social context are valuable in the studies of individual ballads if (1) the student does not permit his concept of a "proper" ballad style or a "proper" traditional history to affect his judgments; and if (2) he does not neglect a rigid analysis of the narrative and textual traits of a ballad in terms of their chronological development. Considering the latter condition, Cazden presents a poor example of a useful technique.

In addition to the broadside types, a number of other noncanon narratives offer opportunities for study. Despite valuable preliminary work on such examples as "The Frog and the Mouse" [152] and "Father Grumble," [153] the old songs, now almost universal nursery favorites, invite significant scholarly study, as do some allegedly ritualistic songs like "The Derby Ram." And the development of tune scholarship is demonstrating new opportunities and values in the study of noncanon narratives. For example, the investigations of the "Captain Kidd" ballad provide the history not of a text or theme, but of a tune and text pattern.[154]

CHILD BALLADS

Studies of individual Child ballads have been many or few, depending on how we define the word *study*. Notes and brief articles on aspects of individual ballads have appeared frequently in the United States and seldom in Great Britain. Reference to Coffin's *The British Traditional Ballad in North America* will reveal most of the material, since he cites much of the British scholarship. Rare is the ballad recovered in North America that has not been the subject of significant comment. And these comments are the material out of which critical histories grow. But we are interested particularly in studies bearing more directly on the entire tradition of a ballad. In spite of the awe created by Child's compendium [155] and the distractions of collecting variants and debating origins, the opening years of the twentieth century witnessed three attempts at investigation in the "grand style," the historical study of international ballad themes. The studies referred to are Gordon Hall Gerould's "The Ballad of the Bitter Withy," [156] Walter R. Nelles's "The Ballad of Hind Horn," [157] and Paull Franklin Baum's "The English Ballad of Judas Iscariot." [158]

The three articles, excellent in their way, illustrate the methods and some of the limitations of the literary folklorist in the early years of the century. Only Gerould deals with a ballad that has any sort of modern tradition, and only Nelles's work involves a significant number of texts (few of them ballad texts). Nelles studies the relationship of "Hind Horn" to early romances, Anglo-Saxon popular tradition, and "The Kitchie Boy." [159] Gerould seeks to canonize "The Bitter Withy" and to trace the legend it recounts. Baum considers the possible relationship among "Judas," a Wendish folksong, and a fragment from the *Coptic Gospels of the Twelve Apostles*. Extensive textual tabulation is absent because it is impossible. The comparisons, with the possible exception of Nelles's, are extremely broad. The studies, concerned on scant evidence with the behavior of stories over great areas of time and space, leap from peak to peak without being able to venture into the valleys between.

The significance of these investigations is not their inadequacy as critical studies of ballads. None of them pretends to be a full critical history. They are attempts, and reasonably successful ones, to sum up and interpret sparse evidence by the methods of comparative literature. The significant point is that such studies have ceased. The scholars who did not become lost in the clouds of communal metaphysics descended into the valleys of local tradition. They are only now climbing out.

Archer Taylor's frequent criticism of English and American ballad scholars has been directed not so much at their journey into the valleys as their long, uninterrupted sojourn there. More particularly he has chided those who wandered off into the clouds. He wrote in 1931:

> No detailed analysis of any ballad has been undertaken by an English or American scholar since the completion of that monumental work [Child's]. . . . Obviously we must know the history and relations of the existing texts before we can profitably indulge in speculations about ultimate origins. Such speculations . . . have been unduly generous with quotations from ethnological writers on the South Seas and other parts of the globe equally remote from direct connection with the English and Scottish popular ballad.

They have totally ignored Scandinavian texts and studies. It is wiser to stay at home and determine, as well as may be, the life-history of a single ballad; to seek the information to be derived from a study of the texts themselves, instead of visiting Malaysia.[160]

It is useless to dispute the truth of these words. But in our impatience at the narrowness and fatuity of the Ballad War we must not fail to observe the pattern, the salutary pattern, that is emerging in Anglo-American ballad studies. The historic-geographic method seems to begin with the tabulation of far-flung versions, followed by the examination of regional variations. In practice, the regional studies can and perhaps should come first. The scholars must climb *up* the peaks.

The process is not the even one the metaphor implies. Activities proceed simultaneously at different levels. Regional, national, even international studies need not wait until every scrap of tradition is assembled and analyzed. And certainly the results of studies in other areas should not be ignored. Nor does the metaphor indicate exactly the course of Anglo-American scholarship. But the pattern is perceptible. The constructive work of the first three decades of the century was spent in collecting. In 1931 the Folk-Song Society ceased to exist as a separate entity because of the diminishing returns of English field collection. And in 1932 appeared Anne G. Gilchrist's study of the English tradition of "Lamkin." [161] Barry began collecting in New England in 1903, and by 1929 he and his associates had studied and reported ballad traditions in Maine, New England, and the United States at large. In 1931 Barry announced work on an international study of "The Two Sisters," [162] and Taylor published *"Edward" and "Sven i Rosengård."* The surveys of Gerould and Entwistle treated broadly the traditions of a number of ballads, and by the mid-forties scholars were seriously studying the traditions of individual ballads or portions thereof. The appearance of national syllabi at mid-century confirms the trend, a trend that considers *oikotypes* before *archetypes*.

The two approaches, the study of regional tradition and the international search for a hypothetical original are not antagonistic.

They complement and tend to confirm each other's conclusions, as can be seen in the investigation of "Edward." Taylor's *"Edward" and "Sven i Rosengård"* is not a complete study of the ballad, and he seems to have considered it a pilot study, a demonstration of the method, and an encouragement for future study. Taylor contents himself with a postulation of the original, a determination of the center and routes of migration, and a few broad remarks on the subsequent vicissitudes of the ballad. He does not study regional variation in detail. In spite of a rather small number of variants—forty-eight, not counting those he did not see and excepting the stanza of "The Wexford Girl" mistakenly included—he arrives at certain logical and convincing conclusions on the basis of a tabulation of traits; stylistic, logical, and verbal fitness; and principles of folk narrative. Coffin's excellent summary follows:

1. Much of the original story of the ballad is missing in current texts, although the Scandinavian tales retain in certain versions at least an inconclusive trace more of the old material than do the British.
2. "Edward" was originally a British song which traveled to Scandinavia. The texts we now have represent two separate degenerate traditions—one a modern British version that contains only vestiges of the old tale, and the other a Scandinavian version that is related to the modern English texts only through the extinct original.
3. The ballad originally tells a tale of fratricide; patricide, sororicide, and so forth, have entered the tale by chance substitution.
4. The mother is not originally an accomplice to the crime, but has entered into the song through corruption with some similar tale.[163]

Three other points need to be discussed: the authenticity of the much-admired Percy version, the motive for the murder, and the relation of "Edward" to other ballads.

To prove that the "Edward" ballad as a whole is, as Child said, "unimpeachable," did not require a historic-geographic study, for a Swedish text of 1640 had been reported in *Danmarks gamle Folkeviser* in 1895 (though the ballad itself was not available for Taylor's use). The course of the ballad in English tradition made it very doubtful, at the very least, that the oral versions represent "merely a debased form of the Percy version." [164] But Taylor's study demonstrates on the basis of overwhelming evidence from England, Scandinavia, and Finland that Percy's text not only represents "an individual variation in detail" but is "a revision of a folk song, a rewriting which we can justly compare with Goethe's 'Heidenröslein.' " [165] In 1940 (apparently without knowledge of Taylor's work), Bertrand H. Bronson arrived at a similar and more detailed conclusion by an intensive comparison of the style and structure of the Percy text with the norm of English ballad tradition.[166] And Margaret Morton Blum has since shown that the Percy text has had almost no effect on folk tradition.[167] Still to be explained are the *who* and *why* of the alterations. Bronson emphasizes the relations between Lord Hailes (Percy's informant) and Lady Wardlaw, the fabricator of "Hardyknute." And Barry suggests personal and psychological reasons for alteration by Percy.[168] But these are conjectures.

In reconstructing the original of "Edward," Taylor was unable to establish the motive for the murder. Barry and Coffin have been able to suggest a probable one, and in doing so have demonstrated the basic validity of Taylor's method, but have also shown how it must depend on narrower studies. Taylor's analysis of traits gave him the answer, but he was unable to recognize it. At opposite ends of the geographical spectrum Taylor found motives. If he had recognized an agreement, he would have been convinced that the trait was old. Unfortunately, he saw no relationship between the Anglo-American

> *What about did the plea begin?*
> *It began about the cutting of a willow wand*
> *That would never been a tree.*

and the Finnish

> *Why did you stab your brother?*
> *Because he put my wife to shame.*

Barry, knowing that a singer had explained to Sharp that the "breaking of a little bush" was a kenning referring to a very young girl, was able to detect the theme of the fatal rivalry of two brothers for the love of their sister.[169] Reexamining the problem, Coffin concludes that the motive involves an incestuous relationship between brother and sister, but he can find no evidence to establish the jealous rivalry.[170] The evidence for this tentative conclusion comes from the notebook of a field collector and from the tendency of "Edward" to attach itself to incest ballads. The latter point reveals a weakness in Taylor's approach. He tends simply to strip from "Lizie Wan" and "The Twa Brothers" the stanzas he concludes are "Edward" without fully inquiring into the relationship. Bronson, who finds the symbolism proposed by Barry "alien to the popular habit," does find a melodic relationship between "Edward" and "Lizie Wan," but not "The Twa Brothers." [171] Whether or not the discovery of the lost Swedish A text [172] will change the picture remains to be seen.

In *"Edward" and "Sven i Rosengård"* Taylor follows closely the historic-geographic or Finnish technique, developed primarily in the study of folktales before the turn of the century by Kaarle Krohn and continued by his disciple, Antti Aarne, and others. Although the principles were known previously—as far as folksong is concerned, they are implicit in the work of Grundtvig and Child— and would sooner or later have been codified elsewhere,[173] the Finnish formulation has become the practical guide for serious study of widespread ballads. The Finnish method is common sense, but, as Taylor has pointed out, "common sense codified into a rigid procedure and not applied at random." [174]

Although the technique has been summarized and demonstrated many times,[175] it might be well to emphasize its important features. The Finnish method depends upon the availability of a large number of versions (of a tale, song, or ballad) which are arranged by linguistic groups. The narratives are analyzed into their principal traits, which are tabulated in terms of their frequency and variation, and studied in terms of their extent of distribution, relation to the complete tale, etc. From this point on, the student must study minutely and interpret the evidence, with special attention to special developments in geographical areas or literary versions, in view of the known possibilities—not laws—of oral transmission. In this manner the life history of a narrative can be constructed. There is provision for close study of the type of formal evidence offered by the verse form of the ballad. In theory, at least, the Finnish method provides for the use of all necessary textual evidence for the study of tale and/or ballad, except that before correction by C. W. von Sydow, it perhaps overemphasized a gradual and wavelike diffusion. In practice, however, the technique in its emphasis on the determination of the hypothetical original may cause the student of a far-flung narrative to slight special regional developments, especially when they do not bear on the older history of the narrative. This observation does not criticize the technique itself but explains the complementary nature of limited, regional investigations and study in "the grand style."

Brief consideration of the recent attention paid to "The Twa Sisters" will further illustrate the point. In 1929 Archer Taylor sought to demonstrate the value of simple and methodical textual comparison of "The English, Scottish, and American Versions of the 'Twa Sisters.' " [176] Barry's contributions beginning in 1931,[177] though they deal with somewhat restricted points in the tradition of the ballad, were actually portions of an uncompleted study which he (fortunately) chose to print from time to time. Barry anticipates later conclusions (such as the connection of the swan in Scottish versions with the nude body in the Scandinavian); he produces musical evidence explaining certain variations in refrain and supporting a diffusion from Norway; he finds in a careful examination of British and American (including non-English) tradition a more complex and useful division than Taylor indicates and makes a number of valuable suggestions about the ballad's previous history that have not yet been fully taken into account. Some of Barry's points are developed or confirmed in Harbison Parker's " 'The Twa Sisters'— Going Which Way?" [178] which is devoted solely to arguing the diffusion from Scandinavia to Britain. Parker is concerned, among other things, with the British introduction of the milldam and the miller (for which his explanation is better than Barry's) and with the fission of characters. Not only are his conclusions independent of Barry's; he makes no reference at all to the latter's work. Furthermore, despite a salutary concern for detail in versions, he does not discuss British and American non-Child versions because "they contain no new motifs having bearing upon the question in hand." Consequently in discussing Knut Liestøl's statement that English versions do not specify the punishment of the elder sister, he is unable to point out that they do so specify. (Although a number of variants outside the Child corpus relate the burning of the elder sister, Parker could have refuted Liestøl's statement without going "out of bounds" had he not overlooked Child Z [II, 509].)

The most recent treatment, Paul G. Brewster's *The Two Sisters* (1953), is a full-scale study of nearly 350 Anglo-Scandinavian variants with some consideration of tale and song parallels in other areas. Brewster shows conclusively the East-West drift of the ballad, probably from Norway, and manages to reconstruct an older version, but possibly not the oldest one. A closer analysis of certain texts, particularly American recoveries, which Brewster considers to have greatly deteriorated, is needed. The recognition of deterioration is, of course, no substitute for determining the *how* and *why* of the degeneration; nor can the possibility that degenerate versions may contain primitive traits be overlooked. Brewster might have considered that some degenerate English and American texts make the lover (the miller) the agent of resuscitation, thus agreeing with the Icelandic version. That the specialized functions of the lover and the harper grew out of the figure of the brother in the Estonian cante fable (which Brewster considers as possibly the most primitive form of the tale) might be entertained. Barry's contention that the reference to the brother in the Child C* version is a recollection or preservation of the earlier story may be a rather wild stab, but it cannot be overlooked. In the same connection, the number of sisters involved needs further scrutiny. On the basis of the age, percentage, and distribution of the ballad trait, Brewster is certainly correct in concluding that the original ballad trait called for two sisters. The presence of three sisters in some versions may be only an accidental agreement with the Estonian cante fable. But the fact that to the scholar the ballad story seems logically to call for only two sisters is not conclusive, particularly when an older tale form contains three. These and other factors indicate that further considerations of "The Twa Sisters" are in order. The Achilles' heel of the Finnish method is not only, as Barry wrote,[179] that it leads to subjective judgment, but that some of its practitioners may place too much emphasis on the results of tabulation which sometimes emphasize widespread traits at the expense of older ones.

An illustration of current problems in ballad study is provided by recent work on the ballad known in English as "Lady Isabel and the Elf Knight" and in the Low Countries as "Heer Halewijn." Iivar Kemppinen, a Finn writing in English, in *Lady Isabel and the False Knight* (1954) develops a theory of the origin and source of the ballad allegedly based on a study of over 1,800 variants scattered from Australia eastward to Russia. Holgar Olaf Nygard's *The Ballad of Heer Halewijn* (1958) [180] is a study of narrative change in northern and western European forms. In this instance, the two approaches seldom complement each other. Kemppinen and Nygard summarize the narrative idea of the ballad in much the same way; they seem to agree that the Low Country forms are the earliest and that the false knight was originally a supernatural being; but so different are their methods and concepts that one is not quite sure that the two scholars are studying the same material.

Though Nygard's study is actually historic and geographic, it is not precisely "Finnish." Nygard disdains the trappings of what he calls "pseudo-science," such as the largely statistical treatment of motifs, and he places less emphasis on the reconstruction of the archetype. For the formalism of the Finnish school, Nygard substitutes an evaluation of the variants and a detailed comparison of texts to determine the pattern of dissemination. He clearly holds that different forms of a ballad are textually related. He finds that ballads, excepting a few repetitious and simple examples, demand a special treatment because of their structural characteristics which resist change and induce substitution or extensive recomposition rather than gradual alteration. A ballad must therefore be studied not in résumés of motifs but as "unit-structures of language" (p. 15), with due attention to their phrasing and their verse and stanzaic structure. Furthermore, "the variants from a single nation or linguistic area have family resemblances that render them recognizable as comprising a national form" (p. 17). Nygard consequently emphasizes the "literary aspect of a ballad's tradition" (p. 12) and developments within linguistic boundaries, without much concern for the geographical or narrative periphery of the tradition.

Within the chosen area of his investigation, Nygard's method produces impressive results, tracing the migration of the ballad from Dutch-German forms to Scandinavia on the one hand and to Britain through France on the other. The relations of texts within an area are ordered so that international relations are clarified. For example, the close study destroys the basic validity of the much-valued Child A and B texts (ironically disposing of "Lady Isabel" as an acceptable title) and demonstrates the priority of English over Scottish texts, thus revealing the French source of British tradition. Nygard plausibly accounts for narrative change in the central traditions of the ballad by the retention of the villain's pleas to the maid after belief in his supernatural character disappeared, or by the maid's loss of heroic stature. His conclusions are limited, and the limitations are generally appropriate, particularly his refusal to postulate the genesis of the ballad. There have been almost as many theories of the source of "Heer Halewijn" and its relatives as there have been investigators, and Nygard finds all the conclusions "improbable possibilities" which "have been fathered by world views, *Zeitgiest*, climates of opinion, attitudes, partialities, rather than by the evidence that the subject itself, the ballad, affords" (p. 33). But whatever subsequent steps may be taken, study such as Nygard's provides the only stable basis.

Kemppinen takes a broader view both of the area necessary for study and of the forms of the ballad: "It is not until we reach right out to the boundaries of circulation of the folk poem, where the transformation of the ballad must be examined in connection with the question of its identity, that the changes pose the problem correctly" (p. 13). Kemppinen's approach is, as he terms it, *holistic*, identifying a unit of the *ballad entity* by its combination of certain motifs in the "spirit of the ballad" (p. 8). It is this method (together with the individual entries for successive appearances of identical texts) which produces 1,865 variants and leads Kemppinen to include narratives rejected by Nygard. But once accepted, all forms seem to have equal rank, and their precise relationships are not inquired into. Kemppinen is studying the origin and sources of the ballad, not the history of a ballad's development from a center. He is *himself* the center from which the variants, considered relatively equal, are equidistant.

Kemppinen's work, irresponsibly based as it is, raises questions largely avoided by Nygard. There is, of course, no brief for Kemppinen's eager grasping at any straw from any stage of "Heer Halewijn" tradition as long as it will support his theory that the knight is Herlewin or the devil's son. Kemppinen deals in dubious philology and even more dubious mythology.[181] But his emphasis on peripheral tradition and disregard of textual connection introduces the problem of the derivative or secondary ballad. Both Nygard and Kemppinen recognize the recasting of ballads, particularly at linguistic and cultural frontiers. And Nygard stresses the role of the more or less sophisticated ballad maker. But the two writers hold positions on the problem of ballad identification so far removed from each other that the precise nature of the derivative ballads falls unheeded between the two poles. Nygard treats as different ballads the national forms without verbal and phrasal parallels and international forms without strict narrative parallels.[182] Kemppinen, holding that "individual features are generally of a more lasting nature than the poetic entity" (p. 6), includes as a "literary variant," a lone American text of "The Cruel Ship's Carpenter." If he is correct in this inclusion, he fails to follow up the full implications of his method. As Samuel P. Bayard has pointed out, there are not only many more variants of "The Cruel Ship's Carpenter," but a number of other western ballads which can therefore be regarded as "spalds of this ancient ballad": "The Wexford Girl," "The Undaunted Female," "Rose Connoley," "Poor Omie," "The Banks of the Ohio," and "The Maid on the Shore." [183] To these might be added not only other late ballads of the murdered girl, but "James Harris (The Daemon Lover)," which, as Bayard writes of the other ballads, is no more drastically revised than some of the peripheral Baltic versions which Kemppinen includes. If these narratives are to be considered derivative or secondary, their relation to the "original" and to the primary tradition of the ballad is important in a consideration of the ballad's history and particularly in relation to Kemppinen's contention that the plot and theme of a ballad become increasingly obscure as it moves toward the periphery of its tradition. It is the more recently developed forms of such ballads as "The Cruel Ship's Carpenter" which are closer to the basic narrative of "Heer Halewijn." Does the answer lie in coincidence, "reversion," or the influence of the parent tradition?

Obviously, the studies of the traditions of older ballads are not merely adding to knowledge but are constantly raising problems of methodology and classification. Study of the traditions of "Lady Alice" and "Clerk Colvill" has united them as well as thrown light on their diffusion.[184] Examination of the French-British-Scandinavian versions of "Lord Thomas and Fair Annet" points to a French original and questions the traditional status of the Percy version.[185] Problems of origin, identification, variation, and editing are raised by Norman Cazden's consideration of the Yarrow ballads.[186] He has advanced good reasons for accepting Child's A-C versions of "Rare Willie Drowned in Yarrow" as a part of the tradition of "The Braes o' Yarrow." And his argument that the "make my bed" stanza of "Barbara Allen" is probably, in this rhyme form at least, original with "The Braes o' Yarrow" deserves consideration. But his insistence that "The Braes o' Yarrow" originally concerned a high-born lady and a lower-class lover needs the support of a methodology stricter than the perception of "poetic validity." Cazden's own emphasis on the "highly stylized rhyme-scheme" casts doubt on the originality of the "servant lad in Galla" stanzas. If Cazden's argument is correct, not only Scott's copies but those collected by William Robertson, Mrs. Murison, Robert Lambe, William Motherwell, and others all involve "aristocratic" rewriting. Cazden is correct in emphasizing the social framework of the ballad; but that framework alters with that of the ballad singer. And Child does not, as Cazden implies, completely accept Scott's account of the background of the ballad; he notes that such events "are likely to have occurred often in history" and cites a Scandinavian parallel [187] which must be examined before any determination of origin be made.

What may amount to a crisis in contemporary ballad study is revealed in the dispute over the origin, diffusion, and antiquity of "Sir Aldingar." In *European Balladry* (pp. 66–67, 195, 233–234), W. J. Entwistle, following Grundtvig (and apparently Child) treated "Sir Aldingar" as the representative of the earliest-known English ballad, which was the parent of the Scandinavian "Ravengaard og Memering." Six years later E. K. Chambers in *English Literature at the Close of the Middle Ages* (pp. 154–155) denied that Entwistle's chief witness, William of Malmesbury, in his twelfth-century *Gesta Regum Anglorum* account of the Gunhild tradition and the song of her wedding, was referring to a ballad identifiable as "Sir Aldingar." And he further pointed out that Scandinavian versions are closer to the accounts of Malmesbury and others. In 1948 Entwistle reviewed the evidence [188] and restated his case that Malmesbury and Matthew Paris described "a typical ballad performance," probably in assonating distichs, and that the subsequent evolution in Scandinavia was influenced by other ballads and by other legends of the accused queen, even while preserving elements of the original lost in English evolution. Entwistle's argument was then attacked by Donald S. Taylor,[189] who, on the same evidence, refused to hypothesize a Gunhild ballad behind Malmesbury's account, was cautious in postulating the existence of Gunhild ballads even by the middle of the thirteenth century, and denied that the present texts of "Sir Aldingar" could be directly descended from such ballads. Further, he favored a Scandinavian original.

Finally, Paul Christopherson produced a lengthy study of *The Ballad of* Sir Aldingar: *Its Origin and Analogues* (1952), which partially supports Entwistle in that it postulates a parallel spread of the Gunhild story (or ballad) from Flanders to England *and* Denmark in the twelfth century, a combination of the Gunhild tradition with the story of another accused queen, Gundeberg (which may have occurred before the tradition reached England), and the alteration of the Scandinavian ballad by the English Gunhild-Gundeberg ballad, which was exported to Norway in the thirteenth century.

Clearly Entwistle and Christopherson hold a wider concept of ballad and the tradition of a ballad than do Chambers and Taylor. And Entwistle and Christopherson find it much easier to equate oral tradition and *"in triviis cantitata"* with ballads, easier to assume that a legend in an English chronicle is drawn from an English ballad, and to place the origin of a ballad as early as possible. The problem of date is exceedingly important, but another matter is of even greater concern for ballad scholarship. Christopherson's study is an important treatment of a popular theme (the queen accused and vindicated of infidelity) which may stretch back even to the story of Susannah and the Elders. The infidelity tale is told in a number of romances and has been attached to a number of historical figures. Christopherson makes a full survey of the material and even turns up a bit of new evidence; he also adumbrates the ballad tradition represented by the comparative handful of texts themselves. Most interesting is the fact that the evidence of the texts themselves hardly agrees with the conclusion Christopherson draws on the basis of material not provided by the ballads themselves. Therefore, the more credence placed in Christopherson's reconstruction, the less trust one can give to distribution studies based on the evidence of the texts alone.

Keeping largely to the ballads themselves, one might support a theory that two waves of tradition reached Scandinavia, but not from the direction Christopherson thinks. The first was the German Gunhild story of a falsely accused queen freed after a trial by ordeal. Such a ballad survives on the Scandinavian periphery: in Iceland and, slightly influenced by a later arrival, in the Faeroes. The Scandinavian ballad became greatly modified by the Gundeberg story, which contained a trial by combat between two unequal antagonists. The modified Scandinavian ballad reached England, where the "loathly bedfellow" was introduced from some member of the Oliva-Sibella group of stories and the ballad associated with "our comely queen" Eleanor. Contradicting this we have "those whispers of local tradition, those fragments from documents and hints from works of art" that Entwistle speaks of,[190] and Christopherson's philological evidence for the development of the names of the combatants in "Ravengaard og Memering." The appearance of the story, including the names *Rodogan* and *Mimecan* and a drawing of the combat, in English chronicles of the twelfth and thirteenth centuries is important evidence. But can an English ballad be postulated on such evidence? Christopherson finds that the names of the combatants in the Scandinavian ballads are best explained by development from the English *Rodigar* and *Mimecan*. But are the principles of regular linguistic development applicable to the variation of proper names in a ballad? Further, the names *Rögnvald*, *Roysning*, and *Roysnigur* appear in the older Scandinavian ballad, and Christopherson himself believes *Mimecan* to have been formed on the Continent, from whence it could have been carried directly to Scandinavia. The problems raised by the "Sir Aldingar" studies are vital to ballad research. If on the one hand Entwistle and Christopherson have emphasized the importance of thematic study, they have on the other questioned the basic techniques of study.

Whatever questioning of study techniques results, the enlargement of the horizon of the Anglo-American ballad critic seems destined to continue. The limitation imposed by the Child-Grundtvig emphasis on Anglo-Scandinavian relations, which Nygard in an unpublished paper has viewed as rather unfortunate, is being re-

moved. Entwistle in *European Balladry* and since [191] has contributed immeasurably to the widening interest; and Archer Taylor's
articles have called attention to important thematic relations of
British ballads and those of Germany and Spain.[192]

A word needs to be said regarding the neglect of "the other half
of the ballad" in the studies thus far considered. Barry is clearly
right when, in reviewing Taylor's study of "Edward," he demands that "since there is a *musical* as well as a *textual* tradition
to every ballad, all the evidence be used." [193] There are valid reasons
for the neglect of the music. In the first place, the evidence of associated tunes is so scanty, because of the textual emphasis of early
collectors, that conclusions based on such evidence tend to be
dangerous. Texts are sometimes "set to forms of a tune so common,
widespread, and variously associated that it cannot be used as evidence one way or another in the solutions of problems of ballad
history." [194] Valuable textual studies can certainly be made independently of tune study. Yet the musical evidence can solve problems puzzling to the textualist, as Barry shows in his examination
of the refrains to "The Twa Sisters" and "The Cruel Mother"; [195]
and few authors of textual studies have made any attempt to examine the musical record. There is no need to continue the warfare
between the textualist and the tune investigator. Students now
recognize the importance of ballad music, and one cannot condemn
the scholar who recognizes his limitations and works within them.

At the risk of a slight digression, we note another symptom of
the quickening of ballad study: the recrudescence of interest in
Robin Hood. Child's judgment that the hero was the creation of
the ballad muse [196] has been recently challenged by ritualist and
euhemerist alike. A goodly number of English scholars, loosely
called the *Cambridge School*—for example, Margaret Murray (*The
God of the Witches*, 1933), Robert Graves (*The White Goddess*,
1948), and Pennethorne Hughes (*Witchcraft*, 1952)—see Robin
Hood as a grand master of a witch coven and therefore the survival
of a pagan god. Perhaps most influential of all has been Lord Rag-
lan's *The Hero* (1937), which presents the Robin Hood legend

(and everything else the writer recognizes as folk narrative) as an outgrowth of ritual drama. Lewis Spence (*Myth and Ritual in Game, Dance, and Rhyme,* 1947) and Douglas Kennedy (*England's Dances,* 1949) are convinced that Robin Hood is a vegetation spirit; and even Evelyn Wells (*The Ballad Tree,* 1950) seems impressed with the mythological background of the hero. An effective answer is made in England by Barbara Lowe,[197] who examines and refutes point by point those characteristics allegedly connecting Robin Hood with the ritual hero or the witch cult. She traces the connection of Robin Hood and his companions with the May Games. She finds Robin Hood a flesh-and-blood man, if only a fictitious one.

But two English antiquarians, J. W. Walker (*The True History of Robin Hood,* 1952) and P. Valentine Harris (*The Truth about Robin Hood,* 1952) have spoken out again for the historicity of the legend. Following up the investigations of Joseph Hunter (*The Great Hero of the Ancient Minstrelsy of England,* 1852), they have unearthed in the Wakefield Manor Court Rolls and other Yorkshire sources a number of interesting details of the life of a fourteenth-century Robin Hood, who may very well be connected with the legend.

Most American students,[198] like Bacil F. Kirtley, view the ritualists as *fantaistes,*[199] but do not overemphasize the historicity of the legend. With sturdy good sense and not a little humor, W. E. Simeone has carefully examined Robin Hood's late entrance into the May Games and has reevaluated the historical evidence.[200] His considered defense of Child's judgment makes room for whatever evidence even the ritualist can provide:

> A historic figure may be at the matrix, and he may wear the tatters of a god, but certainly the legend has been built, ballad by ballad, overwhelmingly, if not exclusively, by the ballad maker. His imagination wove a rich diversity into the ballads which, surprisingly enough, will support almost any theory for the origin of the great English outlaw.[201]

More recently, Simeone has restored Robin Hood to his rightful place in a pattern, not of ritual myth, but of the outlaw from before Hereward the Saxon to Jesse James and beyond— "a story that has been created before and will undoubtedly be created again." [202]

THE STUDY OF OTHER
TYPES OF FOLKSONG

The territory outside the circle of narrative folksong is largely uncharted. The limits of the material are uncertain, let alone the divisions. It is doubtful that there will ever be a complete, not to speak of a consistent, outline of the varieties of folksong. None has been attempted. This brief section cannot include all the contributions to knowledge in such a broad field. But because intensive and significant studies have been few and limited to a few genres, a brief discussion may suggest the richness of the field and indicate the value of intensive studies of a few areas.

It should be made clear at the outset that editorial treatment of nonnarrative folksong has been similar to that accorded ballads. In the *Journal of the Folk-Song Society* and in American academic collections, the songs appear with bibliographical and comparative notes. That the information is usually less full is often due as much to lack of information as to lack of interest. And comparative notes sometimes develop into stimulating study, such as Anne G. Gilchrist's article on *lying songs*.[203] Three types of songs have received important study: religious folksong, work song, and the American play-party song. A fourth type, the folk-lyric, is now coming into more prominent notice. The following discussion will consider briefly the work song and the play-party song, devoting more space to the religious song because of the accomplished work, and to the folk-lyric because of its promise.

The work song proper, that is, the song accompanying rhythmical labor, is not a widespread type. Excepting the waulking songs of the Western Isles of Scotland,[204] Anglo-American examples seem limited to the sea shanties and the gang songs of Negroes. The two bodies of song have become mingled, although that is no argument for their common genesis. Polygenesis seems more probable.

The work songs of sailors are undoubtedly ancient, at least as far as the custom is concerned. Miss Broadwood pointed out references in *Daphnis and Chloe* (A.D. 200–400) and *The Wanderings of Brother Felix* (1480–1483).[205] *The Complaynt of Scotland* (1549) contains texts of what we would call shanties, and one extant shanty, "Haul on the Bowline," has been shown on internal evidence to be at least as old as the early seventeenth century. But the modern custom did not come into notice until the 1830s, and the term is not mentioned before 1856 (in reference to happenings of the late 1840s). Texts appeared sporadically during the later nineteenth century, and collections with tunes appeared before the turn of the century. Two early English collections, Frederick J. Davis and Ferris Tozer's *Sailor's Songs or "Chanties"* (1887) and Laura A. Smith's *The Music of the Waters* (1888) are not very helpful. Davis's shanties were apparently remembered from a rather late tradition, and the tunes are highly arranged. Miss Smith's book contains much besides shanties and much that has no connection with the seaman's repertoire. Her efforts to collect songs at sailors' boardinghouses in the Tyne ports were somewhat hampered by her sex; but it should be added that there is not yet a published collection of unexpurgated shanties. W. B. Whall, a ship's officer with academic and musical training who went to sea in 1861 and took down the shanties in the eleven years following, compiled the best early collection and published it in *The Nautical Magazine* and *The Yachting Monthly*, 1906–1910, and as *Ships, Sea-Songs, and Shanties* in 1910. Collections have since issued from retired seamen, travelers, and folksong collectors.[206] Unfortunately, collectors most qualified musically did their collecting ashore, and one must depend on descriptions for the full performance, which was dying before it was discovered. Recent recordings from shantymen have been helpful in preserving the ornamented singing style.

Although the communalists took some interest in shanties as products of the "singing throng," most of the study has been connected with the origin of the name, which many writers confounded with the origin of the songs and/or the custom of shantying. The controversy over the spelling (as representative of the original pronunciation) and the derivation of *shanty* or *chanty* has generated a good deal of heat. Writers who, like Joanna C. Colcord (*Roll and Go*, 1924) and David W. Bone (*Capstan Bars*, 1931), preferred the *chanty* spelling derived the word from the French or Norman-French. Some, like Whall, urged the spelling *shanty* on phonetic grounds. Richard Runciman Terry (though he referred to his theory as "more plausible still, and equally unconvincing") connected the word with the moving of waterfront huts of Negroes in West Indian ports, where the "object moved was a *shanty*; the music accompanying the operation was called by the negroes a *shanty* tune; its musical form (solo and chorus) was identical with the sailor *shanty*; the pulls on the rope followed the same method which obtained at sea; the soloist was called a *shantyman*." [207] Other writers (but not Terry) even credited the Negro with the origin of the sailor songs. That the name has anything to do with the origin of the songs is, to say the least, uncertain. William M. Doerflinger has made it clear that the original spelling seems to have been *chanty*, pronounced *tSænti*, and that the pronunciation *Sænti* developed in generations of use.[208] Though the word may have come simply from *chant* or from the French through Negro roustabouts, the best evidence seems to be that

> coloured seamen, famous singers all, influenced both words and song in sailors' chanties . . . but they did it as seamen, not as coloured men.[209]

As in other fields, study has shifted to more verifiable history and analysis of the songs themselves. There seem to be Negro shanties and white shanties and songs showing both influences.

The Negro work songs bring us even closer to the Afro-American-origin problem. Here it is sufficient to indicate the opportunities for study which have grown out of the collections and, paradoxically, the almost futile argument. Like the shanties, Negro work songs were collected during a period of decay, and the texts received attention first. One must depend on inadequate descriptions for singing prior to the twentieth century. Fortunately, John and Alan Lomax discovered and recorded gang singing in Southern prisons (see p. 186). Therefore a good deal more objective data is available. Although writers have been prone to assert opinions rather than to study the problem of African survivals in Negro song,[210] outspoken students have shown a tendency to compromise.[211] African work songs, including the call-and-response technique, must have been part of the baggage brought by slavers, but it is equally obvious that the custom in question absorbs and re-creates song material. Scholars are now separating the problems: the origin of the custom, its development in America, the origin and treatment of textual and melodic material, and (but only recently) the relation of the performance to the labor, the study of which would require sound films. A thorough study of Negro work song may even aid in determining the history of songs and song types nominally placed in a different category. Work songs have both received and disgorged material, if not technique.

"The American play-party song is unique to the history of folksong," yet it has ancient roots. It is "game, dance, and song all in one and yet no one of them in particular." [212] Collection of these songs began early. Play-party songs were included in W. W. Newell's *Games and Songs of American Children* (1883), and the first song text printed in the *Journal of American Folklore* was "My Pretty Little Pink." [213] Thereafter, play-party songs appeared almost regularly in journals and collections. The notes to collected items frequently dealt with the place of the play-party in the community and revealed that the custom was not confined to children. The reports laid the foundation for a new type of investigation.

The orthodox study of children's games has been concerned with their preservation of customs and beliefs of primitive man, as in Lady Alice Bertha Gomme's *The Traditional Games of England, Scotland and Ireland* (1894–1898). Newell's work was concerned with similar problems, including the preservation in singing games of other folksongs and popular poetry. This approach naturally continued, but as more and more information accumulated, the play-party came to be viewed as a function rather than as a survival.

B. A. Botkin in *The American Play-Party Song* (1937) has surveyed and interpreted the material. His chief contribution is the separation of the play-party from games, singing games, and ring games. The literature of the subject has a common tenor: the play-party developed because of the religious prohibition against dancing. Botkin does not completely disagree with this conclusion, but he finds it not the sole explanation of the play-party, which he views as a natural development of frontier conditions (pp. 18*ff.*). Certainly the survival of play-parties is not contingent upon the prohibition,[214] and the play-party did satisfy social needs on the frontier (if we include rural New England in the frontier). But overwhelming evidence still favors the initial influence of the religious prohibition.

One more point: the functional study of folksong—which must be continually emphasized—must not obscure other values. The play-party preserves and adapts current material, and the material and its adaption are open to serious study. In this sense, the survival approach is not outmoded.

Religious folksong represents more a subject matter or functional division than a genre. Within the broad boundaries of the group there are songs which, on other grounds, might be separated into ballads, cumulative songs, lyrics, and so on. Furthermore, in terms of their study, it is useful to separate religious folksongs into folk carols and spiritual folksongs.

Though a few of the songs have taken root in North America, the folk carol, "either in its Christian application or in the pagan, seasonal survivals almost inseparable from the 'luck visit' . . . or 'wassailing' as it is called," [215] belong to the Old World.[216] Interest in these songs has been mainly English and has manifested itself in brief articles and notes by Miss Gilchrist, Miss Broadwood, and others in the *Journal of the Folk-Song Society*. No attempt has been made to apply the historic-geographic method to the songs.

Commentators have carefully examined texts and made minute, sweeping, and perhaps intuitive comparisons with medieval material. The suggestions are interesting and sometimes impressive. Miss Gilchrist's study of "Corpus Christi" [217] laid the foundation, for she deals with a song found in a manuscript of about 1400 as well as in modern tradition. Her interpretation of the symbolism in terms of the Grail legends was imitated by other students. Miss Gilchrist concludes that "Come All You Little Streamers" is a "degraded relic of a symbolic hymn in honor of the Virgin and in praise of the Heavenly Paradise"; [218] but M. J. C. Hodgart insists that it be interpreted in Freudian terms.[219] The fact is that "symbolic" judgments, whether of the "parable of birth" in "Thomas Rymer" and "James Harris" [220] or of the connection of "The Bold Young Fisherman" with the legend of the Fisher King [221] must be taken *cum grano salis*. Yet the known fact of rationalization demands that all the possibilities be considered. And the ritual background of the "Pace Egging" song, "Hunting the Wren," and others must be conceded and further studied. Miss Gilchrist's studies have the virtue of considering the songs individually,[222] but one must guard against the tendency to interpret folksongs according to a single pattern. Less ambitious but more disciplined studies, such as the investigations of "The Carol of the Twelve Numbers" by W. W. Newell [223] and Leah Rachel Clara Yoffie [224] seem more promising at present.

The other body of religious folksong to receive important study is that which grew up largely from the need for "folky religious song" among the Anglo-American Protestant dissenters in the second and third decades of the eighteenth century. Before 1770 the practice began of setting religious texts to folk melodies. Although the practice was common on both sides of the Atlantic, the songs flourished in the rural United States and grew in the great revivals of the early nineteenth century. With the emergence of urban culture the great popularity of the songs became restricted to the rural South, where they still survive in individual memories and in cultural islands of group singin's. Aspects of this material must be considered in connection with the study of folk tunes and the controversy over Negro spirituals, but a few observations on the development and progress of the study are apposite here.

Three main developments contributed to the study of spiritual folksongs: (1) unrestricted collection; (2) two origin controversies; (3) an investigation into local culture. Because the oldest traditional element in spiritual folksongs is the music, we might have expected Cecil Sharp to recognize their prevalence and importance in the repertoire of the Southern Appalachian singer. But he did not believe hymns to be folksong, so he did not listen. He writes of his singers:

> Very often they misunderstood our requirements and would give us hymns instead of the secular songs which we wanted; but that was before we learned to ask for "love songs." [225]

Therefore, his 1917 collection contains only two religious songs (one of which is "The Cherry Tree Carol"), the 1932 edition but half a dozen, and the manuscripts only a few more. Although most American collectors lacked musical competency and had no knowledge that church music could be folk music (in fact, they often lamented that for religious reasons their singers had sloughed off the "devil's ditties" for hymns), they tended to record and publish all sorts of material in the repertory of their informants. Therefore religious texts creep into early collections. Not until the late twenties do spiritual songs appear in significant numbers.

Two great controversies are more important. The Ballad War caused some attention to be paid to the revival spirituals because they seemed to be products of a homogeneous throng. It was to the Negro spiritual, however, that the communalists more often turned, and it was the controversy over the origin of the Negro spiritual that brought white religious song to the fore.[226] (See Appendix I). The discovery of a relationship between Negro and white religious song grew largely from textual comparison, though Miss Pound in an early contribution to the controversy [227] did point out a similarity in tune between "Weeping Mary" as printed by

Krehbiel and as sung by her mother. Newman I. White's argument in *American Negro Folk-Songs* (1928) for the white genesis of the Negro spiritual drew upon the texts of revival song books. Guy B. Johnson in *Folk Culture on St. Helena Island, South Carolina* (1930) called attention to musical analogies not only in white hymn books but in white secular song. The way was prepared for George Pullen Jackson, who entered the area by another route.

Jackson learned of country singings by "pure accident" [228] and then began to follow the trail "in the middle of the 1920s outside the circle of the folklorists and in complete ignorance of the facts that what was sought was genuine folk material." [229] Jackson's search led him through the singing conventions and the shape-note hymn books to the discovery of not a "survival in culture" but a creative folk tradition which had built up an impressive body of song. He learned that the old rural hymn books were important collections of orally transmitted religious songs and that these songs consisted of religious verses set to secular folk tunes by folk composers. In her own earlier examination of a few American hymn books, Miss Gilchrist had noted that

> there are . . . various tunes which one would class as folk-airs were there not composers' names attached to them. This leads to the conclusion that either the alleged composers were merely adapters, or else that these more or less untrained musicians unconsciously formed their simple tunes on lines familiar to them from traditional ballads and songs sung in their homes and villages. [230]

Jackson shows that the ascriptions often indicate either the arranger or the person from whom the compiler learned the song. [231] He further shows that tunes were *southernized*; that is, they were deliberately revised to fit the style of the Southern singing folk. [232]

To this great body of printed music Jackson applied internal and external tests [233] to cull out the folk tunes. The result was a history of the song movement—the singing schools, the compilers and folk composers, the camp-meeting recompositions, presented in *White Spirituals in the Southern Uplands* (1933), *White and Negro Spirituals* (1943), and the introductions to Jackson's collections—and a three-volume collection of religious ballads, folk hymns, and revival spirituals—*Spiritual Folk-Songs of Early America* (1937), *Down-East Spirituals* (1943), and *Another Sheaf of White Spirituals* (1952)—that is almost definitive. Jackson's studies were analytical, historical, comparative, and functional. They furnish a background for future studies, particularly of individual songs. His researches into hymn books and group singin's have been supplemented by collection from individual singers.[234] There is hardly an aspect of Anglo-American folksong on which the study of spirituals has not shed some light.

The term *folk-lyric* loosely designates a type of song lacking a coherent, developed story and consisting of images held together by a tune or mood. "With its endlessly wandering groups of stanzas, interchange of cliché, and lack of plotted action, folk lyric often appears beyond definition and even description." [235] The songs differ greatly in age, origin, and stability. Relatively stable pieces like "The Pale Amaranthus" ("Wildwood Flower") offer fewer problems and may be fairly new sentimental pieces adopted by the folk. Complexes such as that comprised of "The Inconstant Lover," "The Wagoner's Lad," "Old Smoky," and others, which may represent one or a number of originals, are more interesting and offer greater difficulties. The apparently free combination of stanzas and clichés makes us wonder if some of them do not exist as free agents. Granting that floating stanzas, like story incidents, had a time and place of origin, they may be actually "floating around in a vacuum awaiting a chance to attach themselves." [236] There is yet little information to provide an answer, though J. W. Allen has demonstrated that it is sometimes possible to trace elements of a composite lyric to their earlier and apparently original home." [237] Generally, editors in their notes have commented on the problems of the type, but, as Coffin writes, students seem to have been "scared off and discouraged" by the difficulties.[238]

There are a number of ways of approaching the problem, of which the most fruitful initially would seem to be the method Coffin has shown, the historic-geographic study of identifiable lyrics. The first step is to select the identifying element in the song, which may be melodic or textual, and thus to limit the material. Otherwise the investigator will involve himself in the study of countless songs and tunes. (And he will in any event, if he pursues the subject far enough.) The subject of Coffin's research, "Green Grows the Laurel," [239] is a "typical folk lyric" in that it is of average stability, a fact which enables the student to determine rather easily the core of the song while presenting problems of accumulation and dispersal. Coffin's work thus far has been concerned with only the identifying element: the chorus. He has tentatively established its main types and the pattern of its diffusion. He has yet to reach conclusions concerning the associated stanzas and the relation of this song to others. But the approach seems promising and deserves emulation.

Tune Scholarship

The devotion of a separate and relatively minor section to the study of the folk tune unfortunately follows the pattern of Anglo-American folksong study. The folk tune is not simple nor can its study be dismissed casually. But this section must reduce the complexities to a few major points. There are convenient analogies between text and tune scholarship, and these facilitate an abbreviated discussion. But there are notable divergencies which require careful delineation.

The student approaching the study of folk music faces almost every problem of the textualist. The record of folk tunes before the eighteenth century is, if anything, less clear than that of the texts. The early collectors extended, emended, and otherwise disfigured their material. (And there are significant differences in the individual interpretations of the careful collectors of later years.[240]) The tune presents problems of origin, style or technical peculiarities, diffusion, and variation, and is reciprocally related but not married to the text. In the early work of Sharp and the Folk-Song Society, the study of the tune was beclouded with evolutionary concepts which possibly mistook a number of technical peculiarities for actual steps in a developmental process. And then, justifiably, of course, students became engrossed in technical details.

But there have been significant differences in the material itself and in the development of techniques to deal with it. True, one may find an apparent similarity in the allotment of the text to the literary scholar and the tune to the musician. But the texts found a more congenial and a more fit place in the disciplines of philology and literary folklore than did the tune in the tradition of art music. Folk music fell into a vacuum between musicology and anthropology.[241] It cannot be said that folk music is finally more complex than folk poetry. But it is more baffling at the outset. The difficulty presents itself in the immediate and basic problem of identifying cognate tune items. The textualists can more easily recognize the fundamental relationship among variants and ignore nondiagnostic commonplaces than can the tune scholar, who "does not have recurrent corresponding stanzas, or runs of stanzas, a correspondence or identity of situation and thought, and a perceptible story to guide him" [242] and thus cannot readily isolate musical formulas. Problems of classification have therefore been more acute and confused.[243]

There have been two interrelated approaches to the study of folk tunes: the analytic and the genetic. The analytic deals with scales, modes, rhythm, structure, contour, formulas, and the like. The genetic seeks to trace the history and development of an air in all its variants. Falling between the two, and uniting them, is the study of variation. Although the studies have been to some extent concurrent, analytical study naturally had priority. As genetic study grew, the problems and aims of analysis altered. Therefore this brief survey will not rigidly separate the studies and will emphasize problems seemingly of pressing importance.

The founding of the Folk-Song Society in 1898 gave great emphasis to analysis. Members of the Society were not unaware of genetic problems, but their immediate tasks were: (1) collection and preservation of accurately transcribed material; and (2) display and propagation of authentic folk tunes in English national life. These needs led to a preoccupation with the technical qualities of folk music and perhaps to an undervaluation of the earlier record.[244] Modal peculiarities in particular were stressed, but when Sharp made his summary in 1907, other qualities received attention.

In addition to his description of modality and rhythmic irregularity, Sharp in *English Folk-Song: Some Conclusions* notes important characteristics of scale and structure. He points out the relative strength of the first, fourth, fifth, and eighth degrees of the scale and the weakness or wavering character of the third and seventh degrees, where neutral or quarter tones often occur. This vagueness seems to give rise to melodic figures different from those of harmonic music. He recognizes that folk tunes are composed predominantly of four-phrase combinations of two phrases, e.g., ABBA, AABA; occasionally of three phases, e.g., ABAC; and rarely of four, e.g., ABCD—a conclusion which has been recently severely modified.

During the years of collecting that followed, notes in the *Journal of the Folk-Song Society* dealt alternately with analysis and genetic relationships. Understandably there was neither time for elaborate study nor material to base it on. Loose terminology developed, particularly in the varying use of the word *type*. Sometimes the commentator seems to refer to some sort of "national style";[245] at other times the reference seems to be genetic.[246] But parallels clearly meant as genetic occur in other notes (of varying value [247]). The annotations recognize genetic relationship among highly divergent tune items, but present no coherent pattern for determining the relationships. More carefully worked out analyses had more immediate influence.

Pentatonic scales, rare in England but extremely popular in the Southern United States, have been of considerable importance in modal analysis. Most widely followed has been Miss Gilchrist's system developed on the basis of Francis Tolmie's collection of Gaelic tunes.[248] Briefly, Miss Gilchrist's system is a numbered order of five pentatonic modes derived from c d f g a ć by a progressive inversion, with an indication of their relationship to "derivative" hexatonic and heptatonic modes by the filling of the gaps. On the basis of her material and theories, she finds two heptatonic modes derivative of each pentatonic. Her formulation has been the basis of almost all subsequent analysis. Sharp modified the system twice, the second time on the basis of his Appalachian collection. Hilton Rufty, Herman Reichenbach, George Pullen Jackson, and Annabel Morris Buchanan have made various formulations, all based on Miss Gilchrist's original chart, but differing in the modes to be derived by filling the gaps.[249] The revisions (except Reichenbach's) are extensions of the system to cover new possibilities. Mrs. Buchanan added a sixth basic scale, Mode 6, Neutral, a neutral or Mixolydian form of Mode 2 in which the neutral third and seventh are stressed and predominant.[250]

A reformulation of the entire system has been made by Bertrand H. Bronson.[251] Finding that historical expositions tend to obscure melodic relationships among modal scales, Bronson has reordered his scales on a common tonic and thus has indicated the correspondences among individual pentatonic, hexatonic, and heptatonic forms of a tune. He concludes that a tune varies from one mode to another along certain well-defined routes. An Ionian tune becomes Mixolydian by first becoming an Ionian/Mixolydian heptatonic (losing the seventh degree of its scale) and then replacing the missing tone with a flat seventh; the tune can then become Dorian through the Mixolydian/Dorian (hexatonic missing the third). An Ionian may become Dorian by losing its third and seventh degrees (becoming Bronson's Pentatonic Mode 2) and replacing them with a minor third and a flatted seventh. Bronson also suggests that melodies may vary from one mode to another because of authentic-plagal relationships. Thus a plagal variant of an Ionian tune may become Mixolydian because of its correspondence with the Mixolydian authentic form. The processes described may, of course, be reversed. Without affirming or denying evolutionary theories, Bronson has devised a convenient method of arranging, even explaining, variants.

Most heartening, perhaps, is that musicologists, turning to the analysis of Western folk music, are escaping the tyranny of the concepts and symbols developed in the study and notation of art music. In his notations of North Carolina ballads,[252] Jan P. Schinhan attempts to present what he finds, dispensing, for example, with useless and misleading key signatures. His analysis is not regimented by the concepts of the pentatonic, hexatonic, and heptatonic modes: of 512 tunes he lists 220 as triadic, tetratonic, pentachordal, hexachordal, heptachordal, or irrational. Folk music is difficult to notate and well nigh impossible to represent by the conventional and inaccurate symbolization. The International Music Council has recommended the retention of staff notation with supplementary signs "because of its convenience and universality," pointing out that "a notation tending to mathematical exactitude must necessarily depend on physical principles and would therefore entail the use of signs intelligible only to specialists." [253] The problem of *hearing* the peculiarities is, however, also involved, and there have been efforts to devise a reasonable mechanical notator. Recent experiments by Charles Seeger [254] are promising in terms of both accuracy and cost of apparatus.

If we exclude modal analysis, Anglo-American tune study prior to 1936 was not extensive. One should not, of course, underestimate the importance of certain observations and studies. Alexander Keith in his 1917 comments on Greig's collection called attention to the large number of variants of a few recognizable tunes circulating in Aberdeenshire, the prevalence of one-strain melodies, and the ability of singers to separate words and tunes.[255] Singing style received some attention. Sharp contrasted the active style of the Southern Appalachian singers with the rigid passive style he encountered in England [256] and which W. Roy MacKenzie found among the older singers in Nova Scotia.[257] Phillips Barry described an "old" or *rubato parlando* technique in New England.[258] A number of problems were receiving attention from a few students, but only Phillips Barry was in any great degree concerned with the identification and study of widespread tunes.

A summary of Barry's studies of tune versions cannot be undertaken here. They are many, though limited, and they give evidence of his developing recognition of what are now termed *tune families.* Tentatively outlining the descent of the "Lord Randall" tune in 1910, he notes its relationship to a number of other English melodies.[259] Partial histories of tune versions appear throughout his writings, but never does he give a complete exposition of the problem. Yet his many discussions of the "way of the folk" with their tunes reveal his grasp of the complex reshapings that create a tune family. Had he outlined the identifying or diagnostic features amid the flux, perhaps the next phase of study might have proceeded more smoothly.

In 1936 George Herzog published his report on *Research in Primitive and Folk Music in the United States* for the American Council of Learned Societies, and Sigurd Bernhard Hustvedt completed "A Melodic Index of Child's Ballad Tunes." [260] In 1937 the Committee on Folksong of the Modern Language Association published a report devoted almost exclusively to the music of folksong,[261] and Herzog ordered the contents of Arthur Palmer Hudson's *Folktunes from Mississippi* musically instead of textually. It is now clear that these publications indicated the shift of the center of tune scholarship from England to the United States. Both the "Suggestions and Recommendations of the Committee" and Herzog's report emphasized the accurate recording of folksong and its study, Herzog commenting on vocal technique, relationship of text and tune, variation, and the cultural and psychological setting. The particular problems of genetic study are treated in Hustvedt's index, Herzog's edition of Hudson's tunes, and Herzog's article, "Musical Typology in Folksong," issued as a part of the report of the MLA Committee on Folksong.[262]

The problem of the indexer is to organize tunes in an order that will reveal their genetic relationship to other tunes within and without the index. English scholars had merely classified songs according to modes. The two American experiments are based on Continental experience with melodic indexes: [263] Herzog employing the Krohn-Bartók system based on "phrase finals" [264] and Histvedt using a formula for the melodic contour of the first phrase. Both methods suffer from a mechanical approach. Herzog, recognizing that "no system of classification or typology can give complete satisfaction or safe clues to where some or all relatives of a given melody may be found," [265] could not claim a success for his experiment and has pointed out succinctly that Hustvedt's system "leads to the same kind of results that we would get if we considered all songs whose first line is identical to be genetically related." [266] But Hustvedt's work cannot be viewed as a total failure which merely indicated the trend of genetic study, for he devised a useful and economical method of transcribing tunes without staff notation.[267]

Herzog is clearly right in stating, "The study of a melody *begins* after it has been placed in some system or index"; [268] on the other hand, study is needed to determine fundamental rather than haphazard traits in tune variants before a workable system can be devised. Significant efforts at determining relationship have shifted from a concentration on parts of a melody to consideration of the whole tune in the *Gestalt* principle. Sirvart Poladian has demonstrated that the most stable element in folk tunes is melodic contour.[269] The most important aspect of such studies is that they come *after the fact* of identification. This rather obvious comment points to the necessity of studying individual items or complexes before the devising of elaborate indexing systems. Had the musicians considered more carefully the course of textual scholarship, they might have arrived earlier at the conclusion that the tune, like the ballad text, is an *idea*. Does this not explain the production of the most noteworthy recent tune scholarship by men ostensibly scholars in language and literature?

George Pullen Jackson began his tune comparisons by considering the first few notes of the tunes.[270] Then he began to notice resemblances in "tonal vestment" among what he considered separate songs and applied the term *tune family* to these traits recognizable in apparently distinct tunes.[271] The work of Samuel P. Bayard and Bertrand H. Bronson has established the term, defined by Bayard:

> A *tune family* is a group of melodies showing basic interrelation by means of constant melodic correspondence, and presumably owing their mutual likeness to descent from a single air that has assumed multiple forms through processes of variation, imitation, and assimilation.[272]

Bayard has justified the approach in closely written articles which sum up knowledge of Anglo-American folk music beyond further compression.[273] It is sufficient to indicate the guiding principles.

Amid the wealth of Anglo-Irish-American song, dance, and instrumental music (with foreign affinities as well) there are more than forty families, each embracing many versions in many variants. Members of a family vary in range, rhythm, phrase order, and formulas, but are relatively united by similar melodic lines and corresponding stressed tones. These melodic ideas, not random collections of formulas or rigidly patterned tunes, have been subjected to conscious and unconscious variation, adapted to various uses, extended or contracted, but can be identified if a tune is examined completely. Lexicographical treatment is therefore impossible. The researcher must familiarize himself with the outlines of tune families and search for members displaying a number of features. The first task is the identification of related tunes, which can be done independently of texts.

There are also independent tunes, borrowed or created, but the common repertory is everywhere dominant. Evidence of this dominance is the fact, which is not helpful in the study of tune migration, that there do not seem to be localized tune versions. Though tunes show stylistic variations in certain areas, similar variations of widespread tunes turn up in area after area.[274] The lack of localized versions may attest the age of the tune families (one of which goes back to at least the tenth century) or their small number, which has resulted in interchange among and differing uses of members of the same family. Bayard has discussed the seven most widely encountered families and has published studies of three smaller ones.[275] Following the Finnish method of "recurrent motifs," Bronson has, with the help of an IBM machine,[276] established a tentative melodic contour for archetypes of two tune families,[277] the "inner core of identity." It is being demonstrated again that each bit of folklore is a study in itself and that only from such studies come reliable accounts of "the way of the folk."

Needless to say, the study of individual tunes is not the only approach productive of important data. Studies of tune-text fit, such as those of Bronson [278] and George W. Boswell,[279] reveal various degrees of relationship. Boswell demonstrates the influence of the tune on prosody, structure, and, to a slight extent, on pitch of words. Bronson is concerned not only with fit in a mechanical sense, but with modal semantics, tempo, and rhythm in relation to narrative tone, and with relations and shifts of tunes among ballads. Bronson's reports are based on the study of the tunes associated at one time or another with Child's texts. He has advanced thus far stimulating remarks on, among other things, the role of tunes in crossings and mergers, and the relations of gapped scales, rounded melodies, and even traditional instrumental accompaniment on the tone of ballads.[280] His study of shifts in types of refrains supports the admission of a "single and sudden . . . conscious shift" instead of a gradual transition in the creation of ballad versions, but it contrasts the passive transmission of recent tradition with a creative period that for the texts was at its height perhaps in the eighteenth century in Scotland, and that for the tunes continued much longer. In this "golden age" there is not "a perfectly pure traditional text . . . over which the individual transmitters from generation to generation have exercised no conscious control" but instead a constant creation and re-creation applied to melodic and textual ideas.[281] Bronson thus furnishes further support for the concepts of the ballad as idea and the folksinger as artist.

Turning his machine on nongenetic problems, Bronson has achieved results which set forth interesting generalizations and challenge older formulations. Turning to the common rather than to the unusual in ballads, he has elicited from the tunes of the seven most popular Child ballads in Anglo-American tradition "the *commonest* preferences." The discovery that the favorite forms are in the authentic range of the major, have four nonrepeating phrases and usually a triple beat, end on the tonic, and usually have a mid-cadence on the first degree of the scale is a step that has yet to be fully interpreted.[282] Also needing interpretation, but valuable in correcting previous statements made on less evidence, is Bronson's determination of the most popular modes in the Child ballad tunes. Ionian still holds first place but is followed by the Ionian/Mixolydian (hexatonic minus the seventh) and Pentatonic 1 (minus fourth and seventh), and Mixolydian. Of perhaps more immediate importance is his revision of Sharp's evolutionary principles of continuity, variation, and selection. Bronson finds, with Bayard, that folk tunes do not tend to vary themselves out of existence but remain within the traditional norm. The removal of the third principle, *selection*, still leaves us with a valid explanation of the melodic record. Despite the operation of the second principle, *variation*, the tune is kept within certain bounds by the working of the first principle, *continuity*, which inhibits change beyond a traditional norm, just as Sharp's *selection* purports to do, excepting that his selection is tied to his theory of evolution. Bronson establishes the fact of *relative stability*, actively resisting with varying strength at varying points the forces of change.[283]

The studies of Bayard and Bronson outline a melodic process traceable before the sixteenth century and bearing evidence of "the uninterrupted continuation of a long-lived and downright archaic tradition of music-making among the unschooled people." [284] Whatever the influence of art music, it has been swallowed up in a folk tradition. The dominant tunes in tradition crop up in broadsides but are not direct derivations of broadside tunes. The tune is the unit, recognizable whether re-created according to individual whim or in a regional style. Future study is needed to confirm these generalizations, but they can hardly be overturned.

If the pattern of the past is to be repeated, a new era of ballad study is announced by the present appearance of the first volume of

Bronson's *The Traditional Tunes of the Child Ballads* (1959). Here the student will have a reasonably complete, impeccably edited, and eruditely annotated arrangement of the tunes *together with the texts* from print and manuscript. This vast work is thus both complementary and supplementary to *The English and Scottish Popular Ballads*. The evidence is here displayed—not completely, for Bronson did not ferret out every private collection and, perhaps wisely, refrained from the reduction of recent sound recordings to symbol. But it is displayed in such bulk and with such skill that Bronson's judgment of Child's volumes can be applied to his own: "So far as he carried it out, his work is complete and sufficient, and will never have to be redone" (p. xviii). One would be impetuous, indeed, were he even to adumbrate the meaning and value of this work in the course of future scholarship. Yet one can confidently predict that the next historian of Anglo-American folksong scholarship will find in these volumes his incipit.

The Functional Approach

This survey of scholarship ends with a mention of a subject about which too little is known: the place of folksong in its setting and how it functions as a part of a social group. This very book represents one facet of the problem: the comparative isolation of folksong from other folklore. And the neglect of the functional approach in folksong study has been paralleled in other fields of folklore. Superstitions have been divorced from their social context and merely listed, just as bare songs have been displayed. Tales have been viewed as texts divorced from the teller and his audience. But interest in functionalism in recent years has pervaded the whole area of folklore study and has tended to unite it. The days of the collector of proverbs, string, songs, and bits of broken glass, in so far as serious study is concerned, seem numbered.

Some types of folksong can be recognized as more clearly functional than others. Thus one might distinguish songs closely related to work, dance, religion, seasonal festivals, *rites de passage*, etc., from the nonfunctional or esthetic songs. But such a distinction is not only loose, but tends to overlook the esthetics of function as well as the function of esthetics. For example, in *The Singing Englishman*—a book devoted mainly to the social background of English folksong—A. L. Lloyd finds expression of a "longing for a better life" in the relative dearth of protest songs.

> Generally the English folksinger . . . did not deny the facts of life nor did he sing about changing them, but he coloured them and wrapped them up in fantasy and to a certain extent disguised them, and even when they were sordid and stupid and brutal he turned them into something beautiful and tragic and honorable (p. 30).

But the distinction between functional and nonfunctional songs serves to point out the lack of emphasis on the functional aspect of Anglo-American folksong. In the first place, songs with an explicit function or directly related to the social life of the singers are of less importance in the Anglo-American repertoire (excepting perhaps that of the Negro) than elsewhere. Further, a number of the socially important songs are often local or of types other than those the collector has prized. And academic and esthetic emphasis on the isolated text and tune has tended to minimize the functional aspect of all types of folksong. The American collector particularly has tended often to confuse subject matter and function, to treat songs concerning work as work songs, songs about sailors as sailor songs, or songs about courtship as courting songs.

There is a good deal of scattered information concerning the folksinger and his attitude toward his songs. Why most of it is American evidence has already been explained in the discussion of collectors. But the reliability of the evidence is far from assured. Such matters as the singer's general attitude toward his song, which are learned from the difficulties of collecting, can be confirmed, but too many generalizations are based on apparently random evidence. Collectors have too often been either untrained outsiders or prejudiced natives. The romantic picture of Appalachian singers given by Sharp in *English Folk Songs from the Southern Appalachians* may be contrasted with the progressive view of Harvey H. Fuson in *Ballads of the Kentucky Highlands.* Sharp's singer who associated her song with driving home the cows [285] is paralleled by MacKenzie's informant who could remember a song when riding a rake.[286] But how representative are these oft-quoted examples?

Collectors' notes or introductions are not the only source of information concerning the function of folksong. MacKenzie's *Quest of the Ballad* (1919) is an early example of a book that devotes more space to singers than to songs. But, like much other work, it is written almost entirely from the viewpoint of the collector, and it is his quest and difficulties that entrance the reader, and, of course, teach valuable lessons in doing just what he did. The same point of view (with much more color) is maintained in Dorothy Scarborough's *A Song Catcher in the Southern Mountains* (1937). The two books present a contrast between communities in which songs are to be plucked from every cranny and those in which the collector can pick the brains of the aged only. One is tempted to accept them as examples of "early" and "late"; yet it must be remembered that after MacKenzie's singers were gone, other collectors harvested songs from the generation that had supposedly rejected them. Was the Nova Scotia tradition a bit more virile than MacKenzie thought, or was there a fundamental difference between Northeastern and Appalachian tradition?

A number of other examples emphasize the background of the material. Emelyn E. Gardner's *Folklore from the Schoharie Hills, New York* (1937) treats folksong as a part of the entire regional culture. The paucity of folksong in this isolated, illiterate group gives pause to the romantic critic and still demands adequate explanation. Vance Randolph has done a more thorough job in his many writings on the Ozarks, such as *The Ozarks* (1931) and *Ozark Mountain Folks* (1932), which provide the setting for his collections of songs, tales, and superstitions. Occupational collections such as those by Mrs. Ekstorm and Mrs. Smyth, George Korson, and most especially William M. Doerflinger have not wrenched the song from its setting. And Jean Ritchie's *Singing Family of the Cumberlands* provides our best portrait of Appalachian familial tradition. Howard W. Odum and Guy B. Johnson pioneered in studies of the function of Negro song; the Lomaxes have given a good part of the story of one Negro folk artist and biographical approaches to a number of other singers; and Zora Neale Hurston in *Mules and Men* (1935) is almost uniquely able to penetrate the "protective mask" of the Negro.

Without listing other examples, consider the important questions formulated by George Herzog in 1938:

> We may well wonder, for example, just why it is that people find delight or satisfaction in singing about things so remote as castles and kings and princes, whose existence in actual life would clash with what they know and practice of democracy. How and why do songs concerned with actual local happenings become localized elsewhere, so that other places and other actors become substituted for the original ones? What songs does the singer like, which ones does he care less for, and why? How much does he respond to subject matter, literary quality, local color, or to musical quality, or other factors? Is there a folk-artist's personality and psychology? Does he play some particular role in his community? Is music something that endows him with social prestige? What is the difference between the repertoires of the young people and of the old? How does one become an accomplished singer? How does one learn songs? What are the standards of criticism? What are the attitudes of the audience? [287]

On the basis of collectors' notes and background sketches, can one answer Herzog's questions? Far from completely, and with little assurance. Herzog's own excellent survey article on "Song: Folk Song and the Music of Folk Song" in the *Standard Dictionary of Folklore, Mythology, and Legend* (2, 1950), full of insights as it is, must be viewed as most important in indicating "some possible leads for future study in the functional aspects of folk song." For Herzog concludes in reference to world-wide study that the "relation of the life of the group to its expression in its songs remains an intricate one that needs much further study."

Apparently no student of Anglo-American song has ever carefully collected and analyzed all the material bearing on questions such as Herzog poses. If and when the effort is made, a great many contradictions may appear. Comments bravely made in handbooks do not always represent the full picture. Evelyn Wells writes that it was natural for the Kentucky mountaineer of Sharp's time "to sing, for the lines of the ballads slipped from his tongue like his own spoken language." [288] Of the same time and place, Josiah H. Combs writes, "Words and irregularities occurring in these songs are, as a rule, not common to the highlander's every-day speech. The highlander strives to use better English in his folk-songs." [289] The difference may not be great, but it is important. And Alfred Williams [290] stated that his English singers tended to avoid even their own dialect in their songs. Most of Herzog's queries cannot be answered by casual observation. They require the investigator to ask the singer questions which the collector seldom asks, and some which the singer can hardly answer. Above all, the formulations require intensive and careful fieldwork foreign to literary, musical, antiquarian, and historical collectors.

Herbert Halpert has pointed out the lack of fieldworkers and a methodology for investigating folk communities.[291] Halpert himself, influenced by Herzog, has made notable investigations of "how and why folk singers operate." With the aid of a systematic questionnaire, he elicited important information in his collecting in New York, New Jersey, the Southeast, and elsewhere. The small portion of his findings now published concerns the singers' belief in the truth of their songs and some functions of songs in folk communities.[292] Because Halpert often asked the right questions, full publication of his materials should be highly instructive. He has shown that songs with the most significance for the student of folk culture may be those least esteemed by the orthodox collector. William Hugh Jansen's investigations of contemporary singing in Kentucky [293] point toward a similar conclusion.

If there is no trend toward the training of a corps of workers to descend with analytical skill on Anglo-American folk communities, there is a tendency to emphasize the performance and background of the singer. One of the factors has been the public release of folksong recordings in the last decade. The editor has no longer only a text and tune to account for; he must explain and justify a personality and a singing style. And one may with little hesitancy place style in the realm of function, not only because it has been neglected but because the manner of rendition is intimately related to the folk culture. How else account for Alan Lomax's tale of how city children listening to an Aunt Molly Jackson program likened her singing to a cat's yowling, whereas children in Enid, Oklahoma, wrote that it was the most beautiful music they had ever heard on the air? [294] As Charles Seeger has pointed out, a singing style "consists of a complex of dispositions, capacities and habits built into the bodily processes and personality of the individual carrier of a song tradition when he is very young by the social and cultural environment into which he is born and by which he is nurtured." [295]

Generally speaking, the early collectors emphasized the text and tune themselves rather than the performance. Often all that survives is that portion of singing style which could be noted as part of the tune, and only the most skillful collectors were able to preserve more than the skeleton of the tune. In *English Folk-Song: Some Conclusions,* Sharp preserves important notes concerning his Somerset singers, including mention of the singing matches often referred to by later collectors in England and America (but apparently never witnessed by any); and he gives the classic description of the older singing style: austere, high-pitched melody rigidly and undemonstrably performed, with the last line or title spoken. The description has been confirmed by MacKenzie, among others, in Northeastern America. But have students pondered sufficiently the fact that Sharp's singers (as well as those of MacKenzie and others) were always aged? Sharp points out that women did not maintain such rigidity and that this was a "ritual on formal occasions. . . . A man will sing naturally enough, and without any formality, by his own fireside" (p. 106). Barry pointed out the occurrence of *rubato parlando* and *declamando* in the folksinging of Maine and the Provinces, a style differing from that of the South,[296] but no one has attempted to account for these regional differences. George Herzog pointed out in 1936 the necessity of studying regional and functional styles,[297] but excepting for important work with Negro singers, there has been too little accomplished since Herzog's outline of needed investigations. The regional pattern of collection has resulted in less attention being paid to difference in styles, and interest has not brought into being needed summaries of collectors' notes and descriptions.

Not only regional differences, but historical developments—again excepting Negro style—have not been studied. And there still exist, at least in the Southern United States, layers of singing style. Jazz enthusiasts, unmindful of the shibboleths of the folklore scholar, have traced Negro style from commercial records to folk origins. Students of folksong have, by and large, considered more recent styles as degenerate. Only Southern style is represented on early commercial folk recordings, and the taint of commercial issue prevented serious consideration of hillbilly songs, even though folksong collectors and record companies sometimes shared informants. It should also be mentioned that the jazz investigators have written off with a sneer the newer white styles, though the relation between Negro and hillbilly performance and repertoire is manifest.

In recent years, however, the general release of field recordings is causing an alteration of viewpoint. There are many hopeful signs that the style of performance will be given more serious attention. Notes to record albums have been discussing performance rather than merely giving historical notes. Such album notes, one feels, are the prelude to more serious consideration. Folk instruments, whose connection with style is clear, are being studied. The "dulcimore" especially has been receiving serious attention.[298] Bayard has produced a study of "Some Folk Fiddlers' Habits and Styles in Western Pennsylvania," [299] which supplements his earlier *Hill Country Tunes* (1945) in giving a picture of the development and perpetuation of folk artistry. Most striking, perhaps, is the demonstration that even British scholars can no longer reject out of hand a harmonic performance as nontraditional, for A. L. Lloyd has shown that "The Singing Style of the Copper Family" [300] has been traditional for a number of generations and most likely is not a survival of some ancient form of polyphony but "an example of rural harmony evolved by folk singers with at least the nodding acquaintance with musical theory that was once common in our villages."

Just how much scope there is for functional study of folksong may be seen in the suggestions set forth in Charles Seeger's recent article on "Singing Style." He proposes four categories of data: (1) of the culture-community in which the tradition of song flourishes; (2) of the singer who carries the tradition; (3) of the repertory; (4) of the singing style.[301]

It is possible, of course, to approach any or all the categories without dealing with function at all. And Seeger's article is concerned with an incisive, but nonfunctional, discussion of folksong style and plans for highly technical study. In fact, because orthodox scholarship has concerned itself largely with repertory—seldom considered functionally—all else has fallen by default into the domain of function. In so far as there seems to be no danger that the functionalist's stress on the meaning of the material and its use in and to the community and the singer will overwhelm the historical-comparative approach, a precise distinction is less important than the encouragement of collection and many-sided study of all the data. But it is well to remember that neither approach is complete without the other, which complements it. In speaking of folk instruments and their use, Felix Hoerburger has written that "we cannot rely any longer upon our objective opinion, but we must ask for the opinion of the folk. . . . For us the essential matter is the value of the object in the life of the people." [302] The student who follows the advice literally is not a folklore scholar; the student who ignores it completely is not a folklorist.

THE NEGRO-WHITE SPIRITUAL

The dispute over the origin of the Negro spiritual has many points in common with the Ballad War. At the heart of the Anglo-African contention has been the confusion of origin and essence. The antithesis of spontaneity and borrowing pervades the air. Early evidence is scanty and confused; the authority of print has been opposed to internal evidence; and both sources have been variously interpreted. In fact, the same evidence has nourished both sides. Etymologies have been constructed to support opposing views. Students have misunderstood or misstated opponents' arguments. Folk authority has been advanced. But this major dispute has unfortunately involved sectional and racial friction, pride and prejudice. Furthermore, the issue is not resolved. Like the problem of "original form" of the English and Scottish popular ballads, the origin of the Negro spiritual may be past determination; but opposing forces are not completely convinced.

A full history of the slave-song controversy may someday be written. But because of the part the Afro-American argument played in the broad field of twentieth-century folksong scholarship, it must be considered here, if only in this brief appendix. The final history may present the dispute in the light of the sympathies and prejudices of those involved. The present discussion will make every effort not to do so. Too many opinions have been judged on these grounds already. Certain motives existed, stimulated the disputants, and possibly colored their judgments. Beyond that this brief outline cannot go.

To define the nature of the argument, one may pose the problem: what elements in the Negro spiritual have been borrowed from the music of the North American whites and what are due to an African heritage and/or the Negroes' own creation in America? Whatever the confusion in some minds, no serious student has imagined that Negroes disembarked in Virginia singing "Deep River" or "Roll, Jordan." And whatever the confusion in some minds, no reputable scholar who has studied the problem has ever said that Negroes merely imitated or echoed white song. The issue lies between the extremes; and it is unfortunate that a few early commentators and the hysterical fringes of both sides have obscured the problem.

The problem and its history are difficult because of the nature of the songs and their record, and because of the nature of their critics. There is no trustworthy evidence before the Civil War. There are few examples of American Negro tradition that we can accept as pure. Too little is known of African song, and analyzable elements seem to prove little. Critics of Negro song have not been competent in all the required fields and have usually based their arguments on only a part of the evidence. Even all the evidence is not enough, for there are elements in the songs to which we are not yet able to apply objective analysis. As long as a subjective chink remains, the argument will continue.

Although there are earlier references to Negro song, the record begins in the "crossed and disguised" songs of the black-face minstrels of the second decade of the nineteenth century (unless we hold with certain students that turn-of-the-century hymn books also give white versions of Negro songs [1]). How many and what elements the minstrel stage borrowed from the Negro will probably remain in dispute. But it is clear that the Ethiopian song craze resulted in a stream of burlesques entering folk tradition—Negro and white. And this exchange of material must have only added to a mutual influence which had been occurring for over a century.

Negro song next came into wide public notice through contacts of Northern soldiers and civilians with the Southern Negro during the Civil War. "O Let My People Go," from the singing of "contrabands" at Fortress Monroe, was published in 1861, and the following year Lucy McKim printed in *Dwight's Journal of Music* a small collection made at Port Royal. Out of experiences with Negroes during and after hostilities grew *Slave Songs of the United States* (1867), bearing the names of William Francis Allen, Charles Pickard Ware, and Lucy McKim Garrison, but containing songs gathered by many other collectors.

Considering the sympathies and understandable ignorance of these collectors, their conclusions are surprisingly moderate. They were not folklorists, anthropologists, or musicologists. They knew little of the South, their acquaintance with the "Western and Southern Camp-meetings" must have been superficial, and they knew nothing of folksongs among the white population. But they recorded a body of song, religious and secular, that differed from any they knew. They discovered the shout and the work song. They described the nonpart harmony of the singers. They heard irregularities, *slides,* and *turns,* and noted what they could. They recognized adaptations of camp-meeting hymns, such as "The Ship of Zion," and rejected some songs paralleled in Methodist hymnals. For the rest, they turned to the only authorities they knew, the Negroes themselves.

We recognize as reasonable Allen's conclusion that

the chief part of Negro music is *civilized*—partly composed under the influence of the whites, partly actually imitated from their music. In the main it appears to be original in the best sense of the word. . . . In a very few songs . . . strains of a familiar tune can be traced; and it may easily be that others contain strains of less familiar music, which the slaves heard their masters sing or play (p. vi).

He found the words to be from Scripture and from the hymns heard at church, but he discovered few tune analogues. The sad songs of slavery then seemed to be the creation of a race "imbued with the mode and spirit of European music—often, nevertheless, retaining a distinct tinge of their native Africa" (p. viii).

The period which followed was one of popularization of the spirituals and general praise, slight study, but growing emphasis on their African nature. In 1871 the Fisk Jubilee Singers made their first tour to raise funds for their school, and *Jubilee Songs* was published the following year. *Cabin and Plantation Songs as Sung by the Hampton Students* appeared in 1874, and similar collections followed. Though the emphasis was on religious song, some attention was given to secular music, particularly in David C. Barrow's description of "A Georgia Cornhusking" [2] and in George W. Cable's articles on New Orleans secular music.[3] Commentators generally agreed on Negro origin and African survival of duple rhythm and pentatonic scales. The Negroes told how the songs grew spontaneously or were brought from Africa; whites repeated the stories. By 1914 the African-Negro origin of the spirituals was widely held, and the presence of Negroid elements in "popular songs of the day" was being noticed.[4] It seemed that there was "no true American music but the wild sweet melodies of the Negro slave." [5]

There were two important dissenting opinions, however, both from foreign observers. Julien Tiersot in his *La Musique chez les peuples indigènes de l'Amérique du Nord* (1911) failed to find African survivals in American Negro songs; and earlier Richard Wallashek in his *Primitive Music* (1893) had stated crushingly that, "speaking generally, these negro-songs are very much over-rated and . . . as a rule they are mere imitations of European compositions which the negroes have picked up and served again with slight variations" (p. 60). But Wallashek did not pretend to have examined the problem. The only other dissent came from scattered American writers who took another tack and denied that slave songs were American. Therefore Henry Edward Krehbiel had few challenges to meet, but had to meet them on a wide range. In *Afro-American Folk Songs* (1914) he set out to show that the songs of American Negroes are folksongs, that they are American folksongs, and that they contain certain "idioms that were transported hither from Africa" (p. 22).

Krehbiel experiences little difficulty in establishing his first two contentions, but he does so in a way that points out the fundamental basis of the argument. To prove that Negro songs are American folksongs (i.e., spontaneous utterances voicing the joys, sorrows, and aspirations of a people [6]), he maintains that they are the *only* American folksongs.

> Nowhere save on the plantations of the South could the emotional life which is essential to the development of the true folksong be developed; nowhere else was there the necessary meeting of the spiritual cause and the simple agent and vehicle. The white inhabitants of the continent have never been in the state of cultural ingenuousness which prompts spontaneous emotional utterance in music. . . .
>
> It did not lie in the nature of the mill life of New England or the segregated agricultural life of the Western pioneers to inspire folksongs; those occupations lacked the romantic and emotional elements which existed in the slave life of the plantations in the South and which invited celebration in song—grave and gay. Nor were the people of the North possessed of the ingenuous, native musical capacity of the Southern blacks (pp. 22–23).

And to justify his attribution of an African background to the idioms of the slave songs he writes:

> There is but one body of specifically national song with which the slave of the United States could by any possibility have become

familiar—the Scottish, with its characteristic pentatonic scale and rhythmical snap; but the singing of Scottish ballads was not so general in the South that their peculiarities could become the common property of the field-hands on the plantations (p. 83).

In fairness to Krehbiel we must recognize that the existence and character of American folksong had not then been widely recognized. Still, by 1913 sufficient criticism, texts, and even tunes were in print to challenge Krehbiel's statements. His approach became typical of those who supported the autochthonous character of the slave songs. The proponents of Negro genesis were to remain largely outside the official tradition of folklore study in the United States. They tended to consider the Negro song in relative isolation from other American song and looked to Africa alone for parallels. They saw no link between white and Negro song—and looked for none.

Therefore Krehbiel's recognition of the wide occurrence of many elements common to the slave songs—gapped scales, unorthodox intervals, the snap or syncopation, the solo and chorus organization, for example—did not deter him from seeking Africa as the sole source of influence. Though he found numerous technical correspondences between the meager record of African song and the slave song, he failed even to look for parallels in Anglo-American tradition. His emphasis was, at least in part, due to ignorance. Among his successors, the ignorance hardened into a refusal to consider the possibility of other influences.

Krehbiel's emphasis on religious song also influenced the course of the argument. Though he provides references to secular songs and summarizes the available material on New Orleans and West Indian dances, he is interested in them only as a background for the important creations, the spirituals; and the spirituals turned out to be the weak link in the African chain. For more than a decade Krehbiel's study remained the point of departure for discussions of Negro song, and the commentators did not depart very far.

Behind the rhapsodies of John Wesley Work's *Folk Song of the American Negro* (1915), whatever their validity, lies too little evidence. The important matters of rhythmic emphasis, "turns, twists, and intonations," and the characteristic use of the voice are dealt with only in generalities. And there is no recognition of parallels in Anglo-American tradition for the verse and chorus plan, introduction of extra syllables, the "African" pentatonic scale with added flat seventh, and the chant with interjections. John Work presents folk authority for the origin of many songs, but does not take a full view of the tradition in which the songs were composed. The narrowness of his approach extends even to Negro tradition. Though he refers to African secular and work songs, he slights the secular tradition of American Negro song. He writes of the "uncommon character" of the Negro's religious songs and "the paucity and utter worthlessness of his secular songs. So few and so inferior are these latter that we may justly state that the Negro Folk Music is wholly religious" (p. 27).

James Weldon Johnson's introduction to *The Book of American Negro Spirituals* (1925) is an excellent recapitulation of the evidence and does emphasize the distinction between the spiritual and the ring shout, but it offers little that is new. The only truly independent work was done by Natalie Curtis Burlin [7] and Nicholas George Julius Ballanta.[8] Mrs. Burlin, who had done fieldwork in Indian music, recorded and transcribed both African and American Negro songs. Her findings, in terms of "intuitive harmonies," rhythm, and tonality, tend to confirm those of Krehbiel, though she concedes a good deal of white influence and calls for more evidence. This was provided by Ballanta's theory of African music, which he found demonstrated in his American collection as well. Briefly, he holds that the African pentatonic results not from any concept of the scale, but from a rudimentary harmonic sense of a fifth above and a fourth below any given tone. The rhythm he finds based on vibration rather than division of the pulse, thus explaining the effect of two or four against three. These concepts he finds reflected in the American Negro song. But his contrasts with European music fail to take into account the evidence of Cecil Sharp and other collectors of Anglo-American folk music.

Despite the emphasis on religious song, students were beginning to notice other manifestations in folk and popular song. Collectors such as Odum and Johnson and Dorothy Scarborough were bringing to light all sorts of secular song. Jazz had succeeded ragtime, and the Krehbiel-Ballanta evidence was applied to the "new" manifestations very effectively by Abbe Niles in his introduction to W. C. Handy's *Blues: An Anthology* (1926).

A reaction from the Krehbiel school was inevitable. Whatever the validity of their evidence, proponents of Negro-African genesis seldom looked outside their chosen field. They tended to sneer at any suggestion of white influence, but sometimes displayed almost total ignorance of white folksong. Thomas W. Talley, for example, illustrates a "negro rhyming pattern" with a version of "Froggie Went A-Courting" and finds that a rhyme entitled "Bought Me a Wife" preserves African social patterns.[9] But "Bought Me a Wife" is a version of the Anglo-American "Barnyard." Some of the musical examples in other collections were to turn out no better. Furthermore, folklorists and cultural historians were beginning to discover evidence which considerably enlarged the picture drawn by the Krehbiel school.

The enlargement came from the discovery of parallel songs and parallel song-making conditions in white tradition. Works such as Louis F. Benson's *The English Hymn* (1915) called attention to the crude songs springing from the early nineteenth-century revivals, compositions called *spiritual songs.* In 1918 Louise Pound noted that one of the Negro spirituals printed by Krehbiel, "Weeping Mary," had been learned by her mother at a New York Methodist revival between 1826 and 1830.[10] But if we except the usual forcefulness of Miss Pound's style and the unfortunate language of Edmund S. Lorenz,[11] the attitude of those opposing the Krehbiel thesis was conciliatory. They sought not to displace but to modify.

The storm of protest broke in 1928. In January, E. M. von Hornbostel printed an article on African music in which, after outlining what was known of the subject, he wrote that the negro slaves in America and their descendants, abandoning their own musical style, have adapted themselves to that of their white masters and produced a new kind of folk-music in that style.[12]

These words from a student of African music were perfectly timed to introduce the rebellion. Edward Sapir, in a review of James Weldon Johnson's *Book of American Negro Spirituals*, paid tribute to the musical gifts of the Negro, but found both the "poetic titles" and the music itself within the European tradition. That another group under the same conditions could have developed the spirituals and blues, he wrote,

is all but inconceivable. [But] it does not follow . . . that American negro music is merely a carry-over of a specifically African tradition, that it owes little or nothing to the white man's musical stock in trade. The truth seems to be far from simple and not at all easy to state either historically or psychologically. No doubt the African tradition as such was entirely lost or nearly so. . . . It is simply not true . . . that the rhythms of American Negro music are African rhythms.[13]

James Weldon Johnson had issued a challenge:

The Negro Spirituals are as distinct from the folksongs of other peoples as those songs are from each other; and, perhaps, more so. One needs to be only ordinarily familiar with the folk music of the world to see that this is so.[14]

Scholars began to compare, and found likenesses instead of differences.

First in the field was Newman Ivey White, whose *American Negro Folk-Songs* (1928) embraced a collection begun in 1915 and a study pursued in the American academic tradition, textual and historical. White does not hold with the theory that Negro song is mere imitation or borrowing. He finds that assumption "fully as unjust and inaccurate, in the final analysis, as the Negro's assumption that his folk-song is entirely original" (p. 19). Disqualifying himself as a judge of the musical evidence, he adds only an emphasis on the strong Scottish element in American songsters and in white songs in the slave-holding areas. He finds it "reasonable to conclude that the Negro brought African music with him to America, and that it is a considerable element in the songs he sings today," and his over-all conclusion is that the "songs of the Negro today are beyond question the Negro's songs, not the white man's" (pp. 24–25). But to the Krehbiel school White's words seemed but an uncharitable concession. He had discovered a "white man in the woodpile."

White's textual and historical studies reveal that from the very first, the Negro's songs have been influenced by the songs of the white people. Through variational imitation of the revival songs of the early nineteenth century, the early minstrel songs (only 10 per cent of which seem to have been actually Negro), and the later "coon" songs, the Negro created his own distinctive music. The core of the argument emerges in White's re-creation of the milieu out of which the Negro spiritual grew: the primitive religious practices of the whites during the camp-meeting period, which produced crude spiritual songs. These songs, with their references to spiritual bondage, were taken over by the Negroes and perhaps reinterpreted in terms of physical bondage. This conclusion White documents with contemporary description of the emotional fervor of the camp meetings, a few hymn books containing examples of "less illiterate" spiritual songs, and a few survivals among the "backwoods" whites. "The American Negro song was not at first original with the Negro. It originated in an imitation frustrated by imperfect comprehension and memory, and by a fundamentally different idea of music" (p. 25).

Similar opinions were being advanced by other students. Robert W. Gordon, for example, wrote in a similar vein in his *New York Times* articles of 1927–1928, although he found some indication of an older stratum of Negro religious songs.[15] But the next step was to include the music in "the white man's burden." Milton Metfessel made an attempt to transcend the limits of conventional notation in determining the African and European qualities of American Negro song. But, as he reports in *Phonophotography in Folk Music* (1928), comparison was made only between Negro folksinging and European-style art singing. Important contributions however, used the forms of analysis developed by students of folksong.

The musical approach was pioneered by Anne G. Gilchrist, who discovered folk tunes in the hymn books of the Primitive Methodists and analogues in American Negro songs.[16] Two years later, in 1930, Guy B. Johnson attacked the problem in a study of *Folk Culture on Saint Helena Island*. For comparative purposes, Johnson used two camp-meeting song books and Cecil Sharp's collection and conclusions drawn from the Southern Appalachians. He found the subject matter and words similar, sometimes identical. The tunes themselves are markedly similar. The distribution of major and minor tunes shows no significant difference. Every deviation from conventional scale in Negro song is also found in the white song. The Negro spirituals employ a higher percentage of pentatonic tunes than do the white religious songs which Johnson examined, but almost the same proportion as do the secular songs found by Sharp. Absence of the fourth and seventh tones is not distinctive of Negro song; and the flat seventh is rarer in Negro than in white song. The results of Johnson's study of tempo and rhythm are less conclusive. He is willing to connect the preponderance of duple rhythm in the Negro songs with the Negro habit of bodily motion, but notes that fewer than 10 per cent of the most "folksy" of the published white songs have triple time. Although syncopation is present in white song, Johnson concedes it to be "one of the few elements in the spirituals which is (*sic*) unmistakably traceable to African patterns" (p. 115).

The remaining element is that of possible melodic relationship. On the basis of his limited material, Johnson discovers four tunes "undoubtedly borrowed" by the Negroes, and eight more traceable "in whole or part" to white song. An effort, writes Johnson, "to check up on the relations between 500 spiritual tunes and about as many white religious tunes, to say nothing of the vast possibilities of white secular music, is a task which might well require ten years of study" (p. 115). And Johnson was right, for George Pullen

Jackson's summation of his own studies of *White and Negro Spirituals* was published in 1943.

Though Jackson was not the only scholar establishing white sources for Negro spirituals,[17] his work is the most complete. It has firmly established the contention that the melodic core of Negro religious songs developed from white spirituals. His textual and musical analysis is set in the frame of American religious folksong, whose history he has written (see pp. 324–325). His examination of the tunes is both analytic and genetic.

In *White and Negro Spirituals,* Jackson gives the results of a comparison (of 892 Negro tunes with 555 white spirituals) which reveals 116 genetic relationships. These relations are the heart of the argument, for sixty of the tunes have been collected from oral tradition in the British Isles, fifteen more are widespread in the secular tradition of the whites of North America, and seventeen are by known composers of the nineteenth century; fifteen are what Jackson terms *general melodizing,* and the source of the remaining nine is unknown. But who made the rest of the Negro songs? The Negro, writes Jackson, just as the whites made their songs "by endless singing of heard tunes and by endless, inevitable, and concomitant singing differentiation" (p. 267).

Jackson's analysis of the tunes generally confirms Guy B. Johnson's earlier study. Jackson finds that the Negro tends to borrow more pentatonic tunes and in singing to slenderize their tonal content still further. The Negroes have preferred more major sequences than have the whites, but the Negroes have seldom altered modes, tending to sing the songs as they heard them. Jackson identifies Krehbiel's "wild tones" (weak or variable thirds and sevenths, and raised sixths) in both singing traditions, as well as in all folksong "since time immemorial," but he gives the Negro credit for bringing about the reintroduction of these deviations into modern art music.

Jackson goes further than some other writers in accounting for other features of Negro spirituals. The call and response, the repetition, the syncopation more prevalent in Negro song he holds not to be connected with Africa. These he finds grew from white singing in the camp-meeting period heightened by the Negro's racial emphasis. This emphasis may correspond with a similar one in Africa, but it did not necessarily come from Africa. The most exotic and "African-sounding" of Negro songs are the *surge songs*, which Jackson identifies as a survival of the old-style country manner of singing eighteenth-century psalm tunes, now reserved by the Negro for "Dr. Watts."

Jackson's writing is not always urbane, but his tone is easily accounted for. This transplanted New Englander became a champion of the Southern yeoman class, the poor white. His early writing, if directed against anyone, chastised "the professional Southerners of big-plantation presumptions" and "the Southern urban church folk," although his reference to those with a "vested interest in the perpetuation of the *untruth*" cuts a wider swath. But his "Farewell to Africa" chapter of *White and Negro Spirituals* was called forth by the attacks, many of them personal, which had arisen as he published his various studies. Followers of the Krehbiel school never contradicted his evidence. They first merely repeated and expanded Krehbiel's one-sided argument, adding a few sneers at "library scholars" and "paper scholarship." They next intimated that the white hymns were borrowed from the Negro. One might ignore such hysterical works as Maud Cuney Hare's *Negro Musicians and Their Music* (1936), but the investigations of Melville J. Herskovits are another matter.

Herskovits is hunting bigger game, of course. His studies of the influence of Africanisms on New World civilization are distinguished. His most important observation on the Negro-white controversy concerns the overemphasis on religious songs and on the Negro songs of the United States. But Herskovits is not willing to write off the spirituals and devote himself to other manifestations of Negro song. Faced with the patent connection of Negro religious song with the American revivals, he seeks to show that the revivals themselves are a "reflex of those Africanisms in Negro behavior which, in a particular social setting, take the form of hysteria." [18] He maintains that European religious possession was a private, not a social phenomenon and that there is an intrinsic difference between the manifestations of the Great Awakening and those of the later camp meetings. Herskovits' suggestion is not exactly new, for William Edward Burghardt Du Bois wrote in 1903 that "the religion of the poor whites is a plain copy of Negro thought and methods," [19] but it has a firmer and more far-reaching basis. Herskovits provides much evidence from Africa and the New World which establishes at least an independent Negro basis of many elements—musical and behavioral—found in the spirituals. But his own evidence reveals that the shouting spiritual is found only after exposure to Protestant revivalism. Herskovits is careful to recognize parallels in African and European tradition that "have coalesced and reinforced each other in New World Negro music," [20] but he seems to impute to Negro influence on white revivalism an importance out of proportion to the probabilities. On the other hand, unacknowledged borrowings by white tradition had received too little attention. Music knows no color line, but to attribute to Negro influence elements possibly developed in white tradition is as erroneous as to postulate the Negro's borrowing of elements which can be African survivals.

Important discussion has been contributed by investigators of the genesis of jazz. Though all such writers are not agreed on origins, they have generally viewed jazz as largely a development from Negro—and hence African—art. They have had the advantage of recent recordings of African and American Negro folk music and have been basically interested in performance, rather than written music. Further, they have seen the spiritual as a small part of the larger picture, and therefore more objectively.

One of the most important students has been Rudi Blesh, whose *Shining Trumpets* (1946) is the most thorough treatment of the problem. Blesh depends to a great extent on the African and New World materials of Herskovits and the unpublished studies of M. Kolinski. He seeks not to discredit the conclusions of Jackson and George Herzog,[21] but to supplement and interpret them. He thus accepts without question the melodic origin of many spirituals in the white hymn, but he emphasizes the adoption of "white melodies and harmony that are amenable to the peculiar scalar, tonal, antiphonal or polyrhythmic treatment of African music" (p. 343)— a selective borrowing and transformation. Consequently the investigator finds African or European elements, depending on which he is seeking. *Matter* tends to be European, and *manner* African. Blesh —to oversimplify his discussion—finds predominantly African elements in the early rural work songs, and in the spirituals and their offspring, the blues, a process of adaptation and transformation that creates a new musical form in the African tradition of songs intimately related to daily living.

With all due respect to Blesh's evidence and careful investigation, his work reveals the fault common to most proponents of African genesis, a failure to take into account the characteristics of Anglo-American folk music, a consideration of which might even strengthen his theory of selective borrowing and tranformation but would reveal the greater complexity of the problem. Blesh's listing of African survivals is most soundly based in the areas of "the hot concept" (variation and improvisation of melody and rhythm), rhythmic patterns, and timbre or tone quality. In other areas he fails to note correspondences with Anglo-American folksong. His comparisons are almost invariably with European cultivated music, not folk music. Pentatonic and hexatonic scale structures and microtonal flatting, especially of thirds and sevenths, may be African survivals; they are also a part of Anglo-American folk music. Glissandi, pitch wavering, and wide vibrato are distinctive of Negro singing, but their occurrence in lesser degree in white folksong must also be observed. And antiphony (call and response) is an African technique that has some slight parallel in the rendition of the American white folk hymn. Blesh's list of types of Negro folk music prior to jazz is enough to indicate many possible interrelationships with white folksong. A small indication of the problem is his dismissal as "pseudo-blues" of "a rural type of song the white singers call blues and which certain writers designate as white blues. This

. . . is not blues, nor is it even an established form. It preserves faint echoes of the real Negro blues, but in mountain districts it is hill-billy song and in the Southwest it is a cowboy tune" (p. 146). But is it parallel to or derivative from Negro singing? Though the latter seems likely, the concept of "white blues" cannot be summarily dismissed, nor can those elements of contemporary American white folksinging not found in Great Britain. The problem of their origin is tied up in one way or another with the problem of African survivals. When Blesh treats "Casey Jones" as a Negro adaptation of a white ballad, he unwittingly points out the difficulty. Blesh's "white ballad" is an adaptation of a Negro ballad, itself widespread in a railroad tradition shared by Negroes and whites. The age and character of the blend assumes great importance.

Marshall W. Stearns' recent *The Story of Jazz* (1956), though less technical than Blesh's study, is an improvement in that it takes more direct account of the white folk tradition and certain similarities of European folk and West African music that enter into the blend of Afro-American music. Stearns notes the presence in both traditions of the diatonic scale and "a certain amount of harmony. . . . The main difference is that European folksong is a bit more complicated harmonically and African tribal music is a little more complicated rhythmically. . . . When the African arrived in the New World the folk music that greeted him must have sounded familiar enough, except for a lack of rhythm. The blending has proceeded on many levels and in a variety of ways" (p. 14). He points out how the white religious tradition in its lining out "confirmed the West African in his use of the call-and-response pattern" (p. 10) and in its part singing and freedom from other than accidental harmony "gave a melodic and rhythmic liberty which proved attractive to the West African ear" (p. 82). But when, describing the growth of revival song in camp meetings, he writes that "the blend of British hymn and folk song became partly Africanized" (p. 83), is he speaking of a parallel development or of the influence of Negro participants? On the one hand he seems to be merely saying that the Negro adopted and adapted the type of worship and song with which he was most familiar and at which he excelled. Yet he writes later, "searching for the origin of the harmony of the spiritual (and sometimes its melody) *as written down* can lead to the conviction that all spirituals were taken from the Protestant hymn. But the truth is that only the harmony of the spiritual could have come directly from the Protestant hymn, and even that was transformed at once by the cry into an over-all blue tonality that is unknown in the Old World" (p. 138).

One of the problems (in addition to Stearns' failure to comment on intervals common to white and Negro song) is the term *spiritual*. Stearns differentiates roughly among ring shout, song-sermon, jubilee, and spiritual. In discussing the evolution of the last, he does not always differentiate clearly between the folk process and the interference of the recorder who wrote down one of a number of tunes for the words. In fact, he leaves the impression that the pioneers created the spirituals by noting fragments of ring shouts or jubilees. Granting that little can be proved by citing the origin of a term, one could wish that Stearns in his many references to the Protestant hymn would note that the term *spiritual* was applied by the whites to their camp-meeting songs. And, "searching for the origin of 'fixed' melodies," Stearns adopts the "spontaneous combustion" theory, improvisation "along traditional lines within a fixed form" (p. 134), making no reference to Jackson's researches. But his over-all position that many types of American music and the widespread shanty as well are a blend of European and West African elements seems sound, even if it still leaves much of the analysis of the blend incomplete.

The implication of Herskovits's suggestion that American revivals derive at least in part from Africanisms has been developed in another direction by Miles Mark Fisher. The thesis of his *Negro Slave Songs of the United States* (1953) is that, although there has been some influence of European song, the slave songs are historical documents created by the Negroes to record contemporary happenings and to pass on a record to future generations. The songs preserve the Negroes' reaction to everyday events of slavery, slave uprisings, the efforts of the African Colonization Society, the secret meetings continuing the African cult. This is the most ingenious interpretation of the spirituals yet seen. The proof is even more interesting.

Fisher has first the evidence of African song and cult, which supports a "worldly" interpretation of Negro song. He has a bit of external evidence in that Negroes sometimes served as choir singers in early Southern churches. But his proof comes largely from the internal evidence of the spirituals themselves. He connects specific songs with events many years prior to the appearance of the cognate white songs—a sort of "higher chronology." But he must date the songs by interpreting their symbolism, which is not static.

> Moses was understood in the eighteenth century to be Bishop Francis Asbury. Later he stood for a Negro and frequently attended camp meetings. All at once he was transported to Africa. . . . Such evolution gave color to the spirituals (p. 178).

Fisher also gives color by his restoration of texts to what he considers their original form.

> *I am huntin' for a city, to stay awhile,*
> *I am huntin' for a city, to stay awhile,*
> *I am huntin' for a city, to stay awhile,*
> *O believer got a home at las','*

becomes

> *I see home,*
> *I see home,*
> *I see home,*
> *O Believer (Po' Sinner) got a home at las'* (p. 45).

The voice of the euhemerist and the hand of the solar mythologist!

According to Fisher, the slaves first created songs in which *heaven* meant the North or Africa; then the whites, to whom *heaven* meant heaven, borrowed the songs. It is difficult to believe, even with Fisher's help, that the slaves created and communicated this symbolism. Fisher has amassed a good deal of evidence to show that the religious songs may have had a private meaning, and no one doubts that many of the songs were symbolically understood or that certain of the slave songs were in code, but the theory seeks to prove too much.

Fisher's approach is fortunately not typical of recent criticism. Though hysterical outbursts appear from time to time,[22] the strongest position is that of the "compromise theorists" who, as Bruno Nettle writes in *Music in Primitive Culture* (1956), "do not hold that the melodies of the American Negroes originated in Africa, but assume that the Negroes have taken over tunes of the whites and combined with them African stylistic traits—hot rhythm, much variation, preference for part-singing, antiphony, and response" (p. 129). Nettle accounts for the survival of African traits by Richard A. Waterman's theory of syncretism—that traits in African music similar to features in European music tend to survive—and by the postulation of strong traits that defy acculturation. Taking another point of view, we might add that strong traits in African music have tended to reinforce and heighten corresponding traits in American white folk music. Thus study is revealing that a simple concept of *origin* is not only misleading, but nonsensical.

To America from Africa the Negro brought a song tradition differing from and yet in some respects resembling the European folk tradition (with which, in fact, it had some historic connections). From the songs of the whites, the Negro borrowed what was congenial to him, and the whites were debtors as well as creditors. The resulting hybrid is a folk music which sounds African in the Negro tradition and European in the white tradition. There are certainly African survivals, even in tunes, as Lydia Parrish has recently demonstrated.[23] The ring shout undoubtedly has African ancestors (the attempt to connect it with shouting in the Old Testament seems beside the point[24]); yet we need not derive *shout* from *saut*[25] or connect the circular dances of the Shakers with African songs. Though a West African river cult may help to explain the popularity of the Baptist sect among the Negroes, it has no necessary connection with the number of Southern white Baptists; rather, the efforts of the Southern Baptists may have reinforced an African survival. The Negro has preserved, borrowed, and re-created, as has the white. The two races share a tradition which they tend to treat distinctively. In the absence of trustworthy reports from the eighteenth and nineteenth centuries, we can only hope that an increasing knowledge of African music and study of recent field reports from American areas will enable us not merely to sort out elements, but to understand the hybridization of not only the spiritual but all American folk and popular music.

APPENDIX TWO

A SELECTIVE DISCOGRAPHY
OF FOLK MUSIC PERFORMANCES
ON LONG-PLAYING RECORDS

For the scholar and teacher recorded folk music is a tool. For others it may be a source of enjoyment or education or both. Perhaps the scholar alone requires absolute authenticity of performance, in so far as *authentic* means a field recording of a traditional performer. For certain purposes the field recording may not be as useful or desirable as one that preserves the essence of authenticity without some of the drawbacks of field conditions. And unless concealed equipment is used, no recording may preserve even all the aural aspects of a traditional performance. On the other hand, the scholar is or should be interested in recordings of performances not always purely traditional, the hillbilly and race recording, for example. Indeed, if writers who insist that the current folksong renaissance is spawning a new oral tradition are in any sense correct, the scholar must be extremely interested even in current "citybillies" and concert performers who also represent one of the effects of folksong on the broader cultural pattern. An analytical and critical folk music discography which approaches completeness is consequently needed. A bare beginning was made in *Folksongs on Records* (Issue Three, 1950) by Ben Gray Lumpkin, who has apparently discontinued his project. A complete discography of folksongs in English on long-playing records has been undertaken by Kenneth S. Goldstein, Ed Cray, and the present writer. But a less ambitious list should be presently helpful to anyone interested in traditional music.

The following list makes no pretense at completeness; rather the opposite. It resembles Alan Lomax's 1947 listing in *Folk Song: U.S.A.* in that it is not analytical and seeks to provide illustrations rather than a complete listing. But the amount of available material and the approach of the compiler have made the list even more selective than Lomax's. For the Lomax list lies on the other side of the. watershed of the LP recording and the current folksong revival and is hospitable to a wide variety of material and many types of performance. The standards of the present list would exclude perhaps half the material in the Lomax list; the extension of the present list to parallel that of Lomax would multiply the number of items *at least* by five.

The recordings in the following list were selected primarily on the basis of stylistic authenticity. Therefore a printed source or a composite version did not determine exclusion. The aim has been to select from recently available albums of recorded folk music those which give a reasonably accurate representation of the performance of British and American folk music. The performances are both primary and secondary—the renditions of traditional performers, whether recorded in the field or in a studio, and attempts on the part of collectors and entertainers to re-create such renditions. But it has not been possible to classify the recordings on these grounds, if only for the reason that many albums—even some issued by the Library of Congress Archive of American Folk Song—include performances of both sorts.

Selection of stylistically authentic items is not an easy task, particularly in America. There is not one folksong style, but several, based on region, culture, and acculturation. Once outside the field of primary performance, judgment is unfortunately subjective. Furthermore, the traditional performer is not always an absolute. His performance is affected by his audience, even when the audience is only the collector or recorder. And the traditional singer who becomes a popular entertainer is an equivocal figure. Or consider Bascom Lamar Lunsford—folksinger, collector, hillbilly recording artist, festival performer and promoter. In figures such as Lunsford, Lead Belly, Woody Guthrie, Josh White, and others it may be possible to determine on the basis of their many recordings the stylistic changes resulting from various pressures. But that is not the purpose of this listing. Recordings have been included on the basis of the norms of somewhat distinctive folk performance, with the recognition that such judgment is not absolute. The list does not include all honest attempts to reproduce folk music, nor does it include all recordings useful to the scholar and teacher. Especially important is the omission of a number of recordings designed to illustrate historical periods, song types, et cetera. Though they are often useful and informative, by their very nature they seldom give an accurate picture of the folk style of performance. And how can a recording illustrating Percy's *Reliques of Ancient Poetry* re-create the folk style of the period? Furthermore, the authenticity of renditions in an album may vary considerably, and judgment has been rendered on the album as a whole.

The recordings are American issues of British (including Irish, though this area was hardly touched in the summary of scholarship) and North American folk music. The albums have been chosen to illustrate the English-language tradition, though some few happen to include material in other languages as well. The division of North American tradition into white and Negro represents a distinction that is in some instances less than academic, but it may be helpful in locating material or performers. Separate listings have been made of some albums fitting into more than one category. The point at which a discographer of Negro folksong should yield to the student of jazz is also arbitrary, but if the limits set here are too narrow, there are jazz discographies which include material omitted here.

Most items in the following list are at this writing still available from the issuing agencies. A few discontinued 10-inch records may soon be reissued on 12-inch, and most out-of-print material can be found in libraries maintaining record collections or on the private market.

1. *The British Isles*

1. Barry, Margaret: *Songs of an Irish Tinker Lady.* Recorded by Ewan MacColl; notes by Kenneth S. Goldstein. Riverside RLP 12–602. 12".

    Irish street songs by folksinger with a magnificent voice.
2. Cameron, Isla: *Through Bushes and Briars and Other Songs of the British Isles.* Tradition TLP 1001. 12".

    Singer with folk background does manage "to catch feeling and style from the inside," although renditions here are uneven in relative authenticity.
3. *English Folk Songs,* ed. Peter Kennedy and Alan Lomax. Columbia World Library of Folk and Primitive Music, III. Columbia KL–206. 12".

    An extremely important recording including shanties, instrumentals, a sword dance, part of a Mummer's play, as well as ballads and other songs. Sung by both folk and "revival" performers.
4. Ennis, Seamus: *The Bonny Bunch of Roses: Uillean Pipes, Tin Whistle and Folk Songs of Ireland,* ed. Liam Clancy. Tradition TLP 1013. 12".

    Rendered by collector and performer in thoroughly traditional style. Notes inadequate.
5. *Irish Folk Songs,* ed. Seamus Ennis and Alan Lomax. Columbia World Library of Folk and Primitive Music, I. Columbia KL–204. 12".

    Songs, keening, instrumentals from the Western counties. Gaelic and English materials by traditional and "revival" performers. An important recording.
6. *Irish Jigs, Reels and Hornpipes.* Notes by Henry Cowell and Esther Brown. Folkways FW 6819. 10".

Traditional performances by Michael Gorman of County Sligo and Willy Clancy of County Clare on fiddle and Uillean pipes.

7. *Irish Popular Dances.* Folkways FW 6818. 10".

   Recorded in Ireland and the United States, apparently from traditional performers. Notes on Irish dance by Esther Brown.

8. *The Lark in the Morning: Songs and Dances from the Irish Countryside,* ed. Kenneth S. Goldstein. Recorded by Diane Hamilton. Tradition TLP 1004. 12".

   English and Gaelic material from traditional performers, recorded in 1955. Inadequate notes.

9. Lloyd, A. L.: *English Drinking Songs,* ed. Kenneth S. Goldstein. Notes by A. L. Lloyd. Riverside RLP 12–618. 12".

   Songs from an East Coast tavern sung in traditional style by one of the finest reproducers of folksongs.

10. ———: *English Street Songs,* ed. Kenneth S. Goldstein. Notes by Lloyd. Riverside RLP 12–614. 12".

    Important street ballads in traditional style.

11. ———: *The Foggy Dew and Other Traditional English Love Songs,* ed. Kenneth S. Goldstein. Notes by Lloyd. Tradition TLP 1016. 12".

    Includes many forthright songs often expurgated by twentieth-century collectors.

12. ———, and Ewan MacColl: *Champions and Sporting Blades: British Songs of Sporting and Gambling,* ed. Kenneth S. Goldstein. Notes by Lloyd. Riverside RLP 12–652. 12".

    Rarely recorded songs in sympathetic presentation in spite of guitar accompaniment.

13. ———, and ———: *The English and Scottish Popular Ballads* and *Great British Ballads,* ed. Kenneth S. Goldstein. 5 vols. Riverside RLP 12–621/2, 623/4, 625/6, 627/8, 629. 9/12".

    A major production, containing seventy-two ballads represented in the Child collection and ten others of great importance. Songs are from recent tradition and from the great collections, sung unaccompanied in traditional style. Full critical notes.

14. ———, and ———: *Haul on the Bowlin',* ed. Kenneth S. Goldstein. Notes by Lloyd and MacColl. Stinson SLP 80. 10".

    Shanties re-created in traditional style. Well done.

15. ———, and ———: *Off to Sea Once More and Other Foc'sle Songs and Shanties,* ed. Kenneth S. Goldstein. Notes by Lloyd and MacColl. Stinson SLP 81. 10".

    Another excellent restaging.

16. Lloyd, A. L., and Ewan MacColl: *Thar She Blows: Whaling Songs and Ballads*, ed. Kenneth S. Goldstein. Notes by Lloyd. Riverside RLP 12–635. 12".

    Shanties and foc'sle songs. Traditional singing although, as in some other albums by Lloyd and MacColl, the accompaniment is not in the older British folk tradition.

17. MacColl, Ewan: *Bless 'Em All and Other British Soldiers' Songs*, ed. Kenneth S. Goldstein. Notes by MacColl. Riverside RLP 12–642. 12".

    Important songs in acceptable style. The accompaniments here and on the following albums, however, are seldom traditional.

18. ————: *Fourpence a Day and Other British Industrial Folk Songs*, ed. Kenneth S. Goldstein. Stinson SLP 79. 10".

    With few exceptions, these are important and rarely noticed songs in an excellent presentation.

19. ————: *Scots Drinking Songs*, ed. Kenneth S. Goldstein. Notes by MacColl. Riverside RLP 12–605. 12".

    A wide selection of virile ballad and song.

20. ————: *Scots Folk Songs*, ed. Kenneth S. Goldstein. Notes by MacColl. Riverside RLP 12–609. 12".

    An excellent variety of material well presented.

21. ————: *Scots Street Songs*, ed. Kenneth S. Goldstein. Notes by MacColl. Riverside RLP 12–612. 12".

    A few important native songs, and many important imports.

22. Robertson, Jeannie: *Songs of a Scots Tinker Lady*, ed. Kenneth S. Goldstein. Riverside 12–633. 12".

    A valuable album from one of the finest contemporary Scots traditional singers.

23. *Scotland, Folk Songs from*, ed. Alan Lomax *et al.* Columbia World Library of Folk and Primitive Music, VI. Columbia KL–209. 12".

    Songs and instrumentals from the Lowlands and Highlands, largely by traditional performers. An outstanding recording.

2. North America

A. THE WHITE TRADITION

24. *American Banjo Tunes and Songs in Scruggs Style*, ed. Ralph Rinzler. Recorded by Michael Seeger. Folkways FA 2314. 12".

    Excellent documentation of contemporary three-finger banjo style recorded from traditional and commercial hillbilly performers.

25. *American Sea Songs and Shanties,* ed. Duncan B. M. Emrich. Library of Congress Archive of American Folk Song L26. 12″.
   Field recordings from old shantymen. This and the following album constitute the most reliable recordings available.

26. *American Sea Songs and Shanties,* ed. Duncan B. M. Emrich. Library of Congress AAFS L27. 12″.
   See No. 25.

27. *Anglo-American Ballads,* ed. B. A. Botkin. Library of Congress AAFS L7. (Reissue of Album 7, 78 rpm.) 12″.
   Field recordings from Southern tradition.

28. *Anglo-American Shanties, Lyric Songs, Dance Tunes, and Spirituals,* ed. Alan Lomax. Library of Congress AAFS L82. (Reissue of Album 2, 78 rpm.) 12″.
   Field recordings largely from Southern tradition.

29. *Anglo-American Songs and Ballads,* ed. Duncan B. M. Emrich. Library of Congress AAFS L12. (Reissue of Album 12, 78 rpm.) 12″.
   Field recordings from Southern tradition.

30. *Anglo-American Songs and Ballads,* ed. Duncan B. M. Emrich. Library of Congress AAFS L14. (Reissue of Album 14, 78 rpm.) 12″.
   Field recordings from Southern tradition.

31. *Anglo-American Songs and Ballads,* ed. Duncan B. M. Emrich. Library of Congress AAFS L20. (Reissue of Album 20, 78 rpm.) 12″.
   Field recordings, including songs and instrumentals from Southern tradition and cowboy songs.

32. *Anglo-American Songs and Ballads,* ed. Duncan B. M. Emrich. Library of Congress AAFS L21. (Reissue of Album 21, 78 rpm.) 12″.
   Field recordings from Northern and Southern tradition, including instrumental music.

33. *Banjo Songs of the Southern Appalachians.* Recorded by Kenneth S. Goldstein and William A. Grant. Notes by Goldstein. Riverside RLP 12–610. 12″.
   Good examples of contemporary Southern styles by folk performers at the North Carolina Folk Festival, 1955.

34. Brand, Oscar (assisted by Fred Hellerman): *G.I.—American Army Songs,* ed. Kenneth S. Goldstein. Riverside RLP 12–639. 12″.
   Generally well-selected material. The lack of distinctive folk style is suitable to most of the material.

35. *Canadian Folk Songs*, ed. Marius Barbeau and Alan Lomax. Columbia World Library of Folk and Primitive Music, VIII. Columbia KL–211. 12".

    Relatively small section devoted to Anglo-American music is well done, though not all by traditional singers.

36. *Cowboy Songs, Ballads, and Cattle Calls from Texas*, ed. Duncan B. M. Emrich. Library of Congress AAFS L28. 12".

    Largely field recordings of widely known songs seldom available in this form.

37. Driftwood, Jimmy: *Newly Discovered Early American Folk Songs.* Victor LPM 1635. 12".

    Ozark folk performer and collector who also composes for professional hillbillies. Some of the songs seem to bear his touches. Included is a rare example of mouth-bow playing.

38. *Eight Traditional British-American Ballads from the Helen Hartness Flanders Collection, Middlebury College, Middlebury, Vermont.* New England Folksong Series No. 1. 12".

    Child ballads by traditional singers from a quite literate tradition.

39. Greenway, John: *American Industrial Folksongs.* Recorded and ed. Kenneth S. Goldstein. Notes by Greenway. Riverside RLP 12–607. 12".

    Important material, not all of which is generally accepted as folksong. Sung in reasonably authentic style by compiler. See also No. 65.

40. ———: *The Great American Bum: Hobo and Migratory Workers' Songs*, ed. Kenneth S. Goldstein. Riverside RLP 12–619. 12".

    Includes IWW and Woody Guthrie material. Reasonably authentic singing by compiler.

41. Grimes, Anne: *Ohio State Ballads*, ed. Kenneth S. Goldstein. Folkways FH 5217. 12".

    Sung by collector approximating folk performance. Authenticity varies greatly.

42. Guthrie, Woody, and Cisco Houston: *Woodie Guthrie Sings*, ed. Kenneth S. Goldstein. Stinson SLP 44. 12".

    From repertoire of folksinger and contemporary folk composer. Not all songs are traditional. Style ranges from hillbilly to somewhat older Southern manner.

43. ———, and ——— (with Sonny Terry): *More Songs by . . .* , ed. Kenneth S. Goldstein. Stinson SLP 53. 12".

    Renditions of Southern repertoire mainly in hillbilly style.

44. Guthrie, Woody, and Cisco Houston: Sonny Terry, Alec Stewart, et al.: *Southern Mountain Hoedowns.* Stinson SLP 54. 10″.
   Authentic though not outstanding renditions in contemporary style.

45. Hilton, L. M.: *Mormon Folk Songs.* Recorded and ed. Willard Rhodes. Folkways FA 2036. 10″.
   Fine selection of material by traditional singer.

46. *Instrumental Music of the Southern Appalachians.* Recorded by Diane Hamilton, Liam Clancy, and Paul Clayton. Notes by Clayton. Tradition TLP 1007. 12″.
   Field recordings of outstanding folk artists of Virginia and North Carolina, 1956.

47. Kazee, Buell: *Buell Kazee Sings and Plays.* Recorded and ed. Gene Bluestein. Folkways FS 3810. 12″.
   Interviews including song and banjo playing by former folk performer who was an early commercial recording artist. Contains secular and religious material.

48. Laurel River Valley Boys: *Music for Moonshiners,* ed. Kenneth S. Goldstein. Judson J 3031. 12″.
   Performances by semiprofessional North Carolina entertainers in hillbilly style.

49. Lunsford, Bascom Lamar: *Minstrel of the Appalachians,* ed. Kenneth S. Goldstein. Riverside RLP 12–645. 12″.
   Religious and secular songs by outstanding folk performer, collector, and festival promoter.

50. ————: *Smoky Mountain Ballads.* Notes by Lunsford. Folkways FA 2040. 10″.

51. *Nova Scotia Folk Music from Cape Breton.* Recorded and ed. Diane Hamilton. Elektra EKL 23. 10″.
   Field recordings made in 1956 of largely Gaelic tradition.

52. Old Harp Singers of Eastern Tennessee: *Old Harp Singing,* ed. Sidney Robertson Cowell. Recorded by Sam Eskin. Folkways FA 2356. 12″.
   White spirituals by New Harp of Columbia Singers.

53. *Ontario, Folk Songs of.* Recorded with notes by Edith Fowkes. Folkways FM 4005. 12″.
   Wide variety of important material sung by traditional singers in old and new styles.

54. Peacock, Ken: *Songs and Ballads of Newfoundland.* Folkways FG 3505. 12″.

Good selection sung by collector, preserving essential elements of style—with, however, certain nuances of art singer.

55. Pegram, George, and Walter "Red" Parham: *Pickin' and Blowin'*. Recorded by Kenneth S. Goldstein. Notes by Robert Black. Riverside RLP 12–650. 12".

Contemporary Southern style and repertoire of festival and part-time folk entertainers.

56. Ramsay, Obray: *Banjo Songs of the Blue Ridge and Great Smokies*. Recorded and ed. Kenneth S. Goldstein. Riverside RLP 12–649. 12".

Contemporary Southern style by North Carolina Folk Festival entertainer.

57. *The Ritchie Family of Kentucky: Jean Ritchie Interviews Her Family, with Documentary Recordings*. Folkways FA 2316. 12". Excellent report from important singing family of Kentucky.

58. Ritchie, Jean: *Children's Songs and Games from the Southern Appalachians*, ed. Kenneth S. Goldstein. Folkways FC 7054. 10". Sung by a representative of one of America's best-known singing families whose style has remained essentially traditional. Most of the material is from her Kentucky family tradition.

59. ———: Elektra EKL–125. 12".
Reissued from but not completely replacing EKL–2 and EKL–25. Ballads, lyrics, dulcimore pieces.

60. ———: *Saturday Night and Sunday Too: A Weekend with the Ritchies of Kentucky*. Recorded and ed. Kenneth S. Goldstein. Notes by Jean Ritchie. Riverside RLP 12–620. 12".
This recording is organized with some regard for the function of the material.

61. ———: *Singing Family of the Cumberlands*. Recorded and ed. Kenneth S. Goldstein. Riverside RLP 12–653. 12".
Readings from the singer's autobiographical volume. Some songs included are not in her book.

62. ———: *Songs from Kentucky*. Westminister WN 6037 (formerly SWN 18021). 12".

63. *Sacred Harp Singing*, ed. George Pullen Jackson. Library of Congress AAFS L11. (Reissue of Album 11, 78 rpm.)
Field recordings of one of the important traditions of Southern religious songs.

64. Seeger, Pete: *American Ballads*. Folkways FA 2319. 12".
Though he sometimes deals in questionable material and his performances are often composites, Seeger has schooled himself in

largely Southern folk style. This album, though a bit uneven, is one of his better performances. The notes are not completely dependable.

65. Seeger, Pete: *American Industrial Ballads*. Folkways FH 5251. 12". The important material on this recording is not all strictly folksong. The album is more historically oriented than No. 39.

66. ————: *Darling Corey*, ed. Alan Lomax. Folkways FA 2003. 10".

67. ————: *Frontier Ballads*. Notes by Moses Asch. Folkways FH 5003. 2/10". (Available singly as FA 2175 and 2176.)
Generally authentic in style, despite a few flamboyant performances.

68. *Songs and Ballads of American History and Songs and Ballads of the Assassination of Presidents*, ed. Duncan B. M. Emrich. Library of Congress AAFS L29. 12".
Primary recordings from Northern and Southern tradition. Includes rare material.

69. *Songs and Ballads of the Anthracite Miners*. Recorded and ed. George Korson. Library of Congress AAFS L16. (Reissue of Album 16, 78 rpm.) 12".
Field recordings by outstanding collector and editor.

70. *Songs of the Mormons and Songs and Ballads of the West*, ed. Duncan B. M. Emrich. Library of Congress AAFS L30. 12".
Largely field recordings of traditional singers.

71. *Southern Mountain Folksongs and Ballads*, ed. Kenneth S. Goldstein. Recorded by Goldstein and William A. Grant. Riverside RLP 12–617. 12".
Sung by North Carolina Folk Festival performers, 1955. Largely contemporary style.

72. Steele, Pete and Lillie: *Banjo Tunes and Songs*. Recorded and ed. Ed Kahn. Folkways FS 3828. 12".
Varied repertoire of ballads, religious and secular lyrics, and instrumentals by Kentucky folksingers now resident in Ohio.

73. Stoneman Family *et al.*: *Old Time Tunes of the South*, ed. Ralph Rinzler. Recorded by Michael Seeger. Folkways FA 2315. 12".
Field recordings of Southern artists most of whom performed on early commercial recordings or radio shows.

74. Warner, Frank: *Our Singing Heritage, III*. Notes by Anne Warner. Elektra 153. 12".
Warner is a collector-performer who re-creates (sometimes unfortunately mimics) the style of his informants, usually quite well. This album includes both Northern and Southern tradition.

75. Warner, Frank: *Songs and Ballads of America's Wars*. Notes by Anne Warner. Elektra EKL–13. 10".
From Northern and Southern tradition.
76. ————: *Frank Warner Sings American Folk Songs and Ballads*. Notes by Anne Warner. Elektra EKL–3. 10".
Important material from Northern and Southern tradition.
77. West, Harry and Jeanie: *Favorite Gospel Songs*, ed. Kenneth S. Goldstein. Folkways FA 2357. 12".
Two young Appalachian singers who perform in hillbilly style and learn many items from commercial recordings. This album contains recent gospel tradition and is useful for comparison with Negro gospel tradition represented, for example, on Nos. 113, 115.
78. ————: *More Southern Folk Songs*. Notes by Harry West and Kenneth S. Goldstein. Stinson SLP 74. 10".
Varied selection of secular and religious song.
79. ————: *Smoky Mountain Ballads*, ed. Kenneth S. Goldstein. Esoteric ES–545. (Issued on stereophonic as Counterpoint CPST–545.)
Secular and religious song, a number not generally accepted as traditional.
80. ————: *Southern Mountain Folk Songs*. Notes by Harry West and Kenneth S. Goldstein. Stinson SLP 36. 10".
Secular and religious song.
81. *Wolf River Songs*. Recorded and ed. Sidney Robertson Cowell. Folkways FM 4001. 12".
Wide selection of field recordings from repertoire of a Wisconsin family. Especially important for logger songs.

B. THE NEGRO TRADITION

82. *Afro-American Blues and Game Songs*, ed. Alan Lomax. Library of Congress AAFS L4. (Reissue of Album 4, 78 rpm.) 12".
Field recordings from the Lomaxes' important Southern collecting.
83. *Afro-American Spirituals, Work Songs, and Ballads*, ed. Alan Lomax. Library of Congress AAFS L3. (Reissue of Album 3, 78 rpm.) 12".
Field recordings, largely from Southern prisons.
84. *American Skiffle Bands*. Recorded and ed. Samuel Barclay Charters. Folkways FA 2610. 12".
Field recordings of remnants of three street jug bands in Alabama, Texas, and Tennessee, 1954–1957, including interviews.
85. Anderson, Pink, and Gary Davis: *American Street Songs*, ed. Ken-

neth S. Goldstein. Recorded by Paul Clayton and Goldstein. Riverside RLP 12–611. 12".

Sacred and secular Negro street singing from South Carolina and Harlem, 1950 and 1956.

86. Beck, Elder Charles, and Congregation: *Urban Holiness Service.* Recorded and ed. William H. Tallmadge. Folkways FR 8901. 12". Recorded in the Church of God in Christ, Buffalo, New York, 1956. Urban development of Afro-American tradition.

87. *Big Bill Broonzy Interviewed by Studs Terkel.* Introduction by Charles Edward Smith. Folkways FG 3586. 12".

Songs and discussion of blues by race recording artist who retained country blues style.

88. *Big Bill Broonzy Sings Country Blues.* Notes by Charles Edward Smith. Folkways FA 2326. 12".

89. *Cat-Iron Sings Blues and Hymns.* Recorded and ed. Frederick Ramsey, Jr. Folkways FA 2389. 12".

Field recordings of excellent Natchez folksinger and guitar artist.

90. Cotten, Elizabeth: *Negro Songs and Tunes.* Notes by Michael Seeger. Folkways FG 3526. 12".

Important for guitar style by traditional artist.

91. Davis, Gary: *Blind Gary Davis with Sonny Terry and Mouth Harp.* Stinson SLP 56. 10".

Religious song by Harlem street singer and former race artist (see No. 90) supported by an outstanding Southern folk performer.

92. Fuller, Jesse: *Frisco Bound.* Cavalier 6009. 12". (Reissue, with additions, of Cavalier 5006. 10".)

Blues and hymns by modern itinerant minstrel.

93. ———: *Jazz, Folk Songs, Spirituals, & Blues.* Good Time Jazz L–12031. 12".

94. ———: World Song EG 10–027. 10".

95. *Jazz, Volume I: The South,* ed. Charles Edward Smith. Folkways FJ 2801. 12".

Includes important secular and religious song recorded for Folkways or reissued from commercial recordings of the 1920s. A few items fall outside the scope of this discography.

96. *Jazz, Volume II: The Blues,* ed. Frederick Ramsey, Jr. Folkways FJ 2802. 12".

Largely outside the scope of this discography, but includes reissues of recordings by Blind Willie Johnson and Blind Lemon Jefferson.

97. Jefferson, Blind Lemon: *Classic Folk Blues*. Notes by Orrin Keepnews. Riverside RLP 12–125. 12″.

Reissues of commercial race recordings by legendary street minstrel of great importance in folk and jazz tradition.

98. ——: *Blind Lemon's Penitentiary Blues and Other Folk-Blues*. Notes by Orrin Keepnews. Riverside RLP 1053. 10″.

99. ——: *The Folk-Blues of Blind Lemon Jefferson*. Notes by Orrin Keepnews. Riverside RLP 1014. 10″.

100. *Blind Willie Johnson: His Story Told, Annotated, and Documented*, by Samuel B. Charters. Folkways FG 3585. 12″.

Reissues of commercial race recordings by important street minstrel; interviews with singer's wife and acquaintances. Included are reissues of commercial recordings by Blind Lemon Jefferson, Blind Boy Fuller, and another Blind Willie.

101. [Ledbetter, Huddie]: *Lead Belly's Last Sessions*. Recorded and ed. Frederick Ramsey, Jr. 2 vols. Folkways FA 2941–2942. 4/12″.

Of the performances of this probably most-recorded folksinger, *relatively* few are available. Those in print include a good sampling of his vast repertoire from 1935 when he first reached New York from the Louisiana State Farm until shortly before his death in 1949. This last sampling, including song and story, was made in relatively informal sessions in a New York apartment the year before his death.

102. ——: *Lead Belly's Legacy, Vol. 1: Take This Hammer*, ed. Alan Lomax. Folkways FA 2004. 10″.

Blues, work songs, and spirituals.

103. ——: *Lead Belly's Legacy, Vol. 2: Rock Island Line*. Notes by Frederick Ramsey, Jr. Folkways FA 2014. 10″.

Ballads, blues, and prison songs.

104. ——: *Lead Belly's Legacy, Vol. 3: Early Recordings*, ed. Frederick Ramsey, Jr. Folkways FA 2024. 10″.

From American Record Company masters, most previously unissued, made early in 1935. Blues.

105. ——: *Lead Belly's Legacy, Vol. 4: Easy Rider*. Folkways FA 2034. 10″.

Includes some of his later compositions.

106. —— (with Sonny Terry): *Lead Belly Memorial*, Vol. 1. Stinson SLP 17. 12″.

107. ——: *Lead Belly Memorial*, Vol. 2. Stinson SLP 19. 10″.

108. —— (with Sonny Terry *et al.*): *Lead Belly Memorial*, Vol. 3. Stinson SLP 48. 12″.

109. [Ledbetter, Huddie]: *Lead Belly Memorial*, Vol. 4. Stinson SLP 51. 10″.
110. ———: *Play-Parties sung by Lead Belly*. Stinson SLP 39. 10″.
111. ———: *Lead Belly Sings More Play-Party Songs*. Stinson SLP 41.
112. McGhee, Brownie: *Blues*. Notes by Charles Edward Smith. Folkways FA 2030. 10″.
   Folk artist with a good deal of professional finish, but a less deviant style than that of Josh White. Includes some current material modeled in traditional country-blues style.
113. *Music from the South*. Recorded and ed. Frederick Ramsey, Jr. 9 vols. Folkways FA 2650–2658. 9/12″.
   A major release. Field recordings from Alabama, Louisiana, and Mississippi, 1954. Vol. 1. *Country Brass Bands*: report from surviving tradition of the transition from pre-Civil War Negro music to jazz. Vols. 2, 3, and 4. *Horace Sprott*: religious and secular songs by and interviews with "an eloquent summation of Negro music." Vol. 5. *Song, Dance and Play*: blues, string bands, and children's songs. Vols. 6 and 7. *Elder Songsters*: spirituals. Vol. 8. *Young Songsters*: gospel song. Vol. 9. *Song and Worship*: portions of services. Extensive notes.
114. *The Music of New Orleans*. Vol. 1. Recorded and ed. Samuel B. Charters. Folkways FA 2461. 12″.
   Field recordings of street cries, street musicians, and parade music.
115. *Negro Folk Music of Alabama*. Recorded and ed. Harold Courlander. 6 vols. Folkways FE 4417–4418, 4471–4474. 6/12″.
   A major release of field recordings made 1950. Vol. 1. *Secular*: hollers, blues, ring games, lullabies, work songs, tale. Vol. 2. *Religious*: spirituals and prayers. Vols. 3 and 4. *Rich Amberson*: religious and secular songs and tales from important informant. Vol. 5. *Spirituals*. Vol. 6. *Game Songs and Others*: includes work songs, spirituals, and gospels. Extensive notes.
116. *Negro Prison Camp Work Songs*, ed. Peter Seeger. Recorded by Toshi and Peter Seeger, John Lomax, Jr., Chester Bower, and Fred Hellerman. Folkways FE 4475. 12″.
   Field recordings of work songs sung indoors after labor on Texas state farms, 1951.
117. *Negro Prison Songs from the Mississippi State Penitentiary*. Recorded and ed. Alan Lomax. Tradition TLP 1020. 12″.
   Interviews, ballads, hollers, and work songs (many recorded on

location) in 1947. Should be compared with earlier recordings
made by the Lomaxes for the Library of Congress, e.g., No. 83.
118. *Negro Religious Songs and Services*, ed. B. A. Botkin. Library of
Congress AAFS L10. (Reissue of Album 10, 78 rpm.) 12".
Excellent field recordings.
119. *Negro Work Songs and Calls*, ed. B. A. Botkin. Library of Con-
gress AAFS L8. (Reissue of Album 8, 78 rpm.) 12".
Field recordings, especially important for hollers and chants.
120. Reed, Dock, and Vera Hall Ward: *Spirituals*. Recorded and ed.
Harold Courlander. Folkways FA 2038. 10".
Field recordings of Alabama singers made in 1950. These re-
cordings are also part of Folkways FE 4473 (see No. 115).
121. *Ring Games from Alabama*. Recorded and ed. Harold Courlander.
Folkways FC 7004. 10".
Field recordings extracted from collector's larger issue (see
No. 115).
122. *The Society for the Preservation of Spirituals in Concert.* 2 ser.
Siegling Music House, Charleston, S.C. 2/12".
Songs learned from plantation Negroes by older white genera-
tion, preserved orally among members of this unique group.
Creditable reproductions of Negro style. Unusual recordings.
123. Terry, Sonny (with Alec Stewart): *City Blues*. Notes by Marshall
W. Stearns. Elektra EKL–15. 10".
French harp and vocal by outstanding North Carolina folk artist.
124. —— (with Alec Stewart): *Folk Blues*. Notes by Edward Tatnal
Canby. Elektra EKL–14. 10".
125. ——: *Harmonica and Vocal Solos*, ed. Frederick Ramsey, Jr.
Folkways FA 2035. 10".
126. —— (with Alec Stewart): *Sonny Terry and his Mouth Harp*,
ed. Kenneth S. Goldstein. Notes by Marshall W. Stearns. Riverside
RLP 12–644. 12".
127. —— *et al.*: *Sonny Terry's Washboard Band.* Notes by Harold
Courlander. Folkways FA 2006. 10".
Good example of performance now fashionably known as
skiffle. Terry and harmonica dominate this group.

C. COMBINATIONS

128. *Anglo-American Ballads*, ed. Alan Lomax. Library of Congress
AAFS L1. (Reissue of Album 1 and *Friends of Music*, 78 rpm.)
12".

Field recordings of imported and native material, largely from white tradition, but including two Negro prison songs.

129. *Anthology of American Folk Music*, ed. Harry Smith. 3 vols. Folkways FA 2951–2953. 6/12".
Reissues of hillbilly, race, and Cajun recordings, 1927–1932. Includes secular and religious music recorded commercially by folk artists, many of whom exerted a tremendous influence on later tradition. Important introduction to this material.

130. *Folk Music from Nova Scotia*. Recorded and ed. Helen Creighton. Folkways FM 4006. 12".
Field recordings of a wide variety of material: land and sea songs in English from white and Negro informants; moose and bear calls; Indian and French songs.

131. *Folk Music U.S.A.*, Vol. 1. Compiled by Harold Courlander. Notes by Charles Edward Smith. Folkways FE 4530. 2/12".
The first volume is a projected series illustrating Anglo-American, Negro, Cajun, Spanish-American, and American Indian tradition. Sung and played in the main by traditional performers. Some of the material is drawn from previously issued Folkways recordings.

132. Lomax, John A.: *The Ballad Hunter*. 5 vols. Library of Congress AAFS L49–53. 5/12".
Reissues of transcribed lectures by John A. Lomax originally prepared for the Federal Radio Education Committee. Discussion of many types of American folksong is illustrated largely from field recordings. Lectures are popularly oriented though historically important. Music excerpts are excellent.

133. *1, 2, 3, and a Zing Zing Zing: Street Games and Songs of the Children of New York City*. Recorded and ed. Tony Schwartz. Folkways FC 7003. 10".
Field recordings largely of Negro and Puerto Rican children. Unusual.

134. *Play and Dance Songs and Tunes*, ed. B. A. Botkin. Library of Congress AAFS L9. (Reissue of Album 9, 78 rpm.)
Field recordings, largely instrumental music and ring plays from the South.

135. *A Sampler of Louisiana Folksongs*. Collected and edited for the Louisiana Folklore Society by Harry Oster. LFS 1201. 12".
Field recordings of white and Negro performers, including French, Gumbo French, and Cajun, as well as English material.

136. Wood, Hally: *American Folk Songs of Sadness and Melancholy.* Elektra EKL–10. 10″.

   Sung by trained musician who has successfully absorbed the nuances of Southern folk style. Secular and religious songs.

137. ———: *Hally Wood Sings Texas Folk Songs.* Stinson SLP 73. 10″.

3. Comparative Recordings

138. Ritchie, Jean, *et al.*: *Field Trip.* Recorded by Jean Ritchie and George Pickow. Notes by Jean Ritchie. Collector Limited Edition 1201. 12″.

   Versions from Kentucky Ritchie family tradition (see Nos. 57–62); matched with versions sung by English, Scots, and Irish singers. Ballads, lyrics, game songs.

NOTES

PMLA: *Publications of the Modern Language Association.*
PTFS: *Publications of the Texas Folklore Society.*
SFQ: *Southern Folklore Quarterly.*
SP: *Studies in Philology.*
TFSB: *Tennessee Folklore Society Bulletin.*
WF: *Western Folklore.*
YWES: *The Year's Work in English Studies.*

INTRODUCTION

1. "Trends in the Study of Folksongs, 1937–1950," *SFQ*, XVII (1953), 112.
2. For a brief review, see Donal O'Sullivan, *Irish Folk Music and Song*, Dublin, 1952.
3. Phillips Barry, "Das Volk Dichtet Nichts," *BFSSNE*, No. 7, p. 4.
4. "A Glance at the Ballad and Folksong Field," *SFQ, I* (1937), No. 2, p. 17.

CHAPTER ONE

1. "The Popular Ballad," *Atlantic Monthly*, CI (1908), 276.
2. Robert Chambers, *The Romantic Scottish Ballads: Their Epoch and Authorship* (1859); Norval Clyne, *The Romantic Scottish Ballads and the Lady Wardlaw Heresy* (1859); James Hutton Watkins, *Early Scottish Ballads* (1867).
3. *American Journal of Philology*, V (1884), 466–467.
4. "Professor Child and the Ballad," *PMLA*, XXI (1806), 755ff.
5. "Primitive Poetry and the Ballad," *MP*, I (1903), 478.
6. *Old English Ballads*, p. lvii.
7. *Harvard Studies and Notes in Philology and Literature*, V (1896), 41, 46.
8. *Folk-Lore*, IV (1893), 234ff.
9. Gordon Hall Gerould, *The Ballad of Tradition*, 205–206.
10. *JAF*, XLVI (1933), 59.
11. Gummere uses the word *tradition* in at least two major senses. It may mean the process of preservation and attendant change which a ballad undergoes among a homogeneous and unlettered people, or it may mean the process and relic of communal composition. Here the latter sense seems intended.
12. *JAF*, XXIV (1911), 253.
13. "The Ballad," in *Library of the World's Best Literature* (1896), vol. 3, 1308–1309. This seems to be his first recorded use of the term.
14. Gummere never touches on the connection of the triad with choral origins except to assert it. He rejects the explanation that the ballad formula is derived from folktale, for such an explanation "leaves unexplained that decrease of incremental repetition with the increase of epic elements . . . ignores the obvious connection of ballad and dance [and] . . . jars absolutely, fatally, with the facts of poetic evolution" (*Popular Ballad*, p. 120). This begs the question.

15. *Scottish Vernacular Literature* (1898); ed. *Minstrelsy of the Scottish Border* (1902); *The Ballad in Literature* (1912).
16. *The Transition Period* (1900).
17. *A Literary History of Scotland* (1903).
18. *MP*, I (1903), 381.
19. "Wilhelm Müller and the German Volkslied," *JGP*, II (1898–1899), 283*ff.*
20. *University Studies of the University of Cincinnati,* ser. II, vol. I, no. 1 (Jan.–Feb., 1905).
21. In his study of *The Gest of Robin Hood* (1909), William Hall Clawson reaches a similar conclusion. He finds the *Gest* to be the production of a highly skilled poet who fused popular ballads and other literary materials into a unified whole. He fails to emphasize his own evidence that the poet was certainly working from manuscripts.
22. Two years later, answering Henderson's sneers, Lang denied ever saying that ballads were of communal origin, explaining his extravagant statements as metaphor. But he admitted that his 1875 article was "insufficiently informed." (*Folk-Lore,* XIV [1903], 147*ff.*)
23. *Epic and Romance* (1896); "On the Danish Ballads," *Scottish Historical Review,* I (1904), 357*ff.*; V (1908), 385*ff.*; "Spanish and English Ballads" (Address to the Anglo-Spanish Society in King's College, London, June 14, 1918), *Collected Essays,* II (1925), 11*ff.*; "On the History of Ballads," reprinted from *Proceedings of the British Academy,* IV (1910); *English Literature: Medieval* (1912).
24. Here again we must note that not the evidence, but its interpretation, was new.

CHAPTER TWO

1. *JAF,* I (1888), 4.
2. *English Folk-Song: Some Conclusions,* pp. ix–x.
3. *JFSS,* I (1899), 1–3.
4. See the excellent biography by A. H. Fox Strangways and Maude Karpeles, *Cecil Sharp* (1934; 2d ed., 1955).
5. *Ibid.,* p. 66.
6. The pioneer folksong scholar, Frank Kidson, disagreed radically. Believing folksong to be "frequently a spontaneous production," he saw in conscious or unconscious alteration no evidence of evolution or communal origin. He recognized that the folksinger composes in a traditional pattern, but he accepted none of the explanations and offered none of his own. (*English Folk-Song and Dance,* pp. 11–35.)
7. *National Music* (1935), pp. 113–114.
8. *JFSS,* II (1905), 3.
9. *Folk-Lore,* XIX (1908), 133–134.
10. *JAF,* VIII (1895), 17. Newell's emphasis on the individual as the creator of folk material agrees with that of many English folktale scholars, except that

the latter have often insisted upon "cultured" origin and subsequent degeneration. See Moses Gaster, *Folk-Lore*, XX (1909), 23–24; W. R. Halliday, *Folk-Lore*, XXXIV (1923), 117ff.; *Folklore Studies* (1924), pp. xff.

11. *JAF*, XIX (1906), 10.

12. *BFSSNE*, No. 3 (1931), p. 11.

13. See the bibliography in *The New Green Mountain Songster* (1938) ed. Helen Hartness Flanders, *et al*. A number of Barry's significant articles were collected in *Folk Music in America* (American Folksong Publication No. 4, W.P.A., 1939), a mimeographed work of limited circulation. Except as otherwise indicated, the discussion of Barry's early work is based on his articles in the *Journal of American Folklore* and *Modern Language Notes*, 1903–1914.

14. *SFQ*, I (1937), No. 2, p. 30.

15. His first recorded use of the term *communal re-creation* seems to be in *JAF*, XXII (1909), 76.

16. *MLN*, XXVIII (1913), 4–5. Two years earlier he had written: ". . . folksong is in reality an idea, of which we can get but the process of actualization, traceable as history" *JAF*, XXIV (1911), 332.

17. "The Bitter Withy" had by this time received the accolade of the communalists and had been added to the sacred 305 of the Child canon. See Gummere, *Popular Ballad*, p. 228.

18. *MP*, II (1905), 573ff.

19. *JAF*, XXV (1912), 4.

20. *JAF*, XXIV (1911), 4.

21. *JEGP*, VIII (1909), 114ff.

22. Belden's discussion of these matters will be found in *JAF*, XXIV (1911), 1ff.; XXV (1912), 1ff.; *Sewanee Review*, XIX (1911), 213ff.

23. *JAF*, XXII (1909), 327ff.

24. Stanley Edgar Hyman, *The Armed Vision*, p. 138.

25. *BFSSNE*, No. 11 (1936), p. 24.

26. "Cowboy Songs of the Mexican Border," *Sewanee Review*, XIX (1911), 1–2. Lomax seems to have borrowed not only some of his song material but some of his language as well from earlier magazine articles. In "Songs of the Old Cattle Trails," *Out West*, XXVIII (1908), 217, Sharlot M. Hall writes that the "Cowboy's Lament" is "a song that grew like the grass, verse by verse, as it was sung up and down the Texas trails." The phrase was of course not original with Hall.

27. *Sewanee Review*, XIX, 16.

28. "Some Types of American Folk-Song," *JAF*, XXVIII (1915), 1ff.

29. Similar songs had, however, been introduced into evidence previously. For example, see *JAF*, XIX (1906), 16ff.

30. "Ballads Surviving in the United States," *MQ*, II (1916), 109ff.

31. "The Negro and the Ballad," *Alumni Bulletin of the University of Virginia*, 3d ser., VI (1913), 93.

32. "Ballad Literature in North Carolina" (reprinted from *Proceedings and Addresses of the Fifteenth Annual Session of the Literary and Historical Association of North Carolina, Dec. 1–2, 1914*), p. 4.

33. A *Popular History of English Poetry*, p. 46.

34. "Ballads," in *Studies in Literature*, 1st ser. (1918).

35. *PMLA*, XXIX (1914), 473ff.

36. " 'Omission of the Central Action' in the English Ballads," *MP*, XI (1914), 391ff.; "The Influence of Transmission on the English Ballads," *MLR*, XI (1916), 385ff.

37. "American Folksong: Origins, Texts, and Modes of Diffusion," *SFQ*, XVII (1953), 114ff.

38. *PMLA*, XXXIX (1924), 440ff.

39. Hartley Alexander, quoted in *American Scholar*, V (1936), 383.

40. H. S. V. Jones, *JEGP*, XXII (1923), 136.

41. *Literary Review*, March 5, 1921, p. 6. Compare Miss Pound's reply, *ibid.*, March 26, 1921, p. 14.

42. For example, see Reed Smith, *South Carolina Ballads*, pp. 27–28; Albert H. Tolman, "Mary Hamilton: The Group Authorship of Ballads," *PMLA*, XLII (1927), 430–431; Roland Palmer Gray, *Songs and Ballads of the Maine Lumberjacks*, pp. xv–xvii. Gray's account is discredited by Fannie Hardy Eckstorm, *Minstrelsy of Maine*, pp. 176ff.

43. See Reed Smith, *op. cit.*, pp. 31–32; Miriam Gabriel, *English Journal*, XVII (1928), 394ff., and Miss Pound's reply, *ibid.*, XVIII (1929), 495ff.

44. *JAF*, XLVI (1933), 58n.

45. *YWES*, VIII, 1928 (1929), 118.

46. We hardly know how to deal with the nonscholarly noncollector like Lauchlan MacLean Watt, whose criticism is half effusion over primitive and spontaneous origin, and half vague reference to minstrel and aristocratic origin. We conclude only that the ballad is "soaked in folk-song." (*The Scottish Ballads and Ballad Writing*, p. 22).

47. See the Grundtvig-Child correspondence in Hustvedt, *Ballad Books and Ballad Men*, pp. 248–336, and Child's comments in *ESPB*, *passim*.

48. In *The Ballad of Heer Halewijn*, Holger O. Nygard considers the problem of Buchan's texts and casts more than considerable doubt on their allegedly traditional source, but presents evidence that some of his texts passed into limited tradition. Nygard's conclusions carry weight because they are based on the wider tradition of a ballad instead of a simple comparison of Buchan's texts with others recovered in Aberdeenshire.

49. *Folk-Song in Buchan* (reprinted from the *Transactions of the Buchan Field Club*, 1906), (1907), pp. 14–15.

50. "Scottish Ballads: Their Evidence of Authorship and Origin," *Essays and Studies by Members of the English Association*, XII (1926), 100ff.

51. "The English Ballad in Jamaica: A Note upon the Origin of the Ballad Form," *PMLA*, XXXIX (1924), 455ff.

52. *MP*, XXI (1923), 22.

53. "A Recent Theory of Ballad Making," *PMLA*, XLIV (1929), 622.

54. *The Ballad of Tradition*, pp. 170–171n.

55. Albert H. Tolman, *PMLA*, XLII (1927), 432.

388 Anglo-American Folksong Scholarship Since 1898

56. Pound, PMLA, XLIV (1929), 622.
57. As published in the *New York Times*, the articles were abridged by the editors. The articles were printed from the original manuscripts as *Folk-Songs of America* (1938). References are to the latter form.
58. *BFSSNE*, No. 7 (1934), p. 4.
59. *The Science of Folklore*, p. 175.
60. "Literary Anthologies and the Ballad," *SFQ*, VI (1942), 129.
61. "On the Dating of the English and Scottish Ballads," *PMLA*, XLVII (1932), 10ff.; "Sizing Our Ballads," *American Scholar*, V (1936), 360ff.
62. *BFSSNE*, No. 7 (1934), p. 4.
63. *JAF*, LIV (1941), 98.
64. The summary of Barry's final statements is reordered from *BFSSNE*, No. 1 (1930), p. 1; No. 5 (1933), p. 4; No. 6 (1933), p. 8; No. 7 (1934), p. 19; No. 8 (1934), p. 17; No. 11 (1936), pp. 16ff.; "American Folk Music," *SFQ*, I (1937), No. 2, pp. 29ff.
65. John Goss, *Ballads of Britain*, pp. viiff.
66. "The Battle of New Orleans," *SFQ*, I (1937), No. 3, pp. 25ff.
67. See Bartlett Jere Whiting, *Traditional British Ballads*, pp. x–xxi; Albert B. Friedman, *The Viking Book of Folk Ballads*, p. xxxiii.
68. *The Growth of Literature*, vol. 3, 692n.
69. *English Literature at the Close of the Middle Ages*, pp. 137ff.

CHAPTER THREE

1. Surveys of published and unpublished materials are given in Chapter 4.
2. See Barrett, *English Folk Songs*, p. iii; Broadwood and Fuller-Maitland, *English County Songs*, pp. iv–v. Baring-Gould, who at first asserted that folksongs were the legacy of a cultured past and that peasants composed only rubbish (*Songs and Ballads of the West*, pp. ix–x), had by 1895 come to agree with his collaborator, Sheppard, that the tunes were "genuine productions of the folk muse." (*A Garland of Country Song*, p. ix.)
3. A somewhat more liberal attitude characterizes Miss Gilchrist when she writes, ". . . composed tunes of a century or two centuries ago have become simplified and translated, as it were, into the native dialect of the untutored singer . . . but such adapted songs are generally recognisable—unless, indeed, the transformation has been so complete that the tune has become, in the course of time, by continued transmission, a genuine folk-tune, recomposed—not *decomposed*, as some would have us think—by the folk who sing it" *JFSS*, II (1906), p. 220.
4. *JEFDSS*, V (1948), 116.
5. *English Traditional Songs and Carols*, pp. ix–x.
6. See Sharp's comments on the texts he fails to print, *JFSS*, IV (1910), 121.
7. *JFSS*, III (1907), 60ff.
8. *An Index of English Songs Contributed to "The Journal of the Folk-Song Society" and its Continuation "The Journal of the English Folk Dance and*

Song Society," compiled by the Rev. E. A. White and edited for publication by Margaret Dean-Smith, p. xi.

9. *JEFDSS*, V (1948), 153*ff*.
10. Sharp's collection of English texts is quite similar to his treatment of Appalachian texts discussed below.
11. For an excellent annotated list of English publications, see Margaret Dean-Smith, *A Guide to English Folk Song Collections*, pp. 25–44.
12. *Word-Lore*, I (1926), 14.
13. Two other writings are useful in this connection. Michael Macdonough in 1903 ("The Ballads of the People," *The Nineteenth Century and After*, LIV, 458*ff*.) discusses the low-class music-hall songs which spread to "the remotest corners of the Kingdom." A. Stanley Davies, in *The Ballads of Montgomeryshire*, includes not only eighteenth- and nineteenth-century Welsh broadsides, but topical ballads in English collected as late as 1927.
14. *Ships, Sea Songs, and Shanties*, p. xiii.
15. *English Folk-Song: Some Conclusions*, p. 119.
16. *Word-Lore*, I, (14).
17. *Ibid.*, 191–192.
18. *Last Leaves*, p. xiii.
19. *Ibid.*
20. Keith gives "The Gaberlunzie Man," which Child printed in the appendix to No. 279, a separate entry as No. XCVI in *Last Leaves*. Thus we must reduce the 108 entries by one. Keith's classification parallels that of many American scholars in that he includes "Kilboggie, which in the United States would be called a secondary form," as a version of Child 228.
21. Although the ballad list for North America now stands at 125 titles, by deducting fragments, traces, and secondary versions, we arrive at a figure of 106, one fewer than Greig found in the northeast of Scotland. The total of American recoveries reported by 1914 was 73.
22. *Last Leaves*, p. xlii.
23. *Ballads of Britain*, p. xviin.
24. Josiah H. Combs, *Folk-Songs du Midi des États Unis*, p. 125.
25. Olive Dame Campbell and Cecil J. Sharp, *English Folk Songs from the Southern Appalachians*, p. xxi.
26. Kittredge's estimate reported by Reed Smith, *JAF*, XXVII (1914), 58, verified for me by Branford P. Millar. The combined total is 81 variants of 38 ballads.
27. *JAF*, XXI (1908), 241*ff*.; XXII (1909), 105*ff*.
28. *JAF*, XXII (1909), 238*ff*., 327*ff*.; XXV (1912), 137*ff*.
29. Kittredge to Arthur Palmer Hudson, expressing regret that *JAF* was unable to print introductory material. Reported by Hudson, *Folksongs of Mississippi and Their Background*, p. viii.
30. *JAF*, XXVIII (1915), 144*ff*.
31. "Ballads and Rhymes from Kentucky," *JAF*, XX (1907), 251*ff*.
32. *JAF*, XIX (1906), 231.
33. *JAF*, XXVIII (1915), 199*ff*.

34. Barry, "A Garland of Ballads," *JAF*, XXIII (1910), 446–454.

35. *A Syllabus of Kentucky Folk-Songs*, p. 29.

36. "Religious Folk Songs of the Southern Negroes," III (1906), 265*ff*.

37. *JAF*, XXIV (1911), 259.

38. *JAF*, XIV (1901), 286.

39. *JAF*, XXV (1912), 268*ff*.; XXVII (1914), 289*ff*.; XXVIII (1915), 262*ff*.

40. *JAF*, XXII (1909), 238.

41. Belden, "The Study of Folk-Song in America," *MP*, II (1905), 578.

42. *JAF*, XXV (1912), 23.

43. "Ballads and Songs," *JAF*, XXX (1917), 283*ff*.

44. "Ballad Literature in North Carolina" (reprinted from *Proceedings and Addresses of the Fifteenth Annual Session of the Literary and Historical Association of North Carolina, Dec. 1–2, 1914*).

45. "Some Songs Traditional in the United States," *JAF*, XXIX (1916), 155*ff*.

46. "Folk-Lore in Michigan," *Kalamazoo Normal Record*, May, 1914.

47. At the turn of the century Charles F. Lummis was recording Spanish-American folksongs in California and by 1905 had almost 400 songs. See *CFQ*, I (1942), 179–183; 359–367.

48. *Folk-Songs of America*, pp. 101–102.

49. Printed in *Ballads and Songs Collected by the Missouri Folk-Lore Society*, pp. 401–402. Ironically, Belden cites *Cowboy Songs* and *American Ballads and Folk Songs* for the Gashade name, apparently unaware that the name came from his own version.

50. *Pardner of the Wind*, in collaboration with Neil M. Clark, pp. 21–44, and *passim*.

51. *Ibid.*, p. 42.

52. See especially *PTFS*, VI (1927), 131, 207, and compare with the latter citation, the printings of "Springfield Mountain" in *American Ballads and Folk Songs* and *Cowboy Songs* (1938).

53. See Fannie Hardy Eckstorm and Mary Winslow Smyth, *Minstrelsy of Maine*, pp. 40–41.

54. Howard Brockway, "The Quest of the Lonesome Tunes," *The Art World*, II (June, 1917), 228.

55. Bertrand H. Bronson, *JAF*, LXVII (1954), 95.

56. In A. H. Fox Strangways, *Cecil Sharp* (1933), pp. 143*ff*. (2d ed., 1955, pp. 142*ff*.).

57. *English Folk-Songs from the Southern Appalachians* (1932), I, xv. The full itinerary is given, xxiii–xv.

58. *Midwest Folklore*, III (1953), 123.

59. *The Ballad Tree*, p. 263.

60. *Ibid.*, pp. 265–266.

61. Quoted by William Hugh Jansen, "From Field to Library," *Folk-Lore*, LXIII (1952), 156. The statement was made in public discussion at the Mid-century International Folklore Conference, Indiana University, 1950.

62. Letter to Arthur Kyle Davis, Jr., printed in *Traditional Ballads of Virginia*, p. 54.

63. The department had been conducted previously, without great success, by John A. Lomax and Robert Frothingham.
64. Hustvedt, *Ballad Books and Ballad Men*, p. 207.
65. *Adventures of a Ballad Hunter*, p. 107.
66. MQ, XIV (1928), 297ff.
67. B. A. Botkin, "The Archive of American Folk-Song: Retrospect and Prospect," *The Library of Congress Quarterly Journal of Current Acquisitions*, II (1945), 65.
68. Leah Jackson Wolford, *The Play-Party in Indiana* (1916), and B. A. Botkin, *The American Play-Party Song* (1937) are examples.
69. Two important collections are Samuel Preston Bayard, *Hill Country Tunes* (1944), and Ira W. Ford, *Traditional Music of America* (1940). Ford's book includes song and game material, but as an afterthought.
70. For example, the collections of George Pullen Jackson, *Spiritual Folk-Songs of Early America* (1937), *Down-East Spirituals and Others* (1943), *Another Sheaf of White Spirituals* (1952); and Annabel Morris Buchanan, *Folk Hymns of America* (1938).
71. See Appendix One.
72. But see Louis W. Chappell, *John Henry: A Folklore Study* for notes of variations in successive printings of "John Hardy" and "John Henry" texts. Chappell concludes, "Very probably some of them are typographical errors, and others may have resulted from confusions in handling a large number of manuscripts, possibly during years when he was overtaxed with other work" (p. 5).
73. New variants and new songs are being provided by the volumes containing the music.
74. "Folk-Songs from Ohio," the manuscript intended for publication, is in the J. G. White Collection, Cleveland Public Library. A manuscript collection sent to Harvard reached Kittredge first and was never deposited in the Harvard Library, though a later supplement is in the Houghton Library. The A. H. Tolman collection in Houghton also contains a number of Miss Eddy's collected songs.
75. For the eighty-five songs in *Minstrels*, Korson provides ten tunes. Of the 136 texts printed in *Coal Dust*, sixty-two were recorded with the tunes, only ten of which were published. Korson names the airs to which thirty-three others were sung.
76. We have already considered such books as *Cowboy Songs* and *North Pennsylvania Minstrelsy*, which might be placed in this category.
77. *The New Green Mountain Songster*, p. v.
78. We refer not merely to analogues—they are present in proportions of one-third to one-half in most American general collections. We mean texts tied rather directly to particular performers or renditions, e.g., the "lost his average" version of "Wreck of the Old 97," the "Waiting for a Train" version of "Ten Thousand Miles from Home," and "T for Texas."
79. *The Maine Woods Songster*, p. 5.
80. *Ibid.*, p. 6.

81. Her "British Folk Songs from Canada," *JFSS*, VIII (1930), 218*ff*. in no way overlaps.

82. *Folk Songs from Newfoundland*, p. iii.

83. The background of Frank Luther's *Americans and Their Songs* might be interesting because of his connection with the commercial recording industry.

84. J. Frank Dobie, "The Traveling Anecdote," *PTFLS*, XXV (1953), 13.

85. *MQ*, XXXI (1935), 109.

86. "Some Types of American Folk-song," *JAF*, XXVIII (1915), 3.

87. *BFSSNE*, No. 11 (1936), p. 24.

88. See Carl Engel, *MQ*, XXI (1935), 110–112.

89. *New Republic*, XLVII (1926), 169.

90. *Ibid.*, 227.

91. *Kenyon Review*, X (1948), 491–492.

92. *The Armed Vision*, p. 137.

93. *Kenyon Review*, loc. cit.

94. *Ibid.*

95. George Herzog, *JEFDSS*, III (1939), 287.

96. *JEFDSS*, I (1933), 105.

97. *Ibid.*, III (1939), 283–284.

98. *Folk-Lore*, LI (1940), 157.

99. *American Ballads and Songs*, p. xiii.

100. W. Edson Richmond, *JAF*, LXVII (1954), 96.

101. *BFSSNE*, No. 5 (1933), p. 4.

102. MacKenzie, *The Quest of the Ballad*, p. 63.

103. *Ballads and Songs of Southern Michigan*, p. 15.

104. Alan Lomax, in *Four Symposia on Folklore*, ed. Stith Thompson, p. 157.

105. Alan Lomax, *New York Times Sunday Magazine*, Jan. 26, 1947, pp. 16, 41–42.

106. B. A. Botkin, in *People's Song Book*, p. 6.

107. Alan Lomax, in *ibid.*, p. 3.

108. "The Ballad of Pete Seeger," to the tune of "Wreck of the Old 97," *The Bosses Songbook*, p. 24.

109. This discussion is based on the American recording industry, concerning which I have information. Until quite recently the only folk recordings available in Great Britain seem to have been an excellent Columbia issue of the singing of Philip Tanner and imported American recordings of the commercialized "folk music for the folk."

110. Columbia 3083: "Tribal Prayer" / "Love Call" / "Hiawatha's Departure" / "My Bark Canoe"; 3084: "Bangum and the Boar" / "The Gallows Tree"; 3085: "Jesse James" / "The Dying Cowboy"; 3086: "Go Down Moses" / "O Graveyard" / "Peter, Go Ring Dem Bells"; 3087: "Old Dan Tucker" / "The Little Old Log Cabin in the Lane."

111. *Negro Workaday Songs*, pp. 23*ff*.

112. "The Bawdy Song . . . in Fact and in Print," *Explorations* 7 (March, 1957), pp. 139*ff*.

113. Letter, 26 December, 1829; printed in William Walker, *Peter Buchan and Other Papers,* p. 67.
114. "Some Problems of Ballad Publication," *MQ,* XIV (1928), 283*ff.*

CHAPTER FOUR

1. *JAF,* XLV (1932), 271.
2. Charles Seeger, *JAF,* LXII (1949), 111.
3. George Herzog, *SFQ,* II (1938), 60.
4. *BFSSNE,* No. 8 (1934), p. 24.
5. For example, see John Harrington Cox, "John Hardy," *JAF,* XXXII (1919), 505*ff.*; Foster B. Gresham, " 'The Jew's Daughter,' an Example of Ballad Variation," *JAF,* XLVII (1934), 358*ff.*; Frances M. Barbour, "Some Fusions in Missouri Ballads," *JAF,* XXXIX (1936), 205*ff.*; Edwin Capers Kirkland, "The Effect of Oral Tradition on 'Robin Hood and Little John,' " *SFQ,* IV (1940), 15*ff.*
6. See particularly Lucy E. Broadwood, "Early Chanty-Singing and Ship Music," *JFSS,* VIII (1928), 55*ff.* A more functional approach is demonstrated in such a collection as W. B. Whall's *Ships, Sea Songs, and Shanties.*
7. *SFQ,* I (1937), No. 3, pp. 17*ff.*
8. *SFQ,* XVII (1953), 158*ff.*
9. *JAF,* XXVII (1914), 58.
10. *JAF,* XXVII (1914), 55*ff.*; XXVIII (1915), 199*ff.*; *The Traditional Ballad and Its South Carolina Survivals,* p. 48; *South Carolina Ballads,* pp. 76–77; *JAF,* XLVII (1934), 64*ff.*; *SFQ,* I (1937), No. 2, pp. 7*ff.*
11. Millar, *SFQ,* XVII (1953), 159.
12. *Ibid.,* 158*ff.* Millar lists five secondary ballads; 119 canon texts, 107 of which are reasonably complete. We have altered his figures for the following reasons: he fails to list "Erlinton" (No. 8) under secondary recoveries; one text (No. 39) he erroneously lists as unpublished; seven texts he notes as unpublished (Nos. 22, 102, 133, 138, 166, 178, 266) have since appeared, and one of these is a fragment; "King Orfeo" (No. 19) has turned out instead to be a text of Child 27, "The Whummil Bore" (see *SFQ,* XXI [1957], 187*ff*). The count might be further reduced by the omission of No. 218, since the alleged informant of the Missouri text has denied any knowledge of such a song (*JAF,* LX [1947], 117) and the text Coffin cites in *Golden Book* is but another printing of the Child A version. We have not reduced to secondary status the recoveries of "Sir Lionel" (No. 18), though Bronson has pointed out that they descend not from the versions accepted by Child, but from a seventeenth-century comic version (*CFQ,* III [1944], 201–203).
13. *JAF,* LXIII (1950), 3.
14. *JAF,* LXX (1957), 231.
15. *SFQ,* XV (1951), 272. Italics added.
16. Gardner and Chickering, *Ballads and Songs of Southern Michigan,* pp. 204–205.

17. Combs, *Folk-Songs du Midi*, pp. 209–210.
18. The source of the Buchan texts affects the matter not at all.
19. *MLN*, XXVIII (1913), 5. See also Wilgus, "Ballad Classification," *MF*, V (1955), 95*ff*.; "A Syllabus of Kentucky Folksongs," *KFR*, I (1955), 31*ff*.
20. "The Ballad of Hind Horn," *JAF*, XXII (1909), 42*ff*.
21. Cra'ster, "George Collins," *JFSS*, IV (1910), 106*ff*.; Bayard, "The 'Johnny Collins' Version of *Lady Alice*," *JAF*, LVIII (1945), 73*ff*.
22. Gilchrist, " 'Death and the Lady' in English Balladry," *JEFDSS*, IV (1940), 37*ff*.; "The Song of Marvels (or Lies)," *JEFDSS*, IV (1942), 113*ff*.; Harvey, "The Unquiet Grave," *JEFDSS*, IV (1940), 49*ff*.
23. Entwistle has written, "Within any given area there is never a doubt but that two ballads of identical content are forms of the same ballad and not spontaneous creations" (*European Balladry*, p. 73). Does this apply to newer forms as well as old?
24. *JAF*, LIX (1946), 432*ff*.
25. See Helen Hartness Flanders, "Index of Ballads and Folk-Songs in the Archive of Vermont Folk-Songs at Smiley House, Springfield, Vt.," *Proceedings of the Vermont Historical Society*, 1940, pp. 214*ff*.; *Check List of California Songs* (1940).
26. *SFQ*, VIII (1944), 201*ff*.
27. *Ballads and Songs Collected by the Missouri Folk-Lore Society*, pp. 473*ff*., passim; *The Frank C. Brown Collection of North Carolina Folklore*, III, 207*ff*., passim. Belden was not able successfully to classify the material, but his perception of the stringing of images to form a lyric may aid students in devising modes of identification.
28. See especially Hyder Edward Rollins, *An Analytical Index to the Ballad Entries (1557–1709) in the Registers of the Company of Stationers of London* (1924; also *SP*, XXI, 1*ff*.); Worthington C. Ford, *Broadside Ballads, etc. Printed in Massachusetts, 1639–1800* (*Publications of the Massachusetts Historical Society*, LXXV, 1922); "The Isaiah Thomas Collection of Ballads," *Proceedings of the American Antiquarian Society*, n.s., XXXIII (1924), 44*ff*.
29. *List of American Folk Songs on Commercial Records* (reprinted with revisions from the *Report of the Committee of the Conference on Inter-American Relations in the Field of Music*, Washington, D. C., Sept. 3, 1940).
30. See, for example, John Speirs, *The Scots Literary Tradition*, pp. 145*ff*. Speirs is a quite sensitive critic, but he sometimes tends to confuse his reactions with those of the folk who composed or sang the ballads. That images of finery in the ballads indicate moral criticism of the upper class seems hardly tenable.
31. Kittredge, in *ESPB*, I, xxx.
32. *American Balladry from British Broadsides*, p. 72.
33. Albert B. Friedman, "A New Version of Musselburgh Field," *JAF*, LXVI (1953), 75*ff*.
34. Andrew Lang in *Sir Walter Scott and the Border Minstrelsy* was not convinced of Scott's sole responsibility, but later opinion has almost unanimously

accepted Scott's authorship. Lang's opinion fluctuated notoriously in regard to "Kinmont Willie," "Auld Maitland," and "The Outlaw Murray."

35. Chambers, *English Literature at the Close of the Middle Ages*, p. 153.

36. *Poetic Origins and the Ballad*, pp. 171ff.

37. "The Bitter Withy" was first printed by Frank Sidgwick in *Notes and Queries* in 1905, but its apparent relative, "The Holy Well," was available in William Sandys' *Christmas Carols* (1833). The folk status of "Corpus Christi" in MS. Balliol 354 was not apparent until 1905, when Sidgwick printed a traditional copy in *Notes and Queries*, though Child may have overlooked a traditional version in *Notes and Queries*, 1862. Later collection stimulated interest in "The Seven Virgins," first printed in William Henry Husk's *Songs of the Nativity* (1868). "The Bold Fisherman" came to notice in Lucy E. Broadwood and J. A. Fuller-Maitland's *English County Songs* (1893).

38. Gerould, *Ballad of Tradition*, p. 4.

39. Hodgart, *The Ballads*, p. 12.

40. Thelma G. James, *JAF*, XLVI (1933), 58.

41. *The Popular Ballad*, p. 340.

42. "Comic Elements in the English Traditional Ballad," *JIFMC*, III (1951), 76ff.

43. *Ballad Books and Ballad Men*, pp. 219–220.

44. *The Science of Folk-Lore*, pp. 178–179.

45. *JFSS*, VIII (1930), 237ff.

46. *JAF*, XLVIII (1935), 352ff.

47. Most of the matter has been summarized by Albert B. Friedman in " 'The Grey Cock'—A Drollery Version," *JAF*, LXVII (1954), 285ff. See also Margaret Dean-Smith, *Guide to English Folk Song Collections*, pp. 23–24.

48. See, for example, Alison White, "Children in the Ballads," *SFQ*, XVIII (1954), 205ff.

49. "Kinship in the British Ballads: The Historical Evidence," *SFQ*, XX (1956), 199ff.; "Kindred and Clan in the Scottish Border Ballads," *Boston University Studies in English*, III (1957), 1ff.

50. Lang, *Encyclopaedia Britannica*, 9th ed., III, 283.

51. W. E. Mead, "Colour in the English and Scottish Ballads," *An English Miscellany Presented to Dr. Furnivall* (1901), 321ff.; B. J. Whiting, "Proverbial Material in the Popular Ballad," *JAF*, XLVII (1934), 22ff.; W. Edson Richmond, "Ballad Place Names," *JAF*, LIX (1946), 263ff.

52. *The Ballad of Tradition*, p. 116.

53. *European Balladry*, pp. 27, 117.

54. *The British Traditional Ballad in North America*, pp. 81, 165ff.

55. "Edward" and "Sven i Rosengård" (1931), pp. 40–42.

56. *JAF*, XLVII (1934), 22ff.

57. See *The Epithet in English and Scottish, Spanish, and Danish Popular Ballads* (1933).

58. See especially "Studies in the Epic Techniques of Oral Verse-Making . . . ,"

Harvard Studies in Classical Philology, XLI (1930), 73ff.; *ibid.*, XLIII (1932), 1ff. Compare C. W. Bowra, *Heroic Poetry*, pp. 215ff.

59. *The Popular Ballad*, p. 325.
60. *The Ballad of Tradition*, p. 125. His "specimen chosen almost at random" illustrates the accidental choice of an atypical example.
61. "The Meter of the Popular Ballad," *PMLA*, XL (1925), 933ff.
62. See especially Pound, *Poetic Origins*, p. 109.
63. *CFQ*, III (1944), 190–191.
64. "The Vulgar Ballad," *Sewanee Review*, XIX (1911), 213ff.; "Boccaccio, Hans Sachs, and the Bramble Briar," *PMLA*, XXXIII (1918), 327ff.
65. *The New Green Mountain Songster*, p. 131.
66. "The Black Letter Broadside Ballad," *PMLA*, XXXIV (1919), 258ff.
67. *Native American Balladry*, p. 11.
68. *JAF*, XLVI (1933), 59.
69. *American Balladry from British Broadsides*, p. 78.
70. *Ibid.*, pp. 27–28, 79–80.
71. *Ibid.*, p. 81.
72. *Native American Balladry*, p. 263.
73. *Ibid.*, p. 34; *JAF*, LXIV (1951), 163.
74. *The Viking Book of Folk Ballads*, p. xxvii.
75. *American Balladry from British Broadsides*, p. 84n.
76. The collections of Odum and Johnson contain stimulating analyses of the style of Negro folksong. See particularly the chapter on imagery, style, and poetic effort in *The Negro and His Songs*, pp. 269ff.
77. *The Negro and His Songs*, pp. 219–220.
78. *English and Scottish Popular Ballads*, p. xvii.
79. *The British Traditional Ballad in North America*, pp. 3ff.
80. "Nonsense and New Sense in 'Lord Thomas,'" *SFQ*, I (1937), No. 4, pp. 25ff.
81. *JAF*, LIX (1946), 263ff.
82. "Some Effects of Scribal and Typographical Error on Oral Tradition," *SFQ*, XV (1951), 159ff.
83. *BFSSNE*, No. 11 (1936), pp. 16–17.
84. See Foster B. Gresham, *JAF*, XLVII (1934), 358ff.
85. *English Folk-Song: Some Conclusions*, p. 21.
86. *The Quest of the Ballad*, pp. 165–166, 175.
87. See Arthur Kyle Davis, *Traditional Ballads of Virginia*, p. 36; Kirkland, *SFQ*, IV (1940), 16.
88. *The British Traditional Ballad in North America*, pp. 5, 11. Coffin's employment of the terms *version* and *variant* seems to refer specifically to Child's volumes. American scholars have used the terms loosely in the same meaning, i.e., varying copy. Kittredge attempted without success to recall the term *version* to Child's conception, "a copy with distinguishing characteristics in plot, style, age, atmosphere, or the like" (Reed Smith, *South Carolina Ballads*, p. 169). Barry protested that the distinction "has the defect of making the process of tradition rather too simple" (*British Ballads from Maine*,

p. 224). Coffin's use of the term *story types* to indicate what might be called *versions* seems to stem not only from the confused usage, but from the fact that one of his story types might include several of Child's versions.

89. But see Barry, *BFSSNE*, *passim*; Bronson, *CFQ*, III (1944), 185*ff.*; George Boswell, *TFSB*, XVII (1951), 9*ff.*

90. *SFQ*, XIV (1950), 87.

91. *BFSSNE*, No. 8 (1934), p. 24.

92. "The Problem of Ballad-Story Variation and Eugene Haun's 'The Drowsy Sleeper,'" *SFQ*, XIV (1950), 87*ff.*

93. "Mary Hamilton' and the Anglo-American Ballad as an Art Form," *JAF*, LXX (1957), 208*ff.* Compare Holger O. Nygard's "The Icelandic Ásu Kvœthi: The Narrative Metamorphosis of a Folksong" (*MF*, V [1955], 141*ff.*), which emphasizes verbal correspondences among variants.

94. *The Ballads*, p. 108. Hodgart is admittedly reviving, in revised form, the "heresies" of Robert Chambers and T. F. Henderson.

95. For a summary and references, see Stith Thompson, *The Folktale*, pp. 437*ff.* For a conclusion based on American field experience, see Wm. Hugh Jansen, "From Field to Library," *Folk-Lore*, LXIII (1952), 152*ff.*

96. *Native American Balladry*, p. 80.

97. *American Balladry from British Broadsides*, pp. 104*ff.*

98. See, for example, Frances C. Stamper and Wm. Hugh Jansen, "'Water Birch': An American Variant of 'Hugh of Lincoln,'" *JAF*, LXXI (1958), 16*ff.*

99. In "'Lord Thomas' in America," *SFQ*, XIX (1955), 257*ff.*, Miss Anne Beard concludes that most American variants of Child 73 are derived from an unknown broadside differing from Child D. Also of interest is Jansen's contention that "an American *oikotype* is quite distinct and rigidly restricted to the small geographic area in which one folk-performer's reputation holds sway" (*Folk-Lore*, LXIII [1952], 155).

100. Information from Mrs. John J. Futrelle, stepdaughter of the Rev. Jenkins, and Polk C. Brockman, through the courtesy of Archie Green. A study of the compositions and recompositions of the Rev. Jenkins has been undertaken by Green and D. K. Wilgus.

101. MacEdward Leach, *The Ballad Book*, p. 31.

102. *Records Roundup*, February, 1947, p. 6. Mullican's recording is "New Pretty Blonde," King 578.

103. *The New Green Mountain Songster*, ed. Flanders, *et al.*, p. 114; *SFQ*, I (1937), No. 2, p. 30.

104. *BFSSNE*, No. 8 (1934), p. 17.

105. *Standard Dictionary of Folklore*, I, 498.

106. *BFSSNE*, No. 8 (1934), p. 24.

107. Belden, "A Study in Contemporary Balladry," *Mid-West Quarterly*, I (1914), 162*ff.* (dealing with ballads of the Meeks family murder, Missouri, 1894). This was not the first article dealing with the origin of an American folksong. Perhaps that honor should go to H. C. Mercer's "On the Track of the 'Arkansas Traveler,'" *Century Magazine*, LI (1896), 707*ff.*

108. See Herbert Halpert, "Truth in Folk-Songs," in John Harrington Cox, *Traditional Ballads Mainly from West Virginia* (1939).
109. *Native American Balladry*, p. 71.
110. *Ibid.*, p. 60.
111. Eckstorm, "How Dan Golden Made up a New Song," *Minstrelsy of Maine*, p. 139. For a meticulous comparison of a ballad with the facts on which it is based, see Daniel G. Hoffman, "Historic Truth and Ballad Truth: Two Versions of the Capture of New Orleans," *JAF*, LXV (1952), 295*ff*.
112. J. Frank Dobie, "Ballads and Songs of the Frontier Folk," *PTFS*, VI (1927), 143.
113. "The Pursuit of a Ballad Myth," *Minstrelsy of Maine*, pp. 176*ff*.
114. "The Origin of a Ballad," *MLN*, L (1935), 465*ff*.; for a summary and interpretation, see Laws, *Native American Balladry*, pp. 62–63.
115. Flanders, *et al.*, *The New Green Mountain Songster*, pp. 112*ff*.
116. *John Henry: A Folk-Lore Study* (1933). Because of his unfortunate presentation of his material, Chappell's study has not received the recognition it deserves. Chappell charges that his unpublished report of investigation of John Henry at Big Bend Tunnel, West Virginia, fell into the hands of Guy B. Johnson, who hurriedly made an investigation and published a book (*John Henry: Tracking Down a Negro Legend* [1929]) using some of Chappell's material and making no acknowledgment. Chappell also points out variations in texts printed more than once by Johnson, Cox, and Combs. Chappell's pugnacious tone and carping criticism disfigure his book. But his ugly charges remain unanswered.
117. The apparent connections of one John Henry with Big Bend Tunnel and with reports of informants would, as Chappell puts it, "be sufficient for the identification of Chaucer's Wife of Bath" (p. 77).
118. *Native American Balladry*, p. 65.
119. *Ibid.*, p. 66. See Barry, "Fair Florella, *AS*, III (1928), 441*ff*.
120. Belden, *Mid-West Quarterly*, I (1914), 162*ff*.
121. For such a recent attribution of "Charles Guiteau," see Maggie J. Lowe, "An Old Ballad Composer of the Nineties," *TFSB*, XIX (1953), 93. A recently collected variant of Child 2 in the Western Kentucky Folklore Archive of D. K. Wilgus is attributed by the informant to her father.
122. "Peter Emberly," once attributed to Gorman (Laws, *Native American Balladry*, p. 159) is now assigned to John Calhoun (Doerflinger, *Shantymen and Shantyboys*, p. 225).
123. Dobie, "More Ballads and Songs of the Frontier Folk," *PTFS*, VII (1928), 167.
124. Eckstorm, *Minstrelsy of Maine*, p. 36.
125. John White, *D. J. O'Malley: "Cowboy Poet," passim*.
126. Rudi Blesh, *Shining Trumpets*, p. 147.
127. Douglas Gilbert, *Lost Chords*, p. 221.
128. *Brown Collection*, II, 512*ff*.; John A. Lomax, "Half-Million Dollar Song: Origin of 'Home on the Range,'" *Southwest Review*, XXXI (1945), 1*ff*.;

Levette J. Davidson, " 'Home on the Range' Again," *CFQ*, III (1944), 208*ff*.

129. *BFSSNE*, No. 8 (1934), pp.19*ff*.
130. *Shantymen and Shantyboys*, pp. 256, 348.
131. Letter, February 15, 1958. Ives is preparing a critical study of Gorman and his songs.
132. "Signature in Ballad and Story," *PTFS*, XXV (1953), 87*ff*.
133. *Native American Balladry*, p. 44.
134. William A. Owens, *Texas Folk Songs* (*PTFS*, XXIII, 1950), p. 96; see also *Brown Collection*, II, 679*ff*.
135. Eckstorm and Smyth, *Minstrelsy of Maine*, p. 50.
136. "Willie Moore," sung by Burnett and Rutherford, Columbia record 15314-D. A variant in the John A. Lomax papers gives the signature, J. R. G. (which could be what is sung on the record).
137. *JAF*, XXV (1912), 156*ff*.; *BFSSNE*, No. 12 (1937), p. 27; *The New Green Mountain Songster*, pp. 112*ff*.
138. *Minstrelsy of Maine*, p. 196.
139. *BFSSNE*, Nos. 7–12 (1934–1937), *passim*.
140. *Native American Balladry*, p. 214.
141. *SFQ*, I (1937), No. 2, p. 40.
142. *Ibid.*, p. 39.
143. For what it is worth, we quote Lucy E. Broadwood's comment on "The Blackwater Side," recorded in County Waterford, Ireland: "This song is included as a specimen of the way in which untaught country people still make their own ballads. Such compositions are very reminiscent, but so also are the older folk-songs; for stock phrases in tunes or verse are peculiar to what has long been communal and traditional" (*JFSS*, III [1907], 37). See also pp. 226–227.
144. *BFSSNE*, No. 6 (1933), pp. 15*ff*. Laws is rather inconsistent in accepting "The Little Mohea" into *Native American Balladry* as an American adaptation and failing to include "The Indian Lass" in *American Balladry from British Broadsides*, though the English form is found in America.
145. "The Riddle of the Flying Cloud," *JAF*, LXVI (1953), 123*ff*.
146. *PMLA*, XXXIII (1918), 327*ff*.
147. See "Popular Song in Missouri—The Returned Lover," Herrig's *Archiv*, CXX (1908), 62*ff*., and the notes to relevant pieces in *Ballads and Songs Collected by the Missouri Folk-Lore Society*.
148. " 'The Lady and the Dragoon': A Broadside Ballad in Oral Tradition," *JAF*, LXX (1957), 221*ff*.
149. *JAF*, LXVIII (1955), 201*ff*. Greene's study of "The Bold Soldier" was apparently completed before he had an opportunity to see Cazden's work.
150. It is perhaps ironic that Cazden may have, in a reference to a text in the *Echo, or Columbian Songster*, of 1800, identified one of the "indeterminate number of printed texts" of the Coverly broadside that Greene postulates but did not find.

151. *JAF*, LXX (1957), 221. The tone of the comment seems, unfortunately, to justify Cazden's criticism that orthodox ballad scholars "come uncomfortably close to an unwitting aristocratic bias."

152. *JAF*, XXXV (1922), 394*ff.*; *PTFS*, V (1926), 5*ff.*; Iona and Peter Opie, *The Oxford Dictionary of Nursery Rhymes*, 175*ff.*

153. Arthur K. Moore, "Types of the Folk Song 'Father Grumble,'" *JAF*, LXIV (1951), 89*ff.*

154. Bertrand H. Bronson, "Samuel Hall's Family Tree," *CFQ*, I (1942), 47*ff.*; George Pullen Jackson, "The 400-Year Odyssey of the 'Captain Kidd' Song Family—Notably Its Religious Branch," *SFQ*, XV (1951), 239*ff.*

155. It is well to point out that, as Archer Taylor has written, Child "does not often or consistently make any endeavor to explain the variations, to point out their significance, or to deduce from them the ballad's history" (*"Edward" and "Sven i Rosengård,"* p. vii).

156. *PMLA*, XXIII (1908), 141*ff.*

157. *JAF*, XXII (1909), 42*ff.*

158. *PMLA*, XXXI (1916), 181*ff.*

159. Compare William Henry Schofield, "The Story of Horn and Rimenhild," *PMLA*, XVII (1903), 1*ff.* William J. Entwistle has since linked "Hind Horn" and the Danish "Hertig Henrick" with a tradition he traces to a tenth- or eleventh-century Akritic ballad ("The Noble Moringer," *Modern Language Forum*, XXXIV [1949], 2*ff.*).

160. *"Edward" and "Sven i Rosengård,"* p. vii.

161. *JEFDSS*, I (1932), 1*ff.*

162. *BFSSNE*, No. 3 (1931), pp. 11*ff.*

163. "The Murder Motive in 'Edward,'" *WF*, VIII (1949), 315.

164. T. F. Henderson, *The Ballad in Literature*, p. 25.

165. "The Texts of 'Edward' in Percy's *Reliques* and Motherwell's *Minstrelsy*," *MLN*, XLV (1930), 226; *"Edward" and "Sven i Rosengård,"* pp. 23, 26.

166. "'Edward, Edward. A Scottish Ballad,'" *SFQ*, IV (1940), 1*ff.*; "A Footnote to *Edward, Edward*," *SFQ*, IV, 159*ff.*

167. "'Edward' and the Folk Tradition," *SFQ*, XXI (1957), 131*ff.*

168. *BFSSNE*, No. 5 (1933), pp. 19–20.

169. *Ibid.*, pp. 6, 20.

170. *WF*, VIII (1949), 314*ff.*

171. *CFQ*, III (1944), 198.

172. *Arv*, V (1949), 69*ff.*

173. See Archer Taylor, "Precursors of the Finnish Method of Folk-Lore Study," *MP*, XXV (1938), 481*ff.*

174. *Ibid.*, 486.

175. See especially the discussion and references in Stith Thompson, *The Folktale*, pp. 430*ff.*

176. *JAF*, XLII (1929), 238*ff.*

177. *BFSSNE*, Nos. 3, 6, 7, 9, 10, 11, 12, *passim.*

178. *JAF*, LXIV (1951), 347*ff.*

179. *BFSSNE*, No. 5 (1933), p. 20.

180. Portions of this study were previously printed in *JAF*, LXV (1952), 1*ff*; LXVIII (1955), 141*ff*; *MF*, V (1955), 141*ff*.
181. A number of other dubious techniques are ably criticized by Samuel P. Bayard, *WF*, XIV (1955), 114*ff*. See also Nygard, *The Ballad of Heer Halewijn*, pp. 18–20.
182. For example, the German *Nicolai* form, in which the maid is killed, almost fails of inclusion because "the song has undergone such a great change that we have in effect a different ballad, whose relations to the rest of the tradition are assured only by the phrasal parallels" (*The Ballad of Heer Halewijn*, p. 85). It is only fair to note that in terms of his purpose, Nygard's limitations are justified, and that he does not advance his specific method as applicable to the study of all ballads, maintaining only that his approach reveals adequately the movements of this one particular ballad (*ibid.*, p. 17).
183. *WF*, XIV (1955), 119–120.
184. Samuel P. Bayard, "The 'Johnny Collins' Version of *Lady Alice*," *JAF*, LVIII (1945), 73*ff*.; Harbison Parker, "The 'Clerk Colvill' Mermaid," *JAF*, LX (1947), 265*ff*.
185. Hodgart, *The Ballads*, pp. 88–95, 106–108.
186. "The Story of a Catskill Ballad," *NYFQ*, VIII (1952), 245*ff*.
187. *ESPB*, IV, 164.
188. "Sir Aldingar and the Date of English Ballads," *Saga Book of the Viking Society for Northern Research*, XIII (1947–1948), 97*ff*.
189. "The Lineage and Birth of Sir Aldingar," *JAF*, LXV (1952), 139*ff*.
190. *Saga Book of the Viking Society*, XIII, 98.
191. "New Light on the Epic-Ballad Problem," *JAF*, LXII (1949), 375*ff*.
192. "The Themes Common to English and German Balladry," *MLQ*, I (1940), 23*ff*.; "Una Comparación Tentativa de Temas de Balada Inglesas y Españolas," *Folklore Americano*, IV (1956), 3*ff*.
193. *BFSSNE*, No. 5 (1933), p. 20.
194. Bayard, *JAF*, LVIII (1945), 103*n*.
195. *BFSSNE*, No. 3 (1931), pp. 13–14.
196. *ESPB*, III, 42.
197. "Robin Hood in the Light of History," *JEFDSS*, VII (1955), 228*ff*.
198. But see Jay Williams, "More About Robin Hood," *JAF*, LXV (1952), 304*ff*.
199. "Theories and Fantasies Concerning Robin Hood," *SFQ*, XX (1956), 108*ff*.
200. "The May Games and the Robin Hood Legend," *JAF*, LXIV (1951), 265*ff*.; "The Historic Robin Hood," *JAF*, LXVI (1953), 303*ff*.
201. "Still More About Robin Hood," *JAF*, LXV (1952), 420.
202. "Robin Hood and Some Other Outlaws," *JAF*, LXXI (1958), 27*ff*. See also Simeone's "The Mythical Robin Hood," *WF*, XVII (1958), 21*ff*., for an examination of the mythic view of Robin Hood as a glossing game.
203. *JEFDSS*, IV (1942), 113*ff*.

204. *JFSS*, IV, No. 16 (1911).
205. "Early Chanty-Singing and Ship Music," *JFSS*, VIII (1928), 55ff.
206. For an excellent bibliography, see Doerflinger, *Shantymen and Shantyboys*.
207. *The Shanty Book*, Part I (1921), p. vi.
208. *Shantymen and Shantyboys*, pp. 100–101.
209. Bone, *Capstan Bars*, p. 21.
210. See Appendix One for a survey of the controversy.
211. For example, see Alan Lomax, "Reels and Work Songs," in *75 Years of Freedom: Commemoration of the 75th Anniversary of the Proclamation of the 13th Amendment to the Constitution of the United States* (1943), pp. 27ff.
212. B. A. Botkin, *The American Play-Party Song*, p. v.
213. II (1889), 104.
214. My experience in Oklahoma, where Botkin collected, confirms this conclusion, in that the young people dance at honky-tonks and "play games" in the home.
215. Dean-Smith, *A Guide to English Folk Song Collections*, p. 20.
216. Songs are treated as folk carols because of their subject or function. They are not to be confused with the formal carol, defined by Richard Leighton Greene as: "A song on any subject, composed of uniform stanzas and provided with a burden" (*The Early English Carols*, p. xxiii).
217. *JFSS*, III (1910), 52ff.
218. *JFSS*, IV (1913), 316.
219. *The Ballads*, p. 168.
220. *Ibid.*, p. 167.
221. *JFSS*, V (1915), 132ff.; Dean-Smith, *A Guide to English Folk Song Collections*, p. 54.
222. See her contention that "I Saw Three Ships" is a "version of the story of the translation to Cologne of the crania of the Magi in 1162 by the Emperor Frederick Barbarossa," *JEFDSS*, V (1946), 34.
223. *JAF*, IV (1891), 215ff.
224. "Songs of the 'Twelve Numbers' and the Hebrew Chant of 'Echod Mi Yodea,'" *JAF*, LXII (1949), 382ff.
225. *English Folk-Songs from the Southern Appalachians* (1917), p. ix; (1932), I, xxvi.
226. The origin controversy does not seem to have been the main stimulus for Miss Gilchrist's pioneer article, "The Folk Element in Early Revival Hymns and Tunes," *JFSS*, VIII (1928), 61ff. More probably her discovery of Primitive Methodist material among Dr. John Clague's collection of traditional Manx songs furnished the lead.
227. "The Ancestry of a Negro Spiritual," *MLN*, XXXIII (1918), 442ff.
228. *White Spirituals in the Southern Uplands*, p. 3.
229. *Spiritual Folk-Songs of Early America*, p. 3.
230. *JFSS*, VIII (1928), 93.
231. *Spiritual Folk-Songs of Early America*, pp. 10–11.
232. *White Spirituals in the Southern Uplands*, pp. 209–211.

233. External tests include the ascription to a man who was a compiler not a composer, the label "Western Melody" or "Southern Melody" in an authorized hymnal, and, less frequently, a parallel in oral tradition. Internal tests are based on the "folky" character of words and tune. Subjective tests, dangerous when applied restrictively to songs in oral tradition, are sometimes necessary as an aid in identifying "unwritten music" in print. Later comparison of Jackson's findings with secular folksong has confirmed his judgments.

234. For example, see Hilton Rufty, Annabel Morris Buchanan, and John Powell, *Twelve Folk Hymns from the Old Shape Note Hymnbooks and from Oral Tradition* (1934); L. L. McDowell, *Songs of the Old Camp Ground* (1934); Annabel Morris Buchanan, *Folk Hymns of America* (1938).

235. Tristram P. Coffin, "A Tentative Study of a Typical Folk Lyric: 'Green Grows the Laurel,'" *JAF*, LXV (1952), 341.

236. Taylor, *"Edward" and "Sven i Rosengård,"* p. 40; compare Thompson, *The Folktale*, p. 439.

237. "Some Notes on 'O Waly Waly,'" *JEFDSS*, VII (1954), 161ff.

238. *JAF*, LXV (1952), 341.

239. *Ibid.*, 341ff.; LXVII (1954), 295f.

240. Bertrand H. Bronson, "Some Observations about Melodic Variation in British-American Folk Tunes," *Journal of the American Musicological Society*, III (1950), 121.

241. See Charles Seeger, "Professionalism and Amateurism in the Study of Folk Music," *JAF*, LXII (1949), 107ff.

242. Samuel P. Bayard, "Prolegomena to a Study of the Principal Melodic Families of British-American Folk Song," *JAF*, LXIII (1950), 7.

243. We might also point out that linguistic barriers have naturally been of less importance, but until relatively recently only Gaelic items from Britain and Ireland and Pennsylvania German items in the United States have been used for comparative purposes. There are, however, few examples of tune-text units crossing national boundaries.

244. See Sharp, *English Folk-Song: Some Conclusions*, pp. 112ff.

245. See Bayard, *JAF*, LXIII (1950), 10, for a discussion and examples.

246. Miss Broadwood writes, "The tune is of the type used so often for the ballad of 'Lord Bateman,' but is seldom met with the minor third. The cadence and general structure of the tune point to some connection with a class of ballad very popular amongst country singers . . ." (*JFSS*, III [1907], 55).

247. Bayard calls attention to the reliability of Miss Gilchrist's notes and the tendency to error in Miss Broadwood's ("American Folksongs and Their Music," *SFQ*, XVIII [1953], 128).

248. "Note on the Modal System of Gaelic Tunes," *JFSS*, IV (1911), 150ff.

249. For a brief exposition of the matter and a comparative chart, see Annabel Morris Buchanan, "A Neutral Mode in Anglo-American Folk Music," *SFQ*. IV (1940), 77ff.

250. *Ibid.*; "Modal and Melodic Structure in Anglo-American Folk Music: A Neutral Mode," in *Papers Read at the International Congress of Musicology Held at New York, September 11th to 16th, 1939*, ed. Arthur Mendel, Gustav Reese, and Gilbert Chase (1944), pp. 84ff.

251. "Folksong and the Modes," *MQ*, XXXII (1946), 37ff. Bronson's numbering of the pentatonic modes is as follows: Bronson No. 1 corresponds to Gilchrist No. 3; B2, G1; B3, G4; B4, G2; B5, G5.

252. *Brown Collection*, IV (1957).

253. *Notation of Folk Music: Recommendations of the Committee of Experts Convened by the International Archives of Folk Music, Geneva, 4–9 July, 1949, and Paris, 12–15 December, 1950* (1952), p. 1.

254. "An Instantaneous Music Notator," *JIFMC*, III (1951), 103ff.; "Toward a Universal Sound-Writing for Musicology," *JIFMC*, IX (1957), 63ff.; "Prescriptive and Descriptive Music-Writing," *MQ*, XLIV (1958), 184ff.

255. *Last Leaves*, pp. xiiff.

256. *English Folk-Songs from the Southern Appalachians* (1917), pp. ix–x; (1932), I, pp. xxvi–xxvii.

257. *The Quest of the Ballad*, *passim*.

258. *BFSSNE*, No. 3 (1931), p. 14; *SFQ*, I (1937), No. 2, p. 42.

259. *JAF*, XXIII (1910), 443ff.

260. *Publications of the University of California at Los Angeles in Languages and Literatures*, I (1936), 51ff.

261. *SFQ*, I (1937), No. 2.

262. *Ibid.*, pp. 49ff.

263. For a summary of European indexing methods, see Hustvedt, *Publications of the University of California at Los Angeles in Languages and Literatures*, I (1936), 59; Gustave O. Arlt, "Lexicographical Indexes of Folk Melodies," *MP*, XXVII (1929), 147ff.

264. In constructing its formula, the method takes into account other aspects: scale construction, melodic range, rhythm, etc. See Herzog, *SFQ*, I (1937), No. 2, p. 54.

265. *Ibid.*, p. 35.

266. *Ibid.*, p. 52; see also Bayard, "Ballad Tunes and the Hustvedt Indexing Method," *JAF*, LV (1942), 248ff.

267. Improved by Entwistle, *European Balladry*, pp. 381ff.; "Notation for Ballad Melodies," *PMLA*, LV (1940), 61ff.

268. *SFQ*, I (1937), No. 2, p. 55.

269. "The Problem of Melodic Variation in Folk Song," *JAF*, LV (1942), 204ff.; "Melodic Contour in Traditional Music," *JIFMC*, III (1951), 30ff.

270. *White Spirituals in the Southern Uplands*, p. 132.

271. *Spiritual Folk-Songs of Early America*, p. 14.

272. *JAF*, LXIII (1950), 33.

273. *Ibid.*, 1ff.; "American Folksongs and Their Music," *SFQ*, XVII (1953), 130ff.

274. Bayard, "Aspects of Melodic Kinship and Variation in British-American

Folk-Tunes," *Papers Read at the International Congress of Musicology Held at New York, September 11th to 16th, 1939,* p. 128.

275. *SFQ,* XVII (1953), 130ff.; "Principal Versions of an International Folk Tune," *JIFMC,* III (1951), 44ff.; "Two Representative Tune Families of British Tradition," *MF,* IV (1954), 13ff.

276. For the explanation of this method (which *follows* identification and analysis) see "Mechanical Help in the Study of Folk Song," *JAF,* LXII (1949), 81ff. Those unable to use IBM cards may be able to employ another system. See G. L. Anderson, "The McBee Keysort System for Mechanically Sorting Folklore Data," *JAF,* LXVI (1953), 340ff.

277. "Melodic Stability in Oral Tradition," *JIFMC,* III (1951), 50ff.

278. "The Interdependence of Ballad Tunes and Texts," *CFQ,* III (1944), 185ff.; "On the Union of Words and Music in the 'Child' Ballads," *WF,* XI (1952), 233ff.

279. "Shaping Controls of Ballad Tunes over Their Texts," *TFSB,* XVII (1951), 9ff.

280. See also "Good and Bad in British-American Folk Song," *JIFMC,* V (1953), 61ff.

281. "Mrs. Brown and the Ballad," *CFQ,* IV (1945), 129ff. Compare Hodgart, *The Ballads,* pp. 102–113.

282. "About the Commonest British Ballads," *JIFMC,* IX (1957), 22ff.

283. "The Morphology of the Ballad Tunes," *JAF,* LXXVII (1954), 1ff. Bronson's principle of *relative stability* differs from Walter Anderson's *law of self-correction* in that the resistance to change lies in the characteristics of the medium, not in the audience.

284. Bayard, *SFQ,* XVII (1943), 125.

285. *English Folk Songs from the Southern Appalachians* (1917), p. viii; (1932), I, xxv.

286. *Quest of the Ballad,* p. 112.

287. *SFQ,* II (1938), 62–63.

288. *The Ballad Tree,* p. 295.

289. "Dialect of the Folk-Song," *Dialect Notes,* IV (1916), 311.

290. *Folk Songs of the Upper Thames,* p. 12.

291. "American Regional Folklore," *JAF,* LX (1947), 355ff.

292. "Truth in Folk-Songs," in John Harrington Cox, *Traditional Ballads Mainly from West Virginia,* pp. ixff.; "Vitality of Tradition and Local Songs," *JIFMC,* III (1951), 35ff. See also "The Piney Folk-Singers," *Direction,* II (September, 1939), 4–6, 15; "A Michigan Lumberjack Singer," *HF,* I (1942), 81ff.; "The Folksinger Speaks," *HF,* III (1944), 29ff., 48ff.

293. "The Folksinger's Defense," *HF,* IX (1950), 65ff.

294. *Four Symposia on Folklore* (1953), ed. Stith Thompson, p. 171.

295. *WF,* XVII (1958), 4.

296. *BFSSNE,* No. 3 (1931), p. 15; No. 9, p. 7; *The Maine Woods Songster,* p. 6. Herzog, in the *Standard Dictionary of Folklore,* II, 1044, points out that *rubato-parlando* occurs in the Southern United States, a statement which may agree with Bartòk's use of the term. We might therefore refer

to Northern style as *rubato-declamando*. The problem may be one of terminology. Alan Lomax, who has compiled—or has helped to compile—a large amount of functional and biographical data but has not yet been able to organize and interpret it in terms of meaningful publication, is turning more hopefully to a stylistic-psychological approach. He is preparing anthologies organizing folksong geographically and characterizing it in terms of psychological and stylistic traits.

297. *Research in Primitive and Folk Music in the United States (American Council of Learned Societies Bulletin No. 24)*, pp. 51–53.

298. Charles Bryan, "American Folk Instruments: I. The Appalachian Mountain Dulcimer," *TFSB*, XVII (1952), 1ff.; "The Appalachian Mountain Dulcimer Enigma," *TFSB*, XX (1954), 86ff.; John F. Putnam, *The Plucked Dulcimer of the Southern Mountains*; Vernon H. Taylor, "From Fancy to Fact in Dulcimer Discoveries," *TFSB*, XXIII (1957), 109ff.; Charles Seeger, "The Appalachian Dulcimer," *JAF*, LXXI (1958), 40ff.

299. *JIFMC*, VIII (1956), 15ff.

300. *JEFDSS*, VII (1954), 145ff. See also Reginald Nettle, *Sing a Song of England*, pp. 190–192.

301. *WF*, XVII (1958), 4.

302. *JIFMC*, IV (1952), 26.

APPENDIX ONE

1. Miles Mark Fisher, *Negro Slave Songs in the United States* (1953), pp. 37ff.
2. *Century Magazine*, XXIV (1882), 873ff.
3. "The Dance in Place Congo," *Century Magazine*, XXXI (1886), 517ff.; "Creole Slave Songs," *ibid.*, 807ff.
4. Natalie Curtis [Burlin], "Folk Music of America; Four Types of Folk-Song in the United States Alone," *Craftsman*, XXI (1912), 414ff.; "The Negro's Contribution to the Music of America," *ibid.*, XXIII (1913), 66off.
5. William E. Burghardt Du Bois, *The Souls of Black Folk* (1903), p. 11.
6. Krehbiel does not deny individual authorship; he insists only that the folk poet must speak for his people in their idiom and about their lives, and that the song must be submitted to anonymous oral tradition (p. 4).
7. *Negro Folk-Songs, Hampton Series*, 4 vols. (1918–1919); *Songs and Tales from the Dark Continent* (1920).
8. *Saint Helena Island Spirituals* (1925).
9. *Negro Folk Rhymes* (1922), pp. 228ff.
10. "The Ancestry of a Negro Spiritual," *MLN*, XXXIII, 442ff.
11. *Church Music* (1923), p. 377.
12. "African Negro Music" *International Institute of African Languages and Cultures, Memorandum IV* (reprinted from *Africa*, I, i), p. 33. See also "American Negro Music," *The International Review of Missions*, XV (1926), 748ff.
13. *JAF*, XLI (1928), 173.

14. *The Book of American Negro Spirituals*, p. 14.
15. *Folk-Songs of America*, pp. 20ff.; see also Gordon's chapter on "The Negro Spiritual" in Augustine T. Smythe, *et al.*, *The Carolina Low Country*, pp. 191ff.
16. "The Folk Element in Early Revival Hymns and Tunes," *JFSS*, VIII (1928), 61ff.
17. See especially Barry, "Negro Folk-Songs from Maine," *BFSSNE*, No. 8 (1934), pp. 13ff.; No. 9, pp. 10ff.; No. 10, pp. 21ff.
18. *The Myth of the Negro Past*, p. 225.
19. *The Souls of Black Folk*, p. 192.
20. *The Myth of the Negro Past*, p. 267.
21. See *JAF*, XLVIII (1935), 394ff.
22. For example, in *The Armed Vision* Stanley Edgar Hyman writes, "Jackson is a Southern white chauvinist who has tricked out with trappings of pseudo-musicology his conviction that the Negro, as an inferior human, could hardly produce a first-rate art like the spirituals" (p. 138).
23. *Slave Songs of the Georgia Sea Islands* (1942), p. 45ff.
24. Barry, *BFSSNE*, No. 9 (1935), p. 10.
25. *Slave Songs of the Georgia Sea Islands*, p. 54.

SELECTED BIBLIOGRAPHY

BOOKS

Collections of Ballads and Folksongs

Adams, James Taylor: *Death in the Dark*, Big Laurel, Va., 1941.

Allen, Jules Verne: *Cowboy Lore*, San Antonio, Texas, 1933.

Allen, Rosa F. and Joseph H.: *Allen Family Songs*, Medfield, Mass., 1899.

Allen, William Francis, Charles Pickard Ware, and Lucy McKim Garrison: *Slave Songs of the United States*, New York, 1867.

Allsopp, Fred W.: *Folklore of Romantic Arkansas*, 2 vols., Kansas City, Kans., 1931.

Anderson, Nils: *The Hobo: The Sociology of the Homeless Man*, Chicago, 1923. (Chapter 14. "Hobo Songs and Ballads.")

Andrews, Edward Deming: *The Gift to Be Simple—Songs, Dances, and Rituals of the American Shakers*, New York, 1940.

Arnold, Byron: *Folksongs of Alabama*, Birmingham, 1950.

Ballanta, Nicholas G. J.: *Saint Helena Island Spirituals*, New York, 1925.

Baring-Gould, Rev. Sabine, and H. Fleetwood Sheppard: *A Garland of Country Song*, London, 1895.

———: *Songs and Ballads of the West*, London, 1889–1892.

Barrett, William Alexander: *English Folk Songs*, London, 1891.
Barry, Phillips: *Folkmusic in America.* (National Service Bureau Publication 180-S, American Folk Song Publication No. 4.) New York, 1939.
——: *The Maine Woods Songster*, Cambridge, Mass., 1939.
——, Fannie H. Eckstorm, and Mary W. Smyth: *British Ballads from Maine*, New Haven, 1929.
Bayard, Samuel Preston: *Hill Country Tunes.* (Memoirs of the American Folklore Society, Vol. 34.) Philadelphia, 1941.
Beck, Earl Clifton: *Lore of the Lumber Camps*, Ann Arbor, 1948.
——: *Songs of the Michigan Lumberjacks*, Ann Arbor, 1941.
——: *They Knew Paul Bunyan*, Ann Arbor, 1956.
Belden, Henry Marvin: *A Partial List of Song-Ballads and Other Popular Poetry Known in Missouri*, Columbia, Mo., 1907; with additions, 1910.
——: *Ballads and Songs Collected by the Missouri Folk-Lore Society.* (University of Missouri Studies, XV.) Columbia, Mo., 1940; reprinted, 1955.
Bone, David W.: *Capstan Bars*, New York, 1932.
Bosses Songbook, The, New York, n.d.
Botkin, B. A.: *The American Play-Party Song.* (University Studies of the University of Nebraska, XXXVIII.) Lincoln, Neb., 1937.
Brewster, Paul G.: *Ballads and Songs of Indiana.* (Indiana University Publications, Folklore Series No. 1.) Bloomington, 1940.
Broadwood, Lucy E.: *English Traditional Songs and Carols*, London, 1908.
——: *Sussex Songs*, London, 1890.
——, and J. A. Fuller-Maitland: *English County Songs*, London, 1893.
Bronson, Bertrand Harris: *The Traditional Tunes of the Child Ballads*, vol. 1, Princeton, N. J., 1959.
Brophy, John, and Eric Partridge: *Songs and Slang of the British Soldier, 1914–1918*, London, 1930.
The Frank C. Brown Collection of North Carolina Folklore, ed. Newman Ivey White, Paull F. Baum, *et al.*, 6 vols., Durham, N. C., 1952–
Bruce, Rev. J. Collingwood, and John Stokoe: *Northumbrian Minstrelsy*, Newcastle-upon-Tyne, 1882.
Buchanan, Annabel Morris: *Folk Hymns of America*, New York, 1938.
Bullen, Frank T., and W. F. Arnold: *Songs of Sea Labour*, London, 1914.
Burlin, Natalie Curtis: *Negro Folk Songs*, New York, 1918–1919.
——: *Songs and Tales from the Dark Continent*, New York, 1920.
Cambiaire, Celestin Pierre: *East Tennessee and Western Virginia Mountain Ballads*, London, 1934.
Campbell, Olive Dame, and Cecil J. Sharp: *English Folk Songs from the Southern Appalachians*, New York and London, 1917.
Chappell, Louis W.: *Folksongs of the Roanoke and the Albemarle*, Morgantown, W. Va., 1939.
Chappell, William: *Popular Music of the Olden Time*, 2 vols., London, 1855–1859.
A Check List of Recorded Songs in the English Language in the Archive of American Folk Song to July, 1940, Washington, D. C., 1940.

Child, Francis James: *The English and Scottish Popular Ballads*, 5 vols., Boston and New York, 1882–1898; reprinted, New York, 1956.

Clements, Rex: *Manavilins: A Muster of Sea-Songs* . . . , London, 1928.

Colcord, Joanna C.: *Roll and Go*, Indianapolis, 1924.

————: *Songs of American Sailormen*, New York, 1938.

Combs, Josiah H.: *Folk-Songs du Midi des États-Unis*, Paris, 1925.

————: *Folk-Songs from the Kentucky Highlands*, New York, 1939.

Cox, John Harrington: *Folk-Songs of the South*, Cambridge, Mass., 1925.

————: *Folk-Songs Mainly from West Virginia*. (American Folk-Song Publications No. 5, National Service Bureau Publication No. 81-S.) New York, 1939.

————: *Traditional Ballads Mainly from West Virginia*. (American Folk-Song Publication No. 3, National Service Bureau Publication No. 75-S.) New York, 1939.

Creighton, Helen: *Songs and Ballads from Nova Scotia*, Toronto and Vancouver, 1933.

————, and Doreen H. Senior: *Traditional Songs from Nova Scotia*, Toronto, 1950.

Davies, A. Stanley: *The Ballads of Montgomeryshire*, Welshpool, England, 1938.

Davis, Arthur Kyle, Jr.: *Folksongs of Virginia: A Descriptive Index and Syllabus*, Durham, N. C., 1949.

————: *Traditional Ballads of Virginia*, Cambridge, Mass., 1929.

Davis, Frederick J., and Ferris Tozer: *Sailors' Songs or "Chanties,"* London, 1887.

Daughters of Utah Pioneers: *Pioneer Songs*, Salt Lake City, 1940.

Dean, Michael C.: *Flying Cloud and One Hundred and Fifty Other Old Time Songs and Ballads of Outdoor Men, Sailors, Lumber Jacks, Soldiers, Men of the Great Lakes, Railroadmen, Miners, etc.*, Virginia, Minn., 1922.

Dett, R. Nathaniel: *The Dett Collection of Negro Spirituals*, 4 vols., Chicago, 1936.

————: *Religious Folk-Songs of the Negro as Sung at Hampton Institute*, Hampton, Va., 1927.

Diton, Carl: *Thirty-Six South Carolina Spirituals*, New York, 1928.

Doerflinger, William Main: *Shantymen and Shantyboys*, New York, 1951.

Eckstorm, Fannie Hardy, and Mary Winslow Smyth: *Minstrelsy of Maine*, Boston, 1927.

Eddy, Mary O.: *Ballads and Songs from Ohio*, New York, 1939.

Fenner, Thomas P.: *Cabin and Plantation Songs*, New York, 1874, 1877, 1901.

————: *Religious Folk Songs of the Negro as Sung on the Plantations*, Hampton, Va., 1909, 1918, 1924.

Finger, Charles J.: *Frontier Ballads*, Garden City, N. Y., 1927.

Flanders, Helen Hartness: *A Garland of Green Mountain Song*. (Green Mountain Pamphlet No. 1.) Northfield, Vt., 1934.

————: *Vermont Chapbook*, Middlebury, Vt., 1941.

————, Elizabeth Flanders Ballard, George Brown, and Phillips Barry: *The New Green Mountain Songster*, New Haven, 1939.

Flanders, Helen Hartness, and George Brown: *Vermont Folk-Songs and Ballads*, Brattleboro, Vt., 1931.

————, and Helen Norfleet: *Country Songs of Vermont*, New York, 1937.

————, and Marguerite Olney: *Ballads Migrant in New England*, New York, 1953.

Ford, Ira W.: *Traditional Music of America*, New York, 1940.

Ford, Robert: *Vagabond Songs and Ballads of Scotland*, 2 ser., Paisley and London, 1899, 1901.

Ford, Worthington C.: *Broadside Ballads, etc. Printed in Massachusetts, 1639–1800*. (Publications of the Massachusetts Historical Society, LXXV.) Boston, 1922.

Friedman, Albert B.: *The Viking Book of Folk Ballads of the English Speaking World*, New York, 1956.

Frothingham, Robert: *Songs of the Sea and Sailor's Chanteys*, Cambridge, Mass., 1924.

Fuson, Henry H.: *Ballads of the Kentucky Highlands*, London, 1931.

Gardner, Emelyn Elizabeth, *Folklore from the Schoharie Hills, New York*, Ann Arbor, 1937.

————, and Geraldine Jencks Chickering: *Ballads and Songs of Southern Michigan*, Ann Arbor, 1939.

Gellert, Lawrence: *Negro Songs of Protest*, New York, 1936.

Gillington, Alice E.: *Old Christmas Carols of the Southern Counties*, London, 1910.

————: *Songs of the Open Road*, London, 1911.

Gomme, Alice Bertha: *The Traditional Games of England, Scotland, and Ireland*, 2 vols., London, 1894–1898.

Goss, John: *Ballads of Britain*, London, 1937.

Gray, Roland Palmer: *Songs and Ballads of the Maine Lumberjacks*, Cambridge, Mass., 1924.

Greenleaf, Elizabeth B., and Grace Y. Mansfield: *Ballads and Sea Songs of Newfoundland*, Cambridge, Mass., 1933.

Greenway, John: *American Folksongs of Protest*, Philadelphia, 1953.

Greig, Gavin: *Folk-Song of the North-East*, 2 vols., Peterhead, 1914.

————, and Alexander Keith: *Last Leaves of Traditional Ballads and Ballad Airs*, Aberdeen, 1925.

Gummere, Francis B.: *Old English Ballads*, Boston and New York, 1894.

Handy, W. C.: *Blues: An Anthology*, New York, 1926.

Henry, Mellinger E.: *Folk-Songs from the Southern Highlands*, New York, 1928.

————: *Songs Sung in the Southern Appalachians*, London, 1934.

Hille, Waldemar, *et al.*: *The People's Song Book*, New York, 1948.

Hudson, Arthur Palmer: *Folksongs of Mississippi and Their Background*, Chapel Hill, 1936.

————: *Folktunes from Mississippi*. (National Service Bureau Publication No. 25.) New York, 1937.

————: *Specimens of Mississippi Folk-Lore*, Ann Arbor, 1928.

Hurston, Zora Neale: *Mules and Men*, Philadelphia and London, 1935.

Jackson, George Pullen: *Another Sheaf of White Spirituals*, Gainesville, Fla., 1952.

————: *Down-East Spirituals and Others*, New York, 1943.

————: *Spiritual Folk-Songs of Early America*, New York, 1937.

Jekyl, Walter: *Jamaica Song and Story*. (Publications of the Folk-Lore Society, LV.) London, 1907.

Johnson, James Weldon, and J. Rosamond: *The Book of American Negro Spirituals*, New York, 1925.

————: *The Second Book of American Negro Spirituals*, New York, 1926.

Karpeles, Maud: *Folk Songs from Newfoundland*, London, 1934.

Kennedy, Charles O'Brien: *American Ballads: Naughty, Ribald and Classic*, New York, 1952.

Kennedy, Robert Emmet: *Mellows*, New York, 1925.

————: *More Mellows*, New York, 1931.

Kidson, Frank: *Traditional Tunes*, Oxford, 1891.

————, and Alfred Moffatt: *Folk Songs from the North Countrie*, London, 1927.

Korson, George: *Coal Dust on the Fiddle*, Philadelphia, 1943.

————: *Minstrels of the Mine Patch*, Philadelphia, 1938.

————: *Songs and Ballads of the Anthracite Miner*, New York, 1927.

————, *et al.*: *Pennsylvania Songs and Legends*, Philadelphia, 1949.

Lang, Andrew: *Border Ballads*, New York and London, 1895.

Larkin, Margaret: *Singing Cowboy*, New York, 1931.

Leach, MacEdward: *The Ballad Book*, New York, 1955.

LeMon, Melvin, and George Korson: *The Miner Sings*, New York, 1936.

Linscott: Eloise Hubbard: *Folk Songs of Old New England*, New York, 1939.

Lloyd, A. L.: *Coal Dust Ballads*, London, 1952.

————: *Come All Ye Bold Miners*, London, 1952.

Lomax, John A.: *Cowboy Songs and Other Frontier Ballads*, New York, 1910; with additions, 1916.

————: *Songs of the Cattle Trail and Cow Camp*, New York, 1919.

———— and Alan Lomax: *American Ballads and Folk Songs*, New York, 1934.

———— and ————: *Cowboy Songs*, New York, 1938.

———— and ————: *Folk Song: U. S. A.*, New York, 1947.

———— and ————: *Negro Folk Songs as Sung by Lead Belly*, New York, 1936.

———— and ————: *Our Singing Country*, New York, 1941.

Lunsford, Bascom Lamar, and Lamar Stringfield: *30 and 1 Folk Songs (from the Southern Mountains)*, New York, 1929.

Luther, Frank: *Americans and Their Songs*, New York and London, 1942.

Mabie, Hamilton Wright: *A Book of Old English Ballads*, New York, 1896.

MacColl, Ewan: *The Shuttle and the Cage*, New York, 1954.

McDowell, Lucien L.: *Songs of the Old Camp Ground*, Ann Arbor, 1937.

————, and Flora Lassiter: *Memory Melodies*, Smithville, Tenn., 1947.

McGill, Josephine: *Folk Songs of the Kentucky Mountains*, New York, London, and Toronto, 1917.

MacKenzie, W. Roy: *Ballads and Sea Songs from Nova Scotia*, Cambridge, Mass., 1928.

Marsh, J. B. T.: *The Story of the Jubilee Singers with Their Songs,* New York, 1883.

Mason, M. H.: *Nursery Rhymes and Country Songs,* London, 1877.

Matteson, Maurice, and Mellinger E. Henry: *Beech Mountain Folk Songs and Ballads,* New York, 1936.

Milburn, George: *The Hobo's Hornbook,* New York, 1930.

Morris, Alton C.: *Folksongs of Florida,* Gainesville, 1950.

Neely, Charles: *Tales and Songs of Southern Illinois,* Menasha, Wis., 1938.

Newell, William Wells: *Games and Songs of American Children,* New York, 1883.

Niles, John Jacob: *Ballads, Carols, and Tragic Legends,* New York, 1937.

————: *Songs of the Hill-Folk,* New York, 1934.

————: *More Songs of the Hill-Folk,* New York, 1936.

————: *Seven Kentucky Mountain Songs,* New York, 1929.

————: *Seven Negro Exaltations,* New York, n.d.

————: *Singing Soldiers,* New York, 1927.

————: *Ten Christmas Carols from the Southern Appalachian Mountains,* New York, 1935.

————, Douglas Moore, and A. A. Walgrean: *The Songs My Mother Never Taught Me,* New York, 1929.

Odum, Howard W., and Guy B. Johnson: *The Negro and His Songs,* Chapel Hill, 1925.

————, and ————: *Negro Workaday Songs,* Chapel Hill, 1926.

Ord, John: *The Bothy Songs and Ballads,* Paisley, 1930.

Owens, William A.: *Texas Folk Songs.* (Publications of the Texas Folklore Society, XXIII.) Austin and Dallas, 1950.

Palmer, Edgar: *G.I. Songs,* New York, 1944.

Parrish, Lydia: *Slave Songs of the Georgia Sea Islands,* New York, 1942.

Parsons, Elsie Clews: *Folk-Lore of the Sea Islands, South Carolina.* (Memoirs of the American Folklore Society, Vol. 16.) New York, 1923.

Pound, Louise: *American Ballads and Songs,* New York, 1922.

————: *Folk-Song of Nebraska and the Central West.* (Nebraska Academy of Science Publications, IX, 3.) Lincoln, Neb., 1914.

Randolph, Vance: *Ozark Folksongs,* 4 vols., Columbia, Mo., 1946–1950.

Reeves, James: *The Idiom of the People: English Traditional Verse . . . from the Manuscripts of Cecil J. Sharp,* New York, 1958.

Richardson, Ethel Park: *American Mountain Songs,* New York, 1927; reprinted, 1955.

Rickaby, Franz: *Ballads and Songs of the Shanty-Boy,* Cambridge, Mass., 1926.

Ritchie, Jean: *A Garland of Mountain Song,* New York, 1953.

————: *The Swapping Song Book,* New York, 1952.

Rufty, Hilton, Annabel Buchanan, and John Powell: *Twelve Folk Hymns from the Old Shape Note Hymnbooks and from Oral Tradition,* New York, 1934.

Sandburg, Carl: *The American Songbag,* New York, 1927.

Sargent, Helen Child, and George Lyman Kittredge: *English and Scottish Popular Ballads,* Cambridge ed., Boston, 1904.

Scarborough, Dorothy: *On the Trail of Negro Folk-Songs*, Cambridge, Mass., 1925.
——: *A Song Catcher in the Southern Mountains*, New York, 1937.
Scott, Sir Walter: *Minstrelsy of the Scottish Border*, ed. T. F. Henderson, 3 vols., Edinburgh and New York, 1902.
Sharp, Cecil J.: *American-English Folk Songs*, New York and Boston, 1918.
——: *Ballads*, London and New York, n.d.
——: *English Folk Chanteys*, London, 1914.
——: *English Folk Songs*, 2 vols., London, 1921.
——: *English Folk-Songs from the Southern Appalachians*, ed. by Maud Karpeles, 2 vols., London, 1932.
——: *Folk Songs of England*, 5 vols., London, 1908–1912.
——: *Folk-Songs of English Origin Collected in the Southern Appalachians*, 2 ser., London, 1919–1923.
——: *One Hundred English Folk Songs*, Boston and New York, 1916.
——, and Rev. Charles L. Marson: *Folk Songs from Somerset*, 5 ser., London and New York, 1904–1909.
Shay, Frank: *American Sea Songs and Chanteys*, New York, 1948.
——: *Drawn from the Wood*, New York, 1929.
——: *Iron Men and Wooden Ships*, New York, 1925.
——: *My Pious Friends and Drunken Companions*, New York, 1927.
——: *More Pious Friends and Drunken Companions*, New York, 1928.
Shearin, Hubert G., and Josiah H. Combs: *A Syllabus of Kentucky Folk-Songs*. (Transylvania Studies in English, II.) Lexington, Ky., 1911.
Shoemaker, Henry W.: *Mountain Minstrelsy of Pennsylvania*, Philadelphia, 1931.
——: *North Pennsylvania Minstrelsy*, Altoona, Pa., 1919; 2d ed., 1923.
Sidgwick, Frank: *Popular Ballads of the Olden Time*, 4 ser., London, 1903–1912.
Sires, Ina: *Songs of the Open Range*, Boston, 1928.
Smith, C. Fox: *A Book of Shanties*, Boston and New York, 1927.
Smith, Laura A.: *The Music of the Waters*, London, 1888.
Smith, Reed: *South Carolina Ballads*, Cambridge, Mass., 1928.
——: *The Traditional Ballad and Its South Carolina Survivals*. (Bulletin of the University of South Carolina, No. 162.) Columbia, S. C., 1925.
——, and Hilton Rufty: *American Anthology of Old-World Ballads*, New York, 1937.
Stout, Earl J.: *Folklore from Iowa*. (Memoirs of the American Folklore Society, vol. 29.) New York, 1936.
Stokoe, John, and Samuel Reay: *Songs and Ballads of Northern England*, Newcastle-on-Tyne and London, n.d.
Sturgis, Edith B., and Robert Hughes: *Songs from the Hills of Vermont*, New York, 1919.
Sulzer, Elmer G.: *Twenty-Five Kentucky Folk Ballads*, Lexington, Ky., 1946.
Sumner, Heywood: *The Besom Maker*, London, 1888.
Talley, Thomas W.: *Negro Folk Rhymes*, New York, 1922.
Taylor, S. Coleridge: *Twenty-Four Negro Melodies*, Boston and New York, 1905.
Terry, Richard Runciman: *The Shanty Book*, 2 pts., London, 1921–1926.

Thomas, Jean: *Ballad Makin' in the Mountains of Kentucky*, New York, 1939.
————: *Devil's Ditties*, Chicago, 1931.
————, and Joseph A Leeder: *The Singin' Gatherin'*, New York and Boston, 1939.
Thompson, Harold W.: *Body, Boots and Britches*, Philadelphia, 1940.
Thorp, N. Howard: *Songs of the Cowboys*, Estancia, N. Mex., 1908; revised and enlarged, Boston and New York, 1921.
Van Wey, Adelaide, and Donald Lee Moore: *Smoky Mountain Ballads*, New York, 1949.
Wetmore, Susannah: *Mountain Songs of North Carolina*, New York, 1926.
Whall, W. B.: *Ships, Sea-Songs, and Shanties*, Glasgow, 1910.
Wheeler, Mary: *Kentucky Mountain Folk-Songs*, Boston, 1937.
————: *Steamboatin' Days*, Baton Rouge, La., 1944.
White, Newman Ivey: *American Negro Folk-Songs*, Cambridge, Mass., 1928.
Whiting, Bartlett Jere: *Traditional British Ballads*, New York, 1955.
Williams, Alfred: *Folk-Songs of the Upper Thames*, London, 1923.
Wolford, Leah Jackson: *The Play-Party in Indiana*, Indianapolis, 1916.
Work, Frederick J.: *Folk Songs of the American Negro*, Nashville, 1907.
Work, John Wesley: *American Negro Songs*, New York, 1940.
Wyman, Loraine, and Howard Brockway: *Lonesome Tunes*, New York, 1916.
————: *Twenty Kentucky Mountain Songs*, Boston, 1920.
York, Dorothea: *Mud and Stars: An Anthology of World War Songs and Poetry*, New York, 1931.

CRITICISM, STUDIES, BIBLIOGRAPHIES, ETC.

Allen, Philip Schuyler: *Studies in Popular Poetry*, Chicago, 1902.
Ames, Russell: *The Story of American Folk Song*, New York, 1955.
Baldwin, Charles S.: *Introduction to English Medieval Literature*, New York, 1914.
Beers, Henry A.: *A History of English Romanticism in the Eighteenth Century*, New York, 1898.
Blesh, Rudi: *Shining Trumpets: A History of Jazz*, New York, 1946.
Borregaard, Meta Catherine: *The Epithet in English and Scottish, Spanish, and Danish Popular Ballads*, Amsterdam, 1933.
Bowra, C. W.: *Heroic Poetry*, London, 1952.
Brewster, Paul G.: *The Two Sisters.* (Folklore Fellows Communications, LXII, No. 147.) Helsinki, 1953.
Brown, Frank C.: "Ballad Literature in North Carolina" (reprinted from *Proceedings and Addresses of the Fifteenth Annual Session of the Literary and Historical Association of North Carolina, Dec. 1–2, 1914*), n.d.
Bryant, Frank Egbert: *A History of Balladry and Other Studies*, Boston, 1913.
Campbell, John C.: *The Southern Highlander and His Homeland*, New York, 1921.

Chadwick, H. M. and N. K.: *The Growth of Literature*, vol. 3, Cambridge, 1940.
Chambers, E. K.: *English Literature at the Close of the Middle Ages*, Oxford, 1945.
———: *The Medieval Stage*, 2 vols., Oxford, 1903.
Chambers, R. W.: *Form and Style in Poetry*, London, 1928.
Chambers, Robert: *The Romantic Scottish Ballads: Their Epoch and Authorship*, Edinburgh, 1859.
Chappell, Louis W.: *John Henry: A Folk-Lore Study*, Jena, Germany, 1933.
Checklist of California Songs, Berkeley, Calif., 1940.
Child, Francis James: "Ballad Poetry," *Johnson's Universal Cyclopaedia*, 1874.
Christopherson, Paul: *The Ballad of* Sir Aldingar: *Its Origin and Analogues*, Oxford, 1952.
Clawson, William Hall: *The Gest of Robin Hood*, Toronto, 1909.
Clyne, Norval: *The Romantic Scottish Ballads and the Lady Wardlaw Heresy*, Aberdeen, 1859.
Coffin, Tristram P.: *The British Traditional Ballad in North America*. (Publications of the American Folklore Society, Bibliographical Series, II.) Philadelphia, 1950.
Courthope, W. J.: *History of English Poetry*, vol. 1, London, 1895.
Dean-Smith, Margaret: *A Guide to English Folk Song Collections*, Liverpool, 1954.
Dixon, W. MacNeile: *English Epic and Heroic Poetry*, London, 1912.
Du Bois, W. E. Burghardt: *The Souls of Black Folk*, Chicago, 1904.
Elliott, Fitzwilliam: *Further Essays on Border Ballads*, Edinburgh, 1910.
———: *The Trustworthiness of the Border Ballads*, Edinburgh and London, 1906.
An English Miscellany Presented to Dr. Furnival, Oxford, 1901.
Entwistle, William J.: *European Balladry*, Oxford, 1939; reprinted, 1951.
Fisher, Miles Mark: *Negro Slave Songs in the United States*, Ithaca, N. Y., 1953.
Geddie, John: *The Balladists*, New York, 1896.
Gerould, Gordon H.: *The Ballad of Tradition*, Oxford, 1932; reprinted, 1957.
Gilbert, Douglas: *Lost Chords*, Garden City, New York, 1942.
Gordon, Robert Winslow: *Folk-Songs of America*. (National Service Bureau Publication No. 73-S.) New York, 1938.
Graves, Robert: *The English Ballad*, London, 1927.
———: *The White Goddess*, London, 1948.
Greene, Richard Leighton: *The Early English Carols*, Oxford, 1935.
Gummere, Francis B.: "Ballads," in *Cambridge History of English Literature*, Cambridge, 1908, vol. 2, pp. 449ff.
———: "Ballads," in *Library of the World's Best Literature*, ed. Charles Dudley Warner, New York, 1896, vol. 3.
———: *The Beginnings of Poetry*, New York and London, 1901.
———: *Democracy and Poetry*, Boston and New York, 1911.
———: "Folk Song," in *Library of the World's Best Literature*, ed. Charles Dudley Warner, New York, 1896, vol. 10.
———: *Handbook of Poetics*, Boston, 1885.

Gummere, Francis B.: *The Popular Ballad*, Boston and New York, 1907.

Halliday, W. A.: *Folklore Studies: Ancient and Modern*, London, 1924.

Hare, Maud Cuney: *Negro Musicians and Their Music*, Washington, D. C., 1936.

Harris, P. Valentine: *The Truth About Robin Hood*, London, 1952.

Hart, Walter Morris: *Ballad and Epic*. (Harvard Studies and Notes in Philology and Literature, XI.) Boston, 1907.

Haywood, Charles: *A Bibliography of North American Folklore and Folksong*, New York, 1951.

Henderson, T. F.: *The Ballad in Literature*, Cambridge, 1912.

———: *Scottish Vernacular Literature*, London, 1898.

Hendren, J. W.: *A Study of Ballad Rhythm, with Special Reference to Ballad Music*. (Princeton Studies in English, No. 4.) Princeton, N. J., 1936.

Herskovits, Melville J.: *The Myth of the Negro Past*, New York, 1941.

Herzog, George: *Research in Primitive and Folk Music in the United States*. (American Council of Learned Societies Bulletin No. 24.) Washington, D. C., 1936.

Hodgart, M. J. C.: *The Ballads*, London, 1950.

Holbrook, Stewart H.: *Holy Old Mackinaw*, New York, 1938.

Hudson, W. H.: *An Introduction to the Study of Literature*, New York, 1910.

Hughes, Pennethorne: *Witchcraft*, London, 1952.

Hunter, Joseph: *The Great Hero of the Ancient Minstrelsy of England*, London, 1852.

Hustvedt, Sigurd Bernhard: *Ballad Books and Ballad Men*, Cambridge, Mass., 1930.

———: *Ballad Criticism in Great Britain and Scandinavia during the Eighteenth Century*, New York, 1916.

Hyman, Stanley Edgar: *The Armed Vision*, New York, 1948.

Jackson, George Pullen: *The Story of the Sacred Harp, 1844–1944*, Nashville, 1944.

———: *White and Negro Spirituals*, New York, 1943.

———: *White Spirituals in the Southern Uplands*, Chapel Hill, 1933.

Jacobs, Joseph: *English Fairy Tales*, London, 1890.

———, and Alfred Nutt, eds.: *Papers and Transactions of the International Folk-Lore Congress, 1891*, London, 1892.

Johnson, Guy B.: *Folk Culture on St. Helena Island, South Carolina*, Chapel Hill, 1930.

———: *John Henry: Tracking Down a Negro Legend*, Chapel Hill, 1929.

Jones, William Powell: *The Pastourelle: A Study of the Origins and Tradition of a Lyric Type*, Cambridge, Mass., 1931.

Kemppinen, Iivar: *The Ballad of Lady Isabel and the False Knight*, Helsinki, 1954.

Kennedy, Douglas: *England's Dances*, London, 1949.

Ker, W. P.: *Collected Essays*, ed. Charles Whibley, London, 1925.

———: *English Literature: Medieval*, New York and London, 1912.

———: *Epic and Romance*, London, 1897.

Kidson, Frank, and Mary Neal: *English Folk-Song and Dance*, Cambridge, 1915.

Krappe, Alexander Haggerty: *The Science of Folk-Lore*, New York, 1930.

Krehbiel, Henry Edward: *Afro-American Folk Songs*, New York, 1914.

Lang, Andrew: "Ballads," in *Encyclopaedia Britannica*, 9th ed., 1875.

————: "The Ballads: Scottish and English," in Chambers' *Cyclopaedia of English Literature*, 1901.

————: *Sir Walter Scott*, London and New York, 1906.

————: *Sir Walter Scott and the Border Minstrelsy*, London and New York, 1910.

Laws, G. Malcolm, Jr.: *American Balladry from British Broadsides*. (Publications of the American Folklore Society, Bibliographical Series, VIII.) Philadelphia, 1957.

————: *Native American Balladry*. (Publications of the American Folklore Society, Bibliographical Series, I.) Philadelphia, 1950.

Leach, Henry Goddard: *Angevin Britain and Scandinavia*. (Harvard Studies in Comparative Literature, VI.) Cambridge, Mass., 1921.

Leach, Maria, and Jerome Fried: *Standard Dictionary of Folklore, Mythology, and Legend*, 2 vols., New York, 1949–1950.

Lloyd, A. L.: *The Singing Englishman*, London, n.d.

Locke, Alain: *The Negro and His Music*, Washington, D. C., 1936.

Lomax, Alan: *List of American Folk Songs on Commercial Records*. (Reprinted, with revisions, from the Report of the Committee of the Conference on Inter-American Relations in the Field of Music, Washington, D. C., September 3, 1940.) n.d.

Lomax, John A.: *Adventures of a Ballad Hunter*, New York, 1947.

Lumpkin, Ben Gray: *Folksongs on Records*, Issue 3, Boulder, Colo., 1950.

MacKenzie, A. S.: *The Evolution of Literature*, New York, 1911.

MacKenzie, W. Roy: *The Quest of the Ballad*, Princeton, N. J., 1919.

Mendel, Arthur, Gustav Reese, and Gilbert Chase, eds.: *Papers Read at the International Congress of Musicology Held at New York, September 11th to 16th, 1939*, New York, 1944.

Metfessel, Milton E.: *Phonophotography in Folk Music*, Chapel Hill, 1928.

Millar, J. H.: *Literary History of Scotland*, London, 1903.

Murray, Margaret: *The God of the Witches*, London, 1933.

Nettle, Bruno: *Music in Primitive Culture*, Cambridge, Mass., 1956.

Nettle, Reginald: *Sing a Song of England*, London, 1954.

Notation of Folk Music: Recommendations of the Committee of Experts Convened by the International Archives of Folk Music, Geneva, 4–9 July, 1949, and Paris, 12–15 December, 1950, 1952.

Nygard, Holger Olof: *The Ballad of Heer Halewijn: Its Forms and Variations in Western Europe; A Study of the History and Nature of a Ballad Tradition*. (Folklore Fellows Communications, LXVII, No. 169.) Helsinki, 1958.

Opie, Iona and Peter: *The Oxford Dictionary of Nursery Rhymes*, Oxford, 1951.

Pound, Louise, "Oral Literature," in *Cambridge History of American Literature*, New York, 1921, vol. 4.

————: *Poetic Origins and the Ballad*, New York, 1921.

Pound, Louise: *Selected Writings of Louise Pound*, Lincoln, Neb., 1949.
Puckett, Newbell Niles: *Folk Beliefs of the Southern Negro*, Chapel Hill, 1926.
Purcell, William E.: *Onward Christian Soldier: A Life of Sabine Baring-Gould*, London, 1957.
Putnam, John F.: *The Plucked Dulcimer of the Southern Mountains*, Berea, Ky., 1957.
Quiller-Couch, Sir Arthur: "Ballads," in *Studies in Literature*, 1st ser., Cambridge, 1918, pp. 22ff.
Ragland, Lord: *The Hero*, London, 1937; reprinted, New York, 1956.
Randolph, Vance: *Ozark Mountain Folks*, New York, 1932.
———: *The Ozarks*, New York, 1931.
Renwick, W. L., and Harold Orton: *The Beginnings of English Literature to Skelton*, 2d ed., New York, 1952.
Ritchie, Jean: *Singing Family of the Cumberlands*, New York, 1955.
75 Years of Freedom: Commemoration of the 75th Anniversary of the Proclamation of the 13th Amendment to the Constitution of the United States, Washington, D. C., 1943.
Sharp, Cecil J.: *English Folk-Song: Some Conclusions*, London, 1907.
Sidgwick, Frank: *The Ballad*, London, 1914.
Smith, G. Gregory: *The Transition Period*, Edinburgh and London, 1900.
Smythe, Augustine T., *et al.*: *The Carolina Low Country*, New York, 1931.
Speirs, John: *The Scots Literary Tradition*, London, 1940.
Spence, Lewis: *Myth and Ritual in Game, Dance, and Rhyme*, London, 1947.
Stearns, Marshall W.: *The Story of Jazz*, New York, 1956.
Strangways, A. H. Fox: *Cecil Sharp*, Oxford, 1934; 2d ed., 1955.
Streenstrup, J. C. H. R.: *The Medieval Popular Ballad*, trans. E. G. Cox, Boston, 1914.
Taylor, Archer: *"Edward" and "Sven i Rosengård,"* Chicago, 1931.
Thomas, Jean: *The Singin' Fiddler of Lost Hope Holler*, New York, 1938.
———: *The Traipsin' Woman*, New York, 1933.
Thompson, Stith: *The Folktale*, New York, 1946.
———, ed.: *Four Symposia on Folklore*. (Indiana University Publications, Folklore Series No. 8.) Bloomington, Ind., 1953.
Thorp, N. Howard, in collaboration with Neil M. Clark: *Pardner of the Wind*, Caldwell, Idaho, 1945.
Vassar Medieval Studies, New Haven, Conn., 1928.
Walker, J. W.: *The True History of Robin Hood*, Wakefield, England, 1952.
Walker, William: *Peter Buchan and Other Papers on Scottish and English Ballads and Songs*, Aberdeen, 1915.
Wallashek, Richard: *Primitive Music*, London, 1893.
Watkins, James Hutton: *Early Scottish Ballads*, Glasgow, 1867.
Watt, Lauchlan MacLean: *The Scottish Ballads and Ballad Writing*, Paisley, 1923.
Welby, T. Earle: *A Popular History of English Poetry*, London, 1924.
Wells, Evelyn K.: *The Ballad Tree*, New York, 1950.

White, Rev. E. A., and Margaret Dean-Smith: *An Index of English Songs Contributed to "The Journal of the Folk-Song Society" and its Continuation "The Journal of the English Folk Dance and Song Society" to 1950*, London, 1951.

White, John: *D. J. O'Malley: "Cowboy Poet,"* Eau Claire, Wis., 1934.

Williams, Alfred Mason: *Studies in Folk-Song and Popular Poetry*, Boston and New York, 1894.

Williams, Iolo Aneurin: *English Folk-Song and Dance*, London, etc., 1935.

Williams, Ralph Vaughan: *National Music*, New York, 1935.

Wimberly, Lowry C.: *Death and Burial Lore in the English and Scottish Popular Ballads.* (University of Nebraska Studies in Language, Literature, and Criticism, No. 8.) Lincoln, Neb., 1927.

————: *Folklore in the English and Scottish Ballads*, Chicago, 1928.

————: *Minstrelsy, Music, and the Dance in the English and Scottish Popular Ballads.* (University of Nebraska Studies in Language, Literature and Criticism, No. 4.) Lincoln, Neb., 1921.

FOLKLORE JOURNALS

Articles in the following, which have been examined in their entirety, are not given separate entry.

Bulletin of the Folk-Song Society of the Northeast. 1930–1937.
Bulletin of the Kentucky Folk-Lore Society. 1931–1937.
California Folklore Quarterly (continued as *Western Folklore*). 1942–
Folk-Lore. 1890–
Hoosier Folklore. 1942–1950.
Journal of American Folklore. 1888–
Journal of the English Folk Dance and Song Society. 1932–
Journal of the Folk-Song Society, 1899–1931.
Journal of the International Folk Music Council. 1949–
Kentucky Folk-Lore and Poetry Magazine. 1927–1931.
Kentucky Folklore Record. 1955–
Keystone Folklore Quarterly. 1956–
Midwest Folklore. 1951–
Miscellanea of the Rymour Club. 1906–1928.
New Mexico Folklore Record. 1947–1956.
New York Folklore Quarterly. 1945–
North Carolina Folklore. 1953–
Northeast Folklore. 1958–
Publications of the Texas Folklore Society. 1916–
Southern Folklore Quarterly. 1937–
Tennessee Folklore Society Bulletin. 1935–
West Virginia Folklore. 1950–
Western Folklore (see *California Folklore Quarterly*).
Word-Lore. 1926–1928.

ARTICLES IN OTHER JOURNALS

Allen, Philip Schuyler: "Wilhelm Müller and the German Volkslied," *Journal of Germanic Philology,* II (1898–1899), 283*ff.*

Arlt, Gustave O.: "Lexicographical Indexing of Folk Melodies," *Modern Philology,* XXVII (1929), 147*ff.*

"Art from the Cabin Door," *Outlook,* CXLI (1925), 268*f.*

Barrow, David C.: "A Georgia Corn-Shucking," *Century Magazine,* XXIV (1882), 873*ff.*

Barnes, Will C.: "The Cowboy and His Songs," *Saturday Evening Post,* CXCVII (June 27, 1925), 14–15, 122.

Barry, Phillips: "An American Homiletic Ballad," *Modern Language Notes,* XXVIII (1913), 1*ff.*

———: "The Ballad of Earl Brand," *Modern Language Notes,* XXV (1910). 104*f.*

———: "The Ballad of the Demon Lover," *Modern Language Notes,* XIX (1904), 283.

———: "Fair Florella," *American Speech,* III (1928), 441*ff.*

Baskervill, Charles Read: "English Songs of the Night Visit," *Publications of the Modern Language Association,* XXXVI (1921), 565*ff.*

Batho, Edith: "The Life of Christ in the Ballads," *Essays and Studies by Members of the English Association,* IX (Oxford, 1924), 70*ff.*

Baum, Paull Franklin: "The English Ballad of Judas Iscariot," *Publications of the Modern Language Association,* XXXI (1916), 181*ff.*

Beatty, Arthur: "Ballad, Tale, and Tradition," *Publications of the Modern Language Association,* XXIX (1914), 473*ff.*

Beckwith, Martha Warren: "The English Ballad in Jamaica: A Note upon the Origin of the Ballad Form," *Publications of the Modern Language Association,* XXXIX (1924), 455*ff.*

Belden, Henry Marvin: "The Ballad of Lord Bakeman," *Modern Philology,* II (1905), 301*ff.*

———: "Boccaccio, Hans Sachs, and the Bramble Briar," *Publications of the Modern Language Association,* XXXIII (1918), 327*ff.*

———: "Folk-Song in America—Some Recent Publications," *Modern Language Notes,* XXXIV (1919), 139*ff.*

———: "Folk-Song in Missouri . . . Bedroom Window," *Archiv für das Studium der neueren Sprachen und Literaturen,* CXIX (1907), 430*ff.*

———: "Popular Song in Missouri—*The Returned Lover,*" *Archiv für das Studium der neueren Sprachen und Literaturen,* CXX (1908), 62*ff.*

———: "A Study in Contemporary Balladry," *Mid-West Quarterly,* I (1914), 162*ff.*

———: "The Study of Folk-Song in America," *Modern Philology,* II (1905), 573*ff.*

———: "The Vulgar Ballad," *Sewanee Review,* XIX (1911), 213*ff.*

Botkin, B. A.: "The Archive of American Folk-Song: Retrospect and Prospect," *Library of Congress Quarterly Journal of Current Acquisitions*, II (1945), 61*ff.*
Bradley, William Aspenwall: "Song Ballets and Devil's Ditties," *Harper's Monthly Magazine*, CXXX (1915), 901*ff.*
Brockway, Howard: "Quest of the Lonesome Tunes," *Art World*, II (1917), 227*ff.*
Bronson, Bertrand H.: "Folksong and the Modes," *Musical Quarterly*, XXXII (1946), 37*ff.*
————: "Some Observations About Melodic Variation in British-American Folk Tunes," *Journal of the American Musicological Society*, III (1950), 120*ff.*
[Burlin], Natalie Curtis: "Folk Music of America," *Craftsman*, XXI (1912), 414*ff.*
————: "The Negro's Contribution to the Music of America," *Craftsman*, XXIII (1913), 660*ff.*
Bush, Douglas: *Literary Review*, Feb. 17, 1923; July 7, 1923.
Cable, George W.: "Creole Slave Songs," *Century Magazine*, XXXI (1886), 807*ff.*
————: "The Dance in Place Congo," *Century Magazine*, XXXI (1886), 517*ff.*
Campbell, Olive Dame: "Songs and Ballads of the Southern Mountains," *Survey*, XXXIII (1915), 371*ff.*
Chickering, Geraldine J.: "The Origin of a Ballad," *Modern Language Notes*, L (1935), 465*ff.*
Combs, Josiah H.: "Dialect of the Folk-Song," *Dialect Notes*, IV (1916), 311*ff.*
Damon, S. Foster: "The Negro in Early American Songsters," *Papers of the Bibliographical Society*, XXVIII (1934), 132*ff.*
Davidson, Thomas: "Professor Child's Ballad Book," *American Journal of Philology*, V (1884), 466*f.*
Davis, Arthur Kyle, Jr.: "Some Problems of Ballad Publication," *Musical Quarterly*, XIV (1928), 283*ff.*
Engel, Carl: "Views and Reviews," *Musical Quarterly*, XXI (1935), 107*ff.*; XXIII (1937), 388*ff.*; XXIV (1938), 297*ff.*
Entwistle, William J.: "The Noble Moringer," *Modern Language Forum*, XXXIV (1949), 2*ff.*
————: "Notation for Ballad Melodies," *Publications of the Modern Language Association*, LV (1940), 61*ff.*
————: "Sir Aldingar and the Date of English Ballads," *Saga Book of the Viking Society for Northern Research*, XIII (1947–1948), 97*ff.*
Evanson, Jacob A.: "American Folk Songs," *Music Educators Journal*, XXXVII (1951), 20*f.*
Flanders, Helen Hartness: "Index of Ballads and Folk-Songs in the Archive of Vermont Folk-Songs at Smiley House, Springfield, Vt.," *Proceedings of the Vermont Historical Society*, 1940, pp. 214*ff.*
"A Folk-Song of Recent Origin," *Literary Digest*, XLVIII (1914), 985.
Ford, Worthington C.: "The Isaiah Thomas Collection of Ballads," *Proceedings of the American Antiquarian Society*, n.s., XXXIII (1920), 44*ff.*

Furness, Clifton Joseph: "Communal Music among Arabians and Negroes," *Musical Quarterly*, XVII (1930), 38*ff*.

Gabriel, Miriam: "Communal Verse Writing," *English Journal*, XVII (1928), 394*ff*.

Gerould, Gordon H.: "The Ballad of the Bitter Withy," *Publications of the Modern Language Association*, XXIII (1908), 141*ff*.

————: "The Making of Ballads," *Modern Philology*, XXI (1923), 15*ff*.

————: "The 'Popular' Ballad," *Literary Review*, March 5, 1921, p. 6.

Gordon, Robert W.: "Old Songs That Men Have Sung," *Adventure Magazine*, July, 1923–November, 1927.

Greig, Gavin: "Folk-Song in Buchan," *Transactions of the Buchan Field Club*, IX (1906–1908), 2*ff*.

Gummere, Francis B.: "The Ballad and Communal Poetry," *Harvard Studies and Notes in Philology and Literature*, V (1896), 41*ff*.

————: "Ballad Origins," *The Nation*, LXXXV (1907), 184.

————: "Primitive Poetry and the Ballad," *MP*, I (1903–1904), 193*ff*., 217*ff*., 373*ff*.

Hall, Sharlot M.: "Songs of the Old Cattle Trails," *Out West*, XXVIII (1908), 216*ff*.

Halpert, Herbert: "The Piney Folk-Singers," *Direction*, II (September, 1939), 4–6, 15.

Hart, Walter Morris: "Professor Child and the Ballad," *Publications of the Modern Language Association*, XXI (1906), 755*ff*.

Higginson, Thomas Wentworth: "Negro Spirituals," *Atlantic Monthly*, XIX (1867), 685*ff*.

Hornbostel, E. M. von: "African Negro Music," *International Institute of African Languages and Culture, Memorandum IV* (reprinted from *Africa*, I [1928]).

Houston, Maude: "The Education of John A. Lomax," *Southwestern Historical Quarterly*, LX (1956), 201*ff*.

"Hunting the Lonesome Tune in the Wilds of Kentucky," *Current Opinion*, LXII (1917), 100*f*.

Hustvedt, Sigurd Bernhard: "A Melodic Index of Child's Ballad Tunes," *Publications of the University of California at Los Angeles in Languages and Literatures*, I (1936), 51*ff*.

Jackson, George Pullen: "The Genesis of the Negro Spiritual," *American Mercury*, XXVI (1932), 243*ff*.

Keith, Alexander: "Scottish Ballads: Their Evidence of Authorship and Origin," *Essays and Studies by Members of the English Association*, XII (Oxford, 1926), 100*ff*.

Ker, W. P.: "On the History of the Ballad. 1100–1500," *Proceedings of the British Academy*, IV (1910).

Kittredge, George Lyman: "The Ballad of the Den of Lions," *Modern Language Notes*, XXVI (1911), 167*ff*.

————: "The Popular Ballad," *Atlantic Monthly*, CI (1908), 276*ff*.

Laubenstein, Paul F.: "Race Values in Aframerican Music," *Musical Quarterly*, XVI (1930), 378*ff*.

Legman, G.: "The Bawdy Song . . . in Fact and in Print," *Explorations*, 7 (March, 1957), pp. 139*ff*.

Lomax, Alan: "America Sings the Saga of America," *New York Times Sunday Magazine*, January 26, 1947, pp. 16, 41*f*.

Lomax, John A.: "Cowboy Songs of the Mexican Border," *Sewanee Review*, XIX (1911), 1*ff*.

——: "Half-Million Dollar Song: Origin of 'Home on the Range,'" *Southwest Review*, XXXI (1945), 1*ff*.

——: "Sinful Songs of the Southern Negro," *Musical Quarterly*, XX (1934), 177*ff*.

MacDonough, Michael: "The Ballads of the People," *The Nineteenth Century and After*, LIV (1903), 458*ff*.

Mercer, H. C.: "On the Track of the 'Arkansas Traveler,'" *Century Magazine*, LI (1896), 707*ff*.

Miles, Emma B.: "Some Real American Music," *Harper's Magazine*, CIX (1904), 118*ff*.

Miller, George Morey: "The Dramatic Element in the Popular Ballad," *University Studies of the University of Cincinnati*, ser. 2, vol. 1, no. 1 (1905).

Moore, John Robert: "The Influence of Transmission on the English Ballads," *Modern Language Review*, XI (1916), 385*ff*.

——: "Omission of the Central Action in the English Ballads," *Modern Philology*, XI (1914), 391*ff*.

Niles, John Jacob: "Shout, Coon, Shout," *Musical Quarterly*, XVI (1930), 516*ff*.

——: "White Pioneers and Black," *Musical Quarterly*, XVIII (1932), 60*ff*.

Odum, Howard W.: "Religious Folk Songs of the Southern Negroes," *American Journal of Religious Psychology and Education*, III (1906), 265*ff*.

Parry, Milman: "Studies in the Epic Technique of Oral Verse-Making," *Harvard Studies in Classical Philology*, XLI (1930), 73*ff*.; XLIII (1932), 1*ff*.

"The Poor Buckra Songs," *Atlantic Monthly*, XCV (1904), 716*ff*.

Pound, Louise: "The Ancestry of a Negro Spiritual," *Modern Language Notes*, XXXIII (1918), 442*ff*.

——: "The Ballad and the Dance," *Publications of the Modern Language Association*, XXXIV (1919), 360*ff*.

——: "Ballads and Illiterate," *Mid-West Quarterly*, V (1918), 4*ff*.

——: "The Beginnings of Poetry," *Publications of the Modern Language Association*, XXXII (1917), 201*ff*.

——: "The English Ballads and the Church," *Publications of the Modern Language Association*, XXXV (1920), 2*ff*.

——: "High-School Ballad Composition," *English Journal*, XVIII (1929), 495.

——: "King Cnut's Song and Ballad Origins," *Modern Language Notes*, XXXIV (1919), 162*ff*.

——: *Literary Review*, March 26, 1921; Jan. 13, 1923; June 9, 1923.

——: "New World Analogues of the English and Scottish Popular Ballads," *Mid-West Quarterly*, III (1916), 171*ff*.

Pound, Louise: "On the Dating of the English and Scottish Ballads," *Publications of the Modern Language Association*, XLVII (1932), 10ff.

———: "The Pedigree of a Western Song," *Modern Language Notes*, XXIX (1914), 30f.

———: "A Recent Theory of Ballad Making," *Publications of the Modern Language Association*, XLIV (1929), 622ff.

———: "Sizing Our Ballads," *American Scholar*, V (1936), 360ff.

———: "The Southwestern Cowboy Songs and the English and Scottish Popular Ballads," *Modern Philology*, XI (1913), 195ff.

———: "The Term. 'Communal,' " *Publications of the Modern Language Association*, XXXIX (1924), 440ff.

———: "The 'Uniformity' of the Ballad Style," *Modern Language Notes*, XXXV (1920), 217.

Reichenbach, Herman: "The Tonality of English and Gaelic Folksong," *Music and Letters*, XIX (1938), 268ff.

Rollins, Hyder E.: "Concerning Bodlean MS. Ashmole 48," *Modern Language Notes*, XXXIV (1919), 340ff.

———: "The Blackletter Broadside Ballad," *Publications of the Modern Language Association*, XXXIV (1919), 258ff.

Seeger, Charles: "Prescriptive and Descriptive Music-Writing," *Musical Quarterly*, XLIV (1958), 184ff.

Sellers, William E.: "Kindred and Clan in the Scottish Border Ballads," *Boston University Studies in English*, III (1957), 1ff.

Shearin, Hubert G.: "British Ballads in the Cumberland Mountains," *Sewanee Review*, XIX (1911), 313ff.

———: "Kentucky Folk Songs," *Modern Language Review*, VI (1911), 513ff.

Smith, C. Alphonso: "Ballads Surviving in the United States," *Musical Quarterly*, II (1916), 109ff.

———: "The Negro and the Ballad," *Alumni Bulletin of the University of Virginia*, ser. 3, VI (1913), 88ff.

Smith, Joseph Hutchinson: "Folk-Songs of the American Negro," *Sewanee Review*, XXXII (1924), 207ff.

Stewart, George E., Jr.: "The Meter of the Popular Ballad," *Publications of the Modern Language Association*, XL (1925), 933ff.

Taylor, Archer: "A Contamination of 'Lord Randal,' " *Modern Philology*, XXIX (1931), 105ff.

———: "Precursors of the Finnish Method of Folk-Lore Study," *Modern Philology*, XXV (1928), 481ff.

———: "The Texts of 'Edward' in Percy's *Reliques* and Motherwell's *Minstrelsy*," *Modern Language Notes*, XLV (1930), 225ff.

———: "The Themes Common to English and German Balladry," *Modern Language Quarterly*, I (1940), 23ff.

———: "Una Comparación Tentativa de Balada Inglesas y Españolas," *Folklore Americano*, IV (1956), 3ff.

Tolman, Albert H.: " 'Mary Hamilton.' The Group Authorship of Ballads," *Publications of the Modern Language Association*, XLII (1927), 422ff.

Turner, Lucille P.: "Negro Spirituals in the Making," *Musical Quarterly*, XVII (1931), 480ff.

White, Clarence Cameron: "Negro Music a Contribution to the National Music of America," *Musical Observer*, XVIII (1919), no. 11, pp. 18ff.; XIX (1920), no. 1, pp. 16ff.; no. 2, pp. 50f.; no. 3, pp. 13ff.

Williams, Alfred Mason: "American Sea Songs," *Atlantic Monthly*, LXIX (1892), 489ff.

Wilson, Edmund: "American Ballads and Their Collectors," *New Republic*, XLVII (1926), 168.

———: "Shanty-Boy Ballads and Blues," *New Republic*, XLVII (1926), 227ff.

Work, John W.: "Plantation Meistersinger," *Musical Quarterly*, XXVII (1941), 97ff.

GLOSSARY

adventure ballad A narrative song treating dramatic experiences not directly related to problems of clan, class, or nation.

antiphony 1. Musical response. 2. Performance of a song alternately by two voices, two groups of voices, or a leader and chorus.

archetype A theoretical approximation of the original form of an item of oral literature, generally based on a careful study of a large number of variants.

art song A song composed in accordance with cultivated traditions and restricted in performance and variation by rules of that tradition.

aube A song of the night visit of a lover and of the parting at dawn.

authentic 1. Lying between the tonic and the octave above: said of a mode. 2. Having all tones lying above the tonic: said of a scale.

ballad A narrative folksong in stanzas set to a rounded or recurrent melody.

ballet A folksong text preserved in manuscript (sometimes print) by a folksinger.

banjo minstrel   A folk entertainer in the southern United States who sang and sometimes composed folksongs to banjo accompaniment, apparently developed in the late nineteenth century: often professional or semiprofessional and itinerant.

banjo song   A lyric or seminarrative folksong of loosely related stanzas performed to banjo accompaniment, in the southern United States.

blackface minstrel   A stage performer mimicking or burlesquing Negro song and culture, beginning in the United States as early as 1828.

blues   Originally a vocal, and later an instrumental, form developed in late nineteenth-century American Negro culture, varying widely, but consisting typically of subjective verse in an antiphonal pattern AAB set to a twelve- (more or less) bar melody with simple harmonic progressions, neutral thirds, sevenths, and sometimes fifths, and the syncopated rhythms of American Negro music.

bothy   A hut or rude cottage provided for Scottish farm laborers.— *bothy songs*   Songs of the laborers, i.e., sung in the bothies.

branle   Sixteenth-century French dance popular in court and country, evidently developed from medieval round dances: distinguished by alternating crablike sidewise movements bearing to the left.

broadside   A large single sheet of paper printed only on one side, usually sold or distributed among the populace, beginning before 1500. The term is applied to garlands, chapbooks, songsters, and—more recently—commercial media for the delectation of the vulgar.

buckwheat notes   See *shape notes*.

burden   A line or group of lines sung sometimes at the beginning and repeated after each stanza of a song, but essentially independent of and external to it. See *refrain*.

call and response   See *antiphony*.

camp-meeting songs   See *revival songs*.

cante fable   A type of folktale in which the narrative is interspersed with verse or song.

cantilenae   Early medieval popular or extraliturgical songs.

carol   Formally, a song in uniform stanzas, beginning with a burden which is also sung after each stanza. The term is generally applied to traditional songs celebrating a special season of the natural or ecclesiastical year.

carole   A dance-song for couples in ring formation, moving from right to left, which spread from southern Europe northward to Scandinavia in the twelfth century.

chanson d'aventure   Medieval French narrative poem with autobiographical incipit: term applied to Anglo-American songs with similar beginnings, e.g., "As I went out one morning to take the pleasant air."

chanson de geste   Old French epic, such as *Chanson de Roland*, dealing with the deeds of historical and legendary figures.

chantey   See *shanty.*

chapbook   Small printed pamphlet containing popular ballads, tracts, tales, etc., formerly distributed by itinerant hawkers. See *broadside.*

Child ballad   A ballad or variant of a ballad found in Francis James Child's *The English and Scottish Popular Ballads* (1882–1898).

climax of relatives   See *sequence of relatives.*

come-all-ye   A commonplace opening of the vulgar ballad entreating the attention of the audience to whom the ballad is addressed: often a synonym for the type. See *vulgar ballad.*

commonplace   A formula, ranging from an epithet or a phrase to a stanza or more, frequently employed to express a similar idea within a given genre of folk literature.

composed   Not composed by the folk, not reshaped by the folk, or perhaps not in the style the critic considers to be folk: used by some critics to characterize consciously devised material.

coon song   Commercial popular song imitating or burlesquing Negro songs, dialect, or expression, and Negro personality.

crossing   Influence or exchange of material among two or more folksongs.

cumulative song   A song in which elements added in each stanza are retained and pile up in successive stanzas.

das Volk dichtet   Literally, the folk says: catchword for the conception, often attributed to Jacob and Wilhelm Grimm, that folk poetry is a spontaneous, communal product of a people.

deaconing   See *lining out.*

diatonic scale   A succession of tones with intervals of major and minor seconds, as the standard major, represented by the white keys of the piano.

diffusion   The principle that items of folklore or culture have spread from a common center, where they first occurred.

Dorian mode   See *mode.*

dulcimore or *Appalachian dulcimer*   A fretted cordophone having three or four strings, a fretboard, and an oblong soundbox; a folk instrument widely but thinly distributed in midland United States.

epic   A long poem of continuous narrative dealing in elevated style with great characters in the heroic age of a people. As an adjective, *epic* has been used by ballad critics to refer to narrative continuity in ballads.

epic song (epos)   A narrative song in continuous verse, heroic in concept and tone, but relatively brief in compass, e.g., the *junačke pesme* (men's songs) of Yugoslavian tradition.

etiological myth   A story told to explain the origin of some phenomenon.

euhemerist   One who holds the theory that myths grew out of the tales and legends of historic events and the deeds of historical heroes who became deified.

fabliau   A coarse, humorous tale in verse, popularized through French versifiers of the twelfth century and following.

fiddle song   Lyric stanzas, at best loosely related, sung in dance rhythm usually to fiddle accompaniment in the southern United States.

fiddle tune   Traditional fiddle music of the American frontier in Anglo-Irish tradition; later, often rendered by other instruments or used for vocal music.

fliting   A satirical or abusive song in which two singers alternately assail each other, sometimes improvised, but now generally traditional in text, as the "answering-back ballads" of the United States.

folk-lyric   A folksong lacking a coherent, developed narrative, often consisting of images held together by a tune or mood.

folksonger   A nonfolk enthusiast engaged in performing folksongs for a nonfolk audience.

foresinger (coryphée, Vorsänger)   The leader of a dance-song who sings the stanzas while the chorus sings the refrain or burden.

Fortey ballad sheet   A broadside issued by a prominent London ballad printer of the nineteenth century.

French harp   American folk name for harmonica or mouth organ.

game song   A song associated with dramatic play, usually of children.

gang song   A song accompanying the rhythmic labor of work gangs, especially of American Negroes, developed in field and construction work.

garland   A small collection of broadsides.

Gessamtgeist   The communal mind; collective soul.

gesunkene Kulturgut   Material originating on the cultivated levels of society but now in the possession of the folk.

gospel song or *hymn*   A religious song with lively rhythm and simple harmony, developed in the United States after the Civil War.

heptachordal   Designating a seven-tone diatonic scale.

hexachordal   Designating a six-tone diatonic scale.

hexatonic   Designating a six-tone scale with gaps or intervals larger than a major second.

hillbilly   1. Of or pertaining to commercialized folk or folkish songs (or the performers thereof) largely derived from or aimed at white folk culture of the southern United States, beginning in 1923. 2. Of or pertaining to that style—a blend of Anglo-Irish-Negro folksong and American popular song—on which the commercial tradition was based and developed.

historic-geographic method   A method of study of the life history of an individual folklore item by means of a rigid procedure involving a minute study of the origin and migration and a comparison of the variations in the details of a large number of versions.

hot music   American Negro music characterized by syncopation and polyrhythms, much variation, and improvisation of melody.

hot rhythm   The syncopation and polyrhythms characteristic of American Negro music.

horizontal transmission   Diffusion of an item of folklore among members of the same generation; tradition in space.

incremental repetition   Repetition of successive phrases, lines, stanzas, or groups of stanzas of a song with slight but significant variation.

Ionian mode   See *mode.*

iteration   Somewhat extended repetition of a linguistic or musical element.

jazz   A type of music developed from American Negro folk music in the late nineteenth century, characterized by duple meter, group improvisation, syncopation, propulsive rhythm, flat thirds and sevenths (blue notes), pentatonic or hexatonic scales, etc.

jig   Anglo-Irish instrumental music and dance: seldom used to refer to American performance, either in the sense of solo virtuosity or patterned figures.

jubilee   An American Negro hymn, usually of the camp-meeting type.

jury text   A fictitious version of a text constructed on the basis of statements of informants or inference from other texts.

kenning   A stereotyped metaphor or paraphrase used in place of a simple noun: a device of early Germanic poetry.

lay (lai)   A short narrative French song of the twelfth century, purported to be based on older songs of Breton minstrels.

legacy motif or *testament device*   A device, usually stereotyped, in song and story whereby a condemned or dying character announces the distribution of his goods, sometimes to indicate the villain of the narrative and sometimes to indicate the generosity of the character.

Liedertheorie   The theory that epics (specifically the Homeric poems) are not the work of single poets, but combinations of preexisting songs: suggested as early as 1722, but clearly enunciated by Ferdinand Wolf in 1795.

lining out or *deaconing*   The reading of each line of a hymn by the song leader before it is sung: current since the seventeenth century.

luck visit (*quête*)   House-to-house solicitation of goods or money by bands of performers at a seasonal festival.

lying songs   Songs containing exaggerations or gross impossibilities; some members of this group, such as "The Derby Ram," may have descended from seasonal rites.

Märchen   A complex folktale, usually concerning marvelous adventures and considered as fiction by the tellers.

maker (pl. *makeris*)   Archaic word for *poet*.

melodic contour   The ascending and/or descending movement of a tune, determined by the pitches of its stressed tones.

metrical romance   See *romance*.

Mixolydian mode   See *mode*.

mode   One of a number of diatonic octave scales differing in the position of major and minor seconds. The six generally accepted modes of Anglo-American folksong are: Ionian (half steps or minor seconds between intervals 3–4, 7–8); Dorian (2–3, 6–7); Phrygian (1–2, 5–6); Lydian (4–5, 7–8); Mixolydian (3–4, 6–7); Aeolian (2–3, 5–6).

motif   The smallest element which may exist independently or make up part of a larger unit of folk narrative.

neutral   A tone occurring between standard pitches of the tempered scale, indeterminate in our notation; an interval smaller than a minor second.

nursery song   A song designed or employed by adults for the entertainment of small children.

occupational song   A narrative or lyric song dealing with a particular employment or with those engaged in that employment: not to be confused with *work song*.

oikotype   A special form of an item of folklore developed within a particular nation or culture.

parlor song   A nineteenth- and twentieth-century melodramatic and sentimental song, whether of professional or folk origin, e.g., "After the Ball" and "The Blind Child."

part singing   The harmonized performance of a song, often unaccompanied, by a number of voices.

passing note   An auxiliary note, not part of the melodic structure of a tune.

pastourelle   A song of the wooing of a shepherdess or country girl in the open air by a man usually of higher rank: originally an Old French type.

pentachordal   Pertaining to a five-tone diatonic scale.

pentatonic   Pertaining to a five-tone scale with gaps, or intervals larger than a major second.

plagal   1. Pertaining to that form of a mode whose tones lie between the fifth above and the fourth below the tonic. 2. Pertaining to that form of a scale in which one or more tones lie below the tonic.

play-party   A combination of game, dance, and song developed in American frontier communities, often employing dance figures (minus the waist swing) but generally without instrumental accompaniment; also, the gathering at which such games are played.

picker   An American folk performer who utilizes a plucked stringed instrument such as a guitar or "banjer."

polygenesis   The principle that similar narratives and narrative elements originated independently in the different cultures in which they occur.

popular   As applied to ballads, the older types, specifically those in the Child canon.

purist   The cuss word of the folk critic. It has been applied to, among others, those who (1) test songs in oral tradition by criteria of age, origin, or style before pronouncing them folksongs; (2) believe that traditional materials should be presented to the general public in as nearly authentic form as possible.

race   Pertaining to material performed by Negroes and distributed to Negro audiences in the United States after 1920.

ragtime   A strongly syncopated form of American popular instrumental music in duple time which developed about 1910, apparently influenced by Negro folk music.

relative climax   See *sequence of relatives*.

refrain   A repeated element in a song which forms a part of the stanzaic structure. (Critics, however, often use *refrain* or *external refrain* in the meaning of burden.)

revenant ballad   A ballad dealing with the return of the dead.

reverdi   An Old French song of the beauties of spring: applied to the "greenwood opening" of such ballads as "Robin Hood and the Monk."

revival song A type of American song growing out of the religious fervor of the Great Awakening and the camp-meeting movement of the late eighteenth and early nineteenth centuries: generally characterized by simple structure, strong rhythm, much repetition, and solo and chorus organization.

riddle ballad A narrative song constructed around a series of enigmatic questions.

rime couée (tail rhyme) A medieval French verse stanza employing among long lines, shorter rhyming lines functioning as "tails" to parts of the stanza, e.g., aa*b*aa*b*cc*b*dd*b*.

ritualist One who contends that "true" myth, folktale, legend, folk drama, folksong, etc. were originally associated with primitive rites.

ring game A circle dance-drama of children, usually accompanied by song.

ring shout See *shout*.

rites de passage Ceremonies and customs accompanying a change in an individual's status within a community, e.g., birth, adolescence, marriage, death, etc.

romance A medieval tale in verse (*metrical romance*) or prose, somewhat loosely constructed, dealing with chivalric love and adventure.

rubato parlando A rhythmically free, highly ornamented style of folksinging in which the rhythm of the tune is adapted to the rhythm of the words.

saut See *shout*.

secondary ballad A ballad related to an earlier one in theme but not in text.

septenarius A seven-stress line employed in medieval poetry.

sequence of relatives A series of stanzas of incremental repetition in which the variation consists of the names of different relatives: brother, sister, etc. When the relatives are introduced in order of their importance, the technique is known as *climax of relatives*.

Seven Dials A section of St. Giles-in-the-Fields, London, in which were located the presses of such nineteenth-century broadside printers as Catnach, Pitts, and Fortey.

shanty A work song of sailors in which a leader (*shantyman*) usually sings a solo part and is answered by the men in a chorus, on the strong accents of which rhythmic labor is performed.

shanty boy A logger; lumberjack.

shape notes or *buckwheat notes* A system of musical notation, developed in early nineteenth-century America, in which the degrees of the scale are indicated by the shape of the notes, the number of shapes in different systems being four or seven.

shout An Afro-American form of worship consisting of strongly rhythmic song (usually in call-and-response pattern) and motor activities increasing in speed, volume, and intensity as the religious exaltation rises; the dancers often move in a counterclockwise circle, shuffling their feet but never crossing them. If *shout* is derived from Arabic *saut*, the term *ring-shout* is somewhat tautological.

signature The "awkward intrusion of the ballad singer, or . . . of the ballad singer as ballad maker"—Robert C. Stephenson; more narrowly, the identification in a song of the person or type of person who allegedly composed it.

simple ballad A ballad dealing with a universal human situation, related without preliminaries, transitions, and temporal or spatial perspective, and employing much dialogue and repetition. Also called *romantic ballad.*

sinful song A secular song of the American Negro, concerned usually with crime, sex, or frolic.

singing book A collection of folksongs arranged for performance by nonfolk readers or singers.

slave song A song of the American Negro prior to the Civil War: sometimes employed as a synonym for *Negro spiritual.*

slide A run of accessory notes leading to a main tone.

solar mythologist One who holds the theory that folktales are broken-down myths which originally described natural phenomena (the sun, in this instance) and seeks to restore the original meaning through the methods of comparative philology.

songster 1. A nineteenth-century song collection, in America usually pocket-sized (16mo or 24mo), containing the texts of music-hall, patriotic, religious, and sometimes traditional songs. 2. A folksinger and/or folk composer: an American Negro term.

spiritual A religious song of American white and Negro folk: applied to English religious song as early as the sixteenth century.

street cry A rhythmical chant or song of a street merchant advertising his wares.

street song A song sold, distributed, or performed by hawkers or itinerant singers (see *broadside*): sometimes applied to a song of children in the streets of contemporary cities.

surge song An American folk hymn performed in slow tempo and highly ornamented style, developed from the psalm singing of New England.

tetratonic   Pertaining to a four-tone scale with gaps or intervals larger than a major second.

traditional   Handed down by tradition, especially oral tradition; as applied to ballads, the term has designated the older types, specifically those in the Child canon.

triadic   Pertaining to a three-tone scale composed of the first, third, and fifth tones of the diatonic scale.

tune family   "A group of melodies showing basic interrelation by means of constant melodic correspondence and presumably owing their mutual likeness to descent from a single air that has assumed multiple forms through processes of variation, imitation, and assimilation."—Samuel P. Bayard.

turn   A melodic ornament consisting of the alteration of a main tone with two subsidiary tones a step or less above and below.

type   1. As used by British folksong students, a tune whose relationships are sometimes genetic, sometimes only structural. 2. As used by students of the folktale, an independent narrative represented by a complex of versions.

ur-form   An original form presumed to lie behind a number of varying forms of an item.

variant   One of a number of differing forms of a folklore item.

version   Often a synonym for *variant*, but sometimes used to mean a distinctive form of a folklore item, itself representative of a number of slightly differing variants.

vertical transmission   Diffusion of an item of folklore from one generation to another; tradition in time.

vocero   An "improvised" funeral song, originally associated with Corsican vendetta custom.

Volkslied   Literally, folksong; though often used by English-language scholars to indicate "true" folksong in the sense of origin or assimilation, the term is in German less precise than the English term *folksong* and refers to all manner of popular or folkish songs.

volkstümliches Lied   Folk-transmitted song, not "true" folksong.

vulgar ballad   1. A street ballad. See *broadside*. 2. A narrative song developed in expository fashion with a commonplace incipit and a series of events and transitions given relatively equal emphasis, often containing sentimental and moral comment.

wassail   A song sung by bands roving from house to house in connection with a seasonal "luck visit," conferring good fortune on contributors.

waulking song A work song of the Hebrides sung by women engaged in the shrinking and fulling of cloth.

work song A song accompanying physical labor, usually in the rhythm of the particular task, facilitating its performance.

zersingen The process wherein the original character of a tune is worn down or destroyed by continued singing.

INDEX

H 11 12—13